Reversing the Colonial Gaze

Exploring the farthest reaches of the globe, Persian travelers from Iran and India traveled across Russian and Ottoman territories to Asia, Africa, North and South America, Europe, and beyond. Remapping the world through their travelogues, *Reversing the Colonial Gaze* offers a comprehensive and transformative analysis of the journeys of over a dozen of these nineteenth-century Persian travelers. By moving beyond the dominant Eurocentric perspectives on travel narratives, Hamid Dabashi works to reverse the colonial gaze which has thus far been cast upon this rich body of travelogues. His lyrical and engaging reevaluation of these journeys, complemented by close readings of seminal travelogues, challenges the systematic neglect of these narratives in scholarly literature. Opening up the entirety of these overlooked or abused travelogues, Dabashi reveals not a mere repetition of clichéd accounts of Iranian or Muslim encounters with the West, but a path-breaking introduction to a constellation of revelatory travel narratives that reimagine and reclaim the world beyond colonial borders.

Hamid Dabashi is the Hagop Kevorkian Professor of Iranian Studies and Comparative Literature at Columbia University in New York. A key figure in the fields of Iranian studies, comparative literature, and postcolonial theory, he has written numerous books on these subjects, most recently *The Shahnameh: The Persian Epic as World Literature* (2019), *Persophilia: Persian Culture on the Global Scene* (2015), and *The Arab Spring: The End of Postcolonialism* (2012).

THE GLOBAL MIDDLE EAST

Arshin Adib-Moghaddam, *SOAS, University of London*
Ali Mirsepassi, *New York University*

EDITORIAL ADVISORY BOARD
Faisal Devji, *University of Oxford*
John Hobson, *University of Sheffield*
Firoozeh Kashani-Sabet, *University of Pennsylvania*
Zachary Lockman, *New York University*
Madawi Al-Rasheed, *London School of Economics and Political Science*
David Ryan, *University College Cork, Ireland*

The Global Middle East series seeks to broaden and deconstruct the geographical boundaries of the "Middle East" as a concept to include North Africa, Central and South Asia, and diaspora communities in Western Europe and North America. The series features fresh scholarship that employs theoretically rigorous and innovative methodological frameworks resonating across relevant disciplines in the humanities and the social sciences. In particular, the general editors welcome approaches that focus on mobility, the erosion of nation-state structures, travelling ideas and theories, transcendental techno-politics, the decentralization of grand narratives, and the dislocation of ideologies inspired by popular movements. The series will also consider translations of works by authors in these regions whose ideas are salient to global scholarly trends but have yet to be introduced to the Anglophone academy.

Other books in the series
1 *Transnationalism in Iranian Political Thought: The Life and Times of Ahmad Fardid*, Ali Mirsepassi
2 *Psycho-nationalism: Global Thought, Iranian Imaginations*, Arshin Adib-Moghaddam
3 *Iranian Cosmopolitanism: A Cinematic History*, Golbarg Rekabtalaei
4 *Money, Markets and Monarchies: The Gulf Cooperation Council and the Political Economy of the Contemporary Middle East*, Adam Hanieh
5 *Iran's Troubled Modernity: Debating Ahmad Fardid's Legacy*, Ali Mirsepassi
6 *Foreign Policy as Nation Making: Turkey and Egypt in the Cold War*, Reem Abou-El-Fadl
7 *Revolution and its Discontents: Political Thought and Reform in Iran*, Eskandar Sadeghi-Boroujerdi
8 *Creating the Modern Iranian Woman: Popular Culture between Two Revolutions*, Liora Hendelman-Baavur
9 *Iran's Quiet Revolution: The Downfall of the Pahlavi State*, Ali Mirsepassi
10 *Reversing the Colonial Gaze: Persian Travelers Abroad*, Hamid Dabashi

Reversing the Colonial Gaze

Persian Travelers Abroad

HAMID DABASHI
Columbia University

CAMBRIDGE
UNIVERSITY PRESS

CAMBRIDGE
UNIVERSITY PRESS

University Printing House, Cambridge CB2 8BS, United Kingdom

One Liberty Plaza, 20th Floor, New York, NY 10006, USA

477 Williamstown Road, Port Melbourne, VIC 3207, Australia

314–321, 3rd Floor, Plot 3, Splendor Forum, Jasola District Centre, New Delhi – 110025, India

79 Anson Road, #06–04/06, Singapore 079906

Cambridge University Press is part of the University of Cambridge.

It furthers the University's mission by disseminating knowledge in the pursuit of education, learning, and research at the highest international levels of excellence.

www.cambridge.org
Information on this title: www.cambridge.org/9781108488129
DOI: 10.1017/9781108768986

First published 2020

Printed in the United Kingdom by TJ International Ltd. Padstow Cornwall

A catalogue record for this publication is available from the British Library.

Library of Congress Cataloging-in-Publication Data
Names: Dabashi, Hamid, 1951– author.
Title: Reversing the colonial gaze : Persian travelers abroad / Hamid Dabashi, Columbia University, New York.
Description: Cambridge, UK ; New York : Cambridge University Press, 2019. |
    Series: The global Middle East ; 10 | Includes bibliographical refereces and index.
Identifiers: LCCN 2019037001 (print) | LCCN 2019037002 (ebook) |
    ISBN 9781108488129 (hardback) | ISBN 9781108738453 (paperback) |
    ISBN 9781108768986 (epub)
Subjects: LCSH: Travelers' writings, Persian–History and criticism. | Persian prose
    literature–19th century–History and criticism. | Travel writing–History–19th century.
Classification: LCC PK6413.5.T73 D33 2019 (print) | LCC PK6413.5.T73 (ebook) |
    DDC 891/.550932–dc23
LC record available at https://lccn.loc.gov/2019037001
LC ebook record available at https://lccn.loc.gov/2019037002

ISBN 978-1-108-48812-9 Hardback

In Memory of Mahmood Bashi (1940–2018)
Born a happy native in southern Iran,
Traveled far and widely,
Then settled and died a proud Swedish citizen –
Father, Husband, Grandfather, Friend

Contents

Figures

Preface

By the sunset
Amidst the tired presence of things
The gaze of someone waiting
Could see the vast expanse of time!
        Sohrab Sepehri (Mosafer/Traveler, Babol, Spring 1966)[1]

[handwritten margin note: vision of time amidst things' presence]

This is a book about travelers – a group of twelve travelers who roamed *[handwritten: 12]* around the globe mostly in the nineteenth but some a bit earlier and some a bit after that crucial century. Somewhere between the Apostolic twelve and the twelve Shi'i Imams, this book determined the course of its narrative. Some of these travelers have been, individually or in twos or threes, studied before – but in this collective gathering, and with the totality of their written prose (and not just the fragment that deals with Europe), have never been examined in this particular manner that I do *[handwritten: HD writes in colonial language]* here in this book. These travelers wrote their travelogues in Persian, my mother tongue, and I write this book about them in English, the colonial language we postcolonial subjects have inherited from our conquerors and made our own. When I am done writing this book and it is published, *[handwritten: spread to subj. of Brit.]* it can be read by people throughout the world, in Asia, Africa, Latin America, and then in immigrant communities around the planet – not because any one of them is British, but because they and their ancestors were the subjects of British imperialism. These travelers have been abused *[handwritten: imperialism]* by generations of their readers who have reduced their travelogues only to the part where they write about Europe. But Europe was only part of their travels – they began writing about their travels and experiences *[handwritten: Europe: just part of exper.]* long before they reached Europe, and long after they had left Europe. These travelers began writing their accounts while they were still in Iran

---

[1] All these translations of Sohrab Sepehri's poem "Mosafer/Traveler" from the original Persian that appear at beginning of all my chapters are mine. For the original, see Sohrab Sepehri, "Mosafer/Traveler," in Sohrab Sepehri, *Hasht Ketab/Eight Books* (Tehran: Tahuri Publishers, 2536/1356/1977): 301–328.

or in India and they roamed the globe writing about what they saw and what they did. In this book I have restored the dignity of their actual words, the totality of their travels and thoughts, and the sense of their prose and purpose, before and beyond Europe. Against the grain of the manner in which they have been systematically abused, I have not privileged Europe as the sole destination of their purpose, for it was not – nor have I ignored the European fragment of their journeys. The result is the exposure of a full-bodied moral imagination that is in fact reversing the colonial gaze cast subsequently upon them and with them us, ignoring the truth that they were in fact remapping the colonial world.

to reverse the col. gaze is to remap the col. world

This book is therefore about reversing the colonial gaze. It covers the vast spectrum of Persian travelers from Iran and India going around the globe fully aware of the colonial gaze cast upon them but not beholden to that gaze. I seek to right the wrong of the terrible epistemic violence that has been historically perpetrated on these travelers and their travelogues by forcibly casting them as "going to Europe." You will read me repeatedly correcting that false assumption and chapter and verse showing how these travelers were actually going around the world and not just to Europe, though Europe certainly was part of their itinerary. They are fully aware of the rising power of Europe around the world but so are they of the power of Russia, of the Ottoman Empire, as indeed of the emerging power of nations around the globe against all these powers. But most of all, my book, in painstaking detail, is about a concerted project of regaining an imaginative grasp of the globe, reversing the colonial gaze, and thereby regaining visual, narrative, moral, normative, and imaginative agency in their contemporary history.

At the time these travelers were writing their travelogues, the European colonial gaze had dwarfed the world to rule it better. The task at hand is not a tit-for-tat; it is not to cast an anti-colonial gaze at Europe to shame, blame, or demonize it. The European colonial gaze has been just one among many other cases of imperial power, though the most recent and technologically the most advanced. Precisely for that reason, reversing the colonial gaze is to regain the world at large against the worst effects of the European colonial gaze. Reversing to correct the colonial gaze means to retrieve the world before in order to facilitate the world after the European colonial conquest. The European panopticon of modernity had a longer colonial window widely opened on the globe, which Michelle Foucault mostly ignored. The world at large, at the receiving end of that European gaze, needs to delve deeply and widely into its own history to retrieve the world when the dehumanizing European conquest was neither final, total, definitive, or terminal. The body of the travelogues I closely examine in this book has been systematically and consistently abused to do precisely the opposite of what they actually do, and I have read them with focused attention to reverse that abuse and to reveal what they actually do. Under the overwhelming power and presence of the colonial Eurocentric imagination, those scholars who have cared to read these travelogues have abusively read them as traveling to Europe. Here I reveal in unprecedented detail how they did no such thing, that they were in fact traveling around the globe, including but not exclusively to Europe. This I do, line by line, paragraph by paragraph, page after page, in order to open the worldly horizons of the time in which these travelers crossed multiple frontiers to see, show, and map out the world they inhabited. In reversing that colonial gaze Europeans had cast upon the world, these travelers, and the travelogues they wrote, I detail the world they witnessed, discovered, and claimed for their posterities, for us, enabling us to retrieve the world lost under the epistemic violence of the European gaze cast on Iranians, Arabs, Indians, etc., who then in turn partook willingly or unwillingly in that colonial cast of mind, becoming the carriers of the colonial grain of humiliation that has denied them authorial agency. I do in pages that follow precisely the opposite of that denial, restoring that authorial agency.

Although the origin of my intention to write this book is much earlier, I began actively working on it during the US presidential election of 2016, soon after which Donald Trump became the US president, and among the first Executive Orders he signed was his "Muslim Ban," disallowing travelers from seven Muslim countries (including Iran) to come to the United States. I continued to plough through my reading and writing one chapter after another with a bit of a bittersweet smile on my face: writing a book about Muslims traveling around the world (including the United States) mostly throughout the nineteenth century as I, the author, despite my US citizenship, was now among those who were subject to travel restrictions, while my friends and their families in Europe, in Iran, and in the Arab and Muslim world were limited in their ability to come and visit me and my family. These were two vastly different worlds: the one I was reading in Persian in these books and the one I was living as I wrote this book in English. But the two worlds were destined to meet, were integral to a colonial cast that had now reached its postcolonial edges, right in the heart of an embarrassingly dysfunctional American empire.

Figure 1 "Isle of Graia Gulf of Akabah Arabia Petraea," 1839 lithograph of a trade caravan by Louis Haghe from an original by David Roberts. [Public domain] – The European gaze and visual imagination had at once romanticized and etherealized their "Orient" as the object of colonial conquest and voyeuristic fantasies. "Oriental" people and places were not real human beings or part of this earth. They were Objet de Curiosité, there to amuse Europeans and tickle their exotic fantasies. The Persian travelers I examine in this book decidedly reverse that colonial gaze against itself and remap the world and people it, before, beyond, and above Europe, for a renewed global conception with detailed realism, purposeful prose, and fiercely insightful reportage. These travelogues are the exact antidote to those Oriental fantasies.

Every traveler I examine in this book had a homeland to return to, the country of their origin Iran or India. I had no such point of return. By the time first Obama and then Trump had issued their travel bans, I had lived in the United States for some forty years, had made a home for myself and my family there, all my four children were born there, and had no reason, interest, or frame of reference in Iran to make it a viable home for us. I was home away from home, in the state of stateless wander that had defined my sojourn to America and beyond. These travel narratives were in effect the origin of my generation's sense of worldly wonder – this is where "Iran" had in effect begun in its postcolonial rendition.

I was working on the final chapters of this book when the US Supreme Court, in a 5–4 ruling late in June 2018, sided with President Donald Trump's Muslim travel ban, putting their legal stamp of approval on a patently racist and xenophobic limitation on Muslims like me being able to travel to the United States any more. I don't therefore think it is any secret that turning to travel narratives as the subject of this book at this stage of my scholarship is prompted by an evident autobiographical urge. Yes, I have had and continue to sustain a course of critical interest in the historic formation of the postcolonial public sphere and its contingent subject in my work over the last decade in particular. This book is therefore certainly in the same trajectory as my books on Shi'ism, or Persian literary humanism, and Persophilia – in all of which I have been trying critically to consider these two concerns of public sphere and corresponding postcolonial subject. But even these crucial theoretical issues are rooted in the existential fragmentation of a spirit of the time that animates us all. I feel a sense of historical responsibility in between what has come before and what might happen after my scholarly records on these issues. "Traveling" has been the defining trope of my generation for as long as I remember – and in this book I wish to expand the active longevity of this collective remembrance. The seminal text of the towering critical thinker of my generation Jalal Al-e Ahmad was in fact not his iconic *Gharbzadegi/ Westoxification (1962)* but far more importantly his Hajj pilgrimage, *Khasi dar Mighat/A Straw where the Pilgrims Gather* (1964). From the time of the earliest generation of Iranian students who packed their meager belongings and left our homeland for good, traveling has been the principal *modus operandi* of our existence. I had always hoped to sit down and think through the larger historical implication of this defining momentum of our history.

Life is strange. I used to love traveling. I have long since lost my own wanderlust. I began writing this book when the memories of my own travels had all faded into the existential homeliness in me no matter where I was. As a project integral to my larger concern with mapping out the contours of the transnational public sphere upon which the postcolonial subject was constituted, no doubt this book sustained my scholarly concerns, but from the very beginning I was also conscious I was attending to a deeply autobiographical dimension of my generation. Who were we, where were we headed, when did such journeys begin, and to what end?

I began reading these travelogues and memoirs quite a long time ago – not just to learn where they went, what they saw, and how they wrote their experiences, but far more importantly to be a witness to their wandering souls, as their worlds were widening, their horizons unfolding beyond their imagination, where the inherited visions of their habitat and humanity were being remapped, expanded, reconfigured. I have a handwritten note in Persian dated Sunday 24 Farvardin 1365, which corresponds to April 13, 1986, in the middle of one of the major sources I have discussed in this book, Yahya Dowlatabadi's *Hayat Yahya* (1893), in which I have scheduled the timing in which I had planned to read that book. The fact that I had written this note in Persian and marked the date on the Iranian calendar indicate that up until this date my mind was still thinking in Persian and my life regulated on the Iranian calendar. It also means the initial idea of this book was with me only a few years after I had left my homeland and came to the United States. I now recall that at that point I wanted to call this book something like "The Troubadours of Modernity." Those initial notes, scattered ideas, and raw sentiments needed decades to simmer and brew in my mind and my soul. I needed to move from the Islamic and Persian calendars to the common Gregorian calendar of my life as a scholar living in the United States and decidedly move from Persian sources into my academic English prose for this book to brew and be ready to be written in a prose that matched the searching souls of those bygone travelers, with whom today I deeply identify. I had come to the United States with an innate worldliness in my self-assured soul. The United States pathologically nativizes its immigrants upon arrival, robs them of the world and worldliness they had brought with them to these shores. The Alien Registration Card (the Green Card) they are issued prior to their fake citizenship effectively alienates them from who they are and what they were. There was always a deep and irreconcilable distance between this sense of alienation and the worldly confidence of poets like Sohrab Sepehri, between the stable but stale confidence of my Persian provenance and the hesitant English prose afforded the newly minted US immigrants. I had to learn and reimagine Sohrab Sepehri's poetic confidence in my English prose – and precisely for that reason I needed to cut deeply into the history that had enabled Sepehri's poetry. I needed to pull back at least two hundred years when these travelogues began to be written to rediscover the emotive and epistemic roots of a poet like Sohrab Sepehri in the latter part of the twentieth century.

The terrorizing world of the boldly racist and xenophobic white supremacy Trump had unleashed upon the globe was narrowing in on us as I was reading and being a witness to a time when these Iranian Muslim travelers were moving exactly in the opposite direction – claiming and mapping the world around them, connecting it East and West, North and South, building upon it moral and imaginative bridges. I too was one of these travelers when I left my homeland some forty years ago, and I am still one of them today hundreds of years after their travels. I was initially unconsciously but eventually quite decidedly digging deeply into the genealogy of my own moral and intellectual heritage – an Iranian reclaiming the mobile heritage of his intellectual predecessors. Who were we – we travelers, the sojourners of truth beyond our existing fields of visions, outside our own home and habitat, far beyond the colonial borders our conquerors had drawn for us, right into the heartland of those who saw us as their enemy? I no longer felt welcome in the United States – nor did I wish to be welcomed there or anywhere else for that matter. But that fact did not bother me. I thought I had finished my journey. The United States was not my destination, nor was the idea of getting back home to Iran. I had no metaphysical conception of a homeland. I was at home in the wanderlust of this shrinking universe, and my last and lasting home was with my four American children, two of them born in Allentown and raised in Philadelphia, Pennsylvania, and the other two in Manhattan, New York.

As I saw my own children growing up with other immigrant children, in the ennobling vicinity of Native, African, Latinx, and myriad of other Americans, I was made more conscious of how these travelers beyond their times and anticipations were in effect reversing the (white) colonial gaze historically cast upon colonized nations. Without these travelers writing the world anew, claiming it all, my generation of Iranians will not have had a pride of place among these other immigrants living in gratitude to the First Nations who had inhabited this landscape. We too could stand up and say "I" against the racist white supremacist that hoped to rule this land by virtue of where these travelers went, what they saw, and what they wrote. I followed the footsteps of these travelers in print as they were remapping the world while I was (literally) walking my younger children to their public school in New York to greet their mostly Latinx classmates – in a dual language education in which they were learning English and Spanish in the same classrooms. At this point I cared far more for them to grow up bilingual in English and Spanish than in English and Persian. As under initially Obama (paradoxical is it not) and then decidedly under Trump I and my ilk were branded as unwanted aliens, it occurred to me that we Iranians living in the United States had in fact joined generations and histories of all other denied and denigrated people on these shores – the Native Americans, the African-Americans, all the subsequent immigrants, generation after generation, coming here to build this country under the racist tutelage of a gang of European settler colonialists who had a bizarre affliction of amnesia and with astonishing arrogance thought this was actually their land.

How do we (Iranians, Indians, Arabs, Africans, Latin Americans, Jews, Muslims, etc.) breach our totality, if I were to ask Emmanuel Levinas's Jewish question in a Muslim mind – is there any infinity left in us? How do we transcend ourselves? Can we even fathom transcending ourselves? It seems to me I have written this book on bygone Muslims traveling at the time of a Muslim travel ban as an occasion to reflect on the im/possibility of a Muslim person ever fathoming to transcend himself, herself, itself. We seem to be condemned, and we seem to have had no say in the matter, to be all potential terrorists, and as such actual threats to our own very existence. We were made to contradict ourselves. We were being denied our own others, our own alterities. We were condemned to be the same, an identity that was cauterized on our forehead without our consent – or even the permission to scream our pain. We did not live in this world except as allegories of terror to others. We were the radical alterity of others, denied having any radical alterity of our own. Are we our own selves, once we have been cast as our self-designated enemies? We did not choose these enemies. They choose us. How can we ever move, from here to there, as James Baldwin once said, without ipso facto threatening their very existence? I went back to these travelers and to the *terra incognita* they were remapping to find the factual footing of where we were and how far we have traveled. We must know how far we have traveled and how before we are certain where we go from here.

I was reading these travelogues, volume after volume, page after page, asking myself: Are we Muslims allowed to transcend ourselves – and more importantly, why should we even ask permission to do so? We are no longer at home in the so-called Islamic world or anywhere else for that matter – for the privileged travelers of yore have now become desperate refugees and migrant labors. We are now the same with this world, our own alterity having escaped and denied us. That is a terrible moral flatness for a people, a culture, a collective consciousness to have allowed itself. The travelers you will encounter in this book were discontented with what and who they were. That discontent was moving toward a transcendence, inclined toward the reconstitution of a mora agent, the particular contours of which they mapped out in thick descriptions and copious notes. Generations of abusive readings have denied these travelers that transcendence by disallowing them the confidence with which they were traveling the world (not just "to Europe"), remapping the globe, as they were writing the inaugural moment of their history. I have tried gently to ease that transcendence from the midst of their thinking, the thicket of their meandering souls – and this not for their sake, for they are no longer here with us, but for our own sake, so from them we may learn how to teach ourselves the terms of the intuitions of our own transcendence.

Acknowledgments

The idea of this book has been with me for decades. I have carried this idea with me around the globe. As I mention somewhere in the body of the book, in the middle of one of the texts I examine in this study I found a handwritten note in Persian in which I had outlined the timetable of reading it. This was at a time when I thought and wrote in Persian; right now I have no idea in what language I think but I write almost exclusively in English. Such is the life of a postcolonial person who is neither here nor there but traveling, as were the subjects of my study in this book, somewhere between here and there, in thoughts, languages, and locations.

The writing of this book would have been impossible without the help of my Iranian friends and colleagues who have procured for me copies of books, essays, articles, and manuscripts in Persian from Iranian libraries and online resources. Chief among these friends is Mahmoud Omidsalar. I am eternally grateful to him.

The two distinguished colleagues who are the general editors of this new book series by Cambridge University Press, Professor Ali Mirsepassi of New York University and Professor Arshin Adib-Moghaddam of University of London, have been instrumental in seeing this book to fruition. It was not until I learned of their book series, "The Global Middle East" by Cambridge University Press, that I was sure my new book had a natural habitat. I am grateful to Ali Mirsepassi and Arshin Adib-Moghaddam for their collegial, friendly, and exceedingly gracious reception of my book in their excellent series. I am honored.

A blind review by an anonymous colleague had offered me detailed and exceptionally helpful comments on the manuscript of this book. I am grateful to this colleague.

Maria Marsh, the Commissioning Editor at Cambridge, and her colleagues Atifa Jiwa and Daniel Brown have been exceptionally helpful in the last stages of preparing this book for publication. I am grateful to them.

My research assistant Laila Hisham Fouad has been hard at work locating high resolution pictures for this book. I am grateful to her.

I am grateful to Mamadou Diouf, my colleague and the chairman of my department at Columbia University, for his unceasing support of my work.

I write these acknowledgments and put other finishing touches on my book while sitting at a café called Joe and the Juice in midtown Manhattan, in the neighborhood of my two younger children's public schools. This book has been with me literally around the globe. The fact of my life, one Iranian traveler among others I have read in this book, is the premise and promise of all their work – I am a New Yorker.

Introduction

What strange valleys
[We traveled –]
And the horse, do you remember?
It was white
And just like a pure phrase
Grazing upon the grass-like greenery of silence.
                    Sohrab Sepehri (Mosafer/Traveler, Babol, Spring 1966)

Just look at the grace and the confidence of Sepehri's lines! Where did these beautiful poems come from – what moral, imaginative, and historical forces inform and sustain the aesthetic sublimity, the poetic purity of these lines? Sohrab Sepehri (1928–1980) was born early in the twentieth century and died late in that century. To come close to the poetic timbre of his voice and see how he arrived there, we need to pull back, way back, and cast a much longer look at the history that enabled him and his poetic voice.

Rewriting Histories

"All historians," Mir Seyyed Abd al-Latif Shushtari, the author of *Tohfat al-Alam/Gift from the World* (1788), writes early in his travel book, "be they Jewish, Christian, or Muslim, believe that after Noah's Flood the entire civilized world was destroyed and only a precious little part of it survived ... All of course except the Indians who do not believe any such flood ever take place, or if it did it may have reached some countries but not others, and certainly it had no effect on India." This is a moment of wonder and pause for the learned traveler who has just left his home and habitat for unknown worlds and widening horizons. "They also trace the creation of this world to millions of years earlier," he reports to his readers, "and they completely deny the

1

story of Adam as the Representative of God on earth as we Muslims
and many other historians believe."[1]

Throughout the nineteenth century, scores of prominent Persian
speaking travelers such as Shushtari traveled from Iran or India around
the world, and a few of them kept a diligent diary of what they saw,
places and persons they met, and what they thought. Who were these
travelers, what attracted and drew them to travel to the Arab and
Muslim world and then beyond to Europe and the United States, what
did they see, how did they interpret what they saw, and how did their
published accounts of their experiences and observations transform
their nations into the modernity of the age they lived?

In this book, I intend to look closely at a number of such travelogues
and address these and similar questions. These journeys were not
exclusively to Europe, some did not even include Europe, but all had
an awareness of Europe as the site of a monumental thing called
"modernity" to which they were exposed through European colonialism, and that grabbed their attention and sent them searching around
the globe. Merchants, diplomats, students, and ultimately an emerging
cadre of what today we would call "public intellectuals," these travelers were at once enamored of modern achievements of this colonial
modernity and yet aghast at the state of affairs in their own homeland.
The travelogues that they wrote, as a result, became a narrative record
of an encounter with colonial modernity in motion, and in the context
of a worldly consciousness. "Europe" was indeed a key character in
the *dramatis personae* of this age and stage, but not the sole interlocutor or the defining moment of their experience. The goal was the very
experience of traveling, to be *on the road, dar safar/in journey*, as
opposed to *dar hazar/at home*. These travels were vastly changing
the very conception of "the world," opening as they did the very
experience of living to new horizons.

The purpose of this book is a close examination of a succession of
travelogues written by Iranians traveling around the world, beginning
late in the eighteenth down to the early twentieth century. This period
is crucial, for it is at this time when Iran as a nation-state and Iranians
as a people begin to emerge from the crumbling sites of their former

---

[1] See Mir Seyyed Abd al-Latif Shushtari's *Tohfat al-Alam*. Edited with an
Introduction and Notes by S. Movahhed (Tehran: Tahuri Publishers, 1363/
1984): 32.

empires and assume a national self-consciousness as they enter a world
dominated by European colonial modernity. These journeys were first
and foremost to get out of a closed-circuited history, through a geographical venue, but evident in them was also a search for the secret of
the global condition of this colonial modernity that had a European
imprint on it, a modernity, to be sure, understood in a worldly
context that now embraced Iranians (as it did people anywhere else
in the world) and gave them a renewed understanding of themselves.
This purgatorial passage from communal to regional and then imperial
consciousness on one hand, and the encroaching contours of a colonial
modernity on the other, is exceptionally important as a foregrounding
of postcolonial nation formations, the public sphere upon which
they were formed and the modes of postcolonial subjectivity they
entailed and enabled. As you see in the case of Shushtari, these travelers did not all go to Europe, nor in fact was Europe their final or sole
destination. Shushtari went to India, where he saw the effects of
European colonial modernity. Wherever they went, these travelers
had already inhabited a world, a towering, imperial, cosmic world,
which now they saw expanding in emotive and topographical terms
they did not completely anticipate or comprehend. They were the
pioneering explorers of this unfolding planetary consciousness of
themselves.

Throughout the twentieth century, these mostly nineteenth century
travelogues have been read as indices of an encounter with "the West,"
a reading that is only partially true, a fragmentary and therefore flawed
reading performed at the expense of a much larger imaginative geography evident in the texts of this body of evidence. I do not wish to rob
these texts of their eventual awareness of Europe but intend to place
that awareness in the more global context of a worldliness that is
patently evident in their texts and that, as such, defines the normative
and moral imagination of those travelers who wrote them. We rob
these travelers of the totality of their worldly experiences as indeed
recorded in these travelogues if we think "the West" was their final
destination, as we would deny that totality a key component of their
wonder and amazement if we were to disregard their European experiences. We should neither privilege nor downplay their European visits.
We must embed those visits in their much more extended wanderings
before and after those visits – as all evident (in black and white as it
were) in the very pages of their travel narratives.

Righting Wrong Readings

Because of the extraordinary significance of these and similar travel narratives, they have been the subject of a number of scholarly investigations, each critically important in one way or another.

In his *Muslim Discovery of Europe* (1982), Bernard Lewis provides a typical example of reading these and similar texts by picking only one aspect of their varied narratives and magnifying it, thereby repressing the rest and thus constitutionally distorting their worldly disposition. In my book, which I write against the grain of such limited and forced readings of the much wider topography of emotive sensibilities they entail, I wish to retrieve their own world and worldliness, without suppressing that seminal colonial encounter with Europe (not with the vacuous abstraction Lewis and other Orientalists call "the West"). Bernard Lewis and likeminded Orientalists habitually comb through these and similar narratives and tease out such oddities as how Muslim travelers were amused by European women's behavior, or their clothing items, or the European homosexuals, or European men's habits of shaving, or other such amusements at Orientalized narratives.[2] I will not disregard or dismiss such encounters, but place them in the context of their textual idiomaticity and the community of self-conscious sensibilities they evoke.

Europe was not the destiny or the destination of these travelers. It was part of a much larger and more enabling world they were rediscovering. The world that they discovered, dwelling as it did more on the distance between a morning ride and an evening rest, included Europe but was not limited to it. The coupling of "Islam and the West," a dangerous delusion that has been handed down as the handiwork of nineteenth to twentieth century European Orientalism and the colonial modernity it enabled and served, exacerbated by militant Islamism that emerged ostensibly to oppose but in effect to consolidate it, continues to be the source of much carnage around the world. We need radically to alter and reverse the historical narrative that has engendered that false and hostile binary, and there is no better way to do that than to retrieve the cosmopolitan worldliness that once mapped the world, and remembering the travelers that traveled that

---

[2] See Bernard Lewis, *Muslim Discovery of Europe* (New York: W. W. Norton, 1982): 279–294.

map. The map these travelers navigated informs a different and much neglected public sphere, enables a much different but maligned subject, and announces a different but concealed emotive universe. Printing machines would soon be introduced, Persian prose would be much simplified, newspapers published, and the public persona all of these enabled have all been lost under the heap of the rubric of a "Muslim discovery of Europe." Yes, these travelers were Muslims, but Muslim was not the only thing they were. Yes, they traveled to Europe, but Europe was not the only place they visited. "Europe," to borrow Fanon's insight, was not yet completely invented by the "Third World." A much vaster geography of sense and sensibility, politics and prudence, mapped the itinerary of these travelers. I wish to draw a new attention to that map.

To be sure, Bernard Lewis's *Muslim Discovery of Europe* was not the first or the only study of such texts to single out "Europe" as the primary focal point of these journeys. Ibrahim Abu-Lughod's *Arab Rediscovery of Europe: A Study in Cultural Encounters* (1963), based on his doctoral dissertation at Princeton University (1957), had done so almost a quarter of a century earlier.[3] Even before Abu-Lughod, Mojtaba Minovi, in his seminal essay, "Avvalin Karevan Ma'refat/The First Caravan of Knowledge" (1953), had also singled out the journey of the first group of Iranian students out of their homeland as exclusively to Europe, disregarding the journeys that were done before and after that visit and the fact that they were not done just to Europe.[4] The concerns of Abu-Lughod and Minovi, however, were different. Though equally fixated on their own colonially manufactured notion of "Europe" and thus oblivious to the world that these travelers were now discovering, they were the products of a time that "the West" had become a categorical imperative and a measure either to embrace or to dismiss. Scholars such as Abu-Lughod and Minovi were primarily concerned with the earliest accounts of Arab, Iranian, and Muslim encounters with Europe by way of excavating a genealogy of their own contemporary political preoccupation. For them, the towering binary of "Islam and the West" had become so politically consolidated and paramount that they never thought to question or dismantle it.

---

[3] See Ibrahim Abu-Lughod, *Arab Rediscovery of Europe: A Study in Cultural Encounters* (Princeton: Princeton University Press, 1963).

[4] See Mojtaba Minovi, "Avvalin Karevan Ma'refat/The First Caravan of Knowledge," *Yaghma* 6:7 (Mehr 1332/September 1953).

Their wounded pride was deeply agitating in their respective scholar-
ships, which in fact became anachronistically integral to the spirit of
the primary sources they were investigating. Preoccupied with the
overpowering politics of their time, they did the texts they were reading
a serious disservice.

Far more in tune with Bernard Lewis's take on these journeys was Sir
Dennis Wright's *The Persians amongst the English* (1990), later complemented by *The English amongst the Persians: Imperial Lives in
Nineteenth-Century Iran* (2001), which also singled out Europe, and
England even more specifically, as the very reason for these journeys.
Studies such as those of Lewis and Wright are emblematic of a particular phase of European and US Orientalism when a condescending
prose of imperial benevolence continued to look down at their former
colonies as the source of pathological insight into the nature and
disposition of the nexus holding the colonizer and the colonized
together. In this respect, these studies too are symptomatic of a particular phase of the politics of knowledge production forcing the
belated preoccupations of these scholars onto the texts they had excav-
ated to read.

But soon, a much more robust and wholesome body of scholarship
emerged around these texts. Muzaffar Alam and Sanjay Subramanyam's groundbreaking work, *Indo–Persian Travels in the Age of
Discoveries, 1400–1800* (2007), reversed and corrected that previous
trend and concentrated on the inner worlds of Asia that these travelers
traversed and discovered, with exquisite details of social history in such
travel narratives within the Indo–Persian sources dealing with India,
Iran, and Central Asia between around 1400 and 1800.[5] These
authors' concerns were primarily with the Mughals, Safavids, and
Central Asia in a period of historic transformation. Equally important,
though still unduly privileging the European "destination" of these
travelers, is a subsequent monograph by Naghmeh Sohrabi, *Taken
for Wonder: Nineteenth Century Travel Accounts from Iran to Europe*
(2012), in which she has selected a few of these Persian sources and put
a significant theoretical twist on them, suggesting that they can in fact
reveal much more about the concerns and agenda of their authors back

---

[5] See Muzaffar Alam and Sanjay Subramanyam, *Indo–Persian Travels in the Age
of Discoveries, 1400–1800* (Cambridge: Cambridge University Press, 2007).

in their homeland rather than where they were visiting.[6] In an excellent edited volume, Roberta Micallef and Sunil Sharma's *On the Wonders of Land and Sea: Persianate Travel Writing* (2013), some of these travel accounts have also been examined for their literary and linguistic aspects.[7] More recently, Nile Green's *The Love of Strangers: What Six Muslim Students Learned in Jane Austen's London* (2015) offers a close reading of just one of these travelogues, Mirza Saleh Shirazi's *Safarnameh*, and produces a lovely read that hinges on the idea of these "adaptable Muslim migrants" adventuring with their "mission ... to master the modern sciences behind the rapid rise of Europe."[8] Though Green's account reverts back to the Lewis and Wright phase of Orientalist amusement with these "Muslim travelers," it happens in a much healthier environment where more serious scholars such as Muzaffar Alam and Sanjay Subramanyam have set a more robust academic agenda.

Discovering a Cosmopolitan Worldliness

Conscious of these significant works of scholarship done on aspects of this substantial body of literature, my book has an entirely different purpose: It offers a decidedly different angle; relies on a much wider body of primary sources, specifically concentrating on the critical period between 1788 and 1924; and seeks to correct a decidedly distorting emphasis on the European "destination" of these travelers at the expense of overshadowing their more global concerns.

In retrieving the worlds, and even more importantly the passage to those worlds that these travelers were discovering, we need to go back to the formative nineteenth century (and here the globalized Christian almanac is the key colonial calendar – though it is crucial to keep in mind that these travelers were mostly using the Islamic calendar) because it was precisely in this fateful period when "Islam and West," as two opposing camps, two Manichean poles of enmity, were being

---

[6] See Naghmeh Sohrabi, *Taken for Wonder: Nineteenth Century Travel Accounts from Iran to Europe* (Oxford: Oxford University Press, 2012).

[7] See Roberta Micallef and Sunil Sharma (eds.), *On the Wonders of Land and Sea: Persianate Travel Writing* (Cambridge, MA: Ilex Series/Harvard University Press, 2013).

[8] See Nile Green, *The Love of Strangers: What Six Muslim Students Learned in Jane Austen's London* (Princeton: Princeton University Press, 2015).

authoritatively narrated into a normative hegemony. The Orientalist construction of "Islamic civilization" (or Chinese or Indian "civilization") was definitive to the normative bourgeois manufacturing of the "the West." In the world that we will discover in these travelogues, however, the planetary vision of these travelers is not divided along an East–West axis. They have a worldly conception of the planet they are traversing, a cosmopolitan vision of the realities they witness and report. To show this, I will dwell on the entirety of their travel itinerary, from home to the worlds they were discovering and back to their tumultuous homeland. These journeys were neither exclusively to Europe nor were they sites of self-reflection within their Asian contexts; they were neither accounts of wide-eyed encounters with outside worlds nor a ruse for political commentary about their homelands. They were all of those and yet much more than all such things put together. They were and they remain what they write in black and white, a journey from home to the world and back to their homeland, which they now rediscover differently, for their own eyes are now equipped with richer sensibilities and more perceptive lenses. To think they just left home to go to Europe and bring back "modernity" is vastly to distort the very narrative logic, every road and every highway, every valley and every mountain they traveled to see the world differently.

These are narratives in motion, literally: books written on horseback, inside moving carriages, while walking, traversing between an origin and a destination that keeps moving, corners of midway teahouses and caravansary, perhaps under a tree or by a brook, through a valley, over a mountaintop, or when you reach a rambunctious urbanity and rest in wonder. Today's destination was tomorrow's origin for these travelers – peripatetic (literally) were these philosophers of the mobile modernity they thought they were chasing, but in effect inventing, overcoming, surpassing. Instead of dwelling on the moment, these narratives dwell on the duration, instead of now or then, on while, instead of here or there, on the distance in-between. This book, mimicking theirs, is about duration, about all the while, about the distance, about the liminality of time and space before here has become there, now then. I wish to dwell as much on the narrative disposition of these travelogues as to the lay of the land they traveled and narrated. In a profound and enduring way, I too have been a traveler like them, though I opted not to return home to Iran, made a home and stayed right here at my destination in the United States, and kept writing books and articles about what I had learned on this journey. So, this book is as much about bygone ages and their record in some exquisite travel narratives as about the rest of Iranian history in its unfolding encounter with the world, with multiple worlds we keep encountering, discovering, overcoming, dreaming.

With this foregrounding, my principal contention in this book, which sets it categorically apart from all other scholarly attentions hitherto paid to some of these sources, is the formation of an alternative geography that these travel itineraries imaginatively posit, narratively perform, and emotively map out. These narratives, I contend, respect no colonial or postcolonial boundaries, observe but trespass all fictive frontiers, and effectively collapse and cross over every and all fictive formations of "East and West," or "Islam and the West," or, a fortiori, "the West and the Rest." Old Muslim empires from the Mughals to the Safavids to the Ottomans are falling down, the weakling Qajar dynasty is clueless about the worlds it encounters as the European empires are encroaching on their ruins, and these traveling troubadours of the emerging worlds are wandering around their known and unknown worlds in search of new meanings for the dawning of a new age, and more than anything else trying to find out who and what they are, their writing hands searching the dark of their white pages in order to narratively locate themselves. Their narrative fluidity stages the overriding topography of the worlds they discover, map out, populate, and narrate, not just outside in the opening horizons, but also inside, mapping the unfolding frontiers of their own searching souls. As they discover and map out the world in which they live, they navigate and place signposts within the soul that will inhabit that world.

In this book I wish to demonstrate how these travelers map a much richer travel itinerary than just going from East to West. That assumption both simplifies and distorts the multilayered worlds they encounter and record in their narratives. I will also show how the systematic simplification of Persian prose in these very narratives was a formidable feature of their reach and significance. They effectively created a reading public for themselves and their prose outside the royal court and deep into an emerging reading public. The rate of public literacy at this point is not significant enough to warrant the assumption of any wide circulation. But the simplicity of their prose and the novelty of the worlds they encounter already force their Persian prose into an eventual assumption and gradual rise of a public readership.

Those emerging public readerships, I will then argue, were definitive and constitutional to the transnational public sphere upon which the post-imperial nations (nations that emerged in the aftermath of the collapse of Muslim empires) were now taking shape. Through a close reading of these sources I intend to identify the principal institutions of civil liberties and the rule of law their authors begin to identify, celebrate, and advocate. As they traveled far and wide, these travelers knew exactly what they were looking for and marking for a particular attention of their countrymen back home. I will therefore introduce the authors of these texts as the first specimen of "public intellectuals," for their prose was definitive to the formation of that public sphere upon which they then laid a legitimate leading claim, and finally how they became definitive to the introduction of a civic discourse in the emerging nations.

Those emerging nations are the way stations, the space in between the itinerary of these troubadours of the rising truths of what it means to be in the world. Paramount to the moment of the in-between is the overarching world that is forming in the minds of these travelers as they move from here to there, from now to then, from past to present. That world is worldly, material, palpable, and aware of the distance between cities and habitats, customs and cultures, in the multiple pluralities of their whereabouts. I wish to discover that world of the in-between, the terra incognita that is waiting to be discovered, covered as it is under the site-specific territoriality of our conception of time and space, and today of a deeply colonial conception of "modernity." A mobile conception of being-in-the-world is what I am after discovering here, where we are neither in the East nor in the West. We are somewhere in between, and what is our West today is our East tomorrow.

Journey as Metaphor

With that mobility of East and West as our master metaphor, I place the central argument of this book in contrapuntal position to the American historian Frederick Jackson Turner's "Significance of the Frontier in American History" (1893), and propose the deliberate crossing of frontiers to be definitive to the post-imperial history these

accounts document.[9] My contention is that these travelogues were
written at a time when their authors had an *active memory* of Muslim
empires (the Mughals, the Safavids/Qajars, and the Ottomans), *a
passive awareness* of European empires that had just descended upon
them, and therefore *a paradoxical disposition* toward the colonial
context of their immediate surroundings. We are catching these travelers at a very crucial period in Muslim history, when imperial frontiers
are falling but colonially mitigated national borders have not been
drawn yet. So, the landscape of the travels that they map out and detail
stages the transnational public sphere upon which postcolonial nation-
states are thereafter artificially engineered. My purpose is to document
that transnational public sphere upon which the postcolonial subject is
formed, precisely through these mobile texts as the most potent evidence of a territorially expansive age now aggressively repressed under
the thick shadow of postcolonial nation-states.

   To turn the abiding master trope of "East versus West" around and
upside-down, I propose reading these travel narratives also as metaphor, deeply rooted in their literary, poetic, and philosophical pedigree. I will therefore suggest the sixteenth century Iranian philosopher
Mulla Sadra's Shirazi's (ca. 1571–1640) philosophical summa, *al-Hik-
mat al-Muta'aliyah fi-l-Asfar al-'Aqliyyah al-Arba'ah/Transcendental
Wisdom of the Four Intellectual Journeys*, as the model and blueprint
for these physical journeys. In these journeys the philosopher travels
from the Multitude/Khalq to the Truth/Haq first, before in the second
journey he travels in Truth and with Truth. Then in the second journey
the One and the Many (the traveler and his scattered belongingness in
the world) efface in the presence of Truth/Haq. The Third journey is
back from Truth/Haq to the Crowd/Khalq, or the Multitude, though
this time with a different vision enabled by his encounter with Truth.
The fourth and the final journey is now with Truth/Haq through the
Crowd/Khalq, the traveler having attained a vision of reality that he
now casts back at the world. Just like Mulla Sadra's philosophical
journeys, these Iranian travelers left the multitude of their known
habitats and traveled toward an unknown Truth of which they knew
not what or where. Once they reached the vast expanse of that destination (which was the journey itself), they abandoned their known

[handwritten margin note: Mulla Sadra: 4 intellectual journeys]

---

[9] See Frederick Jackson Turner, *The Significance of the Frontier in American
History* (Eastford, CT: Martino Fine Books, 2014).

habitat and traveled with the truth they had discovered there through that truth, and once embedded inside that truth, now they traveled back to the multitude they had known before but now armed with a truth they did not know before.

I am not suggesting the travelers I plan to study here consciously modeled their journeys on Mulla Sadra's opus. I am proposing that these travelers do not appear from nowhere, that they come from a rich and diversified culture of traveling, in both physical and metaphysical senses, and therefore Mulla Sadra's monumental philosophical work offers us a manner of reading their writing in a more enabling way. I propose a Weberian "elective affinity" between Mulla Sadra's imaginal philosophical journeys and these later geographical journeys. The resonance I propose between Mulla Sadra's philosophy and these travelers' journeys posits a common imaginative universe, a shared affective ethos, between the towering Safavid philosopher and these late Qajar travelers. The echo of one in the other was somewhere between the subconscious of the traveler and the unconscious of their travelogues, between the enabling metaphor of "journey" and the bold and barren horizons of unknown worlds.

Why is it important to place these later travelogues in a larger metaphoric universe of "journey?" I propose to do so in order to demonstrate how these travel narratives were exceptionally significant in the eventual rise and subsequent formation of the multifaceted public spheres in the Persianate world, extending from India to Central Asia to Iran and Western Asia – and the formation of that public sphere was not a mere manifestation of European colonial modernity, and therefore performed *ex nihilo*. Upon these public spheres we then witness the political foregrounding of the eventual formation of post-imperial nations, persons, and their subjectivities, which are all upstream from the formation of the postcolonial state. I contend that the mapping and the contours of these travel narratives reveal a much richer and more diversified, exciting, and enabling topography than the simplistic and misleading assumption of "East meets West" or else hermetically sealed postcolonial nation-states that have long cast a distorting light on them. I therefore trace the origin of these travel narratives to the genre of *Safarnameh* in Persian and *Rihlah* in Arabic that predates them by a significant distance – let's say back to Naser Khosrow (1004–1088) and Ibn Battuta (1304–1369). This will locate the unfolding drama of Iranian travelers' encounters with a changing world in the emotive universe of travelers roaming the earth within their received Islamic geography.

But even that factual, historical, and geographical expanse upon which these travelers wrote their narratives is not sufficient. I will therefore also place these travelers next to two poets, one long before and one long after them. In his prose and poetry, for Shaykh Sa'di Shirazi (1210–1291), traveling around the world, all the way from India to Palestine, became a central metaphor. Though these travelers were discovering new worlds on the ruins of previous Muslim empires, their prose was squarely rooted in Persian literary humanism. They were projecting that humanism upon newer horizons. I will draw on Sa'di's traveling narratives to place these later travelers in a wider literary and poetic domain. Long after Sa'di, these nineteenth century travelers appeared, and long after they were gone yet a more visionary Persian poet, Sohrab Sepehri (1928–1980), appeared, to whose poetry, too, traveling became a paramount parable. I will therefore look at the traveling tropes of poets such as Sepehri to see in what directions what these nineteenth century poets had discovered resonated later in the next century. The result of this narrative fusion of what these travelers saw and wrote with what had enabled them and what they later enabled in others is a narratively textured, but thematically located, assessment of these travelogues at once rooted in a much older and enduring tradition and yet emblematic of something decidedly new in and about the world they were thus discovering, mapping, narrating, and creating.

The Itinerary of This Journey

Let me now map out the itinerary of my own journey through these travel books, how I will read and interpret them for you. As I have argued in detail, I believe there are two fundamental problems with most of the scholarship so far produced on this body of traveling literature: (1) They have been mostly read as if the final destination of their itinerary were Europe, and thus going to "the West" has been given a disproportionate significance in reading these travelogues and (2) They have been read in sporadic isolation and as an end in themselves and therefore never placed next to each other and within the larger frame of any narrative context and the "worlds" these texts create together. I intend to address and remedy these serious flaws by navigating the full spectrum of their traveling itinerary that includes Europe but is not

destined or directed to Europe, and also place the texts I choose in a
narrative context, forming a distinct body of literature, and therefore
coming together to offer a distinct perspective upon unfolding worlds
and an alternative geography these travelers visit and narrate.

Each of these texts I have selected carefully and for a specific reason, for
a particular angle they offer on how to read the spirit of the age they
document. Each one of these texts has a specific peculiarity hitherto lost to
those who have occasionally read and sought to understand them with a
prior intention to see how "the West" is depicted in them. When we
falsely assume the intention of these travelers was to "discover" Europe,
we gloss over the multiple worlds they visit and narrate in the body of
their texts, each in a slightly different way. It is the particularities of those
worlds, or what you will see me identify as their "cosmopolitan worldliness," that informs the totality of the texts I have selected and placed in
this narrative informed by the content of these books not imposing a
misplaced destination on them. The authors of these texts were only
subconsciously aware and informed by the world they thus inhabited.
My intention is to bring that unconscious world into full consciousness.
This, perhaps, is my singular ambition in writing this book.

Toward these complementary objectives, my book will unfold along
the following texts, pursuing the chronological order of their appearance
by their traveling authors. Although some of these texts have been
examined in other scholarly studies (including my own), the specific
constellation I offer here, with detailed attention to the multiple worlds
they have detected, created, and narrated as well as the literary universe
that had enabled them to do so, have never been so closely studied in the
manner I propose here. There are multiple atlases of a cosmopolitan
worldliness evident in these texts I intend to unearth and map out.

In Chapter 1, "Mr. Shushtari travels to India," I begin with a close
study of Mir Seyyed Abd al-Latif Shushtari's *Tohfat al-Alam/Gift from
the World* (1788). Born and raised in Shushtar in Southern Iran,
Shushtari was one of the earliest travelers of this period, whose travel
itinerary eventually took him to India where he became directly
involved with the British colonial administration of the subcontinent.
Upon his return to Iran, he wrote one of the earliest accounts of Iranian
encounters with European colonial modernity in India. The text is
extraordinary evidence of an imaginative geography of the global
south fully aware of the British and European imperial topography.
What is peculiar to Shushtari's travelogue is that he went East not

West, exactly in the opposite direction of what these travelers are believed to have been destined. It is in India that he encounters the institutional impact of British (European) colonialism, for which he has both a positive appreciation and a critical stand. Shushtari therefore stands at a critical point in a changing world where the Ottoman, the Qajar, and the Mughal Muslim empires are beginning to yield their cosmopolitan hegemony to alternative European imperial imaginings.

Figure 2 "19th century drawing of the Chahar Bagh school, in Isfahan by French architect Pascal Coste." [Public domain] – Iran itself was integral to the European colonial gaze, part of their Orient, subject of their imperial domination. Any Persian traveler leaving his or her homeland was perceived as having walked out of such Orientalist fantasies – straight out of a 1001 Night story. The body of evidence we are examining in this book is the solid archive of how these travelers had an entirely different view of themselves as they traveled and mapped out the world for their contemporaries and posterities. These travelers were real people, coming from real places, traveling around the globe and encountering the real world. They have left for us a detailed record of what they saw and what they thought. Every page of their travelogues is the evidence of the world the European colonial gaze had distorted and sought to recast to rule.

2.   In Chapter 2, "Mirza Abu Taleb travels from India," I turn to Abu Taleb Isfahani's *Masir Talebi/Talebi's Itinerary* (1803). Born and raised in an Iranian family in Lucknow, Abu Taleb Mohammad Isfahani traveled from India to Asia and Europe and wrote a detailed and influential account of his observations. Isfahani's narrative represents an exemplary specimen of Persian prose of his time in South Asia. Known also as "Abu Taleb-e Landani/Abu Taleb from London," he divides his travelogue into three sections: first, a detailed account of his journeys through Europe, second, his observations concerning the social and political institutions he encounters, and third, his thoughts on Muslim lands from Istanbul to Iraq and Arabia on his way back to India. The fact that the English translation of his travelogue was available even before its Persian original may indicate the particularly poignant presence of Persian-speaking thinkers in the formation of "Orientalist" narratives of the East. What is peculiar to *Masir Talebi* is that its author began his journey in India, traveled to the rest of Asia, Africa, and Europe, and then performed his pilgrimages in the Muslim lands, from the capital of the Ottoman Empire to its Arab provinces. In its pages we read a cogent critique of European imperialism, adjacent to a solid appreciation for its global reach. Abu Taleb Isfahani, as a result, offers himself as a singularly important public intellectual on a transnational (global) public sphere that he navigates, narrates, occupies, and critiques at one and the same time.

3   In Chapter 3, "An Ilchi Wonders about the World," I will focus on Abu al-Hasan Khan Ilchi's *Heyrat-Nameh/Book of Wonders* (1809). Abu al-Hasan Khan Ilchi was a statesman and diplomat with many crucial missions in Russia and Europe, during one of which he lived in London for eighteen months and while there kept a detailed diary, *Heyrat-Nameh*, in which we read a firsthand account of the normative imagination of a high-ranking official of the Qajar period. His *Heyrat-Nameh* is replete with insights into the world he sees in front of him, from its highest political aspirations and social changes to varied aspects of a European culture, with which he seems to be completely fascinated. As the very title of his travelogue suggests, we are in the presence of a book of marvels and wonders of a wide-eyed observer who is lost in his uncharted admirations and yet opens up his nation to wondrous new horizons awaiting its future. What is peculiar to Abu al-Hasan Khan Ilchi's travelogue is the fact that he was an official diplomat from the Qajar court, and in his account we encounter the

initial formation of the very idea of "Iran" as a modern (colonial) nation-state. The diplomatic birth of nations as (colonial) nation-states will henceforth dialectically mark the entire course of postcolonial public spheres and their contingent subject formations. Here in Ilchi's text we see the seeds of the dialectic in full spectrum.

In Chapter 4, "A Colonial Officer is Turned Upside-Down," I will turn to James Morier's *The Adventures of Hajji Baba of Ispahan* (1824). The inclusion of this landmark book by a British colonial officer lampooning Iran and Iranians requires some explanation. It is not the actual original book but its exquisite Persian translation by Mirza Habib Isfahani that later assumed a textual reality *sui generis* and became a key text in the course of the Constitutional Revolution of 1906–1911. The original is in fact a work of fiction and not a travelogue. But as a work of fiction it falls into the category of *picaresque* literature, featuring a charlatan who navigates the borders of East and West pursuing his selfish interests. What is peculiar to this text is the reversal of the politics of its reception from its English original to its Persian translation. As much as its original went a long way in detailing the Orientalist fantasies of a British colonial officer, its Persian translation did precisely the opposite in mobilizing a nation against domestic tyranny and foreign domination alike. Mirza Habib Isfahani's Persian translation also reveals the enduring significance of Istanbul where he originally published his translation and where the leading Iranian public intellectuals such as Mirza Aqa Khan Kermani and Sheikh Ahmad Ruhi had gathered to facilitate massive social changes in their homeland. Mirza Habib was a close friend and confidant of such figures, and his translation and its wide reception therefore reveal the transnational public sphere from which the very idea of "Iran" as a nation eventually emerged.

In Chapter 5, "A Shirazi Shares His Travelogues," I follow Mirza Saleh Shirazi's *Safar-Nameh* (1815). Perhaps the most influential public intellectual of his time, Mirza Saleh Shirazi began his career as a courtier with the reformist Qajar prince Abbas Mirza, by whose royal decree he managed to travel to Europe, write one of the most influential travelogues of his time, and bring back one of the earliest printing machines to his homeland with which to publish the very first widely circulated newspaper in his country, *Kaghaz-e Akhbar*. What is peculiar to Mirza Saleh Shirazi and his travel narrative is his pioneering work in helping the formation of a public sphere in his homeland.

Simplification of Persian prose, introduction of the printing machine, description of modern social institutions such as parliamentary democracy and the social functions of media, and undertaking the publication of a newspaper in his homeland all come together to mark Mirza Saleh as definitive to the making of an Iranian (Persian-speaking) public sphere, upon which he or anyone else could claim to be a "public intellectual."

6   In Chapter 6, "A Wandering Monarch," I look closely at Naser al-Din Shah's *Safar-Nameh/Travelogue* (1873). This travelogue by a sitting Qajar monarch represents the widely popular significance of travel narratives in the nineteenth century, in which the royal pen now indulges. The genre was so successful that the ruling monarch wishes to be part of it. Traveling was integral to this arguably most significant Qajar monarch. He traveled widely throughout Iran and abroad and kept diligent records of his travels. His three journeys to Europe (in 1873, 1878, and 1889, successively) are integral to this peripatetic monarch. What is particular to these travels, the first of which I will discuss in detail in this chapter, is the fact that the reigning king had effectively moved the political center of gravity of his realm away from his capital, Tehran, and presided over a mobile court. It is, again, important to remember that Naser al-Din Shah traveled as much in his own realm and around the Arab and Muslim world in the Ottoman Empire as he did to Europe. He financed these trips mostly by selling off major concessions to European colonial interest. Because of the structural link between these colonial concessions and Naser al-Din Shah's extravagant trips abroad, his widely published travelogues were paradoxically the source of much anger and frustration during the preparatory stages of the Constitutional Revolution of 1906–1911. The famous Tobacco Revolt of 1890–1891 was in rebellious reaction to a lucrative tobacco concession the Qajar monarch had granted Major G. F. Talbot, a British colonial merchant, during one of his European trips for a full monopoly over the production, sale, and export of tobacco for fifty years. The Tobacco Revolt was a dress rehearsal for the Constitutional Revolution of 1906–1911.

7   In Chapter 7, "Hajj Sayyah Leads a Peripatetic Life," I dwell on Hajj Muhammad Ali Sayyah's *Khaterat/Memoirs* (1878). In his early twenties, Hajj Muhammad Ali Sayyah embarked upon a journey around the globe that would last almost two decades and take him from Iran to Central Asia, Europe, and finally to the United States, where he lives

for about a decade, becomes a US citizen, and meets with President Ulysses S. Grant. What is peculiar about Hajj Sayyah's travels is that they are decidedly global in their expansive horizons, and therefore they are definitive to the active formation of a non-unitary "nomadic subject." He was about to marry his cousin and forced into a domestic life when he decided to run away and see the world for himself. He in fact fakes his own death while still traveling in Iran, in a gesture of supreme symbolic significance, before he embarks upon his peripatetic life around the planet. He returns to his homeland a harbinger of what at the time was not even recognized as economic and cultural global-ization, yet fully to be grasped and theorized decades later into the future in the age of global and differentiated mobility, when a diffuse form of nomadism will rise to define the location of multiple, inte-grated, and cosmopolitan subjects.

In Chapter 8, "In the Company of a Refined Prince," I examine Abd al-Samad Mirza 'Izz al-Dowleh Salur's *Safar-Nameh* (1883). Abd al-Samad Mirza was a Qajar prince, the son of Muhammad Shah and the younger brother of Naser al-Din Shah. He was appointed as the governor of a number of provinces, and accompanied his older brother during his travels around the world. He commanded a number of languages (Persian, Arabic, and French in particular), led a luxuri-ous princely life in his palatial garden, was occasionally dispatched on ceremonial diplomatic missions, and was an avid follower of global news. He was a poet and a painter. What is peculiar about this travelogue is the fact that its author had a rather remote princely disposition, was not in any significant position of power, and represented a stratum of Qajar royalty that was relatively educated, socially alert, and from his monarchic vantage point deeply concerned about the location of his homeland in the larger regional and global context.

In Chapter 9, "A Wandering Mystic," I turn my attention to Hajji Pirzadeh's *Safar-Nameh/Travelogue* (1886–1889). Hajji Mohammad Ali Pirzadeh Na'ini was an eminent mystic in the Qajar era who came from a prominent Sufi family. In his travelogue, Haji Pirzadeh tells us about his observation as he travels from Tehran to Isfahan, Shiraz, Karachi, Bombay, Cairo, Alexandria, Paris, and London. What will most interest me in this *Safar-Nameh* is Hajji Pirzadeh's mapping out the geography of major cosmopolitan urbanities, paying them all identical attention without privileging one city or country over the other. His description of Shiraz and Isfahan, Karachi, Bombay, or Cairo and Alexandria, are almost identical in detail to those of Paris and London. This narrative in particular categorically dismantles the false notion that these travelers were enamored of or destined toward "Europe," or worse, "the West" and reveals a radically different topography of their own wandering souls and the widening horizons they shared with their readers.

In Chapter 10, "In and out of a Homeland," Yahya Dowlatabadi's *Hayat-e Yahya/The Life of Yahya* (1893) will be the subject of my close reading. Yahya Dowlatabadi was a prominent poet, calligrapher, and social activist of the Constitutional period. His posthumous autobiography, *Hayat-e Yahya*, is a remarkable account of his life as a revolutionary activist. His father was a representative of Yahya Sobh Azal, the successor to Bab, the founder of the revolutionary Babi movement in Iran. He delegated that authority to his son, Mirza Yahya Dowlatabadi, who was a revolutionary social reformist initiating serious educational reform in his homeland. Throughout his life he was either exiled or else traveled extensively in and around the Qajar and Ottoman territories and visited Istanbul, Berlin, London, and Stockholm. In his multivolume autobiography, Dowlatabadi gives a detailed account of his life and travels. What is particular about this text is the deeply involved presence of its author in the most volatile period of his homeland, and therefore his journeys are the spatial extensions of his political activism in a critical period in Iran. His presence in this constellation of travelers is crucial for us to see how there is a narrative and institutional organicity to these travelogues that places the post/colonial subject on an effervescent transnational public sphere.

In Chapter 11, "The Fact and Fiction of a Homeland," I have selected a work of fiction, Zeyn al-Abedin Maragheh'i's *Seyahat-Nameh-ye Ibrahim Beik/Ibrahim Beik's Travelogue* (1903). Born and raised in Iran, and after traveling around the region extensively, Maragheh'i finally settled in Istanbul where he published his pioneering work of fiction and wrote extensively on current affairs for the leading progressive journals of his time. The significance of his magnum opus, *Seyahat-Nameh-ye Ibrahim Beik*, is that its protagonist is an Iranian who lives in Cairo and decides to travel to his homeland, and thus Maragheh'i writes it as a travelogue. The author uses this narrative plot in order to bring his lead character to visit his homeland with the fresh eyes of a familiar foreigner. The significance of this book is not just in being one of the most highly influential documents of the Constitutional period, but the fact that the genre of travelogue had become so widely popular that it informed the writing of one of the earliest works of fiction in Persian. What is particular about this book is the manner in which it reverses the gaze and the angle of vision back on Iran. It is no longer an Iranian who travels abroad, but an Iranian who travels home. This completes the cycle and brings the genre to a symbolic closure.

In Chapter 12, "Professor Sayyah Comes Home to Teach," I will look closely at Fatemeh Sayyah's life and career (1902–1948). Fatemeh Sayyah (aka Fatemeh Reza Zadeh Mahallati) did not write a travelogue, but her life and literary career is emblematic of a peripatetic environment that had made her professional character and literary culture possible. She was related to Hajj Sayyah, whose travelogue I examine in Chapter 7, and was briefly married to his son Hamid Sayyah, from whom she receives her last name. Her father was a professor of Persian literature in Russia, and her mother was Russian, of German descent. She was born and raised in Moscow, received her early and advanced education in Russia, mastered Russian and French literatures, received her doctorate degree in comparative literature with a dissertation on Anatole France, and then traveled to her homeland in 1924 and was a pioneering figure in introducing the discipline of comparative literature to Iranians. What is important about Fatemeh Sayyah is the fact that she was born and raised outside Iran, received her higher education in Russia, was far more comfortable in Russian than in Persian, assumed a leading role in the women's rights movement in her homeland, traveled extensively abroad to represent Iran in various conferences, and thus best personifies the multifaceted cosmopolitan culture that had deeply informed this entire body of travelogues I examine in this book. But, and there is the rub, that personification was marked by a positivist Eurocentrism that went against the grain of the world travelers who had made her possible. In that paradoxical twist we will see the emotive split between the unwavering sovereignty of a nation and the vagaries of states that have sought to rule them.

In my Conclusion, I bring all these observations together for a final reflection by first looking at two related texts by a prominent Shi'i cleric, Agha Najafi Quchani's (1878–1943) *Siyahat-e Sharq/Journey to the East* and *Siyahat-e Gharb/Journey to the West*. While *Siyahat-e Sharq* is an autobiography of the author, *Siyahat-e Gharb* is a fictional journey to the land of ghosts and spirits after death. The combination of these two "travelogues" by an author who really did not travel much beyond his homeland and Iraq to study Shi'i jurisprudence is a remarkable testimony to the power of "journey" as a metaphor for an entirely different imaginative geography upon which learned people of this time mapped out their lives and existence.

My attraction to this body of extraordinary literature in this detailed and multifarious manner is rooted in my recent work on mapping out the historic formation of a transnational public sphere in the wider Iranian world and the eventual rise of the postcolonial subject on its premise. In *Shi'ism: A Religion of Protest* (2011), I have narrowed in on the formation of a nascent public sphere in Isfahan at the height of the Safavid period and concluded with the eventual rise of the post-colonial subject in late the Qajar period and the onset of the Constitutional Revolution of 1906–1911.[10] In *The World of Persian Literary Humanism* (2013), I shifted my attention toward literary humanism as a narrative alterity to Islamic scholasticism as the modus operandi of the formation of the public and parapublic spheres and the multifaceted aspect of the selfsame postcolonial subject and the organicity of its multiple consciousness.[11] In my *Persophilia: Persian Culture on the Global Scene* (2015), I traced the historic formation of a transnational public sphere through cultural border crossings where the postcolonial subject is in fact seen operating far beyond any fictive colonial frontier.[12] Now in this book, *Reversing the Colonial Gaze,* I map out the liminality and conflation of worlds that have come together to form a new word and a corresponding cosmopolitan worldliness on an imaginative geography transnational in its character and far beyond the very assumption of any nation-state. The world I thus navigate and map overrides the dangerous delusion of "the West and the Rest."[13] Upon these interpolated worlds I propose the active formation of a

[10] See Hamid Dabashi, *Shi'ism: A Religion of Protest* (Cambridge, MA: Harvard University Press, 2011).

[11] See Hamid Dabashi, *The World of Persian Literary Humanism* (Cambridge, MA: Harvard University Press, 2013).

[12] See Hamid Dabashi, *Persophilia: Persian Culture on the Global Scene* (Cambridge, MA: Harvard University Press, 2015).

[13] In *A Metahistory of the Clash of Civilizations: Us and Them Beyond Orientalism* (New York: Columbia University Press, 2011), Arshin Adib-Moghaddam has offered a sweeping panorama of the origins and dialectic of such a binary.

cosmopolitan public sphere and an organically multifaceted subject that has asserted historical agency beyond the pale of any coloniality.[14]

The itinerant thinkers of the late eighteenth to early twentieth century I examine in this book were traveling from place to place as peripatetic harbingers of a whole new world that was fast dawning upon them, and they would not know it unless and until they had navigated through and wrote it down. They in effect crafted it by writing it down. Without that writing that world would be lost. Wandering souls, they were moving from city to city, from clime to clime, roaming beyond the limits of their received imagination, marking the lands that were pregnant with possibilities, rethinking and rewriting the world for their contemporaries and beyond for their posterities. With their saddlebags in tow, they were nomadic subjects forming a manner of knowing and being yet to be assayed, migratory in their varied readings of the world, vagrant and vagabond in the transitory disposition of their thinking. They traveled from one city to another, wondering what the new expansive horizons might reveal. The birth of Iran as a nation-state into colonial modernity was through these vagabond sojourners roaming from one end of the world to another – the very metaphor of journey thus became definitive to this age, journey through the homeland, into its familiar environs, and then beyond into its unfamiliar new distances. Wherever they went, they were always drawn to a fictive center that these peripheral wanderings entailed and defined. Where was that fictive center? It is misleading to call that fictive center "Iran," for Iran was being redefined and repossessed by these very travels. That center was a focus of gravity that was to hold the inhabitants of this land together. The final fate of the boundaries and borders of this homeland was a matter of colonial and counter-colonial encounters, of continually changing frontiers of the foreign and the familiar, thus offering a vastly different conception of regional and global history.[15] But the imaginative, emotive, and normative space inside those changing frontiers was always integral

---

[14] In many of his recent works, Ali Mirsepassi has had similar concerns, especially in his *Islam, Democracy, and Cosmopolitanism: At Home and in the World* (Cambridge: Cambridge University Press, 2014).

[15] In Alexander Anievas and Kamran Matin (eds.), *Historical Sociology and World History: Uneven and Combined Development over the Longue Durée* (London: Rowman & Littlefield, 2016), the editors have brought together a massive body of scholarship, radically rethinking the very notion of world history.

to the figurative geography of those wandering souls and the widening horizons they discovered as they traveled. There has always been an unfolding dialectic between those porous postcolonial frontiers and the emotive space these travelers discovered and defined as their *homeland* or *vatan* that was and has remained an irreducibly transnational public sphere, a conversation space between now and then, which is bound by no fictive frontier, and upon which a person becomes a person always already a foreigner in his homeland, as she is always already familiar with any foreign land she visits.

So, as the Iranian poet Mehdi Akhavan Sales (1929–1990) puts it in one of his most iconic poems, "Chavoshi/Harbingering,"

> Let us collect our backpack,
> Get going on the road that has no return and see
> If the sky over everywhere
> Is really the same color?

[handwritten margin note: vatan as emotive space]

1 | *Mr. Shushtari Travels to India*

Shushtar → India
(Iran)
⌐GB in
this context

No Nothing
Can rescue me
From the onslaught of emptiness about me
And I think this sad melodious song
Will be heard forever.
                    Sohrab Sepehri (Mosafer/Traveler, Babol, Spring 1966)

Who is it speaking in Sepehri's poem "Mosafer/Traveler"? Where did this voice dwell, how did it mature, through what echoes did it reach us? The date of this poem is only 1966 – but it reads Biblical and Qur'anic, Nirvanic and Olympian in its power and potency, visionary presence, and poetic timbre. When today we pick up Sepehri's collection of poetry, or any other poet of his generation, and we read through the oracular assuredness of their presence in our mind and soul, there is only so much of it that can be attributed to the worldly genius of a singular poet. That poetic voice needs, as it needed, the dexterity, longevity, and rich complexities of a different sort, of an historical experience that is hidden behind the soft gentility of the lines as they reach us. That longevity, however, is of a recent vintage, hidden but excavatable in the vanishing history of our presence. Sepehri was a traveler, both in person and in poetry, and I am writing these lines in New York, the city where he visited in 1970–1971 for a few months, and where he sat in peace, painted and exhibited a few paintings, composed a few poems, wrote a few letters to his friends. I see him, in my mind's eye, wondering when would I finish writing this book.

Back in the Times of Kayumars and Noah

Sepehri on
NYC?

After Noah's Flood, a small part of humanity survived and eventually managed to gather around a civilized life and continue to procreate. But soon chaos and warfare emerged yet again among them, the

25

powerful preying upon the weak. After a while it occurred to wise people to choose a king to rule over them in peace and harmony. They selected Kayumars, who was a descendant of Adam, to rule over them. People agreed to pay him tribute and tax, from which they made a crown to recognize him as their king, and they called him Kayumars the Pishdad to mark his being the first ever king to rule over men.

This is how Mir Seyyed Abd al-Latif Shushtari (1758–1805) begins his travelogue to India, *Tohfat al-Alam/The Gift from the World* (1788–1801).[1] From here he proceeds to give a full summary of the ancient Persian mythological order of creation until he brings it down to the moment when people made adjacent homes with mud brick, and the city they built was so beautiful they called it Shush (Susa), which in his offered etymology means "good," namely people were pleased with the city they had built. From there, Shushtari proceeds to tell us how King Houshang was hunting one day and chanced upon a lovely area which he called "Shushtar," meaning even better than Shush. He shares this bit of the local lore in order to place his hometown of Shushtar at the very beginning of time, the very epicenter of the universe, and from there link it to other major cities around the world, ranging from Delhi, Isfahan, and Istanbul, all the way to "some cities in Europe."[2]

Is it at all unusual, strange, or outlandish that Shushtari begins his travelogue to India with a thorough description of his hometown of Shushtar – its archaeology, geography, history, climate, environmental properties, architectural monuments, agricultural products, sacred precincts and mausoleums, notable religious and literary elites, etc.? He is indeed very proud of his hometown and takes his sweet time to give his readers a thorough exposition of his place of birth and breeding. He then concludes this initial section of his travelogue with a full chapter on his own family background, who he is, and what great ancestral lineage in Shushtar commends his earthly claims.

Mir Seyyed Abd al-Latif Shushtari is not the first learned man from Shushtar to find his way to India. Generations earlier, one of his own

---

[1] See Shushtari's *Tohfat al-Alam*: 32–33. For my earlier, brief encounter with Shushtari's travelogue, see Hamid Dabashi, *Iran without Borders: Towards a Critique of the Postcolonial Nation* (New York and London: Verso, 2016): chapter 1.

[2] Shushtari, *Tohfat al-Alam*: 34–35.

ancestors, Qazi Nurollah Shushtari (ca. 1542–1611), had also left his hometown and eventually emerged as a towering Shi'a scholar in Mughal India, who under Emperor Akbar had reached highest positions of power and authority. Mir Seyyed Abd al-Latif Shushtari refers to this Qazi Nurollah and many other prominent members of his own family in his *Tohfat al-Alam*.[3] This structural link between the Safavid Iran and Mughal India points to a regional map of commercial and cultural intercourse long before the British or even Portuguese presence and power. Shushtari's observations about the British and other Europeans in his book, as a result, must be considered from the vantage point of a regional history that predates that colonial interlude.

It is only *after* this long section on Shushtar and a detailed account of its history, which takes almost half of his book, that Shushtari turns his attention to his trip from Shushtar, first to Basra in Iraq, and then from there to India.[4] On his way to India, he first provides a full treatise on seafaring and the British conquest of India as well as a casual account of Europe and its marvelous achievements in science and technology, politics, and world conquest. When he finally reaches India, his description of the Indian subcontinent commences in earnest – beginning with a full account of Kolkata and other regions of Bengal and concluding with similar accounts of Hyderabad and other places he visited while residing in India. But everything he says in his travel book is ultimately overshadowed by what he says at the very beginning about his hometown. He first puts his feet down firmly in his ancestral city, where he was born and raised, and links it to the very cosmic origin of the universe, before he ventures out to tell us about the rest of the world. He narratively packs his hometown in his backpack before setting sail to India.

---

[3] Ibid.: 165.
[4] In "Limning the Land: Social Encounters and Historical Meaning in Early Nineteenth-Century Travelogues between Iran and India," Mana Kia has studied two other such pioneering travelogues between Iran and India, in two opposite directions, almost at the same time as Shushtari's. See Roberta Micallef and Sunil Sharma (eds.), *On the Wonders of Land and Sea: Persianate Travel Writing* (Cambridge, MA: Ilex Series/Harvard University Press, 2013): 44–67. Kia rightly draws attention to the Persianate world between Iran and India that such travelers occupied quite independent of any European interest.

Shushtar as the Center of the Universe

Shushtari begins his travelogue by describing his birthplace of Shushtar, rooting it in the myth of creation, which he then uses to offer a theory of civilization. He proposes civilization is contingent on four factors: first, a major capital like Delhi, Isfahan, Istanbul, or any European capital; second, the regularity of seasonal changes that help with agricultural products that this country can then export; third, having access to open sea from which commerce is possible, as they do in China, some European countries, Basra, Jeddah, and southern Iran; and fourth, climes where rainfall during summer is high enough to help with production of silk cotton and cereals that are the source of all other goods.[5] This example typifies the manner in which this travelogue is an occasion for him to express his considered opinion about everything that happens in the world, including his own theory of civilization. The mobility of the interpreter – the fact of systematically recording his movements from this to that city, from this to that port, from this to that ship – is definitive to his prose, giving it an agile disposition that moves from subject to subject with the quick wit of a traveler who must catch a ship here or be quick about a meal there in order to be on his toes and not miss a timetable.

From his own account, we learn that Shushtari comes from a very prominent and learned family in Shushtar. He in fact traces his ancestry to Seyyed Ne'matollah Jazayeri, a renowned jurist of the Safavid period in the sixteenth century. The best source of information about Mir Seyyed Abd al-Latif is in fact his own *Tohfat al-Alam*, which halfway through his narrative he in effect uses as a kind of autobiography. This latter point underlines a crucial aspect of the Persian travel narratives of the nineteenth century, namely the gradual emergence of an autobiographical voice of the person, an authorial "I," from the bosom of these circumambulatory journeys, in which Iranian literati seem to have to leave their homeland in order to find themselves in earnest and confidence. Immediately related to the gradual formation of this authorial "I" is the active articulation of the very idea of "nation" or "homeland," which is also (and quite paradoxically) formed while these travelers are moving away from their homeland. The farther they get from their homeland and the more they reflect on other nascent nations – in this case on Indians, the Arabs, the British,

---

[5] Shushtari's *Tohfat al-Alam*: 34–36.

the Russians, or the French – the more they seem to discover their own homeland, and think of it as a homogenous entity. In the case of Shushtari, however, this notion of homeland seems to be overwhelmingly anchored in his own hometown of Shushtar, which for him, as if as a synecdoche, stands for the whole country. "Iran" in effect becomes an extension of Shushtar. He otherwise scarcely talks about "Iran," but Shushtar is always on his mind. Unbeknownst to himself, he is building the very material from which a public sphere will be crafted, upon which now "Iran" will soon emerge as a postcolonial nation.

Home not Iran

   The narrative logic Shushtari follows is such that every item that he mentions about Shushtar or any other city occasions a short treatise on that subject. He mentions the star coordinates of Shushtar, for example, and bursts into a short commentary on how ancient people believed in astrology but British scientists no longer believe in such things. The same is his commentary on the ebb and flow of seas, which occasions yet another short treatise on astronomy. The history of Shushtar, however, as well as its culture and industries, remains constant in the early part of the book, with consistent references to ancient Iranian history and mythology. He has, to be sure, a critical assessment of his hometown, praises its salt for example, but criticizes its bad agricultural products and repeated famines.[6] Certain passages read like detailed ethnographic accounts of Shushtar, fusing history and ethnography together, occasionally bursting into a comparison of European past and present history. He walks his readers through various neighborhoods, tells them about mosques and minarets, draws their attention to its tourist attractions and ancient ruins, and offers detailed accounts of its prominent families, including a detailed account of his own family that culminates in his own autobiography, while sharing some of the local folktales.[7] What we are reading in these pages of Shushtari describing his hometown is in fact a returned gaze cast upon his birthplace from his Indian vantage point. In his mind he is looking "back" at Shushtar with the trained eyes of a traveler moving away from Shushtar toward India. It is India that is alerting him to Shushtar. He looks at the familiarities of his own hometown from the curious vantage point of a foreigner.

---

[6] Ibid.: 42.
[7] Ibid.: 73: Where he talks about a local wrestler, Pahlevan Reza Qassab/ Champion Reza the Butcher.

Shushtari's prose is consistently and appropriately flavored with poetry. He is having fun writing this book. It keeps him happy company, leads him to think, occasions his reflections on the world around him. Writing the book is therefore itself a journey. You never know, nor does he, what comes next. The fact that Shushtar is so central to his critical imagination gives his book at once both a centrifugal and a centripetal narrative force, a paradoxical tension that draws the world into a physical location and then releases it back into the world. He is not therefore talking in analytic abstractions. He writes with the narrative convictions of a native, from his homeland forward and backward into anywhere and anything else he visits, with Shushtar as the very epicenter of his universe:

My wonder-prone pen has already informed you that the Just Monarch Shapur Zu'l-Aktaf built Shushtar, from where he went to Ctesiphon and built that magnificent city upon Euphrates. Eventually other Persian kings added to that city and turned it into their capital, and it became so splendid that Egypt and China were ashamed of themselves.[8]

Crafting a New Narrative

Shushtari's inordinate attention to his hometown of Shushtar, in more than half of his travelogue, has prompted some scholars, such as the renowned early twentieth-century reformist Ahmad Kasravi (1890–1946), to accuse him of plagiarism in this part of his travelogue from a very important book on the geography of Shushtar *Tadhkereh-ye Shushtar/History of Shushtar*, which was in fact written by his own uncle. This *Tadhkereh-ye Shushtar* is a very important and rather well-known book, and perhaps the most famous book of Shushtari's uncle, whom he in fact discusses in his book and gives a bibliography of his writings, and yet he fails to mention this most famous of his books. As S. Movahhed, the editor of the critical edition of Shushtari's travelogue, has discovered, Shushtari has in fact "plagiarized" not only his own uncle Seyyed Abdollah's book on Shushtar, he has also done the same with another famous book on Shushtar by another author, called Hazin Lahiji, who was a rather prominent poet. As Movahhed points out, Shushtari does to Hazin Lahiji what he does to Seyyed Abdollah, his uncle – copies from their

[8] Ibid.: 76.

[handwritten note:] Plagiarism from Tzk-i Shusht. and from Hazin Lahiji

books on Shushtar, adds a few phrases of his own, and drops the names of
these books from the list of their publications.

While Kasravi accuses Shushtari of being "both a thief and a liar,"[9]
Movahhed is far more patient, generous, and understanding with Shushtari than Kasravi is, while at the same time documenting in precise detail
the specific examples of the passages that he has lifted off both his own
uncle's and Hazin Lahiji's books on Shushtar. As documented in detail by
Movahhed, Shushtari does freely help himself to those sources, but he
also plays with them, adds new material, disregards certain passages he
does not need for his immediate purpose. But, here is the crucial point for
my purpose here: What both Kasravi and Movahhed fail to notice is that
Shushtari himself mentions specifically, halfway through his book, that
writing was a mode of therapy for him; he wrote in order to feel better
when he was depressed. But he also mentions something crucial about not
having access to any library while traveling in India. When writing the
biography of his ancestors while in Hyderabad he says he was not feeling
well and was depressed and writing about his ancestry made him feel
better. Here he also says very specifically he will forego citing the exact
dates of people he mentions, for he does not have access to his or any
other proper library so he writes from memory, for "my nephew who is
like a son to me, Seyyed Razi ibn Seyyed Abu al-Qasem who is always in
my company was very eager to learn about his ancestors." Then in the
same breath, he adds, "I will write a bit about certain aspects of Europe
especially the cultivated English and their quite strange country."[10] In
other words, he may indeed have taken certain passages from some other
sources but has completely embedded them in his own prose.

There is little doubt that when Shushtari is writing about European
countries,[11] he is at times citing, copying, or paraphrasing from sources he
may have recently read or heard, sources to which he may or may not have
had immediate access at the time of his writing, for occasionally words
such as "Asia" or "Engineer" or "Governor" all appear in the Persian
transliteration of their English originals. Was he also copying these passages from some other books, perhaps? It is quite possible that his "plagiarism" extended far beyond the sources that Kasravi and Movahhed
have documented. But what is important about Shushtari and all of these
travelers is the fact of their travels, the reality of their eyewitness accounts,

---

[9] See Movahhed's Introduction to ibid.: 22–27. [10] Ibid.: 96–97.
[11] Ibid.: 327–337.

the impressions they have left of what they saw. Shushtari does not cite any
other source for any other part of his travelogue; therefore, to blame him
for having failed to cite the source of his sections on Shushtar or any other
section is meaningless. He and any other such traveler may exaggerate,
they may stretch the truth, they may claim things they may not have
actually done, they may even lie. But that does not compromise what they
are doing. "Jahan-dideh besyar guyad dorugh/The world traveler tells
much lie" is a famous line from a story of Sa'di in his *Golestan* (1258)
that speaks to a superior truth in manner of reading travelogues.

In that story Sa'di, who is the master model of all these later travelers, tells us about a man, who sports his hair like the Shi'ites do, who
comes to a prince, tells him he has just returned from a Hajj pilgrimage,
and has composed a wonderful new *qasideh* for him. It turns out that
he was a fake Shi'i, had not performed any Hajj pilgrimage, and that
very day they discovered his *qasideh* in the prominent poet Anvari's
divan. About to be punished, the man asked permission to say one last
thing, and he offered this heartfelt poem of his own:

> If a stranger offers you yoghurt,
> Its two spoons of water and a bit of watered down yoghurt –
> If you heard a frivolity from me do not get upset,
> The man who has traveled the world tells much lie.[12]

The weaving of fact and fantasy is definitive to the writing of these travelogues in a manner that is not meant to deceive or abuse anyone of
anything. The original authors of a book on Shushtar have had their
own immediate and appreciative audiences and readership. Books such
as Shushtari's *Tohfat al-Alam* are creatures of a vastly different world, a
wondering world, and as such they are crafting a new prose and narrative,
full of new ideas, phrases, and a vastly different geography of future
readership. At the time of their composition they scarcely have a readership
of their own, which is yet to come, to deceive them of or about anything.

What is significant is the mode and mood of his narrative, on his way
and while in India, giving an account of seas and seafaring, of global
geography based on European sciences, giving us a sense of his state of
mind as he travels. What is important is to see how he talks about
China and Europe in the same section, for he is following navigational

[12] Sa'di, *Golestan*. Edited, annotated, with an Introduction by Gholam Hossein
Yusefi (Tehran: Khwarazmi Publishers, 1368/1989): 81.

roots and not fictive geographies of "East and West." The order and flow of his narrative is important as he writes about the French conquest of Egypt just before he talks about papacy, or when he gives a detailed ethnographic account of the British, including their customs of dueling, their gender relations, their theatres. There is a sense of worldly awareness about Shushtari's prose. He talks about women's rights, venereal diseases, marital relationships, verities of British cuisines and their eating etiquettes. Occasionally there is an orality tone to his writing, reporting how he has "heard" certain things:

Because boys and girls are not concealed from each other, there is much amorous relationship among them and many of them turn to poetry and compose lyrics. I hear they are so incredibly passionate and well-composed. Because upper class girls are not sufficient in number, they engage with lower class boys, and they become so bold in this that nothing can prevent them. Their parents regrettably disown them and yet they go after their desires. I hear streets of London are full of such members of the nobility.[13]

Whether gossip, hearsay, or fact, whether he heard or read them somewhere, whether he is citing or copying from some other source, this is a revelatory prose that palpitates with verve and excitement of discovering an entirely new universe. Shushtari's ethnographic accounts based on what he has read or heard eventually lead to his discussion of the manner in which the British came to conquer India, just before turning his attention back to England to talk about capital punishment, incarcerations, and jails, as well as a detailed account of their legal system. From there he talks about the discovery of America, just before talking about the British financial system, gambling and lottery, taxation, bordello houses, medical practices, childbearing, Copernicus and astronomy, Newton and his telescope, and how the Europeans were thinking about inventing the airplane! There simply is no genre of writing in Persian at this time that matches the effervescence of this probing prose. He writes about military sciences of both the British and the Russians and their respective strategies. If you read Shushtari to find fault with him, catch him take phrases and passages from this book or another, you will not be disappointed. But what you will miss is the narrative tenor of his prose, the purpose of his writing, the cumulative impact that this and other texts like it will have in future.

---

[13] Shushtari, *Tohfat al-Alam*: 295–296.

The test of the authenticity and originality of Shushtari's prose is when he comes to talk about India and its history, culture, literature, and various customs. He does so precisely in the same manner he talks about Europe or about the Americas. He writes about Kolkata and Bengal the same way that he does about London and Paris. Right when he is deep into writing about the climate of the city in which he lives, he writes about his own life and marriage.

Everyone there was very much fond of me and high-ranking officials and nobility wanted me to be related to them via marriage, offering me considerable wealth. So although the matter was inconceivable for me even in my own homeland let alone in India and since when Almighty has ordained something all its wherewithal readily appear … and since our Imams have written much against solitary life and in praise of having a household … my cousin had a chaste daughter whose expenses he could not afford and therefore I obliged and in the spirit of being kind to my relations in Sha'ban 1205/April 1791 I married her.[14]

From this brief passage he moves to the rest of his coverage of India. He has a fascinating passage in which he addresses the thorny issue of sati – in very sober and straightforward language, neither glamorizing nor demonizing it. It is here that he writes about how the Hindu practices have influenced Muslims, and how Hindu and Muslim practices have influenced the British. He does the same about Deccan and Hyderabad, and then in his Epilogue he writes about the attack of the Wahhabis on Karbala, the ideas of Muhammad ibn Abd al-Wahab (1703–1792), and the short-lived mission of the Qajar envoy Hajji Mohammad Khalil Khan to India (he was evidently killed soon after his arrival in the course of a domestic disturbance). Shushtari has a particular interest in various religious sects and religious movements – seeking to provide economic, political, or at times even geographical accounts of their rise and significance. His interest in the rise of religious movements extends beyond India and includes Arabia and the larger region, with a particular interest in the rise of Wahhabism. He knows and reports of Captain John Malcolm's mission to the Qajar court, but he does not know (or he does not tell his readers) Malcolm is there to instigate Fath Ali Shah against the Afghans to prevent them attacking the British interest in India.

Shushtari's text is a historic document in revealing how an Iranian intellectual of his generation thought and reflected upon his

[14] Ibid.: 373–374.

contemporary issues outside the boundaries of his native homeland, how the very idea of that homeland was in fact being formed and informed by events far beyond its fictive frontiers. He reveals alternative geographies of normative sentiments, political prowess, and above all the opening horizons of emerging worlds. That is where the authenticity of his prose resides and offers unparalleled access to a world in the grips of colonial modernity and yet mapping itself beyond its self-contradictory mandates.

Figure 3 "Lord Curzon, British Viceroy of India, entering Delhi on an elephant with Lady Curzon 1902," Photograph. India is a major spot on the global map these travelers are incorporating into their vision of the world. One of these travelers in fact just went from Iran to India and back, never ever going to Europe. Neither his nor any other of these travelogues were written from or to Europe. As a major colonial force, Europe is integral but not definitive to them, as are India, the rest of Asia, all the way to Africa and Latin and North America. These travels are initiated in Iran and India and they map the world over, with no epicenter to their worldly imagination. They are neither Eurocentric nor anti-Eurocentric. Reading them all together, we emerge with a vastly different conception of the Eurocentric world of the colonial heritage. In these books the world is liberated from Eurocentrism. Europe here is decentered, brought into the topography of a decidedly different conception of the world. The fluent realism of these traveling proses cures all of their readers of any lingering Orientalism – if they were to be afforded the dignity of a total and comprehensive, cover to cover, reading. Reprinted with permission from North Wind Picture Archives/Alamy Stock Photo.

Traveling Intertextuality

We have an intertextual reference to Mir Seyyed Abd al-Latif Shushtari
by a close friend of his, Mirza Abu Taleb, the author of *Masir Talebi*
(1804), to which I will turn in the next chapter. Such intertextual
references are important to gather the sense and spirit of the time, the
manner in which these travelers came together to form the spirit of
their age, and the mood of unfolding a different world in front of them.
From Abu Taleb we learn that Shushtari was quite fond of traveling in
his own homeland and its immediate vicinity and had gone for various
visits to Basra, Baghdad, Hillah, Karbala, Najaf, Kermanshah, and
Kurdistan. He had in fact spent much of his life traveling around and
took particular pleasure in talking with the learned elite of the places
he visited.[15]

(elite)

According to Mirza Abu Taleb, Shushtari had arrived in Kolkata in
October 1788, when he was thirty years old. Upon his arrival he went
straight to Morshed-abad in Bengal, where he married his cousin, then
returned to Kolkata and lived there for a period. While he was in
Kolkata, his brother, Mir Mohammad Shafi', who was a successful
merchant in Basra, sent him some money and asked him to be his agent
for buying certain products and sending them to Basra, which he did.
From this transaction, Shushtari had made a serious amount of money
and soon not just his brother but a whole group of other merchants
from Basra sent him money and asked him to buy and send them
merchandise. From his commissions from these transactions, Shushtari
accumulated a small fortune, from which he lived quite comfortably in
India. Soon, Mirza Abu Taleb reports, through one of his cousins,
Shushtari found his way to the palace of the British Governor of
Bengal, which in turn increased his fame and fortune in India.

Mirza Abu Taleb further reports that Shushtari had helped him
financially when he had embarked upon his own trip to England,
and that Shushtari had in fact written a letter to Abu Taleb while the

[15] S. Movahhed cites this reference to Mirza Abu Taleb in his useful introductory
essay to his critical edition of Shushtari's text. See Shushtari's *Tohfat al-Alam*:
11–28. The original reference is in Mirza Abu Talebi's own travelogue. See
Mirza Abu Taleb Khan, *Masir-e Talebi: Ya Safarnameh-ye Mirza Abu Taleb
Khan/ Talebi's Itinerary or the Travelogue of Mirza Abu Taleb Khan.* Edited,
annotated, and with an Introduction by Hossein Khadiv Jam (Tehran: Jibi
Publications, 1352/1973): 452–453.

latter was in England, in which he reported to his friend that because of ill health he was about to leave India and go back to his homeland in Shushtar. His return to his homeland, however, is delayed because of some political problems he had encountered in India, resulting in an accusation that he had misappropriated some funds, and he ended up spending some time in jail in India. The Iranian ambassador in Bengal interferes on his behalf, secures his release, and he leaves for Bombay, where Mirza Abu Taleb finally manages to meet up with Shushtari. According to Movahhed, "Mir Seyyed Abd al-Latif did not live long after the year [Abu Taleb Maki's] *Masir Talebi* was composed, which is 1804, and died in 1805 in Hyderabad of Deccan, because of his chronic disease and the bad climate of India."[16] Shushtari's travelogue was finished in 1801, and later in 1804 he added a short Epilogue to it, just before he died in 1805.[17]

Between Shushtari and Mirza Abu Taleb, one going from Iran to India, the other from India around the world (in a fluid geography such that all these terms are now up for rethinking), with both keeping a written record of their observations, we have joint evidence of an unfolding genre in Persian that informs a nascent reading public yet fully to be realized. There is not much of a circulation to these texts, not much of a reading public, not much of an immediate impact to what they see and what they write. They are the harbingers of widely opening horizons to their people, the forerunners of a prose that will change their world for good, the heralds of an advancing universe, the narrative indications that they are all aware of the ringing bells of a new dawn in history, the complete proportions of which they do not yet thoroughly understand.

Sighting the British in India

While in India Shushtari takes particular pleasure in associating with the political elite, both Indian and British. He is a learned and deeply cultivated man, naturally curious about the world, flaunts his learning effortlessly, and enjoys the company of those who do the same. He puts all his rationalism and all his learning straight at the service of

[16] S. Movahhed's Introduction to Shushtari's *Tohfat al-Alam*: 13.
[17] Shushtari also talks about Abu Taleb in *Tohfat al-Alam*, corroborating the latter's account in his *Masir Talebi* in some detail, of which I will write in the next chapter, which is on Abu Taleb's travelogue. See ibid.: 368–369.

British colonialism in India.[18] He is totally enamored of the British and believes them to have brought peace, justice, and equanimity to the world. He opposes such leaders as Fateh Ali Khan Sahib Tipu, aka "Tiger of Mysore" (1750–1799), for opposing the British and advises them to accept the authority and legitimacy of "Selseleh-ye Jalileh-ye Engelisiyyeh/the Magnificent British Dynasty." He is deeply connected with the East India Company and the British Governor, and even boasts of his attraction to "a European Christian girl." Not despite but in fact because of his deep affection for the British rule in India, he provides detailed accounts of their manners, including unsavory manners, of administrative domination over India. As an Anglophile, Shushtari harbors a deep dislike for the French and their "ill manners" in politics and taste – and yet despite his admiration for the British he boasts about the fact that Iranians were not colonized by the British or any other foreign power.[19]

Despite all the pomp and ceremony afforded him in India, Shushtari deeply misses his homeland and wishes to be able to go there and regrets the day he set foot in India.[20] He also regrets not having spent his life in pursuit of knowledge and having wasted his time with material pursuits. There is a deeply confessional aspect to Shushtari's narrative here – as if the pages of his travelogue provide him with a safe haven in which he can indulge in his private thoughts and anxieties – almost momentarily forgetting that this might also be contributing to the formation of an extended colonial public sphere. In fact, the borderlines of the private and public become quite porous in this travelogue – whereby we cannot quite tell where he is assuming a personal space and where carving a public audience for his travelogue.

Shushtari is an astute commentator on his contemporary politics, early Qajar reign, British colonialism in the region, uprisings and revolts against this domination – and at times provides deeply informed social, political, and economic accounts of a vast region from the Ottoman and Russian empires down to Qajar territories and the British hold on India. While in India, he comes to learn much about Europe and European countries and takes a considerable delight in narrating his learned commentaries on these countries for his Persian-speaking audience. Certain pages of Shushtari's travelogue read like a highly cultivated short treatise on his contemporary politics,

[18] Ibid.: 361–341.   [19] Ibid.: 270.   [20] Ibid.: 466.

particularly on British colonialism and its social and political consequences. His journey to India happens not too long after 1765, when
the East India company had stopped installing puppet rulers and
obtained the power from the Mughal court to collect their revenues
directly, and when in the course of the great Bengal Famine of
1769–1770 millions of people had been starved to death. This is just
eighteen years before Shushtari had arrived in Kolkata in 1788, precisely the year when the impeachment of the first British governor–
general in India, Warren Hasting (governor–general, 1773–1785), on
charges of misconduct and corruption, had started in the British parliament. Shushtari speaks highly of Lord Hastings, however, and
credits him to be a very generous man who had established a Muslim
madrasa in India.[21]

Shushtari's text is one of the earliest accounts of European history
after the Renaissance, the Enlightenment, and the rise of European
colonialism in Persian – from an almost entirely sympathetic and
laudatory perspective. He sees a direct correspondence between the
rise of European colonial power and the advancement of science and
technology, philosophy, and arts in Europe. As Movahhed points
out,[22] Shushtari had no other writing that has survived him except
for this travelogue and its Epilogue. But his *Tohfat al-Alam* was
apparently well-received by his contemporaries (however limited that
reception might in fact be) and cited as an authoritative source.[23]

Perhaps the most crucial aspect of Shushtari's account of the British
imperial prowess and technological achievements is that he sees,
experiences, and in fact admires it from the vantage point of their
receiving end in colonial India. In his book, as a result, we have a quite
sympathetic account of what the British were up to while they ruled
India. Shushtari is completely enamored of the British and in fact
befriends and frequents the company of their leading political elite in
India. His account, as a result, has the peculiar characteristics of an
Iranian observing the British rule in one of their richest colonial possessions. Sympathetic as he is to the British, he is not completely blind
to their treacherous atrocities – but he considers these as integral to the
reign of an empire ruling a land halfway around the globe from its
headquarters on an island in the Atlantic Ocean. His account of the
British colonial presence in India, as a result, cannot be dismissed as

[21] Ibid.: 369.   [22] Ibid.: 16.   [23] Ibid.: 17.

hostile, antagonistic, or belligerent. From his supportive and sympathetic perspective, we see how the British took over an entire continent, transforming it into a settler colony for their expansive commercial, colonial, military, strategic, and imperial interests. Shushtari speaks voluminously about the British military, administrative, judiciary, and every other aspect of their colonial conquests of the world through his immediate observations in this their most lucrative possession (their "Jewel in the Crown"). None of his observations about the British colonial rule in India can be easily dismissed, for the simple fact that he, literally, worked for them – and he worked for them with conviction and admiration.

In between Two Encroaching Genres *ask abt. this .*

The rise of this travelogue genre of critical thinking, such as Shushtari's *Tohfat al-Alam*, occurs in between two encroaching modes of knowledge production: one, the powerful European Orientalist historiography best represented by colonial officers like Captain John Malcolm (1769–1833), and the other, the useless court poetry regurgitated by Qajar poets like Fath Ali Khan Kashani, *nom de plume* Saba (1765–1822). Placing Shushtari's prose and purpose in his travelogue in between these two genres of his contemporary time better highlights its significance.

Just about the time of Shushtari's visit to India, Captain John Malcolm (1769–1833), a prominent British military officer and pioneering Orientalist scholar, was in India and was in fact sent in the opposite direction on a mission to the Qajar court in Iran. Malcolm had arrived in India precisely when Shushtari was there too, in 1783, as part of the East India Company Madras Army. Later Malcolm became the military secretary to none other than Field Marshal Sir Alured Clarke GCB (1744–1832). Clarke was no ordinary colonial officer. He was in charge of all British troops in Georgia in the United States, from where he was sent to Philadelphia toward the end of the American Revolutionary War. From there he became Governor of Jamaica and then lieutenant governor of Lower Canada. From here he was sent to India where he became commander-in-chief of the Madras Army, and many other services to the British colonialism. Malcolm was eventually sent to Iran, where with Prime Minister Haji Ibrahim Khan Kalantar he signed a commercial and diplomatic pact, among the provisions of which was the opening of a commercial interest of the Qajar court in Bombay. The primary concern of the British at this point was to use the Qajars to safeguard their Indian possession against any Russian or even French incursion from Afghanistan.[24] Captain John Malcolm was a pioneering Orientalist with a keen interest in Iran. He wrote and published one of the earliest studies of Iranian history by a British colonial officer, *The History of Persia: From the Most Early Period to the Present Time* (1815), which was a standard staple of Orientalist scholarship for decades. With these and similar studies by leading British and other European colonial scholars, the study of Iran and production of knowledge about Iranians became central to their colonial interest in the region.

Shushtari was also a contemporary of Fath Ali Kashani Saba (1765–1822). Saba began his courtly services with the Zand dynasty (1750–1794) but after its demise shifted allegiance to the victorious Qajar side. He was a gifted neoclassicist poet who praised the reigning monarch, Fath Ali Shah, lavishly and for which he was lucratively compensated by being appointed governor of Qom and Kashan. His claim to fame is *Shahanshahnameh*, which he composed on the model of Ferdowsi's *Shahnameh*, precisely at a time when his favorite monarch, Fath Ali Shah, was embarrassingly defeated by the Russians and lost a vast portion of his territories during the Perso-Russian wars of 1804–1813, which resulted in the two successive treaties of Golestan and Turkamanchai, perhaps the most humiliating (now proverbial) pacts in modern Iranian history.[25]

As the Orientalist historiography on countries like Iran crescendoes to reach the highest plateau of knowledge production at the service of European imperialism, Persian poets like Saba are parroting the masterpieces of the classical period ad nauseam to no social or literary purpose except to praise useless monarchs and enrich their own deep pockets. While Captain John Malcolm has much to teach the British colonial project about "Persia" and how to rule its regions and rob them better, Fath Ali Khan Saba and his ilk have absolutely nothing to

[24] For more on Captain John Malcolm, see the entry "ANGLO-IRANIAN RELATIONS ii. Qajar period" (*Encyclopedia Iranica*), available online here: www.iranicaonline.org/articles/anglo-iranian-relations-ii. Accessed August 29, 2016.
[25] For more details on Saba, see the encyclopedic work of Yahya Aryanpour, *Az Saba ta Nima/From Saba to Nima* (Tehran: Zavvar Publishers, 1971): I: 20–28.

offer their people about how to resist the armed robbery of nations of Asia, Africa, and Latin America. The rise of travel writings of this period, even in places where the authors are in awe of European colonial might, reverberate with a robust prose that is in tune with the spirit of the time.

Paramount in Shushtari's narrative of his trip to India is his flaunting of what he calls *Aql-e Salim/Sound Reason*, with which he measures everything he observes, and then he accepts or rejects its veracity. He is a rationalist through and through – in some uncompromising way opposed to what he believes are unreasonable propositions, super-stitious beliefs, and unsound judgments. With such persistent claims to sound judgment, Shushtari at times demonstrates an uncanny atten-tion to detail of what he observes in India and gives an almost clinical description of what he sees. For this reason, it is safe to assume that he has already a reading public in mind at the time of writing his travel-ogue. While drawn to a rational perspective, still his prose is studded with pieces of poetry that embed his narrative in classical Persian diction. Carrying the best his classical culture had invested in him like a backpack, Shushtari travels onto new horizons to see the world with a set of fresh and inquisitive eyes.

Bringing the World to Europe   → [Not eyewitness]

Shushtari's book can and should be considered in line with the classic text of Alberuni's (1073–1048) *India* as a detailed study of India, a text in Indology proper. It is an eyewitness account of an Iranian traveler going to India and writing down his observations that may indeed be considered proto-anthropological in detail. Once we do that, almost all other texts we are studying in this book and many more like it become also a study of the countries and climes other than India that these travelers had come to visit, leaving a detailed account of their findings and something of their "field notes," as contemporary anthropologists would say. If we did so, this in turn raises another issue: that these books are in fact collectively the earliest "modern" anthropological studies of a wide range of regions that these travelers had visited, which includes Europe but is not limited to Europe. As a result, there is no Eurocentrism to this mode of knowledge production about Europe or about anywhere else. In other words, in this body of literature we have a solid compendium of European and non-European studies by Iranian

(importance of textual sources for authors we are considering here?)

(Muslim) travelers, scholars, literati, and critical thinkers, without privileging Europe or non-Europe, for Europe is placed in a larger frame of global and regional contexts. These contexts are unfolding, overlapping, changing, and exchanging with new frames of reference. The active mobility of these travelers translates into ever-unfolding horizons and worlds they visit, discover, and narrate.

My concern in this book, as I have indicated from the outset, is to allow these authors to teach us about the *entirety* of the unfolding and ever-changing worlds they have visited, and not just the European part of their findings, for which they have been mostly considered, with the notable exception of more recent scholars who have paid attention to the navigational routes of the Indian Ocean or the Persianate world evident in some of these travelogues. But in addition to these regions, there is also the more crucial question of "Europology" without Euro-centrism that is most solidly evident in these texts, a sustained body of literature produced neither from a position of power like Orientalism nor from a position of weakness as suggested by those who have read them as pathological indices of Muslims and Orientals visiting "the West." They are neither exclusively fixated on Europe, nor are they devoid of critical attention (positive and negative) to Europe. Because they travel with ships through the navigational trade routes around their own immediate region and beyond, they have a far more accur-ate, far more materially based conception of their world than the fictional binary that informs "the West versus the Rest" school of historiography. In short, they bring Europe into the bosom of larger worldly contexts, contexts to which Europeans had remained decidedly hostile, aliened, ignorant, condescending.

This particularly powerful epistemic dimension of these texts has been either completely ignored or else distorted by assuming they were wide-eyed Orientals going to Europe to marvel at their glories and bring "modernity" back to their homeland, whereas the reality of these texts is something entirely different. Keep in mind these travelers were producing knowledge about the world (including but not exclusively Europe) at a time when Orientalists were busy casting the world into "the West and the Rest." They, on the contrary, did no such thing. They had a far more generous, open-minded, critical, competent, and caring conception of the world. They did not bring "Europe to their homeland." Quite the contrary: They brought the world to Europe, and they did so writing in Persian, for the whole world to read, for they came from an imperial imagination that linked the active memory of three Muslim empires (in Indian, Iranian, and Ottoman domains) together and thought the whole world must know Persian, or at least the world they thought significant. Contrary to the European Orientalism that is contemporary to them, there is no nativism to these texts, and contrary to the Orientalist discourse, these travelogues had no institutional support within the European or any other colonial project. There is a resounding worldliness to their prose and purpose to which both European Orientalist and Muslim nativist readers have remained oblivious.

What Shushtari in particular offers his readers is an imaginative geography of the global south fully aware of the superimposition of the British and European imperial topography upon it. He went East not West, exactly in the opposite direction of what these travelers are believed to be destined. In India he encounters the institutional impact of British (European) colonialism, for which he has mostly a positive appreciation and occasionally a mild critical stand. He stands at a critical point in a changing world where the Ottoman, the Qajar, and the Mughal Muslim empires are beginning to yield their cosmopolitan hegemony to alternative European imperial imaginings. He appreciates that imperial power but is not beholden to it. He is a proud native son, arrogant even in certain aspects of his own autobiography. But he is not prejudiced against the things that he sees. He is widely curious but never wide-eyed. He does not think his homeland or India "backward," in need of "Westernization," nor indeed does he harbor any critical stand vis-à-vis the British or the Europeans. There are times today when we read Shushtari that we wish he did. But he does not – and in that absence of a critical stand he is much more open-minded to show us a different vision of the world that is dawning on him and the rest of humanity.

That brings us to a full recognition of a different kind of "cosmopolitanism" that travelers like Shushtari had discovered and narrated. There is something fundamentally flawed with the range of thinking about "cosmopolitanism" that has historically originated in Europe and has now reached its glosses and commentaries in North America.[26] From its Western European heritage to its North American

cosmopoli-
tanism

---

[26] As best collected, edited, and with an Introduction by Garrett Wallace Brown and David Held in *The Cosmopolitanism Reader* (Cambridge: Polity, 2010).

extensions, this idea of "cosmopolitanism" is in fact astonishingly provincial, for it takes one particular imperial narrative it calls "the West" and casts it categorically upon the entirety of the globe and the varieties of the worlds in plural it has produced and lived, and is still capable of producing and living, and almost entirely oblivious to the colonial ravages this very idea and practice of "the West" has visited upon the world. From this provincial vantage point it then produces a cosmopolitanism that we are told is good for the world at large to follow and practice as something that we need and we should strive to achieve, entirely oblivious, without even a hint of irony, that this self-privileging of a provincial point of view ipso facto silences and blinds an entire history of other worlds and their cosmopolitanisms that need to be part of this conversation.

The astonishing power of these travelogues we are reading here is the fact that their authors are emerging from the towering imperial narrative of their own – three simultaneous world empires ranging from the Mughals to the Safavids/Qajars to the Ottomans, and are entering upon a full horizon of the European empires fully conscious of the world about them. In between these two colliding worlds, they are navigating the vast expanse of a purgatorial world that is neither here nor there. Their cosmopolitanism as a result is not to universalize their particular; it is not to urbanize their provincialism. It is to discover a whole new worldliness that thrives in between cities and urbanities, cultures and climes, religions and cultures. That space-in-between that they traverse is entirely lost to these European cosmopolitan theorists and philosophers, for they write from the bosom, the very heart, of their own imperial pedigree, while these travelers are daring the elements of the in-between-worlds, in-between-histories, in-between-universes of imagination. These texts are the active evidence of those worlds, in chapter and verse, before those worlds were concealed and condemned under the narrative hegemony of "the West and the Rest."

As an example of these navigational tropes of the emerging worlds, Shushtari's travelogue records how the author begins in his hometown and travels in his own immediate region before sailing for India, where he spends a significant portion of his life as an expat intellectual. While in India, what he misses is not "Iran" in abstraction, but just his own hometown of "Shushtar," for which he has a deeply mystical affection. Somewhere in between mythology, poetry, science, technology, and colonialism, Shushtari is an eyewitness to one of the most transformative periods in the history of his homeland, its regional and global context, and the manner in which he sees the world. Traveling to India is only an excuse, an occasion, for Shushtari to wonder about the world around him. He did not even go to Europe to consider such travelogues as intended to reach Europe and learn from Europeans. He was learning from his own observations, limited or expansive. The result of what he writes is a detailed ethnography; local, regional, and global history; the rise and demise of sectarian violence; the collapse of the last three Muslim empires; and the rise of the Russian, British, Portuguese, and French imperial conquests. He is an eyewitness to the massive globalization of Eurocentric capitalism and imperialism. His prose is easy, accessible, witty, and admonitory here, entertaining there, and always expository at one and the same time. The authorial voice of Shushtari is inaugural, his audience a posterity he knows will arrive, and his purpose to frame the emerging worlds in a new vocabulary it will demand from his readership generations later. As an author, Shushtari writes for a posterity beyond his own lifetime; as an itinerant intellectual, he sees the world in the unfolding organicity of multiple public spheres beyond any imperial claim or control.

2 | *Mirza Abu Taleb Travels from India*

The gaze of the traveler
Was cast upon the earth:
"What beautiful apples!
Life is the ecstasy of solitude."
              Sohrab Sepehri (Mosafer/Traveler, Babol, Spring 1966)

Sohrab Sepehri's poetic voice was long in the making – his sense of solitude rooted in a society he did not have to keep to own. Not just over his own lifetime, and not during the lives and works of other monumental poets of his time, such as Nima Yushij (1897–1960) – but a historical consciousness breathes behind the sublimity of his words. We can of course trace that voice deeply into the history of other philosopher/poet/travelers, such as Naser Khosrow (1004–1088) or Sa'di (1208–1294). But the thick and thriving history of the nineteenth century resonated with a global consciousness that would eventually come down, poet after poet, traveler after traveler, to Sohrab Sepehri and animates his poetic intuition of transcendence. To see the sublimity of an entire existence in a few fresh apples or to mark a traveler as the sojourner of truth was no mean achievement in a singular poetic consciousness, generations in the making. My joyous task in this book is to map out the shifting contours of that consciousness.

Fellow Travelers

What is astonishing about Shushtari is the catholicity of his curiosity, absence of any rancor against "the West," and a balanced and healthy proclivity toward both admiration and criticism, all placed within a solidly comparative and global perspective. Even when they recognize a category as "the West," or "Farang" (and the two terms are not exactly identical, as I will argue in detail shortly), they do so without prejudice or resentment. They go around the world and expand their horizons unencumbered by any false bifurcation between "Islam and the West." Every occasion calls for a specific reading in terms domestic to those circumstances. They move from countries to countries, climes to climes, open to what the new horizons have in store for them, and the new world they signal has to offer. They sail upon seas and ride through valleys, weaving together an entirely different imaginative geography than the one they had inherited or the one awaiting their posterity. It is this abiding sense of wonder and discovery of a new world opening its vistas to them that needs to be uncovered and mapped out.

Let me now turn to Abu Taleb Isfahani's *Masir Talebi/Talebi's Itinerary* (1803). What was Abu Taleb's itinerary? What does it mean when they say he went from India to Europe and came back? Who was this Abu Taleb, anyway?

"An Oriental Man"

Before we get to know Abu Taleb and his travelogue, let's first take a look at the manner in which he has been represented by his British readers, past and present, for the initial Orientalist gaze cast upon him during his own lifetime early in the nineteenth century has now extended to include our own time. First, we need to clear up a bit of confusion before the author of this travelogue can be seen more clearly.

"*The Travels of Mirza Abu Taleb Khan,*" declares Nigel Leask of University of Glasgow, "is perhaps the most significant 'reverse travelogue' published in Europe during the Romantic era, and one of the first published accounts of Britain by an Asian author. Abu Taleb casts a fresh eye on the sites and personalities of Georgian London, combining a sense of wonder at the technical and aesthetic achievements of Britain at the dawn of the nineteenth century with a sharp social and moral critique of the new masters of Bengal."[1] This laudatory review of a

---

[1] See the blurb endorsing Abu Taleb Khan, *The Travels of Mirza Abu Taleb Khan in Asia, Africa, and Europe, during the Years 1799, 1800, 1801, 1802, and 1803.* Edited by Daniel O'Quinn (Peterborough, ON, Canada: Broadview Press, Broadview Editions, 2008). The original edition was published as *The Travels of Mirza Abu Taleb Khan in Asia, Africa, and Europe, during the Years 1799, 1800, 1801, 1802, and 1803. Written by Himself in Persian Language.* Translated by Charles Stewart, Esq., M. A. S. Professor of Oriental Languages in the Hon. East-India Company's College, Herts. Printed by R. Watts, Broxbourne, Herts, and sold by Longman, Hurst, Rees, Orme, and Brown, London, 1814.

recent English version of Abu Taleb Khan's travelogue contains perhaps the most crucial twist European Orientalists past and present have put on it: "Reverse travelogue." What is a "reverse travelogue?" What is that "reverse" doing there? What kind of travelogue is "straight" to which this one is a "reverse" specimen?

"Reverse travelogue" is not the only phrase that thus introduces Abu Taleb Khan's travelogue to a new readership. We also read that in the considered opinion of Ros Ballaster of Mansfield College, Oxford University, "Eighteenth-century readers were so familiar with the fiction of 'reverse ethnography' (the record of travels to Europe by a traveler from a different culture) that reviewers were at first suspicious about the authenticity of these learned, witty, and often satirical writings. As they did for contemporary readers, they have much to tell us now – about political cultures, social interactions, the colonial context, and the attractions as well as fears of the European metropolis."[2] So the book is a specimen of both "reverse travelogue" and "reverse ethnography." The issue is therefore confounded. Why "reverse" both "travelogue" and "ethnography"? What kind of "ethnography" is "straight," to which this is a "reverse ethnography" – and by what authority, and who gave those "straight ethnographers" and "straight travelers" the authority to be the primary kind of anything? This is precisely the continued colonial chutzpah that underlines the continued abuse of these texts with almost total disregard for their textual evidence.

Another, equally curious, word used to describe such travelogues, presumed to be from Asia to Europe but in fact from Asia around the world, is "Counterflows." Why "Counterflows"? Which flow is the real flow, the right flow, the appropriate flow, to which such travels are "Counterflows"? "Counterflows to Colonialism" is the title of a recent book on the subject, subtitle: "Indian Travelers and Settlers in Britain, 1600–1857."[3] Such verbal ticks as "reverse travelogues," "reverse ethnography," or "counterflows" are symptomatic indices of a deliberate or inadvertent attribution of primacy to a genre of travelogues or ethnography or colonial flow that came "down" from Europe to Asia,

---

[2] Ibid. These blurbs are also available online on the webpage of the publisher. See here: https://broadviewpress.com/product/the-travels-of-mirzah-abu-taleb-khan/#tab-description. Accessed September 19, 2016.

[3] See Michael H. Fischer, *Counterflows to Colonialism: Indian Travelers and Settlers in Britain, 1600–1857* (Delhi: Permanent Black, 2004).

Africa, or Latin America. In effect, the fictional work of the Sudanese
writer Tayeb Salih's *Season of Migration to the North* (1966) and its
central character Mustafa Sa'eed's trip to England has cast an entirely
ahistorical shadow upon the historical prose of these travelogues.
There was nothing primary to such flows for the Asian or African
travelers to "reverse" or to counter it. "Europe" is a creation of the
"Third World," as Fanon rightly recognized, and in more than one
way, as I have detailed.[4] Unless and until we begin to look at these
travel accounts as an autonomous narrative – initiative not reactive, a
reality *sui generis* and not contingent – and read them for what they
actually write, before we have butchered their prose and purpose into
something else in order to fit a historical narrative that gives European
colonialism agency and primacy, we will never get to know what
worlds, what histories, what narratives those false sense of "primacies"
have consistently covered and concealed, distorted and stolen, like the
minerals and cheap labor of their colonies, to give autonomy and
agency to their own imperial imagination of the globe.

    Equally troublesome, as I did and will continue to point out, is
singling out the European aspect of these travels at the terrible cost
of ignoring their non-European components. The British Council in
Iran has recently paid a particular attention to Mirza Abu Taleb's
travelogue. They too have singled out the European side of his travels.
"The Persian Abu Taleb Khan," they write on their official website,
"travels from India to Ireland, England, France and the Ottoman
Empire in the 19th century."[5] True. But he first traveled to Africa
before he reached Ireland, and while in the Ottoman Empire he also
performed his Muslim pilgrimages. This map of his itinerary is crucial
to understanding his travelogue. Entirely oblivious to the factual evidence of a precolonial geography of the Indo–Persian world that had
not been divided into postcolonial nation-states (India, Pakistan, Iran,
Afghanistan, Turkey, etc.), this report is also emphatic that Mirza Abu

---

[4] See Hamid Dabashi, "Europe Is the Creation of the Third World" (*Aljazeera*,
    June 26, 2016), available online here: www.aljazeera.com/indepth/opinion/2016/
    06/europe-creation-world-160613063926420.html. Accessed September 26,
    2016.
[5] See Yahya Rafiee, "A Persian Prince in London: The Travels of Mirza
    Abu Taleb" (British Council, Iran, *Underline Magazine*, No date). The blurb is
    available online here: www.britishcouncil.ir/en/underline/literature/persian-
    prince-london. Accessed September 19, 2016.

Taleb Khan was Indian and not Iranian! "Contrary to the usual Qajar era travelogues," the report says, "the author had never lived in Persia, although he had a Persian father and wrote his book in Farsi (he had only seen Iranian islands in the Persian Gulf and Bushehr Port from far away while passing by on a ship)."[6] This emphasis is important, for it dovetails with the superimposition of a Eurocentric geography that then categorically disregards the travelers' African and Ottoman travels and turns him into an Indian who came to visit Europe. Abu Taleb was a product of an Indo–Persian cultural territory that predates the European (the British in particular) colonialism. So, in effect, these commentators misread him not just in terms of the itinerary of his visit as to where he was going but equally significantly as to where he was coming from! Superimposing a Eurocentric colonial map on the factual evidence of the map that Mirza Abu Taleb Khan knew and traveled thus categorically casts him into a whole fantasy world irrelevant to the reality of his lived experiences as evident in the textual authority of what he in fact wrote.

The rest of the British Council report, falsely setting it apart from other similar travelogues by people from this Indo–Persian world, is as flawed and abusive of the original text and the entirely different emotive geography of which it actually reports. The identification of Mirza Abu Taleb as a "Persian Prince" by his British contemporaries and later is as ludicrous as indicative of the aristocratic disposition of those who were receiving or interpreting him. He was neither a "Persian" (his family had gone to India from Tabriz via Isfahan) nor a "prince." He came from a very modest background that could scarcely support his travel expenses, traveling from an Indo–Persian world in which he had taken time from his services to his colonial employers to carve out an impressive literary career for himself, with no aristocratic claim to his name. The key point here in this renewed British Council interest in Abu Taleb again we encounter is this phrase of "reverse travelogue," with the following explanation:

The English translation was published in the peak of popularity of "reverse travelogues," a form in which a usually critical treatise is presented through an often imaginary travel of an Oriental man coming to Europe. So the British reader was confused for some time whether to read Taleb's texts as a real travelogue or an imaginary "reverse" one faked by a British author.[7]

---

[6] Ibid.   [7] Ibid.

That was "the British reader's" problem. Abu Taleb wrote neither in English nor for the British readers, nor was he any "Oriental man" writing any "reverse travelogue." This is how you read him if you sit in London or Paris and think yourself the epicenter of the universe. This is not how Abu Taleb imagined himself or wrote his travelogue once he set sail from India. He was a towering intellectual of his time writing something original, in his own mother tongue, the language of his cultural birth and literary education. He had a history, a genealogy, a culture, a prose and a purpose to his travels and travelogue. We need politely to sit down in his presence and learn from him. Once we do that, from his pages we will eventually gather the momentum of he and other travelers of his time and location writing no "reverse travelogue" or "reverse ethnography," or worst of all thinking themselves, an "Oriental man," but effectively *reversing the colonial gaze* that was cast upon them by the very fact and phenomenon of the colonialism that still reads them in reverse. He did not recognize the authority of any "primary" traveler from any "West" to his "East" for him to have written from his "East" to any "West." He wrote in Persian, which is written in the opposite direction of English or any other European language. But in Persian he wrote the world from his own point of departure. They were not going to Europe to write "reverse travelogues" to Europeans' travelogues. They were, as colonials, traveling the world and reclaiming it for the world, and in doing so they reversed the nasty, demeaning, denigrating, colonial gaze cast upon them and the rest of the colonized world.

In traveling the world, Abu Taleb and other travelers like him did reverse the colonial gaze, corrected it, and expanded the horizons of human consciousness by also visiting Europe and placing it in its proper place in the much larger global references of their itinerary. They wrote and documented what it means to be human, to be worldly beyond the dehumanizing gaze of European colonialism, to have the agency to be the authors of their own destiny. This reversing of the colonial gaze, as I argue in this book, is the worldly vision that measures the effect and power of these travel narratives once we learn how to read them as the *primary* authors of their destinations and destinies. They traveled and wrote the world over, and in the worldliness of their prose they provincialized Europe, de-universalized it to be more precise, put it in its right place, and cast its colonial gaze back and against itself. Without the mediation of European colonialism, evident in the very assumption of "reverse travelogue" and "reverse ethnographies," or "the Oriental man," we will never see the originary power of these travel accounts. We will read these travelogues as "reverse" only if we give primacy to Europe. If we do not, then by the very fact and texture of their traveling and writing the world, these travelogues have reclaimed the world beyond but including Europe, recast the colonial gaze, and turned it into a mirror of its self-universalized tribalism. Seeing these travelogues for how they reclaim the world puts the primary power of reversing the colonial gaze against itself in the pages I am now reading in Persian and re-visioning in English for you to read.

Reclaiming the Man

Let us now look at Abu Taleb from the perspective of a close friend of his, someone who was his contemporary and knew him personally as a friend – none other than Mir Seyyed Abd al-Latif Shushtari, whom we studied in the last chapter. Shushtari gives us Abu Taleb's full name as Mirza Abu Taleb Khan ibn Haji Beik Khan Tabrizi Isfahani. "His father," Shushtari then adds, "came to India during the reign of Nader Shah, lived in Lucknow and Abu Taleb was his only son. He has a brilliant mind, a noble character, a gracious disposition, and exuded an auspicious presence."[8] These are not "Oriental florals," as people with limited colonially mitigated command of the Persian language imagine. These are carefully constructed sentences, composed by someone with intimate knowledge of his friend. Shushtari continues to describe his friend as a finely educated man, a learned poet and literati, "a matchless historian and a rare intellect."[9] He describes him as blessed with a prodigious memory, having mastered and memorized the best samples of Persian poetries, and a brilliant literary critic. Shushtari continues to praise Abu Taleb's taste for poetry, his gracious company, his professional successes.

Shushtari then makes two comments about Abu Taleb's wish to see the world that are of crucial importance to the point I am making here. The first is when he refers to Abu Taleb's move from Lucknow to Kolkata and he predicates it by an allusion to the Qur'anic phrase, "the Earth of Allah is spacious so travel upon it."[10] The phrase Shushtari

---

[8] Shushtari's *Tohfat al-Alam*: 367.   [9] Ibid.   [10] Ibid.

uses is part of the Quranic verse 4:97 and the full phrase is: "Was not
the earth of Allah spacious [enough] for you to emigrate therein?" The
second reference is when Shushtari says about his friend: "After a
while in order to see the world (*beh 'azm-e siyahat-e 'alam*) he traveled
to England."[11] To semi-literate Orientalists with an artificial and
clumsy command of Persian, these nuanced phrasings and allusions
are of course completely lost. But not to anyone else with a superior
command of the language and its textual allusions. In these two
references, Shushtari in effect is giving us both a Qur'anic justification
and a personal testimony that Abu Taleb was eager to "see the
world" – and not just travel to England.

Shushtari concludes his remarks about Abu Taleb by saying that at
the time of his writing, Abu Taleb was in fact still in England enjoying
his visit. He cherishes his friendship with him and in his opinion: "He is
a towering example of chivalry, ethics, good manners, independence of
judgement, above any worldly needs. No matter how difficult his
circumstances he never degraded himself to anyone or became
humbled to those in position of power. I deeply miss him and very
much hope to see him soon."[12] To the ears of colonial officers and
their Orientalist ideologues, all such phrasings sound like "Oriental
hyperbole." But there is an alternative reading of this Shushtari passage in which we need to ask, why would he say any of these things
about his friend if they were not true? He does not need him. Abu
Taleb is not in any position to help him. These are the notes he is
writing in the privacy of his own travelogue. Now compare this with
the nonsense Orientalists have said and made of Abu Taleb.

What emerges from this and Abu Taleb's own travelogue is the fact
that he is a native of Lucknow who traveled from India through Asia
toward Africa, and after visiting Europe he traveled through the Ottoman territories and performed his Muslim pilgrimages. He was born in
Lucknow in 1752. His father, originally from Azerbaijan, had moved
to India from Isfahan. His birth coincides with a tense period in the
course of British domination of India. By 1763 the British were at war
with Mir Kasim, the Nawab of Bengal. The following year, in 1764,
they defeated the Mughals in the Battle of Buxar. The next year the
East India Company effectively ruled and owned India. Abu Taleb's
family leaves Lucknow for Murshidabad, where he lost his father in

[11] Ibid.: 368.   [12] Ibid.: 368–369.

1768 when he had just turned sixteen. By 1775 he enters the bureau-
cratic employment of local governors. But soon he loses his job and
enters the employment of British Colonel Alexander Hannay. Thereafter he is increasingly drawn into the political machinations of the
East India Company, the notorious commercial enterprise paving the
way for the British domination of India and beyond. In the course of
his services to the British interests in India, Abu Taleb became
acquainted with Lord Cornwallis. But by 1787 he fails to find a
position with the company and opts to follow a literary career, which
includes the publication of a collection of Hafez's ghazals, a biographical dictionary, and a universal history. But despite a successful literary
career, he accepts the invitation of a Scottish friend, Captain Richard-
son, who encouraged him to travel the world and visit England, a
journey the result of which was his *Masir Talebi*, which he wrote in
1803, soon after which it was translated into English by an Irish
employee of the East India Company, and published in 1810. Abu
Taleb dies in Kolkata in 1805.[13]

Reclaiming the Text

Part of the problem with the abusive readings of Abu Taleb's travelogue is because before its original version was published or widely
available to Persian speaking readers, the British Orientalist Charles
Stewart had a head start translating it into English and published it in
the United Kingdom. In this translation, Abu Taleb comes across very
much on the model of James Morier's notorious *The Adventures of
Hajji Baba of Ispahan* (1824), a vicious colonial mockery of the entire
Iranian culture through the chicaneries of its lead character. Short of
Hajji Baba's full-fledged charlatanism but still in need of European
moral rectitude and admonitory discipline and explanatory glosses,
Abu Taleb is portrayed here as a wide-eyed, sex-crazed object of
curiosity there to entertain and tickle European Orientalist fantasies.
Stewart's version therefore reads more like a fictional rendition rather
than a translation, given an air of authenticity very much on the model
that Morier uses to cast his fiction in a realistic mode. This case is

---

[13] For a full chronology of Abu Taleb's life, see Daniel O'Quinn's Introduction
to Abu Taleb Khan, *Travels of Mirza Abu Taleb Khan in Asia, Africa, and
Europe, during the Years 1799, 1800, 1801, 1802, and 1803*: 49–52.

therefore exactly the opposite of what happens to Morier's text, which
was translated into Persian by Mirza Habib Isfahani decades after its
original English and in turn became a hallmark of critical thinking in
preparation for the Constitutional Revolution of 1906–1911.[14] In the
original travelogue, Abu Taleb is in total control of his prose, demonstrating an exemplary command of the geopolitics of the regions he
visits, and had he written his own text in English it would have been
worthy of attention at Oxford and Cambridge in courses in sociology
and social anthropology. He is neither beholden to Europe and Europeans he visits nor harbors any undue resentment toward them. He
speaks of the British and the French the same way he does of the Irish,
Turks, and Arabs. This is not the sense you get reading Charles
Stewart's rendition.

[*a goin' now?*]

    The original Persian of *Masir-e Talebi*, or *Safar-nameh of Mirza Abu
Taleb Khan*, is the travelogue that its author wrote while traveling
from India to Asia, Africa, Europe, the Ottoman Empire, with a
particular attention to Muslim pilgrim sites, and finally back to India.
He wrote the travelogue upon his return to India in 1804 based on
scattered notes he kept while traveling. The following year, in 1805, he
dies in Kolkata. The original Persian was published posthumously after
its English appeared in 1810 by Mirza Abu Taleb Khan's son Mirza
Hossein Ali in 1813, three years after its author had passed away.
A Dutch translation was also published in 1813, and the French
version came out in 1819.[15] The English rendition is one of the main
reasons (but not the only one) why this travelogue has been historically
read as one of the earliest accounts of an Iranian from India visiting
Europe, and the United Kingdom in particular. Mirza Abu Taleb was
the intellectual product of an Indo–Persian world that embraces the
postcolonial nation-states of Iran, Pakistan, and India today. This is
particularly evident in his prose, which reflects a literary universe that
extends from India to Central Asia (Tajikistan and Afghanistan) to

[14] I have discussed this transmutation of Morier's English original in Mirza Habib
Isfahani's Persian rendition in detail in my *Persophilia: Persian Culture on the
Global Scene*: 160–174.
[15] The critical edition of the travelogue was published by Hossein Khadiv Jam in
Iran in 1984, and a new edition of the English translation published in
1814 came out in 2008 by Broadview Press, with an introduction by Daniel
O'Quinn. See Abu Taleb Khan, *The Travels of Mirza Abu Taleb Khan in Asia,
Africa, and Europe, during the Years 1799, 1800, 1801, 1802, and 1803*.

Iran. The prose is representative of an Indo–Persian world still not divided along the fictive frontiers of postcolonial nation-states. He traveled long before and long after his visit to Europe, and he wrote as detailed accounts of his visits before he arrived in Europe (England) as of those after he left for the Ottoman Empire.

Let us now look closer at Abu Taleb's itinerary – where did he go, and what was the route he traveled. Based on his full travelogue, published in three segments in one comprehensive volume in its now definitive critical edition, we read a detailed mapping of a world to which Abu Taleb was witness.[16] The first section starts in Calcutta as he sails toward Cape Town, and proceeds by describing sea routes, strange birds and animals and attractive islands, and storms he encounters and the difficulty of traveling with ships. Then he turns his attention to Cape Town and gives a full description of the port city. Then begins his journey from Cape Town to Ireland, again giving a full description of the sea journey from Cape Town to Ireland. While in Cape Town he speaks of his own poverty – "Because I did not have the means and was afraid of the high costs I stayed onboard"[17] – and does not venture into the port city. Eventually he comes to the city, meets with the British dignitaries (at the time Cape Town is taken back and forth by the British and the Dutch), and writes of the number of colonial soldiers and their military fortifications against the French.

Then comes a full, almost exhaustive description of Ireland, giving detailed ethnographic and sociological descriptions of Dublin and other cities he visits. He pays particular attention to the state of poverty in Ireland. "The peasants and the homeless of this country are so poor that Indian peasants look like rich people next to them."[18] He gives an economic account of the causes of Irish poverty. He writes of the high cost of living, of overpopulation, of a brutally cold climate, and of the diet of potatoes because of lack of access to meat. He writes of class differences, how in rich people's houses there is plenty of meat. He writes of poor people running after coaches for a piece of bread.[19] This is not a wide-eyed, sex-crazed, "colonial subject" visiting "the metropole." These passages of Abu Taleb's travelogue are reminiscent of the classic study of Ireland by Alexis de Tocqueville and his lifelong friend

---

[16] All my references to the Persian original of the text are to Abu Taleb Khan, *Masir-e Talebi: Ya Safarnameh-ye Mirza Abu Taleb Khan.*

[17] Ibid.: 29–30.   [18] Ibid.: 60.   [19] Ibid.: 60–61.

and collaborator Gustave de Beaumont, *Ireland: Social, Political, and Religious*, based on his observations in the 1830s, a couple of decades after Abu Taleb's visit.[20] There is scarcely any difference between Mirza Abu Taleb Khan's and Gustave de Beaumont's observations about Ireland, except their names and the fact that one wrote his account almost three decades earlier in Persian and the other in French. Why is it that when these Orientalists, early or late, read Abu Taleb on Ireland, they don't think of Gustave de Beaumont, or even after him of Friedrich Engels, who also visited Ireland in the 1850s and was deeply concerned about its plight?

[weird] →

From Ireland, Abu Taleb moves to England after first visiting Wales and from there going to London, Oxford, Blenheim Park, and Henley, offering full discussions of Freemasonry and the British Museum, and then moves on to the second segment of his book where he writes about the significance of the press, followed by detailed discussions of the English people's habits and customs, the significance of freedom among them, their manner of governance, a description of the positive and negative habits of the British, and their hostility to the French. Abu Taleb pays full and detailed attention to the British state apparatus and divides it into four hierarchical parts: (1) The King or Queen, (2) The Crown Prince, (3) The Cabinet of Ministers, and (4) The Parliament.[21] Reading this section carefully shows Abu Taleb's narrative proclivity, the manner in which he writes. He first says he wants to talk about the condition of governance (*Awza'-e Ryasat*) in England. First, he says, is the person of the king. But he does not immediately tell you what the second layer of power is. He now relates a whole story about an incident in London during his visit that illustrates the power of the king. Then he composes a poem praising the wisdom of a king, and proceeds with other descriptions of the power and majesty of monarchy, before a couple of pages later he tells you what the second layer of power is. One might even speculate that Sa'di's *Golestan* (1258) might very well have been a model in Abu Taleb's mind while writing this travelogue. He was a major literary historian and poet of his time. A thorough knowledge of the history of Persian literature and its masterpieces of prose and poetry – we know for a fact, from Shushtari

---

[20] See Gustave de Beaumont, *Ireland: Social, Political, and Religious*. Edited and translated by W. C. Taylor (Cambridge, MA: Harvard University Press, 2007).
[21] Abu Taleb Khan, *Masir-e Talebi: Ya Safarnameh-ye Mirza Abu Taleb Khan*: 237–284.

himself – was definitive to who he was. One cannot separate the
literary dimension of his travelogues from the masterpieces of Persian
prose and poetry.

The third section of the critical edition of Abu Taleb's travelogue is
the story of his return over land to Kolkata. He writes extensively
about the French territories, then about the Mediterranean scene and
Italy, then about Malta, until he reaches Izmir. While in Paris he offers
a comparative cultural analysis of the minutest aspects of Parisians'
daily lives in public space. He admires the number of Parisian cafes and
bars, and he makes a comparison between the manner of serving a
customer in a London Pub and a Parisian café, where in the former all
the ordered food and beverages are brought at once while in Paris they
are brought one at a time.[22] While in Marseille, he writes about
Egyptians, Berbers, and people from Istanbul and other parts of
Europe gathering in that port city, with a clear indication of his full
awareness of the Mediterranean basin of their common culture.[23] He
also writes extensively of the colonial rivalries between the French and
the British, with a full account of the Napoleonic conquest of Egypt.[24]

From Izmir he goes to Istanbul and gives as detailed account of
Istanbul as he does of London, from where he moves to Baghdad,
which is the subject of his deepest and most critical observations, after
which he travels through the Persian Gulf to Mumbai and from there
sails toward Bengal. While performing his pilgrimage to Karbala he *pilgrim.*
gives a gruesome account of the barbarity of the Wahhabi slaughter of *to Karbala*
the Shi'is in that city and offers a short account of the rise of Wahhabism and the consolidation of their power over the Arabian Peninsula.[25] *(shi'i)*
Here the full spectrum of his Shi'i faith is on display.

"Let it be known," he writes in a beautiful passage toward the end of
his journey, "that during these journeys, my passage took me through
the Indian Ocean, the Southern Ocean, the sea of Rum (the Mediterranean), the Italian Sea, known as the Sea of Venice, the Greek Sea, the
sea of Constantinople, and through the Persian Gulf. Sailing all of
which I sat upon ships, and had my share of storms, as I have had
occasions to describe, the most tumultuous of such storms, though
short in duration, was in the sea of Rum."[26] He has, therefore, a solid
and pronounced conception of his journey through the seas

---

[22] Ibid.: 313–314.   [23] Ibid.: 322–323.   [24] Ibid.: 295.
[25] Ibid.: 408–410.   [26] Ibid.: 440.

surrounding the lands he has visited, from one to another, which, yes, includes *Farang* (not exactly *Europe*), but is not limited to it.

Abu Taleb's journey to England and what he calls *Farang*, and what we today think corresponds to "Europe," is, as is perfectly obvious, entirely bracketed within a much larger itinerary, which cannot be just disregarded and his journey branded a "visit to Europe" or worse, "the West," not even to England. Mirza Abu Taleb was a poet and a literary stylist directly rooted in the Indo–Persian world. He recorded his observations in Asia, Africa, Europe, and the Muslim world with identical precision and detail. There was nothing "reverse" about his observations, neither "reverse travelogue" nor indeed "reverse ethnography." His book becomes "reverse" if we give the primacy of traveling and ethnographic observations to Europeans. Europeans too have traveled and made ethnographic observations. But theirs is not "primary" or "original" to make Abu Taleb's "secondary" or "reverse." The publisher of this most recent edition of its English rendition asserts:

> The narrative's vital and controversial account of British imperial society is one of the earliest examples of a colonial subject addressing the cultural dynamics of metropolitan Britain, and its complex critique of empire challenges many preconceptions about intercultural relations during this era.[27]

Mirza Abu Taleb is anything but "a colonial subject." Throughout his travelogue, Mirza Abu Taleb is a sharp and insightful observer of everything he reports. He is opinionated but not dogmatic, critical but open-minded, witty but not silly. Isfahani's travelogue is an exquisite specimen of the Indo–Persian prose of his time. A sustained critique of European imperialism sits naturally next to a deep appreciation for the social and political institutions underlying that imperialism. Reading the original, we encounter a public intellectual of a fierce critical perspective reflecting on a transnational (global) public sphere that he is literally navigating and occupying at one and the same time.

---

[27] See Abu Taleb Khan, Travels of Abu Taleb Khan in Asia, Africa, and Europe, during the Years 1799, 1800, 1801, 1802, and 1803. Publisher's description on the back cover of the book.

DISCUSSING THE WAR IN A PARIS CAFE.
SEE PAGE 304.

Figure 4 "Discussing the War in a Paris Café," by Fred Barnard, *The Illustrated London News*, September 17, 1870/Wikimedia Commons [Public domain] – If we follow the itinerary of these travelers closely, the map that will emerge places their European destinations, such as Paris, in a larger frame of topographical reference that includes Tehran, Isfahan, Mumbai, Delhi, Moscow, St Petersburg, Istanbul, all the way to New York, Chicago, San Francisco, Tokyo, Rio de Janeiro, Cape Town, Beirut, Damascus, and Cairo. In this book I have sought to correct the distortion that has been historically perpetrated on these texts by only privileging their European destinations at the expense of all other equally if not even more important places these travelers visited and recorded in their travelogues. The factual evidence of these travelogues maps the transnational bourgeois public sphere of the nineteenth century far beyond Europe and deeply into Asia, Africa, and the Americas – where trade, commerce, culture, and colonialism had an entirely worldly character.

"One Night Two Days"

The mischaracterization of Abu Taleb's travelogue is in fact much worse in our time than in his. We have an account of a certain Lady Anne Barnard, "Capetown's chief hostess," writing this note to Lord Dundas about a certain visitor in her company: "He has the Honor to be a particular friend of Lord Cornwallis & travels chiefly to see the world, possibly he may combine some other motive which he will communicate to Lord Cornwallis but both are worthy of your notice I believe."[28] Two indications are crucial here to mark Abu Taleb's global vision of his travels: The fact that this participant observer in his travels meeting him in Cape Town specifically says he "travels chiefly to see the world," and the other – the fact that the person who translated his travelogue even before its Persian edition came out decidedly specified his travel itinerary as including "Asia, Africa, and Europe." There can scarcely be any better indication that Abu Taleb's travelogue was neither exclusive to Europe, nor begun in Europe, nor indeed ended in Europe. Yet having just cited Lady Anne Barnard's statement that Abu Taleb "travels chiefly to see the world," Daniel O'Quinn, the person asked to write an introduction to a new edition of the English translation of Abu Taleb's travelogue, persists in characterizing him as "making his first and only visit to the metropole," marking the purpose of the journey to be "understanding imperial relations as a negotiation between metropole and colony."[29] That may indeed be the case, but Abu Taleb was not "making his first and only visit to the metropole." The very ideas and spatial distinctions between "metropole" and "colony" were in fact alien to him as evident in the very letter and spirit of his travelogue. These are early twentieth century postcolonial sensibilities ahistorically catapulted to late eighteenth century realities.

But these latter-day transfigurations of Abu Taleb are always consistent with old-fashioned Orientalism of his own time. At times some very simple and perfectly normal and natural behavior on the part of Abu Taleb is turned upside-down into a crooked timber of their own perturbed imagination and projected onto their "Oriental" or "Asiatic" object of curiosity. Abu Taleb is in the company of two women while at Lady Anne Barnard's reception. "A person remarked to him

[Handwritten margin note: Not a "visit to metropole"]

---

[28] See O'Quinn's Introduction to ibid.: 9.   [29] Ibid.: 10.

the other evening at our House," she reports in this letter that O'Quinn cites, "that he was supported by a pretty woman on each side, he smiled and pointing to himself, said in English – 'one night–two days' – alluding to his dark complexion of course."[30] Based on this remark, O'Quinn engages his favorite word, referring to the "complex" relationship (everything is "complex" for him – that is his most favorite word in this Introduction) between "East and West," leaving the factual evidence of the original Persian text entirely out of his remote psychoanalytics. He literally considers this travelogue as "a historical problem." What problem, what complexity? A young man in the company of young (or older) women? What is so "complex" about that, and why would this text pose a "problem" – except in the troubled racialized imagination of both Lady Anne Barnard and Mr. O'Quinn himself? The very vocabulary afforded this body of literature is a deeply troubled lexicon of racialized fantasies preventing a direct encounter with the text itself and the literary heritage from which it emerges.

Against such abusive readings, Abu Taleb comes through his travelogue as among the very first specimens of public intellectuals. He worked in circumstances dominated by East India Company and the British colonial domination of India. He was trained in high Persianate culture and wrote a regional history, edited a collection of Hafez's poetry, and demonstrated an elegant command of his own poetic compositions. He had a sharp critical mind, fully conscious of the transnational public sphere he was traversing. Other travelers preceded and succeeded him, and they have all been cast as having first and foremost traveled to Europe and then went back to where they came from. O'Quinn is the epitome of this false and forced reading: "I'tisam al-Din, who helped William Jones in his Persian studies at Oxford in 1768, Mir Muhammad Husain, who visited France and England in 1775 to gain knowledge of European scientific and technological discoveries, and the European travels of Mirza Abu al-Hasan in 1809–10 were a cause célèbre."[31] Each one of these travelers had an imaginative universe far different from these cliché-ridden Eurocentric colonial constitutions of the planet, as if the world at large was hanging on the balance of a visit to "Europe." These travelogues are in fact

[30] Ibid.: 9.   [31] Ibid.: 11.

subjected to these abusive readings precisely to cross-authenticate the very idea of "Europe."

Scholars like O'Quinn occasionally show a sense of unease about their own reading of Abu Taleb. He for example purposes: "The text documents the performance of a form of colonial subjectivity that slides between complicity and resistance that perhaps calls into question the very applicability of such terms."[32] Precisely: These terms are entirely inapplicable and yet O'Quinn forces them back on a history where an author who had an entirely different conception of himself is dragged into these misapplied concepts. O'Quinn begins with a misreading of the text as written by "a colonial subject" that oscillates between complicity and resistance and then reaches a point where he has to dismiss both these terms. The fact is that based on the original Persian, before all these Orientalist machinations, the author is no "colonial subject." He is a self-conscious, proud, confident, deeply informed and globally alert thinker who is as much amused by what he sees in Europe as he is by what he sees in Africa or the Ottoman territories or indeed in his travels through stormy seas in between. Why first cast him as a "colonial subject," give European colonialism so much nonexistent power over the mind of the people they thought they were ruling, and then wonder how in the world they could actually think and criticize things? In effect, the history of European colonialism begins in earnest over the minds of their former subjects after it has ceased to exist over their territories. Yes, the British and other Europeans had their share of native informers and sold out intellectuals – as indeed US imperialism does today. But this does not mean the world rolled backward in submission when the British or other Europeans were ruling the world.

O'Quinn correctly admits that Stewart's "translation" is in fact an Orientalist fantasy of the original:

The translation bears the marks not only of errors in linguistic and cultural interpretation, but also of systematic derogation of the work of the very scholars who enabled its production. These errors and the disregard which proceeded them are part and parcel of the document, and thus inflect any conclusions derived from readings of the *Travels*. Most importantly, Stewart elided most of the poem ... which were embedded in the original and thus

---

[32] Ibid.

[handwritten margin note: elision of poetry in transl.]

brought the text in line with European expectations that travel writing work primarily through factual description.[33]

Here we need to wonder about two points: One is the very idea of a "European reader," which is a recent concoction, and Stewart could not have had anything other than his own employers at the East India Company in mind when translating Abu Taleb into English. Plus: By virtue of the colonial expansion of English, French, or Spanish language, these languages were not exclusive of any "European" provenance. An Indian, African, Australian, South African, or Latin American could have read these translations without being a "European." The other point is, which European travelogue could Stewart, or O'Quinn, for that matter, have in mind when they say these Europeans are used to "factual descriptions"? Certainly not the readers of the works of fear and fantasy going back from V. S. Naipaul's to Marco Polo's!

O'Quinn also offers a false comparison between Abu Taleb's travelogue and Montesquieu's *Persian Letters*.[34] Montesquieu wrote his book to critique European institutions from the perspective of two Persians in order to proceed with planting the foundations of liberal democracy.[35] Stewart did his rendition of Abu Taleb and deliberately distorted a factual document by way of consolidating British imperialism and dishonoring the original author. These are two vastly different tasks. Abu Taleb is not offering much useful information about Iran or the Muslim world for the East India Company to use to further its colonial interests – nor are his extensive observations about Ireland, England, or France of any particular interest to his colonially invested British readers, as judged by this translator at the employment of the East India Company. But both those points are embedded in the textual authority of Abu Taleb's own original text, which is of travels destined to and about the world – a fact alluded to by one woman in Cape Town and inevitably acknowledged by his first translator, who hopefully had to read the whole book anyway, and yet entirely neglected by almost everyone else, including those who wish to write a counterargument to Edward Said's *Orientalism*, which has paradoxically perhaps and perhaps not exacerbated a false binary between the colonized East and the colonizing West at the expense of a much wider

---

[33] Ibid.: 12–13. Emphasis added.   [34] Ibid.: 15.

[35] For more on my reading of Montesquieu's *Persian Letters*, see Dabashi, *Persophilia*: 50–68.

perspective of colonialism and imperialism, that includes pockets of misery and resistance in the so-called "West" (as in the Ireland Abu Taleb visited) and classes of beneficiaries in the so-called "East."

Abu Taleb is a severe critique of British colonialism in both India and in Ireland. But O'Quinn seeks to rob him of this fact by turning him into a "native informer"! This is how he does it:

> Abu Taleb's explicit attack on British governance in India serves the Company's interests quite well. This is why he can both critique legal corruption among government officials in India and promulgate plans for instruction in Persian as a way of improving bureaucratic governance. For British readers committed to colonization, most importantly, for the company officials publishing Abu Taleb's narrative, many aspects of his discussion of British rule, including those that critique past excesses, have the virtue of placing the reformist objectives of colonial rulers in the mouth of a native informant.[36]

This is an entirely flawed, forced, violent, and abusive reading of Abu Taleb, performed by a latter-day Orientalist who to this day has remained clueless about what these texts did and continue to do in their original Persian. O'Quinn, however, makes a very astute observation when he points out that Abu Taleb enters England via Ireland,[37] and is therefore fully conscious of the colonial context of Irish history predating that of India. So even if we were to concentrate on his European sojourn, this critical angle is definitive to our reading of his reading of British colonialism. He leaves India, stops in Cape Town, and enters his European journey toward the Ottoman Empire through Ireland. As evident throughout his travelogue, this encounter between two imperial domains, one European and the other Islamic, is never far from his critical observations.

Reversing the Narrative

One day Abu Taleb is traveling coach on a train and sits next to a "not-so-famous" member of the British aristocracy.[38] The gentleman asks Abu Taleb about the price of goods and services in India. He responds in detail. His interlocutor says that lower prices may appear to be good but they are in fact inimical to accumulation of wealth and therefore

---

[36] Ibid.: 33–34.   [37] Ibid.: 35–36.
[38] Abu Taleb Khan, *Masir-e Talebi: Ya Safarnameh-ye Mirza Abu Taleb Khan*: 275.

capital, which in turn leads to higher prices. Abu Taleb disagrees and reports how in India both the prices are low and wealth is accumulated in abundance. "He could not grasp what I meant," Abu Taleb reports.[39] While they are talking, the English gentlemen invites Abu Taleb to have a meal together and while eating he orders an abundance of wine, which Abu Taleb chooses not to drink. When they bring them the bill, the man divides it completely in half, including the expensive wine, and asks Abu Taleb to pay his share, which causes a significant financial burden on him. From this incident Abu Taleb concludes that conspicuous consumption weakens a nation and does not allow it to accumulate wealth and capital to defend itself, as has happened to Italy and India, he emphasizes. This is early in the 1800s, one complete century before Max Weber wrote his *Protestant Ethics and Spirit of* ~~deny him~~ *Capitalism* (1904–1905). Why is it when they read Abu Taleb they ~~critical~~ never think of Max Weber? Abu Taleb's simultaneous reference to ~~thought~~ Italy and India is among the clearest indications that he has a global conception of the operation of accumulated capital far beyond "the West and the Rest." Why are such clear allusions not picked up by his latter-day Orientalist readers, who persist in portraying him as a wide-eyed Hajji Baba of Ispahan incarnate?

Abu Taleb is falsely cast as having written a "reverse travelogue" or engaged in "reverse ethnography" or even following a counterflows by way of ipso facto making his journey secondary to a primary conquest and knowledge of the world. The later scholarship that has suddenly discovered these texts and began to recast them as "Europology" in reversal of Orientalism is not any better.[40] This "Europology" business was meant to be a corrective lens to Orientalism but in fact actually made it worse, for it continued to rob critical thinkers like Abu Taleb of the totality and organicity of their prose and purpose and helped in manufacturing further false evidence of a binary between "Islam and the West." Lost was what happens before or after the sections of the travelogue that deal with Europe – not just the totality of the text, but equally importantly, the totality of the person writing it – and the world is thus rediscovered for a postcolonial posterity. The point here is not to deny, conceal, or even underestimate the significance of the

---

[39] Ibid.
[40] See Mohamad Tavakoli-Targhi, *Refashioning Iran: Orientalism, Occidentalism, and Historiography* (New York: Palgrave, 2001): 35–53.

European component of the journey. Abu Taleb himself in fact even calls his own travelogue an account of his journey to Farang (which is not exactly Europe, as has been ahistorically and inaccurately approximated to it). The point is to place that European component within the large context of the narrative itself.

NB / Farang ≠ Evro

Let me now explain why I insist "Farang" is not exactly "Europe," as has been falsely assumed. Farang territorially corresponds to but conceptually differs from Europe. As a Persianization of the word "Frank," which in Arabic has become "Faranj" or "Ifranj," "Farang" is not "Europe" in its full idiomatic meaning but it does parallel it; and it most certainly is not "the West." It is imperative for us to distinguish between the genealogy of "Farang" as a word, a concept, a geographical index and "Europe," which is now ill-advisedly used interchangeably. The Persian word "Farang" or the Arabic "Afranj" is a very old geographical designation predating European colonialism in the Arab and Muslim world that we see in numerous sources such as in Yaqut al-Hamawi's *Mu'jam al-Buldan* (1224–1228), and soon after him in Rumi's *Masnavi* (1258–1273), and even before them in the poetry of Khaqani (1121–1190), and after them in Sa'di's *Golestan* (1258). The earliest source in which the word "Farang" appears in Persian is actually by the anonymous author of *Hudud al-'Alam/Boundaries of the World* from the tenth century, and even before in Arabic in the works of Al-Jahiz (776–869),[41] as in the expression "King of Farang" or the region of "Farang." The Franks itself could refer to the medieval Germanic people, to the French people, to the Crusaders, or to the Levantines. In either case, the emotive universe and the political weight much later invested in the word "Europe" (both by Europeans and non-Europeans) are furthest from this word Farang, which was a subject of Muslim geographical lexicon.

Abdolmohammad Rouhbakhshan has done an excellent compilation of all the major and minor references to the word "Farang" and even "Rum" in Persian and Arabic, identifying "Farang" as

---

[41] For a fuller discussion of the word "Farang" in Persian, see Abdolmohammad Ruhbakhshan, *Farang and Farangi dar Iran/Farang and Being from Farang in Iran* (Tehran: Roshan Publications, 1388/2009). I am grateful to my friend and colleague Mahmoud Omidsalar and a few other Iranian colleagues from Tehran who have kindly shared with me their knowledge of the oldest roots of this word in Persian and Arabic sources and for alerting me to Abdolmohammad Ruhbakhshan's learned book.

referring to a region "beyond the western frontiers of Muslim lands whose exact boundaries are not known."[42] Although in texts such as *Fars-nameh* Ibn Balkhi the term is used as a proper name without any geographical designation,[43] it mostly refers to a geographical location, as in the love story of *Vamegh and Azra* in the Ghaznavid period where we have "Parand-e Chin v Diba ye Farang," meaning the silk that comes from China or Farang.[44] What is crucial is how during the Saljuqid period the term "Farang" is used interchangeably with the "Salibi," meaning "the Crusaders."[45] Here is the clearest indication that the term "Farang" keeps assuming new meanings with every encounter between Muslims and invading armies to their west. This is corroborated later by the famous mystic Abu Said Abi al-Khayr (967–1049), who sarcastically suggests a "Farangi dog" is better than him,[46] which means the term relates to Christians. By the time of Sa'di we have reference to "Farangi armor,"[47] and later Rumi uses it to mean "White" as opposed to "Zangi," meaning "Black." In *Golestan*, Sa'di relates an episode when he is captured by the Crusaders whom he refers to as people of "Farang," as in fact does Rumi,[48] who also uses it in reference to the Crusaders.

During the Mongol period in the thirteenth century, the prominent historian Rashid al-Din Fazlollah devotes a whole section of his *Jame' al-Tawarikh* to "Tarikh-e Farang/History of Farang." Meanwhile, in texts such as *Ajayeb-nameh* in the same period, the term refers to a region "beyond Nile, near Abyssinia, and near Sicily,"[49] which means Northern Mediterranean and Christianity are now fused together, while "Darya-ye Farang" or "Darya-ye Rum" is referring to the Mediterranean Sea. Eventually, in the aftermath of the Safavid and Mughal dynasties' encounters with European colonial powers, "Farang" begins to be related to Europe again under a renewed warring context. Poets like Bidel and Ghalib begin to use the term extensively now.[50] Farang and Farangi here become very dominant in their poetry, which coincides with the British presence in the region. The point is therefore clear that "Farang" begins as an object of Muslim geographical imagination and conquest and then eventually, after the Crusaders during the

---

[42] Ruhbakshan, *Farang and Farangi dar Iran/Farang and Being from Farang in Iran*: 5.
[43] Ibid.: 8.   [44] Ibid.: 10.   [45] Ibid.: 13.   [46] Ibid.: 15.   [47] Ibid.: 20–22.
[48] Ibid.: 28.   [49] Ibid.: 18.
[50] Ibid.: 86–88 for Bidel and 100–102 for Ghalib.

Seljuqids period, enters the lexicon of Muslims as referring to the invading Crusaders and then reaches its heights during the Safavids period when it assumes increasing identification with European colonial powers. This history is completely lost when we disregard the crucial element of power politics in meanings people attribute to terms and categorically equate "Farang" and "Europe" together.

So, when Abu Taleb calls his travelogue "Ketab Masir-e Talebi fi Bilad Afranji/The Book of Talebi's Itinerary to the Realms of the Franks," this entire history is in the back of his mind while his later readers have assimilated that word forward to their own post/colonial conception of "Europe." Abu Taleb was deeply steeped in Persian and Arabic literary traditions and this conception of Farang was totally known to hm. But after him there has been a colonially conditioned rush to equate his and similar uses of "Farang" with "Europe," disregarding their significantly different genealogies. Farang is not Europe, for one has been the subject of Muslim knowledge for a very long time, and the other is the very recent object of Muslim *ressentiment* accumulated over the course of European colonialism and colonial knowledge production. These travelers are located exactly at the threshold of the transition period when Muslim subjectivity is still deeply rooted in seeing the world, including Europe, as the domain of their active investigation, as indeed any other part of the world. When Abu Taleb says he is going to Farang he means it in the historic designation of the term as integral to Muslim geographical imagination. When his translators and commentators translate that as Europe, they imply the subordinate position of a sex-crazed "colonial subject" going to do a bit of voyeurism in "the metropole." These are two vastly different subject positions. It is much later that this Europe became their object of envy and *ressentiment*. Their passages about women are a discourse of conquest and discovery and not one of voyeurism and erotic fantasy.[51] Farang is not Europe, for Europe does not become Europe until much later when the third world creates it in material and moral imagination, and certainly not until Oswald Spengler writes his *The Decline of the West* (1918), thereby fetishizing and reifying the European subject.

---

[51] Chiefly responsible for the over-sexualization of these Persian travelogues after old-fashioned European Orientalists is Mohamad Tavakoli-Targhi, in *Refashioning Iran: Orientalism, Occidentalism, and Historiography* : 54–76.

Here in this book one of my principal concerns is with the genealogy of Iranian and by extension Indo–Persian cosmopolitanism as clearly evident in the body of literature I closely examine. There is a wide geographical implication to this literature and in drawing attention to this critical aspect of the texts we read, my foremost and abiding concern is with the worldly, global, and cosmopolitan content of what these authors write. I must particularly emphasize the fact that Europe or England was not the primary exclusive destination of these travelers in order to draw attention to their wider itinerary. As such I will consistently draw your attention to the full, wide spectrum of these travelers, which includes their European visit but is not limited to it. There is no reason for us to distinguish between Naser Khosrow (1004–1088) traveling from Khorasan to Egypt and back and Abu Taleb traveling to Ireland and back. The world they visited was of course vastly different. But the experience of these two journeys reveals two identically critical thinkers making astute observations about what they see. As Naser Khosrow was definitive to the cosmopolitan worldliness of his time, so was Abu Taleb to his. Except Naser Khosrow was not violently abused by latter-day Orientalist interpretations of his work before he was the subject of immense scholarship by those who had critical intimacy with it.

The cosmopolitan worldliness of which Abu Taleb's critical thinking is a perfect example, however, is not contingent on any idealist preconception of the project. Here it is important to recall that Kant's conception of cosmopolitanism is entirely contingent on an abstract and idealist understanding of the human condition. "Since men," he declares at the very outset of his reflection on the issue, "neither pursue their aims purely by instinct, as the animals do, nor act in accordance with any integral, prearranged plan like rational cosmopolitans, it would appear that no law-governed history of mankind is possible."[52] He therefore abandons any attempt to see humanity in its actual lived experiences. "The result," as he puts it, "is that we do not know what sort of opinion we should form of our species, which is so proud of its supposed superiority," which fact in turn leads him to "discover a purpose in nature behind this senseless course of human events, and

---

[52] See Immanuel Kant, "Idea of Universal History with Cosmopolitan Purpose," in *The Cosmopolitanism Reader*, Garrett Wallace Brown and David Held (eds.): 17.

decide whether it is after all possible to formulate in terms of a definite plan of nature a history of creatures who act without a plan of their own."[53] This means he has no patience for the lived experiences of human beings, or to see them in their mortal, fallible, transient, contingent, and fragile conditions, and therefore prefers to see the possibilities of a cosmopolitan worldliness by mandating it from his lofty armchair rather than through the fleeting moments of "public happiness" (as Hannah Arendt would call it) they actually experience. There are such pure moments of bliss in Abu Taleb's travelogue as he travels from one corner of the afflicted world to another, when he feels himself connected to his fellow human beings beyond their fictive differences. Every single time he bursts into a poetic composition we see him basking in that cosmopolitan worldliness and in that public happiness. To me this is the defining moment of what I look for in these travelogues and what I detect as their cosmopolitan worldliness.

[53] Ibid.

Q of temporality
thru poetry.
address differently

3 | *An Ilchi Wonders about the World*

[handwritten: Abu al-Hasan Khan Ilchi]

[handwritten: 1. From Iran → Rum → Farang → New world → Tehran | (London) India (Istanbul) (Rio de Janeiro) (Mumbai)]

And they know only too well
That no fish did ever
Untied the one thousand and one knots
Of the river –
And yet mid through the night
With the old boat of Illumination
They sail upon the rivers of Guidance
All the way to the Immanence of Wonder.

[handwritten: 2. Iran → Russia]

> Sohrab Sepehri (Mosafer/Traveler, Babol, Spring 1966)

In his incandescent poetry, Sepehri single-handedly recast an entire history of mystic wonder – going from here to there and then nowhere, and all of that through a succinct metaphor of traveling, deeply rooted in the effervescent materiality of life, a journey both within and without. Throughout his short life, Sepehri traveled extensively around the globe, and much of such journeys appeared in his poems. But all those physical travels were contingent on a more inward journey from the surface of his world deeply into the hidden labyrinth of passages we never knew we harbored in us under the skin of our consciousness. Concepts such as Illumination, Guidance, Immanence, or Wonder had all been incarcerated in their classical closets – there but not there. Sepehri liberated them and gave them new lives – all made possible by taking his contemporaries to a long, unreturnable journey. That journey, in matter and meaning, had begun a long time before Sepehri. Before he brought the world to us, others had brought the world to him.

Playful Interchange between Prose and Poetry

Abu Taleb's travelogue is studded with some of the finest examples of his own poetry. There is a rhyme and reason to the place and significance of these poems in his narratives. For example, when he enters

73

Maybe show

Henley-on-Thames, he seems to have an amorous interest in the city that he is very eager to see.[1] At this point he wants to get rid of his luggage, which he finds cumbersome. He wants to give it away to the poor. But his friend convinces him not to do so and carefully packs his belongings and ships them to India. It is on this occasion that he bursts into a rather beautiful ghazal describing the beauty of Henley-on-Thames and its landscape and the subtlety and elegance of his amorous desire. His habitual playful interchange between prose and poetry becomes particularly intense in this part of the travelogue. At this point he is in his late forties, and these pages are effectively the mobile literary saloons and courts of yonder Persian princes that his predecessors would praise and entertain in their poetries. We therefore could look at the pages of these travelogues as the transnational spaces between the court poetries of the imperial Muslim contexts, such as the Mughals, and the public sphere that would eventually emerge in contested encounters with European imperialism. This could also account for the preponderance of Abu Taleb's praise for urbanity and cosmopolitan cities he visits along the course of his travels. In the absence of any Persian court in sight or Persianate public sphere to speak of, these pages are the only simulacrum of a "public sphere" on which these poetic pauses might be performed.

Let me now move on to our next traveler, though this time not from India around the world but in fact from Iran around the world, though at a time of similar confusion and mayhem as nations rose to challenge the power of European empires, and when the current postcolonial boundaries of nation-states were very much in flux. Abu al-Hassan Khan Ilchi's *Heyrat-Nameh/Book of Wonders* (1809) is a veritable document for further reflection on how the postcolonial person was born into political agency. Abu al-Hasan Khan Ilchi was a statesman and a diplomat with many crucial missions to Russia and Europe, in a particularly tumultuous epoch in the history of his homeland. He was an utter failure in these diplomatic missions. But even in his failures, or perhaps particularly in his failures, he has left us a veritable account of the very timber of his time.

Q: role of wonder

[1] Abu Taleb Khan, *Masir-e Talebi: Ya Safarnameh-ye Mirza Abu Taleb Khan*: 127–148.

Heyrat-Nameh: A Book of Wonders

"It is most clearly known that someone named Ahmad was the Master of this World"; Ilchi's opening phrasing of his travelogue is august, somber, and formal. By "Ahmad," here he means Prophet Muhammad, one of whose endearing names to Muslims is Ahmad. "He was Muhammad the Chosen One, May the Peace and Benediction of the Almighty be upon Him, and upon his Family be our most gracious Greetings and Praises, and upon his Blessed Children and his Infallible Household, and so also be upon the Imam of all the Easts and the Wests of this World, the Prince of Believers Ali ibn Abi Talib, Peace be upon Him."[2]

In what in classical Persians and Arabic formal prose style we call "Bira'at-e Istihlal," all the proper praising that Ilchi uses in this opening gambit of his travelogue points to the subject of his book, and all such references, without a single exception, refer to "the world": "The travelers of all time and the experienced visitors of the world," he says, ought to know the author of this book is Abu al-Hassan. It was His Majesty the king, whose throne is "high upon the universe," who is "the master of the world, "the king of Arabs and Persians," who commanded him to travel abroad. He continues to say that his journey to "Farang" was through "Rum," and "on the way back through land and sea I returned via the New World, that in Turkish we call 'Yengi Dunya,' and in Farangi expression they call it 'America,' and from there to Mumbai Port, which is among the ports in India, and about five years ago on my way from Bengal I had visited and I revisited some of the ports in India I had already seen."[3] He says he has written his travelogue in detail about places he has visited from the time he left the capital city of Tehran, hoping someday someone would consider his travelogue to be of some use. Then he says that because on his journey he had witnessed "many strange and novel things that will inevitably cause wonder and amusement, I therefore call this book 'Heyrat-Nameh Sofara'/The Wonder Book of the Ambassadors."[4]

---

[2] See Abu al-Hassan Khan Ilchi, *Heyrat-Nameh/Book of Wonders*. Edited with an Introduction and Notes by Hasan Morsalvand (Tehran: Rasa Cultural Institute, 1985): 47–48.
[3] Ibid.   [4] Ibid.: 48.

Right at the very beginning of his book, if people cared actually to read it, Ilchi says very clearly what the itinerary of his journey was, from where he started, where he went, and how he returned home. Before he gets to his itinerary, he makes a crucial remark about the fact that his prose in this book is not going to be floral but by necessity simple and straightforward. He reminds his readers that they should not look for "tasteful and melodious words, or for phrasings with colorful allegories,"[5] for what he reports are of direct daily observations, and asks for forgiveness from the masters of Persian prose among his readers for the simplicity of his prose. Two centuries later we don't just forgive him, but in fact we thank him for thus specifically marking this crucial passage in Persian prose from floral, courtly shackles and the ushering in of a robust and purposeful new prose. This is a crucial turning point in the history of Persian prose when even authors associated with the royal court, as Ilchi was, feel the necessity of addressing an entirely new reading public. With this clearly stated intention and delivery of a simple prose, we may continue to wonder why he should not be read as directly as he speaks, and why nonexistent intentions and purposes of his travels are attributed to him.

Ilchi's travelogue is divided into three *"Babs"* or *"entries:"* The first *Bab* is from the time he obtains permission from Fath Ali Shah to commence his journey until he reaches London. This section, as he says clearly in his own words in his introductory remarks, has four chapters. Ilchi initially says "three" but just a few sentences later he forgets and actually cites four chapters: First from Tehran to Doğubeyazıt in Rum, Second from Doğubeyazıt to Istanbul, Third on Istanbul itself, and Fourth from Istanbul to London. The second *Bab* is on London and has seven chapters each for every month he spent there. In the middle of this chapter outline, he introduces another that consists of the division of his journey from Istanbul to London into land travel and sea travel. The third *Bab* is not cited specifically in his outline but must be extrapolated from his own initial enumeration and consists of his travel from London to the Americas on his way back to India and then Iran.[6] Ilchi's travelogue in the manuscript used by the editor in its only published edition abruptly ends while they are off the coast of Rio de Janeiro, but we know from another extant and more complete manuscript of the travelogue and also other corroborating evidence

---

[5] Ibid.   [6] Ibid.: 49–50.

written by Ilchi's fellow travelers that they had arrived in Rio on September 14, 1810, and after about two weeks on September 27 they leave Rio for Mumbai, and they reach there on January 12, 1811, and from there they sailed to Bushehr and reached there on March 1, 1811.[7]

Based on this very outline and Ilchi's own wordings, there are four major cities that he visits in this particular journey outside Iran: Istanbul, London, Rio de Janeiro, and Mumbai – two in Asia, one in the Americas, and only one in Europe. Here is the question: Why privilege London and Europe against the other two cities and call this "Safarnameh Abu al-Hassan Khan Ilchi beh Landan/Abu al-Hassan Khan Ilchi's Travelogue to London" by its Iranian editor, when in his own words the author says his book is called "'Heyrat-Nameh Sofara'/Wonder Book of Diplomats" – or even worse, "A Persian at the Court of King George, 1809–1810: The Journal of Mirza Abul Hassan Khan," by its English translator? On the basis of which false premise, then, you now have a new generation of young and presumably critical scholars regurgitating the unexamined mantra of "Persianate Europology" or else "Nineteenth-Century Travel Accounts from Iran to Europe"? Why disregard the part of the journey that is before London, and then the parts that are after London, which in fact cover intercontinental travel from the Americas to India? Nothing except an astonishingly Eurocentric and colonized mind can explain this egregious negligence of textual facts and submission to Orientalist fantasy passing for scholarship.

Mirza Abu al-Hassan Khan from Shiraz

Let us now take a closer look at Mirza Abolhassan Khan Shirazi Ilchi Kabir (his full honorific name), the author of this travelogue, and find out more about who he is and what is he up to traveling from Iran to the Ottoman territories and from there to London and then to Rio de Janeiro and India.

---

[7] I take these dates from Henry McKenzie Johnston's *Ottoman and Persian Odysseys: James Morier, Creator of Hajji Baba of Ispahan, and His Brothers* (London: British Academic Press, 1998): 154–164. I will have more uses from this crucial text later.

Abolhassan Khan was born in 1776 in Shiraz to a prominent family of viziers and administrators at the Afsharid and Qajar court.[8] He began his political career quite early when as a young man he was appointed as the governor of Shushtar. But soon his family fell out of favor with the rising Qajar warlords, because they were affiliated with the previous, the Afsharid, dynasty. Ilchi fled to Basra and from there he traveled to Hyderabad, India. This trip is crucial for it shows that from his youth the emerging dynastic politics of his homeland had a wider range of geographical possibilities for him that extended to the Ottoman and Mughal territories. In 1800 he received a royal pardon, returned to Iran, and entered the courtly service of the Qajar monarch, Fath Ali Shah, where he "accumulated considerable wealth."[9]

By this time the colonial interests of the British and the French in the Qajar court had seriously intensified. Napoleon was determined to pivot toward the Jewel in the Crown of the British Empire in India through Fath Ali Shah's territories. Fath Ali Shah needed the French's help to resist the Russian incursion into his northern borders. By 1807, Fath Ali Shah had signed the Finkenstein Treaty with Napoleon to facilitate the French conqueror's ambitions to harass the British interests in India in exchange for militarization of his army to get Georgia and other parts of the Caucasus back from Russia. "But the same year Napoleon made peace with the Russians at Tilsit, and Fath Ali Shah turned to the British."[10] It was during this time that Ilchi was commissioned to represent Iran in a diplomatic mission that included Sir Harford Jones Brydges, the British ambassador, and James Morier, a secretary to the mission and soon to be discovered as one nasty piece of racist colonial officer who thrived and delighted in making wicked jokes about any "Oriental" he met. The mission left Tehran on May 7, 1809, and reached Plymouth on November 25 of the same year. This was the political occasion for Ilchi's writing of his *Heyrat-Nameh Sofara*. From this journey we have a few other accounts. The notorious James Morier also wrote a detailed "satirical" account of this journey, *A Journey through Persia, Armenia and Asia Minor to Constantinople, in the Years 1808 and 1809* (London, 1812), as did

---

[8] For an excellent summary of Abu Al-Hassan Khan Ilchi's biography, see "ABU'L-ḤASAN KHAN ĪLČĪ" (*Encyclopedia Iranica*. Available online here: www.iranicaonline.org/articles/abul-hasan-khan-ilci-mirza-persian-diplomat-b. Accessed October 20, 2016.
[9] Ibid.   [10] Ibid.

Brydges, in *An Account of His Majesty's Mission to the Court of Persia, in the Years 1807–1811* (London, 1834, 2 vols.). But the cake goes to the selfsame James Morier's vicious "novel" *The Adventures of Hajji Baba of Ispahan* (London, 1824), also conceived during this journey and that became a sensation among racist Europeans who delighted in the horrid colonial officer's scornful derision of Iran and Iranians. Much of the interpretation of Ilchi's travelogue, alas, has historically been under the shadow of these almost simultaneous Orientalist diatribes by two nefarious British colonial officers. Be that as it may, these additional travelogues by people who knew Ilchi and traveled with him, plus extant more complete manuscripts of Ilchi's travelogue, provide invaluable additional information.

Ilchi's mission in the London part of his journey was to convince the British to help the Qajar monarch to push the Russians out of their northern territories, which the British of course had no intention of doing. They were playing with Ilchi and procrastinating in his mission until they found a way not to do for the Qajars what they had promised to do, while getting rid of the French menace to their Indian possessions through other means. They wined and dined Ilchi much to his ceaseless delight until they made sure his trip to London was entirely useless. Thus, "none of the objectives of the Iranians was attained."[11] His mission unaccomplished, Ilchi left London and boarded a ship at Portsmouth on July 16, 1810, in the company of "Sir Gore Ouseley (the new envoy to Iran), his family, his brother Sir William Ouseley, and James Morier." Ilchi's journey, however, takes him first to the coasts of the Americas and a landing in Rio de Janeiro. The extant accounts of Ilchi's travels have only scant references to this American part of his journey, but there is corroborating evidence of his visit in other sources by his fellow travelers: Morier's *A Second Journey through Persia ... to Constantinople, 1810–1816* (London, 1818), Sir William Ouseley's *Travels in Various Countries of the East, More Particularly Persia* (London, 1819, 3 vols.), and William Price's *Journal of the British Embassy to Persia* (London, 1832, 2 vols. in 1).[12] Through these sources we can gain a fuller picture of Ilchi's travels beyond London, through Brazil, and on to India before he returned to Iran.

[11] Ibid. [12] Ibid.

While in London, Ilchi was actively courted and recruited into the illicit services of the British colonial interests in Iran, and was evidently very well paid for it. But a contemporary account of his visit indicates he did not quite do as he was recruited to do: "Although he has for a long time past, and I believe still receives a considerable annuity from the English government, and has returned to Persia loaded with its presents, he constantly opposes its interests, and talks of it before his countrymen generally in very slighting terms."[13] Be that as it may, Ilchi was instrumental in facilitating the British colonial interests that culminated in the infamous Treaty of Golestan (March 1813) between Iran and Russia, which the British were instrumental in drafting in order to "safeguard the British and Russian interests and enable the Russians to face the Napoleonic army without being disturbed by Iran."[14] Two years later, in 1815, Ilchi was again dispatched to Russia to help secure the return of the Northern Qajar territories. This journey, which lasted two years, resulted in yet another travelogue he dictated to his secretary, but was as catastrophic in its failure to achieve any result as indeed was his visit to London. In 1819 Ilchi was sent on a second diplomatic mission to England, this time for ten months, and yet again with much fanfare and ceremony and gossip columns in local papers but utterly a fiasco diplomatically for by now Napoleon was defeated and the British had no immediate or urgent interests in their Qajar court connections. He returned to become the Iranian foreign minister during the tense Perso–Russian tensions that resulted in a war that ended with yet another ignominious treaty, the Treaty of Turkamanchai (February 1828), which also bears his signature. In the aftermath of Fath Ali Shah's death, Ilchi sided with the wrong son and ended up running for his life by seeking refuge in a shrine. He was spared his life and returned to serve as the Iranian foreign minister until his death in 1845.

The Good and Evil Men Do

Abu al-Hassan Khan Ilchi was no beacon of moral rectitude or political integrity, but he was an acute observer of the world in which he lived, and from which we need a record to remember it properly. No doubt he was a deeply flawed weakling enamored of the pomp and

[13] As cited in ibid.   [14] Ibid.

ceremony of being an official envoy of Iran in England, where he was treated like a celebrity and taken for his luxurious portraits to be painted by renowned portraitists of the time, among them Sir Thomas Lawrence and Sir William Beechey.[15] Ilchi lived in a tumultuous and treacherous period in the history of his homeland and beyond, caught in between three combative colonial powers: the Russians, the French, and the British. There was very little he or anyone else could do to alter that geopolitical map of the world. But in the midst of his entanglements with political treacheries of the Qajar dynasty he has left us an eyewitness account of a period that has carved an indelible mark for the future of the region as postcolonial nation-states.

He wrote his travelogue with the expressed intention of it being a guide for future generations of Iranian and even Indian diplomats traveling abroad. We read him at the height of a colonial domination of the region when an aging imperial court is yielding reluctantly to the accouterment of emerging nation-states. Throughout his travelogue he seems clueless as to what a fool his British hosts take him to be, delaying his stay until his diplomatic mission was completely useless and made an utterly disgraceful failure, for the British were gauging the threat of Napoleon to their Indian colony and did not wish to alienate the Russians to appease the Qajars. Ilchi is entirely oblivious of these British colonial designs and completely mesmerized by his busy social schedule in London. He was a man of the world, worldly, political, ambitious, exceptionally intelligent, sometimes too intelligent in fact for his own good. He looks and sounds like Alice in Wonderland – and precisely for that reason in his travelogue his guard is down, leaving an accurate record for posterity of the period in which he lived.

As a diplomat he was instrumental in giving birth to Iran as a postcolonial nation-state, though in a manner that brought shame and ignominy to the state and empowered the emancipatory imagination of the nation. One can feel the growing pains of the Persian prose he writes, struggling with the English words he does not quite hear, let alone understand. Much of the travelogue is filled with useless and repetitious accounts of Sir Gore Ouseley's visits, their going out for riding, shopping, and the operas. The travelogue pales in comparison

[15] Ibid.

with the robust and piercing observations of Abu Taleb of almost the same period, which is a clear indication of the superiority of the Indo–Persian environment of his upbringing compared with the corrupt Qajar court atmosphere in which Ilchi had become prominent. Be that as it may, Ilchi's account in general, in both his European and non-European journey, is solid evidence of the clearing of Iranian eyes onto a widening world, a veritable document of his captured and frightened imagination, his bewilderment at the new world, his struggles to read what he sees.

As an influential courtier, Ilchi was the target of much attention by the notorious East India Company, wining and dining him, having his illustrious portrait done, enriching and ingratiating him to serve their colonial interests in Iran and India. Ilchi was a willing partner in these colonial designs, and unlike Abu Taleb, had not a bone of critical thinking about him, or if he did, he kept it mostly to himself. But there was something else that his generation of world travelers had made possible, that today we need to salvage from these violent and abusive Eurocentric readings that categorically disregard his non-European travels that today are crucial for us to reconstruct and remember. We must remember the colonial context of the time. The East India Company was deeply concerned about Zaman Shah of Afghanistan to their northern frontier and the prospect of a Napoleon alliance with Fath Ali Shah that would potentially facilitate an invasion from the west of India. All of these concerns would soon be terminated after the Battle of Waterloo (1815). The Qajar court was being yanked into the colonial intrigues, and as evidenced in this travelogue, it was nowhere near ready or even conscious of how to deal with it. Ilchi simply lacks the political language, the moral imagination, or the critical consciousness necessary for this age.

Ilchi partook in the lucrative hospitalities of his British hosts and forfeited Iranian national interests simply because he was a product of a corrupt dynastic court that still had no clue of what "national interests" were. There was no national will to speak of at this time to expect, demand, and exact from him and his court otherwise. It would be exactly another century before that national will would come to fruition in the course of the Constitutional Revolution of 1906–1911. Ilchi enriched himself and accepted lucrative salaries from the East India Company the same way that Fath Ali Shah received lucrative

gifts from the same company to help them protect their Indian possessions. It was a nasty and brutish time and produced nasty and brutish
people presiding over the fate of nations that were not even conscious
of their own existence as a nation except in periodic revolutionary
uprisings under the banner of one sectarian slogan or another. The
world Ilchi was traveling through was in a state of transition and
limbo. It was not a postcolonial map of "the West and the Rest." That
ahistorical superimposition of a different era has done much damage to
our understanding of the man and of where he went, what he saw, and
what he wrote.

I mentioned in the last chapter that "Europe" is not exactly "Farang," that it corresponds to it but it does not signify the same mental
universe or political punctuation as the new term did. In Ilchi's travelogue we see even more solid evidence for that fact. Ilchi has no idea
where or what is this "Europe." He writes it with three or four
different transliterations in Persian alphabet, for there is yet no standardized way of transliterating it. He tells us he asks his fellow traveler
James Morier to explain to him where exactly is Europe, and writes the
detailed explanation that Morier offers "for the edification of *Sayya-
han-e Ruzegar/World travelers of the time.*" He writes about England,
Scotland, and Ireland and then where France, Spain, Portugal, Italy,
Australia, Hungry, Prussia, and Sweden are located. He asks
about Europe and Morier tells him and he adds: "Europe, which is
the entirety of Farhang, is 3500 miles long and 2500 miles wide."[16]
He then asks Morier about Bonaparte (which he does not quite
hear and writes as "Paneh Pati." We know he is telling the truth and
Morier is the source of his knowledge of "Europe," for Ilchi partakes
in his informant's anti-French sentiments in his understanding of
Europe. It is quite telling that this first understanding of an Iranian of
what exactly is "Europe" is directly received from a nasty colonial
officer.

Why should such crucial facts contained in the travelogue be ignored
and only Ilchi's presumed "erotic fantasies" about "Farangi women"
be noticed and fancifully accentuated and badly theorized? But the
careless misreading of travelogues such as Abu al-Hassan Khan Ilchi's
begins much earlier than these later works and commences with the

[16] Ilchi, *Heyrat-Nameh*: 94.

shabby state of scholarship afforded them from the very critical edition
of the original Persian, its scattered manuscripts, its irresponsible
English translation, and then the categorically flawed Eurocentric
reading of the actual text. The best available "critical edition" of Ilchi's
travelogue, even if we can call it that, the one prepared in 1985 by
Hassan Morsalvand, is a disgrace. It is based on a single manuscript at
Majlis Library in Iran, and like that manuscript it abruptly ends in
mid-sentence at the end, and the editor writes in a footnote that "the
last few pages of the book are missing."[17] This means the rest of his
journey must be reconstructed from other corroborative sources (such
as those of the notorious racist Orientalist James Morier) often hostile
and condescending to him. But this reconstruction is possible if we care
to have a fuller conception of where Ilchi went and what he did.

The printed version prepared by Morsalvand has an embarrassingly
unreadable layout, and the original manuscript in Majlis Library is far
more beautifully written and outlined.[18] We also know that the editor
of this only Persian edition actually censored some of the passages of
even the single manuscript he consulted for some passages he found
insulting to his religious sensibilities.[19] We of course know of
the existence of other manuscripts of the travelogue: "One copy is in
the British Museum (Add. 23, 546) and another in the Majlis Library.
The present writer has seen a third in the possession of the descendants
of Mirza Abu al-Hassan in Tehran, longer and more detailed than the
British Museum copy."[20] We also know of the existence of another
more complete manuscript in Khuda Bakhsh Library, in Putna, India,

[17] Ilchi, *Heyrat-Nameh*: 370.
[18] Through the kind help of my friend Mahmoud Omidsalar and other colleagues
in Tehran, I have obtained the original manuscript in possession of the
Majlis Library, on the basis of which this printed edition is prepared. The
manuscript too, alas, ends abruptly in the same place. To see a digital copy of
this manuscript from the Majlis Library in Tehran, visit here: http://
94.232.175.44/index.aspx?pid=6&ID=55077&CBNID=ac17d33e-b2dd-4d4f-
a79a-d6d5948d100f. Accessed October 21, 2016.
[19] Morsalvand at one point writes he found a passage in the manuscript he was
editing offensive and wanted to delete it but let it go, which means in other
places he actually censored the original. See Ilchi, *Heyrat-Nameh*: footnote 2 on
page 83.
[20] See "ABU'L-ḤASAN KHAN ĪLČĪ" (*Encyclopedia Iranica*).

which includes a more detailed account of Ilchi's return journey to Iran via Brazil and India.[21] From the English translator of the book we also know:

Abul Hassan's own copy of the journal has disappeared, but contemporary copies were made for circulation at the Persian Court, and later copies were made from these – it is impossible to know how many. One is kept in the library of the Iranian Parliament and there is a greatly abridged version in the British Library. Another copy, with the poetry omitted, appeared at auction in London in 1981. The copy I have used for this translation belonged to Abul Hassan's great-great-great-granddaughter, Mrs. Effat Samiian ... Mrs. Samiian's copy of the journal is a 371-page undecorated manuscript in the clear nastaliq of a nineteenth-century scribe.[22]

There are many other issues with these manuscripts. The English translator reports that the copy she has used has dates of the entries added after the manuscript was finished and that the dates are not correct and she has had to find the correct dates from other corroborating sources. She also reports that there are "unexplained gaps" in the manuscript she has used. She also reports the events in the month of March are particularly confused and adds, "The impression is that the scribe was working from unbound sheets which he dropped on the floor and reassembled in haste."[23]

This is the calamitous condition of the travelogue that has gone through all these nasty distortions before it has reached us. Under ideal circumstances these manuscripts should have been collected and collated by a competent and trustworthy scholar and a reliable and complete critical edition prepared. But this was not done because of the combined negligence and incompetence of Iranian and non-Iranian scholars alike. The ruling Islamic Republic dislikes Ilchi because he was a freemason; the Orientalists old and new have ridiculed and treated him like a buffoon or else a character from James Morier's infamous *The Adventures of Hajji Baba of Ispahan*. Sensationalist "historians" such as Isma'il Ra'in have been even worse in their ludicrous

---

[21] Sohrabi, *Taken for Wonder* : footnote 30, page 136.
[22] See *A Persian at the Court of King George 1809–10: The Journal of Mirza Abul Hassan Khan*. Translated and Edited by Margaret Morris Cloake. Introduction by Denis Wright (London: Barrie & Jenkins, 1988): 9–12.
[23] Ibid.: 9–10.

commentaries on him.[24] Meanwhile the younger generation of scholars has even further buried him in their own endemic Eurocentric and colonized mind by useless and flawed speculations about Ilchi's "eroticism."

Istanbul, London, Rio de Janeiro, Mumbai ... St. Petersburg

Be that as it is, there are certain facts clearly evident throughout all the extant manuscripts and the only printed edition of *Heyrat-Nameh*: that Ilchi left Iran, traveled to Ottoman territories, boarded a ship and sailed to England, and from there to the Americas and from there to India before he came back to Tehran, from where he was soon sent on a new diplomatic mission to St. Petersburg, Russia, from which we in fact have another recorded account of his observations. Why disregard all these facts, choose only a fraction of his two travelogues, give primacy to the "European" part of his visits, turn him into a "voyeur" and a sexual predator while he was in England, and thus categorically distort both who he was and his own geographical imagination? Let us now look closer at his travel itinerary.

First and foremost, let us remember that Ilchi traveled from a major cosmopolitan city, from Tehran, the newly established capital of the Qajar dynasty (1776). He traveled from Tehran on May 7, 1809, in the company of James Morier, a nasty, racist colonial officer who would soon turn his privileged position next to Ilchi in this journey into a widely popular (in England and rest of Europe) racist satirical novel based on his impressions of his Iranian fellow traveler.[25] Morier detested everything about Iran and Iranians and was eager to get back to his beloved Europe. It is instructive to read Johnston's carefully reconstructed account of their journey together to see the difference between Ilchi's courteous, polite, and even affectionate attitude toward Morier, in contrast to Morier's foul and racist attitude toward him, as best evidenced in the novel he published lampooning a man with whom he had a close professional affiliation. Johnston offers a perfect psychoanalysis of the jealousy that Morier harbored toward Ilchi:

---

[24] See, for example, the phantasmagoric fusion of fact and fiction woven together by Isma'il Ra'in in his *Mirza Abu al-Hassan Khan Ilchi* (Tehran: Javidan Publications, 1978).

[25] Johnston's *Ottoman and Persian Odysseys*: 120.

"Mirza Abul Hasan was a striking contrast to James. Tall, handsome, a lush black beard below his beautiful dark eyes contrasting with the dazzling white of his teeth, he towered above the rotund James, seven years his junior."[26] It is also imperative to keep in mind that prior to this journey from Tehran, Ilchi had spent two and a half years in India and was perfectly familiar with the colonial context of the journey he was undertaking from this Indo–Persian world all the way to the coast of the Americas and back to India in fact. The colonial context of this departure from Tehran in the company of a British colonial officer who was closely observing him, only later to lampoon him in a novel, casts an entirely different light on this journey.

Between Tehran and Istanbul, Ilchi and his companion passed through Tabriz, a major cosmopolitan city with a vast history of encounters with colonial modernity and global thoughts in the region. Soon after he enters the Ottoman territories, Ilchi reports of an encounter in Izmir where a local dignitary comes to visit him and is deeply excited to find out he is from Shiraz and starts reciting the poetry of Hafez for him, telling him how widely popular the Persian poet is in his region.[27] He reports how happy he was to meet a few Shi'is in Izmir. He goes for a concert of song and dance by some boys in the company of a few friends that he makes there.[28] One of his servant's weapons is stolen while he is in this region. In Istanbul he gives a description of the city, its mosques, churches, parks, and beautiful buildings. He complains of the hilly topography of Istanbul but praises its beautiful buildings.[29] He writes of the diplomatic missions of Austria, Spain, and Switzerland in the Ottoman capital, including how beautiful the wife of the Swiss ambassador was, and how capably she spoke Turkish.[30] In Istanbul Ottoman authorities try to dissuade him from going to England and want to know what kind of treaty he was going to sign with the British. He keeps his diplomatic mission confidential and does not divulge, which fact he reports to his British contacts, much to their delight.[31] He continues his journey through Ottoman territories until he boards a ship for England. James Morier tells him he has instructed the captain to feed him properly, but of course he has lied and played yet another nasty trick on Ilchi, and he complains about his food.[32] On September 5, Ilchi and James ceremoniously board a ship in Smyrna

---

[26] Ibid.   [27] See Ilchi, *Heyrat-Nameh*: 72.   [28] Ibid.: 74.   [29] Ibid.: 78–79.
[30] Ibid.: 82–83.   [31] Ibid.: 83–84.   [32] Ibid.: 96.

and sail toward England, at which point James's racism sends him to his own diary to remark on how Ilchi was now eating his food "with knife and fork."[33] Ilchi is as happy, verbose, curious, and descriptive of his encounters in Istanbul and the rest of the Ottoman region as he is of London and Europe. He is as attentive to women here in Asia (if that is the measure of our reading his travelogue) as he would be later in Europe; thus, we can dispense with the whole hullaballoo of his presumed "fixation" on "*Farangi* women."

Ilchi arrives in England at Plymouth on Saturday, November 25, 1809, with all gun salutes and ceremony, and spends eight months trying to achieve his diplomatic mission but also doing much sight-seeing and socializing. He was not, however, fully satisfied with his reception given the formality his rank demanded, all of which James Morier was recording for his second racist diatribe, *The Adventures of Hajji Baba of Ispahan in England*.[34] Ilchi did manage to have an audience with Richard Wellesley, 1st Marquess Wellesley, at the time the foreign minister, as well as with Prime Minster Spencer Perceval, and King George III himself, much to the delight of the British public curiosities.[35] From then on, British officials and aristocracy were head over heels entertaining him lavishly with parties and operas as they figured out how to renege on their promises of helping Fath Ali Shah regain his lost territories to the Russians.

The English translation of this part of the travelogue, based on a more complete version with its dates carefully corrected, is in fact far superior to the existing Persian printed version. Here we are witness to Ilchi trying his limited best to achieve his diplomatic mission with little to no success, meeting with Sir Gore Ouseley, the British entrepreneur and diplomat, regularly, going out and socializing with the English elite. "The day dawned and an affectionate note arrived from my friend and companion, Sire Gore Ouseley," is a typical entry in this part of his travelogue, this one for Sunday, December 10, 1809, "in which he said that 'since today is Sunday and a holiday for us, I am deprived of the pleasure of the company of my distinguished and true friend. The Foreign Office is closed today, but tomorrow, which is Monday, the Foreign Minister will call on you to discuss your audience with the King.'"[36] He receives constant and multiple invitations to

---

[33] Johnston's *Ottoman and Persian Odysseys*: 126.   [34] Ibid.: 128–129.
[35] Ibid.: 130.   [36] Cloake, *A Persian at the Court*: 45.

dinner parties,[37] nevertheless he is homesick and wants to go back, but the British officials, especially Ouseley, keep him in suspense.[38] He remains fully abreast of the news at home and wary of the East India Company sending Sir John Malcolm to visit with the Shah in his absence.[39]

We know that in July 1810, Ilchi and his seven servants boarded HMS *Lion* in England and headed for the coasts of the Americas. The ship also included Sir Gore Ouseley, his wife, their three-year-old daughter, his diplomatic staff, servants, "and a cow to provide milk."[40] Traveling with them was of course the ever-present James Morier who was not happy to travel to Tehran through a six-month journey via Latin America and India.[41] They reach Rio on September 14, "where they spent a fortnight as the guests of the Portuguese prince Regent."[42] While in Rio, Morier continued his habitual nasty commentaries about Ilchi, Iranians, and Muslims in general. "He was well aware that the agents of a court so ignorant and so proud as are all the Mohammeden courts would never under-stand the diplomatic usages of European courts."[43] Morier's racism was of course not limited to "the Mohammeden" but extended well into his observations of the Brazilians he met. "James found the people generally dirty and uncouth. The natives had the habit of defecating publicly in sight of their residence, but when Sir Gore tried to stop this by having guards posted he soon had them removed because he was even more disgusted by their cruel treatment of the blacks."[44]

Fortunately, somewhere outside the prevalent Eurocentrism of Qajar scholarship, someone has taken Ilchi's journey to Brazil seriously and carefully examined it in some detail.[45] In an excellent essay published in German in 1987, Kamran Ikbal completely and persuasively dis-mantles the notion that Ilchi and his companions went to Brazil "due to bad weather." We already know that Ilchi was there in the company of Morier and Sir Gore Ouseley and his brother William Ouseley,

---

[37] Ibid.: 98.   [38] Ibid.: 139.   [39] Ibid.: 173.
[40] See Wright's Introduction to Cloake, *A Persian at the Court*: 20.
[41] Johnston's *Ottoman and Persian Odysseys*: 153.   [42] Ibid.: 154.
[43] Ibid.: 155.   [44] Ibid.: 155.
[45] See Kamran Ikbal, "Die Brasilienreise des persischen Gesandten Mirza Abu al-Hassan Khan Shirazi im Jahre 1810," *Die Welt des Islams*, New Series 27:1/3 (1987): 23–24.

where there was even an assassination attempt on Ilchi.[46] But from Ikbal's careful examination we also know the route these travelers took from Portsmouth to Madeira, Rio de Janeiro, Point de Galle (Ceylon), Kotschin (South India), Bombay, and finally Bushehr.[47] Ikbal persuasively dismisses the idea of the trip to Brazil being unplanned and due to stormy weather and considers the very idea "absurd."[48] Citing other corroborating sources, Ikbal demonstrates how the journey was perfectly planned and that it progressed apace under normal weather conditions. Ikbal, however, keeps asking why Persian sources are "concealing" this trip, and thus looks for political explanations.[49] Whereas, in both the Majlis Library Manuscript and the printed version we have, it is perfectly clear (as I have cited the specific passages) that Ilchi specifically mentions his journey to Americas, and offers both the Turkish and English terms for the word "America." Ikbal correctly turns to the geopolitics of the region to explain the Brazilian part of the journey, which was in fact the specific purpose of the British hosts of Ilchi. Ikbal makes the perfectly plausible argument that the British wanted to show Ilchi in person to the Portuguese king as the living evidence that they had the Persians under control, and Napoleon's efforts to mount an attack on India were useless.[50] Ikbal also speculates, somewhat less persuasively, that the story of the stormy weather may have had something to do with Ilchi's own "bad conscience" and fear of Fath Ali Shah's wrath that he had entrusted his fate so completely to the British mercy. There is no such evidence in the text of the travelogue. We should also add to Ikbal's apt observations concerning the political purposes of this journey to Brazil the fact that the "Strangford Treaty" was also signed in this very year of 1810, an agreement between the Portuguese government and Great Britain, containing certain commercial, military, and even religious dimensions, and in exchange for such concessions to Britain, Portugal was promised protection against Napoleon's militarism. For Ilchi to be taken along to this visit to Brazil was perfectly logical.

At any rate, this odd company left Rio on September 27, "taking three and half months to reach Bombay."[51] The passage to India was quite miserable, and Ilchi and his entourage were treated with habitual

---

[46] Sohrabi, *Taken for Wonder*: 26–27.
[47] See Ikbal, "Die Brasilienreise des persischen Gesandten Mirza Abu al-Hassan Khan Shirazi im Jahre 1810": 24.
[48] Ibid.: 25.   [49] Ibid.: 28.   [50] Ibid.: 35.   [51] Ibid.: 155.

disrespect, which at one point even resulted in a dramatic revolt, before things calmed down. They reached Mumbai on January 12, 1811, after a journey lasting "five months and twenty-five days covering a distance ... of 18,589 nautical miles."[52] They spend two weeks in Mumbai "sightseeing and attending banquets," where Ilchi, now conscious of his proximity to home, had evidently stopped publicly drinking wine, a fact that Morier of course abuses to ridicule him in his fiction. The journey is finally completed in Bushehr, to which Ilchi and his companions sail from Mumbai and into Iranian territories on March 3, 1811, eventually making their way back to the capital through Shiraz and Isfahan.

Ilchi's journey around the world took place during the crucial period of the Russo-Persian War of 1804–1813, and the undue significance given to the London part of his journey is in part under the influence of the geopolitics of the region when the colonial rivalries among the British, the French, and the Russians had encroached upon the Qajar court and territories. The origin of these territorial disputes between two tired old empires went back to the 1796 Perso-Russian War. Two years after Ilchi returned to Iran empty-handed from the diplomatic aspect of his journey, the war ended in 1813 with the infamous treaty of Golestan, which consolidated the control of Russia over Georgia, Dagestan, Azerbaijan, and certain parts of Armenia. These territorial losses to the Qajars meant very little to the regional culture of these territories that were multilingual and multicultural and remained that way no matter who controlled them. The war between the Qajar dynasty and the Russian empire resumed yet again in 1826 until 1828, during which period Ilchi assumed yet another diplomatic mission to solicit the British imperial help, which was equally useless and an exercise in futility, for the imperial and colonial games were now played well over the Qajars head. The war of 1826–1828, however, was even more humiliating for the Qajars, for they lost even more of their territories and were forced to sign yet another treaty in Turkamanchai and forfeit even more of their claim on a vast swamp of land in the Caucuses.

In between these two wars, Ilchi was dispatched to Russia on yet another impossible mission to oversee the ratification of the ignominious Golestan treaty. Ilchi and his mission left Tehran in June 1814 and

[52] Ibid.: 156.

returned two years later. They reached St. Petersburg in 1815, by which time the British had lost interest after the Conference of Vienna (November 1814 to June 1815), wherein European colonial powers had gathered to address issues arising from the French Revolutionary Wars and the Napoleonic Wars and thus agreed not to interfere in each other's colonial possessions. The first chapter of this particular travelogue is the description of the journey from Tehran to Tbilisi, the second and third chapters on events happening in Tbilisi, the fourth chapter on entering the Caucuses, the fifth chapter on entering the city of Tula, the sixth chapter entering Moscow, and then a chapter on St. Petersburg, with a final chapter on returning to Iran.[53] The most extensive chapters in this second travelogue are first on St. Petersburg and then on Moscow, with detailed chapters on other stops on the way. While in Moscow the authors, Ilchi and his scribe, offer details of the city, its markets, professions, industries, and write of Napoleon's destruction in Moscow.[54] Much of the attention is diverted to the pomp and ceremony they were offered. They write of the wealth of the Russian empire they have seen, and give details of how cold the weather is. We also learn that while they are in Moscow and much throughout their journey, they studied English first thing in the morning.[55] While in Moscow, Ilchi was still in correspondence with Sir Gore Ouseley.[56] The most detailed account of this and the other travelogue put together, by far, is about St. Petersburg. This part of the travelogue contains a full treatise on Russian empire in ten chapters on history, topography of St. Petersburg, architecture, interior designs, cuisine, local cultures and customs, political apparatus, finances, and the army, as well as the legal system.[57] Detailed accounts of their diplomatic

Russia

---

[53] See Mirza Mohammad Hadi Alavi Shirazi, *Dalil al-Sofara: Safarnameh Mirza Abu al-Hasan Khan Shirazi Ilchi beh Rusiyeh/Guide for Ambassadors: Mirza Abu al-Hasan Khan Shirazi Ilchi's Travelogue to Russia.* Edited by Mohammad Golbon (Tehran: Markaz-e Asnad Farhangi Asia, no date).

[54] Ibid.: 85.   [55] Ibid.: 97.   [56] Ibid.: 99.

[57] Ibid.: 131–181. Anna Vanzan has done a close examination of this travelogue in her "Mirza Abu al-Hassan Khan Shirazi Ilchi's Safar-Nama ba Rusiya: The Persians amongst the Russians," in Elton L. Daniel (ed.), *Society and Culture in Qajar Iran: Studies in Honor of Hafez Farmayan* (Costa Mesa: Mazda Publishers, 2002): 347–358. She makes the apt point that both Ilchi and his scribe are the authors of this text. But alas, she too, following the misbegotten trend of scholarship on these travelogues, considers them pivoted toward "Europe," and falls into the trap of laser-beaming on women and sex! See ibid.: 352–356.

banquets abound. We also find out that the relationship between Ilchi and Sir Gore Ouseley is no longer that warm and that Ilchi has discovered his British friend's duplicity.[58]

Now: Just look at Ilchi's itinerary from Asia to Europe to Latin America back to Asia through the Horn of Africa. That is the entire global map of European colonialism and the sites of active resistances to it. What sane person who has actually bothered to read the entirety of this travelogue cover to cover would still write a book on his "travels to Europe"? That one Iranian diplomat traveled in the company of British colonial officers for almost the entirety of the colonial map of the globe and kept a daily record of it is one singularly important document. His own follies, limitations, entrapment within the system that sustained him, all become secondary to a far more significant knowledge of where he was and what he was doing and in the company of what icons of British imperialism. In the span of two volumes, Ilchi connects the capital of his homeland to major and multiple epicenters of power in his world, from Istanbul to London, Rio de Janeiro, Mumbai, and St. Petersburg. That is a veritable topography of both colonial power and rising anticolonial struggles. He was far more integral to the former than attentive to the latter. But the baby of this indispensable knowledge he provides should not be thrown out with the bathwater of his own deeply colonized and compromised mind. He enables us to read beyond his limitations, by way of offering evidence of a reality he is unable to read but has the farsighted wisdom that others might, generations after he was gone. Ilchi and his secretary are scripting the future diplomacy of a nation-state. They offer detailed intelligence on places they visit. No doubt a royal readership may have been included in what they were writing, but they also knew the world they inhabited was at the threshold of a monumental change. They did not quite understand this world, but that it entailed unprecedented dangers and possibilities they intuited very well.

Orientalizing Ilchi

The abuse to which Ilchi's travelogue has been subjected is not limited to its Persian original. It extends well into its irresponsible English translation, which, though based on a presumably complete

---

[58] Shirazi, *Dalil al-Sofara*: 185.

RIO DE JANEIRO
1854

Figure 5 "Rio de Janeiro Brazil 1854" The fact that one of the travelers I examine in this book reached as far away from his homeland as Rio de Janeiro in Brazil is the clearest indication that the undue privileging of "Europe" as the destination of these travels is patently unwarranted. What is crucial here is not just the fact that South America is part of these itineraries, but that such destinations become integral to the counter-colonial remapping of the world as these travelers roam the earth. Their views of the places they visit is decidedly counter-colonial, non-Orientalist, empathetic, embracing, and narratively liberating. What these travelogues lack in visual representation they more than compensate with detailed and realistic prose. They write not to represent and dominate. They write to embrace and acknowledge, and thus to reimagine the world. Reprinted with permission from Andrew Fare/Alamy Stock Photo.

manuscript, the translator cavalierly omits everything before Ilchi arrives in England, as well as what happens after he leaves.[59] To be fair, it is a beautifully manufactured book, printed on expensive glossy paper, with ample and luxurious illustrations from the period. The translator has gone through a lot of trouble fixing the dates of the entries as best as she could. But still, its distorted and incomplete English translation is a key factor in creating the false impression that

---

[59] See Cloake, *A Persian at the Court*: 24.

Ilchi's journey was only to England – as if he descended from the heavens upon a ship nearing Plymouth on November 25, 1809, and then on July 18, 1810, he just disappeared into thin air off the coast of England.

Another serious and related flaw in reading Ilchi's travelogue is its conflation with that notorious colonial officer James Morier's fiction *The Adventures of Hajji Baba of Ispahan*. Sometimes even serious scholars have fallen into this trap. "The book is written in the usual florid style of the period," one such otherwise serious scholar writes, "and illustrates many of the incidents that are humorously described in *Hajji Baba* and its sequel."[60] The Persian original is decidedly not in a "florid style," and the author goes into detail apologizing for its being written in a straightforward simple prose. The English translator of the travelogue, too, opts to begin her rendition with a citation from James Morier, although she acknowledges how Morier abused his friendship with Ilchi to turn him into the fictional character of Mirza Firouz in the nasty, condescending, abusive piece of Orientalist satire of his widely popular fiction *The Adventures of Hajji Baba of Ispahan*.[61]

A younger generation of scholarship has picked up on that Orientalist pedigree and alas helped in turning Ilchi into a sexual pervert fixated on British women he met while in London. The man was thirty-four years old when he visited England, tall, handsome, and exotic to his British hosts, and obviously there were women such as Mrs. Perceval,

---

[60] "ABU'L-ḤASAN KHAN ĪLČĪ" (*Encyclopedia Iranica*).

[61] For an excellent analysis of the thematic and narrative link falsely presumed between the historical figure of Ilchi and the fictional character of Morier's novel, see Naghmeh Sohrabi, "Looking behind *Hajji Baba of Ispahan*: The Case of Mirza Abul Hassan Khan Ilchi Shirazi," in Amy Singer, et al. (eds.), *Untold Histories of the Middle East: Recovering Voices from the 19th and 20th Centuries* (London: Routledge, 2011): 159–175. Alas, Sohrabi, too, falls flat into the flawed Eurocentric narrative that presumes that Ilchi had traveled to Europe and back, subtitling her own book: "Nineteenth-Century Travel Accounts from Iran to Europe," engaging in baseless speculation about the title of Ilchi's travelogue, and ending up as an apologist for the monarchist Qajar historiography. This is particularly disappointing, for she has gone through the trouble of actually locating a more complete manuscript of Ilchi's travelogue that includes the detailed account of his journeys to Brazil and India before he returns to Iran. See Naghmeh Sohrabi's otherwise excellent book, *Taken for Wonder*: footnote 30, page 136. The actual content of her scholarship, however, is far more serious than these unnecessary distractions occasioned by the shaky foundations and misbegotten Eurocentrism of Qajar period scholarship.

the wife of the Prime Minster, or the niece of the foreign secretary who
were attracted to him and he to them. His travelogue makes frequent
references to such attractions and desires in open or concealed ways.
Nothing is strange, unusual, or scandalous about the matter to give
scholarly credence to the notorious Orientalist fantasies of James
Morier and turn Ilchi into a sexual predator. What these scholars
ignore is that Ilchi's travel companion, the blue-blooded British James
Morier, was equally, if not more, attracted to young women he met on
their way: "At Amasya, where he [James Morier] was particularly
struck by the beauty of the unveiled women."[62] They are two young
men obviously attracted to women they meet. Nothing strange or
unusual about that. No one makes a federal case of James's sexual
attractions, but whole chapters and books and bizarre theories of
"refashioning Iran" are devoted to Ilchi's sexual prowess toward
"European women." What these later commentators also fail to report
to their readers is the fact that Ilchi had become something of a rock
star, tickling the Oriental fantasies of his British acquaintances.
"Women of every class and age vied for the attention of this handsome,
exotic man," we read in sources never cited by these young Iranian
scholars, "and were enchanted by the pretty complements he paid in
his quaint English, in which, thanks to James's tuition, he became quite
fluent ... There were some ... who threw himself at him and begged to
be taken back to Persia. Perhaps he was tempted."[63] Of course he was
tempted. Why should he not be tempted? The question is why, in
turning him into a sexual predator on the model of an Oriental
Casanova, we disregard this environment and laser-beam on his sexual
desires at the expense of his intellect, his politics, his social observations. Ilchi was not the only one with an evidently healthy dose of
testosterone about him. Other men in his entourage are reported to
have visited London bordello houses and perhaps even contracted
STDs.[64] It's called life.

The entire texture, timbre, spirit, and the letter of Ilchi's travelogue is
distorted by undue emphasis on his (and other travelers like him)
"imagining European women, comparing women, libertine women,
the scapegoating of women ..."[65] all indices of a bizarre fixation on

---

[62] Johnston's *Ottoman and Persian Odysseys*: 123.   [63] Ibid.: 131.
[64] Ibid.: 131 – for the rest of the romances of both Ilchi and Morier, described with
   vicarious delight, see ibid.: 132–135.
[65] See Tavakoli-Targhi, *Refashioning Iran*: 54–76.

the sexual dimensions of a travelogue written by a man in his thirties, traveling alone in faraway lands. He shows equal attraction to young women (and men) while he is in Ottoman territories, and must have been the same person during his short visit in Brazil, and after that in India. Who said he was only attracted to "Farangi women"? The result of such irresponsible and flawed scholarship is the aggressive and violent transformation of a normal human being into a fictive Oriental predator on the model that Tayeb Salih fictionalized in the figure of Mustapha Saeed in his *Season of Migration to the North* (1966), or more immediately lending credence and authenticity to Morier's *Hajji Baba*, a hateful book, the product of a resentful colonizing mind writing against a more competent, more handsome, more attractive man. The wide popularity of *Hajji Baba* in Europe is itself a damning condemnation of a pervasively racist public that thrived on such works of fiction.

Instead of plucking him out of his natural and cultural habitat and sending him on a singular journey to England and back, and there and then turning him into a crazed sexual object fixated with "Farangi women," we need to liberate Ilchi and let him loose where he belongs, in the long and enduring tradition of *Seyr-e Afagh va Anfos/Journey through Horizons and Souls.* Long before Ilchi, luminary figures of Persian and Arabic literature such as Naser Khosrow, Sa'di, and Ibn Battuta had gone through similar journeys. This time around, Ilchi is mapping out a whole new colonial topography by being integral to it. On this topography, Ilchi is a master of the geopolitics of his region and the world he visits, and thus he is among the earliest specimens of a new breed of public intellectual. We may not agree with his politics (I do not, and I cringe at the very thought of him at those gaudy banquets in London). But we must reconstruct his journeys and what he saw and what he did responsibly. Twice he runs for his life in the course of his political career: once in his youth from Shushtar to India early in the history of a nervous new dynasty, and another time seeking refuge in a sanctuary when he sided with the wrong son successor of Fath Ali Shah. With all his flaws – and he was indeed a deeply flawed, greedy, unprincipled, wide-eyed young man unscrupulously in want of fame and fortune – Ilchi was not fixated on women, was far from the caricature that nasty Orientalists such as James Morier turned him into in his *Hajji Baba*, and in both his faults and in his experiences he has left us a veritable account of the world he witnessed and the life he lived.

When "Farang" Was Still Not "Europe"

What does James Clifford mean when he says: "Theory is no longer naturally 'at home' in the West – a powerful place of Knowledge, History, or Science, a place to collect, sift, translate, and generalize"? Let us read him more carefully:

> Or, more cautiously, this privileged place is now increasingly contested, cut across, by other locations, claims, trajectories of knowledge articulating racial, gender, and cultural differences. But how is theory appropriated and resisted, located and displaced? How do theories travel among the unequal spaces of postcolonial confusion and contestation? What are their predicaments? How does theory travel and how do theorists travel? Complex, unresolved questions.[66]

Upstream from Clifford's apt observations, the towering metaphor of "the West" is where the problem dwells, when we no longer even ask where in the world is this "West," and how did it get there. "The West" is an allegory of power (of reading, interpretation, and fixation) that has now successfully hidden the fact that it is just an allegory. There are real people who think they are from "the West," and there are therefore people who think they are from "the East" and behave that way. The issue is precisely the location of power that authorizes such fictions as facts, and even in the most critical moment we continue to use them to think critically! There are no "unequal spaces," just our colonial thinking makes it so. "Their predicaments" are not just theirs (whoever they might be), they are actually ours. Clifford seeks to disentangle this riddle: "Intellectuals such as Gayatri Spivak, Cornel West, Aijaz Ahmad, Trinh T. Minh-ha, Chandra Mohanty, Renato Rosaldo, [Edward] Said ... to name only a few, move theories in and out of discrepant contexts, addressing different audiences, working

---

[66] See James Clifford, "Notes on Travel and Theory" (*Return to Inscriptions*, Volume 5, 1989): 179. Edited by James Clifford and Vivek Dhareshwar, Group for the Critical Study of Colonial Discourse & The Center for Cultural Studies, University of California, Santa Cruz. Available also online here: www.complit.utoronto.ca/wp-content/uploads/COL1000-Week08_Nov4_JamesClifford.pdf. Accessed October 25, 2016.

their different 'borderlands.'" Long before or any other critical theorists moved any theory, the factual evidence of people's migration did, but the long shadow of the metaphor makes them invisible. Clifford further explains:

Theirs is not a condition of exile, of critical "distance," but rather a place of betweenness, a hybridity composed of distinct, historically connected post-colonial spaces. Lata Mani's essay in this volume is a case in point. A traveling theorist addressing audiences in both India and the United States, she risks misappropriation at every moment of speaking and writing.[67]

As we read these travelogues of the nineteenth century today, there is no longer any "condition of exile." We are all in exile. No one is in exile. The fictive frontiers of homeland have all faded away. "The West" is no longer there: Its fiction is read and resolved. Exile was a fiction that "home" made to make us homesick. We are no longer homesick. We are cured of that sickness. Exile is a condition of disempowerment, of exclusion, of alienation, we self-inflict. I am, with my name, supposed to be in exile in New York, while the Zionist "lone soldier" who goes to Palestine to fight for the Israeli army to steal Palestinian land and murder its inhabitants is supposed to be at home in the selfsame New York? How does that work? This whole thing called "exile" is a sham, a complete sham, fabricated to alienate and disenfranchise critical voices. All those names James Clifford mentions: Said, Spivak, Ahmad, etc., are not, and were not, in exile. They were home, in Palestine, in India, or in the United States. Calling them "in exile" is to weaken their voices, alienate their insights, and disfigure their shapely intellects. "Addressing audiences in both India and the United States" is not a condition of exile, it is a condition of a sculpted urbanity, a cosmopolitan culture beyond the limited imagination of those trapped in the fiction of being a "Native American," or those who have successfully repressed their parental memory of where they came from. The only real "Native Americans" are those fighting for the sanctity of their ancestral territories in Dakota as I write these lines. We more recent immigrants into their land have the privilege of never forgetting where we came from – that makes us amphibian, not marginal, at home in our defiance, not made redundant in exilic irrelevance.

[67] Ibid.: 179.

As he sailed and rode from one end of the colonized world to the next, Mirza Abu al-Hassan Khan Shirazi Ilchi canvassed and marked, early in the nineteenth century, the topography of a new universe dawning on nations yanked out of their habitual homelands. The English, the French, the Portuguese, and the Dutch, as well as every other European colonial power, mapped and mounted the world as if it were their parental inheritance and personal possession. Other nations and their rising consciousness of who they were and how to reconfigure their presence on this new global map were a nuisance to them. They wrote the world but prefigured, transfigured, prejudiced, and preempted any other alternative writing and mapping that could reveal a different story. That epistemic violence done to the world progressed apace into the making of even younger and more critically conscious generations of scholarship down to our time. To retrieve that transfigured universe is to reclaim the unresolved traumas of nations trapped inside disabling narratives of who they were and what they can be. It is precisely that "Western discursive space" that has had a false monopoly over "theory"[68] that needs dismantling before we can imagine the world otherwise.

As we narrow in on these traveling troubadours navigating the world within the contours of European colonial modernity, we are catching the world precisely at the moment when it is right in the process of its ecdysis, sloughing and molting, from one skin to another, from one momentous occasion to another. "The West" or "Europe" is not reciprocated yet by those who do not yet see themselves as "Orientals." These travelers are being indoctrinated and inducted into it, at the very moment that they were writing. We must sail back against almost a century of "Europology" to dismantle the myth and see the world differently, as they were witness to it, yet not knowing what they were watching.

In their close and confident company, we will have to learn how to read them closely. For reversing the colonial gaze means reverse engineering it, zeroing in on its colonial point of origin, and there and then provincializing and de-universalizing it, which is impossible if a different vision of the world is not painstakingly mapped out and peopled against that endemic Eurocentrism. The colonial gaze was perforce Eurocentric and manufactured an ahistorical metaphor and called it

---

[68] Ibid.

"Europe," or "the West," before casting its colonial gaze of power and audacity against the entirety of the world it sought politically to conquer but morally failed to de-author. Reversing that dehumanizing gaze requires not traveling back to Europe, which in fact falsely corroborates and perforce cross-authenticates it, but traveling before and beyond Europe, not bypassing but in fact placing and locating it in the factual evidence of a world it has failed completely to map and manage to eradicate. These travelers, if read carefully, have given us the factual evidence of that world, reverse engineering "Europe" to its provincial nativism, false and quite gaudy self-universalization.

4 | *A Colonial Officer Is Turned Upside-Down*
(Hajji Baba)

"It is a clean solitary room –
What simple proportions it has
For thinking!
I am so terribly sad –
Couldn't possibly go to sleep" –

He went and sat by the window
On a soft cloth chair:

"I'm still traveling
Thinking to myself
As if there's a boat floating
On all the rivers of this world and I
Sailing on this boat
Have for thousands of years
Been singing the living song
Of ancient mariners
Into the hollowed ears of seasons
As I sail forward –

Where will this journey take me?
Where will my footprint cease and
The gentle fingers of rest untie
My shoelaces?

Where's the place
Where I will have arrived –
Where I can spread
A little carpet and sit on it
In peace
Listening to the sound of a dish
Being washed at a nearby faucet?"

                    Sohrab Sepehri (Mosafer/Traveler, Babol, Spring 1966)

102

I translated this passage of Sohrab Sepehri's poem early in the morning on July 10, 2018, in Ocho Rios, Jamaica, where I was traveling with my younger children. What, I wondered as I was translating this poem and working on this book, accounted for the ability of colonized people around the globe – from Jamaica to Iran and India, and from there to the rest of Asia, deep into Africa, Latin America, and back here to the Caribbean Sea – to stand up to injustice and say "No!" Sohrab Sepehri's poem is the most sublime example of a poetic intuition of transcendence that has emerged from the historical ground, up. His poetic voice speaks with such confident consciousness, such transcendent awareness of what it was and what it said, no one in the vicinity of that poem could ever be subject to tyranny and injustice, to mental colonization or moral cowardice. In and with and through Sepehri's poem, "Traveler" in particular, we too traversed upon a path and sang those songs with and to ancient mariners. We were integral to a history that could not have been defeated and ended. We were alive and breathing in and through that poem. European colonialism was no match for the ancient assuredness of that history. I was now fully aware and confident the "I" with which I was reading these travelogues and writing this book was the collective "I" of an entire people, of the quintessence of Sepehri's poetry.

Colonialism at Work

On Wednesday, December 6, 1809, Mirza Abu al-Hasan Khan Ilchi writes in his diary how "Mr. Morier and my other traveling companions came to greet me in my own residence."[1] They are there to inform him that Marquis Wellesley, the former governor of Calcutta, has just been appointed minister of Foreign Affairs. Ilchi praises Wellesley to the moon and loudly sings his virtues in the privacy of his travelogue. Morier also informs Ilchi that the British Crown had appointed a high-ranking member of British colonial administration, Sire Gore Ouseley, as his personal host (*mehmandar*), but because Ouseley lived in the suburb of London he had appointed Morier to be at Ilchi's disposal for any services he might require. "He begged me to carry out in his stead any wishes your Excellency might have."[2] Morier had also brought Lord Radstock, "the husband of Mr. Morier's maternal aunt," as Ilchi

---

[1] See Cloake, *A Persian at the Court*: 37.   [2] Ibid.

tells us, along with him. Soon Sir Gore Ouseley himself shows up at
Ilchi's residence, entirely contradicting Morier's report. Presently,
Ilchi's attention is totally absorbed by Ouseley's command of multiple
languages and forgets about Morier and others in the company. This
Morier character that appears throughout Ilchi's travelogue will inadvertently play a crucial role in the history of the Iranian Constitutional
Revolution (1906–1911). How and why and through what circuitous
way this was the case cast a bright light on the course and significance
of the travel narratives we examine in this book.

In a deeply informed essay, "Persian Travelogues: A Description and
Bibliography," the late Iraj Afshar offers a typically exhaustive outline
of the range of travelogues written in Persian, with a particular
emphasis on the Qajar period.[3] So prevalent have been these travel
narratives that there are even books on the etiquette of traveling.
Afshar begins with the famous travel book of Naser Khosrow
(1004–1088) in the eleventh century and moves on to equally important if less famous travel narratives by the Indian mystic Jalal al-Din
Mohammad Moltani, Abu al-Sharaf Mohammad Hosayni Yazdi,
Ghiyas al-Din Naqqash Samarqandi, and many others in subsequent
eras. Then he moves to the Qajar period in particular and has a whole
section on the "geographical classification" of places that these travelers had visited.[4] Reading this section, it is essential for us not to confuse
traveling in a much larger radius with traveling exclusively to Europe.
Yes, traveling to Europe was part of this body of literature but by no
stretch of imagination was Europe their first, final, or exclusive destination. Visiting Mecca and Medina during their Hajj pilgrimage, for
example, was of course a typical journey of these travelers from Iran
and India, or the Indo–Persian world to be exact. The second destination of travelers from Iran was India, as typified by Mir Seyyed Abd
al-Latif Shushtari's travelogue, which we have already examined.
Equally important are Indian travelers who traveled to Iran and wrote
extensive accounts of their visits. Another major destination for these
travelers was cities such as Bokhara, Samarkand, and other Central
Asian destinations and other regions of the Caucuses. Many of those
travelers who went to Russia and Istanbul and Europe did so through

---

[3] See Iraj Afshar, "Persian Travelogues: A Description and Bibliography," in Elton
L. Daniel (ed.), *Society and Culture in Qajar Iran: Studies in Honor of Hafez
Farmayan*: 145–162.
[4] Ibid.: 150–160.

these Central Asian regions. Travelers from colonial India also went to Europe, visiting a whole range of places including Africa on their way. As early as the time of Amir Kabir (1807–1852), interest in the Americas also emerged among Iranian travelers. Equally important, Afshar tells us, are travelogues written by those traveling within Iran itself.[5] These travelers were interested in seeing the world, and the world was their destination, and therefore worldly was the vision of their own whereabouts.

Now compare the range of these traveling accounts and places these travelers visited with the manner in which Eurocentric diplomats such as Denis Wright, for example, cherry-pick and narrow in on those Iranians who went to England and those Britishers who went to Iran – a nice little two-way street that completely disregards a much wider traffic around it, privileges England and by extension Europe, and casts a long, distorting shadow on an entirely different reality. In two highly influential books, *The English amongst the Persians* (1977) and *The Persians amongst the English* (1985), Denis Wright has been a major architect of this false binary of setting Iranians and Europeans against each other in a deeply flawed category that keeps feeding on itself. Other scholars of the period have joined forces with this British diplomat, altogether disregarding the factual evidence of these texts and what they represent. To be sure, any person can pick any one set of these travel narratives and do with them as he or she desires for whatever particular reason – but only so far as the world remains conscious of the larger frames of reference from which this selection is extracted.

By a bizarre turn of events during the time we are now examining this crucial body of literature, we actually have a textual *pharmakon* (as both poison and remedy) that can act as an antidote to this misguided distortion of truth from the very heart of colonial and colonized imagination that has given birth to this systemic contortion of reality. In every chapter, I have been driving the point home that the body of literature we are examining here has been falsely identified as travelogues to and from Europe, whereas the truth is that these travelers have gone far before and far beyond "Europe"; that in fact what they called "Farang" is somewhat different than what today we call "Europe"; that this false privileging of Europe has in turn distorted the

---

[5] Ibid.: 158–160.

actual world, the crucial imaginative geography, that these travelers had occupied and lived. Now I wish to turn to a work of fiction written by a colonial officer that is the epitome of such Eurocentric colonial imagination of falsely positing an Oriental sojourner destined to and from Europe, and yet in its Persian translation it has turned out categorically to upend that assumption and bring the fictive traveler back home to his worldly habitat, and thus positively to dismantle that fictive colonial geography. Let me explain this twisted turn to truth in some detail.

An utterly nasty piece of colonial literature, James Morier's *The Adventures of Hajji Baba of Ispahan* (1824) offers a unique opportunity to reflect on the nature and functions of travel narratives in this period.[6] Why should we consider a British colonial officer's racist lampooning of Iran and Iranians thinly disguised as a work of fiction (and a very bad work of fiction at that) in this category? The answer lies in the peculiar history of this text and the manner it has itself traveled back into Iran to become something entirely different than its original purpose and provenance. The exquisite Persian translation of this book by Mirza Habib Isfahani (1835–1893), a towering public intellectual of his time, almost half a century after its original publication is the main reason why this book deserves our critical attention.[7] By a bizarre turn of events, this translation assumed a reality *sui generis* almost entirely independent of its original and turned out to become a critical text in the course of the Constitutional Revolution of 1906–1911. The encounter with this text as a result takes place at the critical interface between a nasty colonial exercise in classical Orientalism on one side and its inversion into a critical piece of anticolonial thinking on the opposite side. So successful was Mirza Habib's rendition of this book into Persian, and so definitive became that translation to the anticolonial struggles of his people, that even its original was and to this day still is popularly (and falsely) believed to have been the work

---

[6] I have had two previous occasions on which I have reflected on Morier's novel and its Persian reception. First, in my *Iran: A People Interrupted* (New York: The New Press, 2007): chapter 1; and then in my *Persophilia: Persian Culture on the Global Scene* : chapter 9. But this is by far the most extensive in the context of the central theme and theory of this book.

[7] For a short account of Mirza Habib Isfahani's life, see "HABIB ESFAHANI" in *Encyclopedia Iranica*. Available on line here: www.iranicaonline.org/articles/habib-esfahani. Accessed November 27, 2016.

of an Iranian and done in Persian and then badly translated into English by a British colonial officer with a flawed and awkward command of Persian language! The debate over whether the original was written by an Iranian patriot (perhaps Mirza Habib himself) or a British colonial officer is further testimony to the power of the Persian text to radically transform the intention and authorship of the original.

As a work of fiction, *The Adventures of Hajji Baba of Ispahan* belongs to the genre of *picaresque* literature, featuring a certain career opportunist Iranian named Hajji Baba, a charlatan *par excellence*, who navigates the borders of East and West, home and abroad, pursuing his selfish interests in unsavory ways. Paradoxically, however, James Morier has done a remarkable act of self-projection and invested his own repressed guilty conscience as a careerist colonial officer onto the Oriental character he has created in his book. We may therefore read Hajji Baba as in fact James Morier himself in his Oriental guise. The astonishing history of this text is the exact and complete reversal of its original intention and audience (to ridicule and denigrate Iranians and by extension Orientals to an uproarious delight of its vastly popular European reception), and its Iranian destination and audience that turned it into a piece of auto-critic to mobilize against both Qajar tyranny and British and European colonialism. A key factor in this encounter between the original and its hermeneutic reversal in its Persian translation is the site of Istanbul as a liminal space between Iran and England, where Mirza Habib Isfahani's Persian translation was produced and initially published. Istanbul is where leading Iranian public intellectuals such as Mirza Aqa Khan Kermani and Sheykh Ahmad Ruhi (both Mirza Habib's contemporaries and in fact close friends) had gathered to think through the fate of their homeland. This immediate community to which Mirza Habib belonged was itself in exile from a fictive geography of their homeland, effectively expanding it into Central Asian and Ottoman domains. The transnational public sphere from which the very idea of "Iran" as a postcolonial nation eventually emerged is the *locus classicus* of the expat public intellectuals who were in fact far more at home abroad than in their own homeland, thereby collapsing the porous boundaries of both. By the time Mirza Habib produced his translation of Hajji Baba, the emerging and potent body of travelogues we are examining in this book had already trespassed that idea of homeland and produced a richly potent tertiary space.

He Was Sick of Persia

"I am sick of Persia and everything belonging to it."[8] This phrase of James Morier, cited by Johnston in his book on Morier and his brothers, very much sums up the attitude of the notorious author of *Hajji Baba of Ispahan* by the time he arrived in Bushehr in March 1811 in the company of Seyyed Abu al-Hassan Khan Ilchi, and in fact through much the rest of his visit to the Qajar Iran. His was a classic example of morally depraved British colonial officers who served the imperial interests of their government and yet detested themselves for doing so in faraway lands and were homesick for the comfort and familiarity of their homeland and hence projected their hatred of the job they were doing onto the people they met while doing it. The British imperial history is full of such British and other colonial officers – exuding a racist hatred that has on many occasions resulted in the massacre of those they loathed to rule. Colonel Reginald Dyer (1864–1927), who ordered the massacre at Jallianwala Bagh, known as Amritsar Massacre (April 13, 1919), in the height of Indian anticolonial uprising, is perhaps the best prototype of these colonial officers. James Morier did no such vicious atrocity but still he needs to be understood in the context of self-loathing colonial officers out to find a morally depraved outlet for their psychopathology. By the time Morier arrived in Iran in the company of Ilchi he was a bitter, angry, and vindictive man, at odds with his own superiors Sir Hartford Jones and Sir Gore Ouseley, whom he accused of "parsimony" for not accommodating his whims to travel more luxuriously.[9] Meanwhile he did not miss any opportunity to ridicule and denigrate Ilchi, as he did on April 1 of the same year in this journey when he played an April Fool's trick on the poor man, sending him a message that "James was dying and wanted to see him urgently," only to laugh at and ridicule him when the poor man rushed to see the person he considered to be his friend.[10]

James Morier continued to quarrel with Sir Gore, constantly complaining behind his back that the two had differences of opinion as to how to conduct their business with the Qajar court, whether to bribe or not to bribe the officials, or how much, or in what way.[11]

---

[8] Johnston, *Ottoman and Persian Odysseys*: 164.   [9] Ibid.: 165.
[10] Ibid.: 165.   [11] Ibid.: 166.

The foreground of all such quarrels was Morier's sense of despair for living in Iran. He wrote to his mother: "The life we lead here is more like the pastoral life of our first fathers than that of our modern gentlemen."[12] Desiring to resume his gentlemanly life back in England, he felt obligated to learn more about the people and their culture he deeply despised. "I intend to study Persian," he wrote to a friend:

not because I take any delight in it, but because it is a sort of thing expected from a man who has lived in Persia, that he should be conversant in its literature. My object in reading its best authors ... will be to have the power of judging whether they really possess those excellencies that our oriental scholars are so eager in giving them ... From what little I have seen of Persian literature, I must own that it does not repay the trouble one has in learning it, & that its poets and historians would never bear the test of close criticism – at least according to our northern and logical ideas of excellence.[13]

Who would do that? Why would a human being do what he detests doing? It is a really twisted and dark soul dwelling inside those neatly clean and starched colonial uniforms. It was not just Persian literature Morier disdained. He had a copy of Adam Smith's *The Wealth of Nations* (1776) with him that he never opened, and he said he had not enough money to buy a copy of Robert Malthus's *An Essay on the Principle of Population* (1798), about which he had evidently heard. Instead, his correspondences were filled with his sexual fantasies of the Oriental harem, particularly finding ludicrous things to report, such as Ilchi bringing silk stockings to Iran because he believed and reported that they evidently increased a man's sexual prowess.[14] The depth of his racist hatred of his surroundings became evident when he wrote to a friend how he preferred "to be surrounded by a little population of my own creation instead of that constant succession of bearded muzzles that have so long been my companions."[15] He did fulfill his wish by writing a loathsome book full of his own creations, though in a psychopathological twist it was still entirely populated by those "bearded muzzles."

Morier's Christianity was of an entirely colonial disposition, of a sort that led him toward "comparing local customs with biblical passages."[16] This was in line with his systematic assimilation of Iran and the rest of the colonial world he visited backward into an archaic

---

[12] Ibid.: 166.   [13] Ibid.: 166–167.   [14] Ibid.: 167.   [15] Ibid.: 170.
[16] Ibid.

Biblical age feeding his Oriental fantasies. Practically everything he
encountered while in Iran became material he would gather and abuse
sarcastically and with an intent to mock and deride in his "Hajji
Baba."[17] To be sure, these were wretched times and the politically
incompetent and morally arrested Qajar dynasty gave James Morier
and other British colonial officers every reason and plenty of occasions
to abuse and ridicule Iran and Iranians. On the news of the imminent
victory of Bonaparte over Russians, Fath Ali Shah was mortified by
fear of the French invading his country and went begging with Sir Gore
Ouseley, pleading with the British to come and take over his power to
defend his throne.[18]

Morier ultimately left Iran, declaring gleefully, "Although full five
years in Persia, yet I never left a place with less regret."[19] Thus full of
hatred and not a shred of affection for the people he had spent half a
decade living with, he returned to his homeland to write a book to fill it
with nasty "bearded muzzles" and vicious Orientals to create and craft
out of his own deeply perturbed mind and make them behave as he
wished, like dolls and marionettes out of an "Arabian Harem," to
sooth his own repressed anxieties. In other times and under different
circumstances James Morier would have been committed to a psychi-
atric ward to be treated by behavioral and/or chemical therapies.
Instead he wrote a novel that catered to equally sick racist fantasies
of other Europeans, made "Europeans" by precisely these sick fantasies about other people, who now loved and admired his delusions as a
reflection of their own.

An Orientalist Novel for All Seasons

Hajji Baba has been declared by leading Iranian scholars of the Qajar
era as "the most popular Oriental novel in the English language and a
highly influential stereotype of the so-called 'Persian national character' in modern times."[20] The content and purpose of the novel are
summarized as follows: "*Hajji Baba* lampoons Persians as rascals,
cowards, puerile villains, and downright fools, depicting their culture
as scandalously dishonest and decadent, and their society as violent.

---

[17] Ibid.: 172.   [18] Ibid.: 180.   [19] Ibid.: 190.

[20] See the "HAJJI BABA OF ISPAHAN" entry in *Encyclopedia Iranica*, available
online here: www.iranicaonline.org/articles/hajji-baba-of-ispahan. Accessed
November 28, 2016.

Morier's satire, a bestseller in England and elsewhere, is an entertaining picaresque novel embellished with Orientalist motifs. To English
and other Western readers ... Morier's display of the Persian vagaries
served as a reassurance of Europe's cultural and moral superiority and
the civilizing mission of the imperial powers."[21]
  Written by a nasty and vindictive colonial officer toward the end of
his career in India and Iran, *Hajji Baba* uses the space of a work of
fiction for the author's own belated revenge upon Iranians he had met
in the course of his diplomatic career. He did so by appealing to the
basest common Orientalist delusions of other Europeans like him.
"Morier's success in adopting the picaresque genre for this purpose,"
it has also been rightly suggested, "was in no small measure due to the
style and presentation of *The Thousand and One Nights* ... which was
in vogue at the time."[22] This was the height of European colonial
constitution of their Oriental subject in whatever form best suited to
deny them decency of self-rule. What is the content of the novel, you
may wonder? Here is a short summary:

A long, and at times tedious novel of eighty chapters, Hajji Baba of Ispahan
recounts in the first person the extraordinary adventures of its hero, the son
of a barber from Isfahan who in the course of his many years of travel and
adventure frequently changes guises and professions. He gets into trouble
because of his own mischief and he manages to get out of it through his
resourcefulness. He experiences sharp vacillations between poverty and
wealth and between undeserved power and punishing powerlessness. His
life is dictated in the main by a blind and fickle fate, which Hajji Baba seems
to be able to miraculously turn each time to his own advantage.[23]

The prose of the original English reeks with intentional absurdities to
ridicule Persian language and prose, and yet it also reveals an astonishingly ignorant author when it comes to his knowledge of the language
of his chief character. "His surprisingly weak knowledge of Persian," it
has been generously observed, for there is no surprise here at all,
"evident in many spelling and pronunciation errors, and his poor grasp
of Persian syntax, were offered as justifications for vague or meaningless sentences and phrases in his prose, as though the author had
translated from Persian without grasping its actual meaning."[24] In
other words, Morier's ignorance of Persian language, even after more

[21] Ibid.   [22] Ibid.   [23] Ibid.   [24] Ibid.

than half a decade of living in Iran, is here rendered as an indication of the wretched ignorance of the character he creates. It is for that reason that I continue to propose that *Hajji Baba* is James Morier himself in his Oriental guise.

Equally important for our purposes is the sequel to the novel that Morier published as *The Adventures of Hajji Baba of Ispahan in England* (1828), in which we learn how Hajji Baba joins the Persian mission and comes for a visit to England. Here we learn about "Hajji Baba's journey from Persia to England, his formal engagements and informal encounters there in the company of the Persian envoy, and his reflections on England and the English."[25] It is this second novel that "closely corresponds to Morier's own experience as secretary of a diplomatic mission. The journal kept by the Ilchi during the period 1809–10, known as *Heyrat-Nameh*, also bears a striking resemblance to Morier's fiction." In other words, it is this notorious Orientalist work of fiction that has subsequently cast an enduring shadow over the text of Ilchi and to this day and even among serious scholars continues to distort the totality of the journeys he undertook while away from his homeland. A notorious British colonial officer writes a delusional fantasy about an Oriental's visit to England, and generations of scholarship have been sent after the wild-goose chase of "Persian travelogues to Europe"!

That Morier's work of fiction was taken dead seriously by British colonial administration we know for a fact.

Far beyond its worth as a work of fiction, Hajji Baba was regarded as a true display of Persian roguery and villainy hidden behind deceptive appearances. Not surprisingly, it became standard reading for all Westerners dabbling in Persian, and, in a broader context, any "Oriental" affairs. This included diplomats and statesmen, political commentators, missionaries, academics, archeologists, physicians, educators, travelers, artists, writers and even casual readers who wished to know something about Persia. When C. J. Wills was appointed to serve in Persia as the physician of the Indo–European Telegraph Department, he was strongly advised by F. J. Goldsmith, the Director of this department and an old hand in Persian affairs, to read Hajji Baba: "When you read this, you will know more of Persia and the Persians than you would if you had lived there with your eyes open for twenty years." When, in 1883, he wrote In the Land of the Lion and the Sun or Modern

[25] Ibid.

Persia, Wills endorsed his superior's advice: "It is seventeen years since I went to Persia, and I read 'Hadji Baba' now, and still learn something new from it." It is no wonder that, in 1897, Wills and Goldsmith brought out their own edition of Morier's Hajji Baba.[26]

That single text, it would not be an exaggeration to suggest, became the template of British colonial administration, for anything and anywhere the term "Persian" was applicable, for more than two centuries, from the time James Morier wrote it in the early nineteenth century all the way to British diplomats coming to the Pahlavi court in the mid-twentieth century. In the epistemic foregrounding of their reading of Iran and Iranians, Denis Wright's two volumes, *The English amongst the Persians* (1977) and *The Persians amongst the English* (1985), is still very much predicated on the two volumes James Morier wrote on Hajji Baba a century and a half earlier. This much is not a surprise. Of course, the British and by extension other Europeans would take that obnoxious work of defamation as factual evidence. But the true damage is when this work of fiction is allowed to cast a long and distorting shadow back on the factual evidence of travelogues written by Iranians themselves, and then read backward to generate a "Persianate Europology" anchored on a nonsensical pivot of "imagining European women!"[27]

A Text and a Counter-Text

Now let's turn to the miraculous Persian translation of James Morier's *Hajji Baba* and see how a quick change of readership and reception suddenly and radically altered what it meant and signified. Soon after its translation, the first copy of Mirza Habib Isfahani's rendition of James Morier's *The Adventures of Hajji Baba of Ispahan* reached Iran

---

[26] Ibid.

[27] For an abusive and forced reading of Ilchi's travelogue through Morier's fiction, see Sohrabi, *Taken for Wonder*: 40–45. In yet another treatment of the same subject, published a year earlier, she again juxtaposes Ilchi's travelogue against the backdrop of *Hajji Baba*, this time to denounce the whole "rhetoric of the Constitutional revolution," as she dismissively calls and rejects the most monumental social uprising of a nation in the early twentieth century. See Sohrabi, "Looking behind *Hajji Baba of Ispahan*": 163–166. Fortunately, the scholarship of Haddadian-Moghaddam and Kamran Rastegar has saved the Qajar historiography from these abusive readings. For more on their excellent scholarship, see below.

in a manuscript that was in his close friend Shaykh Ahmad Ruhi's handwriting, and thus people assumed it was in fact Ruhi's, and were delighted to read it, and in fact thought it the first Iranian novel. But as soon as they heard from a certain Major D. C. Phillott, a British diplomat stationed in the city of Kerman in Iran who had published the first edition of Mirza Habib's Persian translation in India, that it was, in fact it is, a translation of an English original, they almost immediately changed their mind and thought it very rude of its English author to have ridiculed Iranians. The British diplomatic corps in the region, ranging from Iran to India, however, including the Viceroy of India Lord Curzon (1859–1925), thought it exceptionally important and insightful for other British colonial officers to read and learn before going on any diplomatic mission.[28] It was therefore perfectly evident from the very beginning that the original text was solidly based on the experiences of a high–ranking colonial officer and was now deemed useful to other such officers dispatched on any diplomatic mission to the Indo–Persian world. But the fate of its Persian translation would be rather drastically different.

   In subsequent editions of the Persian text, it was now read as a work of fiction and thus liberties were taken in "editing" it to match the literary standards of later eras. A later Persian translation appears independently of Mirza Habib's text later in India, from the original English, for by this time the text is used decidedly to train the British colonial officers in Persian "manners"! Meanwhile, the original manuscript of Mirza Habib's translation was finally discovered by the leading Iranian scholar Mojtaba Minovi in 1961, from which he prepared a facsimile copy and took it to Iran. There is also a letter by Shaykh Ahmad Ruhi to the prominent British Orientalist E. G. Browne (1862–1926) that further testifies that this Persian translation was in fact made by Mirza Habib based on its French translation. Decidedly putting it into a very colloquial Persian, Mirza Habib produces an

---

[28] See the detailed Introduction of Ja'far Modarres Sadeghi to his critical edition of Mirza Habib Isfahani's translation of James Morier's Hajji Baba *as* Sargozasht-e Hajji Baba Isfahani/The Life of Hajji Baba Isfahani (Tehran: Nashr-e Markaz, 1379/2000): Nine-Fifty-Nine. Sadeghi's edition is based on the original manuscript of the Persian translation in Mirza Habib's own handwriting.

astonishingly effective prose as if the text was written originally in Persian.[29] In Istanbul of this period, circa 1892, Mirza Habib Isfahani was in the company of Shaykh Ahmad Ruhi, Mirza Agha Khan Kermani, and Khabir al-Molk, three leading revolutionary thinkers and activists who were at the center of a rich and thriving dissident culture. While Mirza Habib was ill, however, his friends were arrested in Istanbul, sent to Iran, and summarily executed. They were suspected in an assassination plot that had just killed the Qajar monarch Naser al-Din Shah (1831–1896). Before his death, Mirza Habib emerged as a leading Persian poet, prose stylist, and grammarian, teaching the language and systematizing its grammar while living in Istanbul and translating European literature into Persian.

In his original English, Morier uses the framing story that the original of his book was given to him by an Iranian. Mirza Habib and all subsequent Iranian readers of this text have taken that framing story literally and to this day some still believe Morier's text is a bastardization of a Persian original, and thus they believe Mirza Habib's was not a *translation* but a *restoration* of that original.[30] Highly influential on Morier was, however, the whole popular genre of picaresque novel as best represented at his time in Alain-René Lesage's *L'Histoire de Gil Blas de Santillane/Gil Blas* (1715 and 1735), which Mirza Habib also translated from French into Persian. In both *Hajji Baba* and its sequel, Mirza Abu al-Hassan Khan Ilchi is the key character that Morier uses and abuses to fit his sarcastic twinge. Both Mirza Abu al-Hassan Khan Ilchi and another Iranian student, Hajji Baba Afshar, who was among the first group of Iranian students sent to London by Qajar Prince Abbas Mirza, were evidently deeply angered and offended by James Morier's fanciful novel.[31] The battle of authorship, intention, reception, and who and why wrote this picaresque novel raged from one generation to another. Constant remain two undeniable facts: James Morier's original demeaning English, and Mirza Habib Isfahani's uplifting and liberating Persian translation.

While during the Pahlavi period (1926–1979) Iranian commentators were critical of the original and appreciative of the Persian translation,

---

[29] Sadeghi's Introduction to *Sargozasht-e Hajji Baba Isfahani/The Life of Hajji Baba Isfahani*: Twelve-Thirteen.
[30] Ibid.: Twenty-One.   [31] Ibid.: Twenty-Five.

soon after the success of the Islamic Revolution (1977–1979) all such
readings were dismissed in favor of a more militantly "nuanced"
appreciation of the original and its Persian translation, accusing the
previous generations of "ignorance" for their harsh judgment of the
original and the under-appreciation of Mirza Habib's Persian.[32] Now
it was the "literary" virtue of James Morier's original that was loudly
and uncritically celebrated, a virtue its Iranian readers of previous
generations were deemed hitherto too ignorant to appreciate,
according to Ja'far Modarres Sadeghi, the editor of its most recent
critical edition and a prominent novelist in his own right who is totally
enamored of *Hajji Baba* and entirely oblivious or dismissive of the
colonial context of its original production and wide circulation and
reception in Europe. He thinks it "innately" a masterpiece. Be that as it
may, Modarres Sadeghi is rightly critical of the manner in which in
post-constitutional period the text of Mirza Habib was abused by
leading Iranian novelist Mohammad Ali Jamalzadeh (1892–1997)
and manhandled in its first edition produced in Iran. Modarres Sadeghi's own critical edition is prepared based on a critical edition relying
mostly on the copy in Mirza Habib's own handwriting. As a major
novelist in his own right, Modarres Sadeghi also spends considerable
time appreciating the healthy and robust prose of Mirza Habib, which
he considers liberated from the arrested and arcane formalism of the
Qajar courtly prose, linking it back to a masterpiece of Persian prose,
Sa'di's *Golestan*.[33] This is indeed a strange Introduction, full of
insights into Mirza Habib's prose, and yet deeply enamored of the
British colonial officer, Major D. C. Phillott, who had published an
earlier edition of the book in India, and concluding by calling Mirza
Habib's Persian translation of an original English novel a "Persian
novel."[34]

---

[32] Ibid.: Twenty-Six.   [33] Ibid.: Thirty-Eight.
[34] Far more nuanced and balanced than Modarres Sadeghi in this Introduction
is an excellent essay by Esmaeil Haddadian-Moghaddam of Universitat Rovira i
Virgili, Tarragona, "Agency in the Translation and Production of *The
Adventures of Hajji Baba of Ispahan* into Persian" (*Target*, Volume 23:2, 2011):
206–234. Available online here: https://benjamins.com/#catalog/journals/
target.23.2.04had/details. Accessed November 27, 2016. In this essay,
developed within theories of translation with a thorough command of primary
and secondary sources, the author examines what he calls "agency in the
translation and production of James Morier's picaresque novel, *The Adventures
of Hajji Baba of Ispahan* (1824) into Persian." His main argument is that:

After all these twists and turns, the fact is that James Morier's *The Adventures of Hajji Baba of Ispahan* is not a Persian novel. It is a nasty piece of Orientalist literature based on its author's vindictive anger against his lived experiences as a colonial officer in Qajar Iran, cleverly fused with the genre of picaresque novel popular in his time to give it a fake aura of respectability to a European audience only too eager to believe anything and everything about the Oriental figment of their own perturbed imagination.[35] Mirza Habib's text meanwhile is an exquisite translation of James Morier's novel originally written to entertain the Orientalist fantasies of his contemporary Europeans and exacerbate the racist predilection of generations of later European diplomats, which in its Persian translation was turned upside-down by an ingenious translator. That's it. As a novelist in his own right, Modarres Sadeghi is too eager to fabricate a genealogy for his craft and thus a bit too enthusiastically calls it "the first novel in Persian language written by an Iranian."[36] Why and how it is that this Persian translation of an English original through its French rendition became

"Mirza Habib Isfahani, the translator, intervened in the text in order to exercise his exilic agency ... for the ethics of political progress was higher than the ethics of fidelity to the foreign text as one way of exercising his agency in exile." He further examines other factors, such as: "the English Major in charge of the editing and publication of the Persian translation in Calcutta [Major Phillott] and a Persian dissident and copyist [Shaykh Ahmad Ruhi] whose tragic death transformed his posthumous agency from a cross-border copyist to a misidentified translator for more than 50 years." Equally important is an earlier study, Kamran Rastegar, "Adventures of Hajji Baba Ispahani as a Transactional Text between English and Persian Literatures," *Middle Eastern Literatures* 10:3 (2007): 251–271. These two studies are far superior and benefit from a much more advanced level of literary scholarship than a previous generation that thought Mirza Habib's attention to Morier's novel was an indication of how "a sophisticated Persian intellectual of his time, was in heart an early example of the masochistic Persian modernists who were fascinated with everything Western, even to the extent of deprecating their own culture" (see "HABIB ESFAHANI" in *Encyclopedia Iranica*).

[35] It is not accidental that with its solid Orientalist pedigree and colorful cast of characters, it was of course just a matter of time before Hollywood finally turned to adapt *Hajji Baba* for the screen. Don Weis's *The Adventures of Hajji Baba* (1954), starring John Derek (as Hajji Baba) and Elaine Stewart, states early in its credit line that it is "suggested by the novel Adventures of Hajji Baba by James Morier." The movie is available online here: www.youtube.com/watch?v=o9D_9xtHkPM. Accessed November 27, 2016.

[36] Sadeghi's Introduction to *Sargozasht-e Hajji Baba Isfahani/The Life of Hajji Baba Isfahani*: Forty.

Figure 6 "The Thames Embankment, 19th century, River Thames in Central London, England." As the capital of the British Empire, London had a compelling attraction to many (but not all) of these travelers. The location of this city, however, was on a transcontinental map that went literally around the globe, irrespective of countries and continents. As one of these travelers once put it, he measured the longevity of his travels with the number of cities he had visited, irrespective of where these cities were located, but most of them extended between India to the Americas, and then to Africa, most particularly Muslim pilgrimage sites in Ottoman territories. Mumbai, Delhi, Cairo, and Istanbul were as, if not more, important to these travelers as Paris or London. Retrieving the expansive geographical imagination of these travelers has been one of the most important concerns of this book. Reprinted with permission from FALKENSTEINFOTO/Alamy Stock Photo.

so critically important in the course of the Iranian Constitutional Revolution requires a bit of more literary critical reflection.

Horizons of Expectations

Safely tucked away from any curriculum with which Qajar period scholarship could be bothered, what Mirza Habib Isfahani was doing when translating James Morier's *Hajji Baba* might now be read as anything but "masochistic" and in fact squarely within the parameters of what "reception theorists" such as Hans Robert Jauss and others have developed over the last half century. What mattered most when the English original was translated into Persian in Istanbul some half a century after its original publication in Europe was the radical change in its audience and readership, in the politics of its reception. This is precisely where Jauss's theory of "reception" can help us relocate Mirza Habib's translation in a different domain than its original. As Jauss puts it:

The relationship of work to work must now be brought into this interaction between work and mankind, and the historical coherence of works among themselves must be seen in the interrelations of production and reception ... literature and art only obtain a history that has the character of a process when the succession of works is mediated not only through the producing subject but also through the consuming subject – through the interaction of author and public.[37]

What Jauss here terms "the relationship of work and mankind" gives a literary work of art the ability in effect to create a new readership for itself far from the original intention of the author. What he considers the "interrelations of production and reception" emotively separates the two domains both temporally and spatially, and in this case also via the loaded power of a different language. What Jauss terms "the consuming subject" is precisely where the reading public becomes so central that "the interaction of author and public" enters a whole new domain. Mirza Habib's translation happens at a crucial moment in the formation of Persian literary public sphere, and effectively becomes definitive to it.

The origin of Jauss's "reception theory" can be traced back to the hermeneutics of Friedrich Schleiermacher (1768–1834). and more recently to Hans-Georg Gadamer (1900–2002), where the effective history of a text is predicated on such concepts as its "reader," "implied reader," or "actual reader." The Reception theory in effect creates a hermeneutic dialectic between the intention of the author and the intention of the reader. This idea effectively opens up the interpretive apparatus of the text into the world at large. As Jauss puts it:

---

[37] Hans Robert Jauss, *Toward an Aesthetic of Reception*. Translated by Timothy Bahti. Introduction by Paul de Man (Minneapolis: University of Minnesota Press, 1982): 15.

A renewal of literary history demands the removal of the prejudices of historical objectivism and the grounding of the traditional aesthetics of production and representation in an aesthetics of reception and influence. The historicity of literature rests not on an organization of "literary facts" that is established post festum, but rather on the preceding experience of the literary work by its readers.[38]

Here we may even expand on Jauss's ideas and extend his theory into the even more potent argument of Umberto Eco who, after the German literary theorist, offers actually three and not just two "intentions": the *intentio auctoris/intention of the author*, the *intentio lectoris/intention of the reader*, and the *intentio operis/intensions of the text*.[39] Here the intention of the Iranian readers of Mirza Habib's translation will assume a much more pointed purpose.[40] But Jauss's ideas are here more immediately related to my point, for he specifically talks about the new hermeneutic space into which a text enters. Jauss says:

A literary work, even when it appears to be new, does not present itself as something absolutely new in an informational vacuum, but predisposes its audience to a very specific kind of reception by announcements, overt and covert signals, familiar characteristics, or implicit allusions. It awakens memories of that which was already read, bring the reader to a specific emotional attitude, and with its beginning arouses expectations for the "middle and end," which can then be maintained intact or altered, reoriented, or even fulfilled ironically in the course of the reading according to specific rules of the genre or type of text.[41]

Mirza Habib's translation of James Morier indeed forced the original to be "altered, reoriented," and its purpose "fulfilled ironically" by turning a deeply colonial ridicule on its head and turn it into an anticolonial cornerstone of national consciousness. Jauss explains that what he calls "the Horizon of Expectations/Erwartungshorizont" is formed through "the reader's life experience, customs and understanding of the world, which have an effect on the reader's social behavior."[42]

---

[38] Ibid.: 20.
[39] See Umberto Eco, *Limits of Interpretation* (Bloomington, IN: Indiana University Press, 1990): 33.
[40] I have made this point in my *Persophilia* in the chapter on James Morier's Hajji Baba. See Dabashi, *Persophilia*: chapter 9.
[41] Jauss, *Toward an Aesthetic of Reception*: 23.   [42] Ibid.: 39.

In this regard, one of the fundamental theses in his "reception theory" is this:

The horizon of expectations of a work allows one to determine its artistic character by the kind and the degree of its influence on a presupposed audience. If one characterizes as aesthetic distance the disparity between the given horizon of expectations and the appearance of a new work, whose familiar experiences or through raising newly articulated experiences to the level of consciousness, then the aesthetic distance can be objectified historically along the spectrum of the audience's reactions and criticism's judgement (spontaneous success, rejection or shock, scattered approval, gradual or belated understanding).[43]

James Morier never expected his "presupposed audience" would be so drastically altered. He never cared to know the "newly articulated experiences" of the people he treated like a nuisance in his life experience. For Morier, Iranians, a people, a nation, did not exist. He saw Ilchi and from him he extrapolated an entire nation. With his translation opening new "horizons of expectation" for Morier's book, Mirza Habib Isfahani set that record straight for the whole world to see.

Traveling Theories

What makes Jauss's "reception theory" and his notion of "horizons of expectations" even more of interest to us here is if we add to it Edward Said's "Travel Theory," which focuses on the production of theory itself, the theoretical product of the critical thinker, and proposes a serious of questions to ask when they travel from one to another location. What happens to Lukács, for example, Said asks, when his thoughts travel to Paris to Lucien Goldman or to England to Raymond Williams. Said's point is to mark the "historical situation"[44] where a theory is produced or reconceived. From an "insurrectionary consciousness" here, it may become a "tragic vision" somewhere else. Therefore, Budapest and Paris pretty much "provide limits and apply pressure" to critical thinkers. Said offers four stages in the itinerary of traveling theories: their point of origin, the distance they travel, the conditions of their acceptance or rejection, and finally when the

---

[43] Ibid.: 25.
[44] Edward Said, "Traveling Theory," in *The World, the Text, and the Critic* (Cambridge, MA: Harvard University Press, 1983): 237.

transformed idea finds a new "time and space."[45] Before we extend
Jauss to Said for our purposes, let us complicate his theory a bit
further.

James Clifford has already noted how Said's thinking is terribly
limited and Eurocentric, for it remains confined to the axis of Budapest, Paris, and London, a very much limited and "linear" trajectory.[46]
Clifford quite rightly improves and expands Said's fetishizing of European theory to include conditions of "immigration and acculturation
of people."[47] Clifford complicates Said's theory further by positing
much more complicated and circular conditions when Gramsci, for
example, goes to India via Subaltern studies collective and returns to
California via thinkers such as Ranajit Guha. By now theorizing Said
himself, and critical thinkers like him, Clifford says: "Theirs is not a
condition of exile, of critical distance but rather a place of betweenness, a hybridity composed of distinct, historically connected postcolonial spaces."[48] To Lukács, Goldman, and Williams, Clifford
attributes a "stable audience," whereas today he believes theorists like
Said are exposed to "complexly literate, politicized, global systems of
cultural flows" and as a result they are all "exposed to discrepant
audiences, in very different locations," thereby marking "several third
worlds" and even minorities and feminists as the site of mis/appropri-
ations of theory.[49]

Here we encounter Clifford's own limitation by observing how he
collapses Said's simple theory into the Pandora's Box of identity politics plunged into a bottomless pit of self-degeneration into nullity, with
no center, no periphery, no order, no logic, and deep in chaos. But
between Said's Eurocentrism and Clifford's theoretical meltdown,
there are worlds that Clifford nervously marks as "third world."
Before those worlds became "third" to any "first" or "second," they
were the center of the universe for themselves. We are now witnessing
these travelers traversing the world, a world to which both Said and
Clifford and indeed the whole production of postcolonial theory is
blind, trapped as they are either in Eurocentrism or Europhobia. These
travelers were mapping a different geography to which the subsequent
colonial and postcolonial theorists and their Euro–American comrades
were, and alas still remain, totally blind: the world that people traveled

---

[45] Ibid.: 227.   [46] See Clifford, "Notes on Travel and Theory": 184.   [47] Ibid.
[48] Ibid.: 184–185.   [49] Ibid.: 185.

from any point on this globe (in our case from the Indo–Persian world) and mapped the topography that unfolded in front of them as they populated and thereby theorized it. These travelers were not carriers of theories – they were theories incarnate. The fundamental problem with this generation of postcolonial critical thinkers was the loose cannon of "interstitial liminality" and "in betweenness" that Homi Bhabha's imaginative insecurity, moving from what he thought was "the Third" to "the First World," had entailed, with no history of alternative geographies tucked into his suitcases.[50]

In reading these travelogues coming from the Indo–Persian world, and here magnificently rendered into a literary *pharmakon* by Mirza Habib, we need to complicate the genre by simplifying the fact of their itinerary; de-Europeanizing their abusive readings; and decentering Europe as the principal destination of where these travelers visited – by unfolding the fact that they traveled to a much wider region than just Europe; that Europe has been falsely privileged and thereby these travelers thickly Orientalized, exoticized, over-sexualized, eroticized, ridiculed, caricatured, and fantasized; and their deadly serious points and purposes satirized, all of which are exacerbated by a later gener-ation of scholars who from the heart of a deeply colonized mind have perpetrated a massive epistemic violence on them. We therefore need to relocate these travelers in the Indo–Persian world they occupied; place them in their proper historical and geographical contexts; take the poetic allusions they make seriously and actively de-Orientalize them; and place them right in the middle of the Persian, Islamic, and Indo–Persian context from which they emerged. Placing these travelers next to Sa'di, Ibn Battuta, Naser Khosrow, and other Muslim travelers will give them back to their world-historical habitat, allow us to rethink theories of travels with other scholars, and thus actively de-Orientalize them. The way the British, the European, and even contemporary Eurocentric Iranian scholars have abused these texts requires an equally concerted effort to reverse gear in how to read these texts. Theorists such as Jauss, Said, and Clifford map out an alternative modality of critical thinking where we can locate the world in which these travelers traversed, mapped out, and narrated before they were forced into a linear trajectory of "the West and the Rest."

---

[50] Homi K. Bhabha, *The Location of Culture* (London: Routledge, 1994): 5.

All of these, however, are preparatory for a third crucial move: rethinking the very idea of *cosmopolitanism* away from its aggressive Eurocentric theorization, which in effect means to be cosmopolitan is to become European as a sign of belonging to the world European colonialism has crafted. The task is exactly the opposite of that assumption of "cosmopolitanism" and to discover and map out existing worlds, such as the Indo–Persian world, of these travelers from which they traveled around the globe. We need to re-examine the very conception of "transnational public sphere," for these travelers enable us to think of a mobile, agile, migratory public sphere, and move toward an expansive, amorphous, and eventually multilingual public sphere, formed on the road, aboard ships, on familiar and foreign lands. This mobile sphere goes beyond a transnational public sphere that takes "the nation" and its public sphere within territorial boundaries as the site of this transnational public sphere. In my *Persophilia* (2015), I have already detected and documented the dialectic of the public sphere beyond any fictive frontiers. In *Iran without Borders* (2016), I brought that sphere to a regional domain. Here in this book I expand that idea even further and well into a mobile metaphor of cross-national, non-national, public sphere: mobile, migratory, and amorphous. What we witness in Mirza Habib's translation of James Morier is even more radical: A categorical reversal of a colonial conception of the world, turning it upside-down against itself and putting it at the service of anticolonial defiance.

This move preconditions a precarious, vicarious, and substitutional subjectivity, and agency, completely overriding the assumption of "liminality," or "contingency" on even a colonial modernity, projecting the discovery of new worlds upon which subjectivity was and remains possible. This conception of *public sphere* therefore prefigures the rise of poets such as Nima Yushij, Forough Farrokhzad, Sohrab Sepehri, Ahmad Shamlou, etc. That mobile conception of public sphere in effect alters the dialectic between *the native* and *the foreign* altogether. It also categorically dismantles the centrality of the myth of "Europe" in our understanding of world history. Here we encounter a potent topography and genealogy of a hidden world before "the West" became the defining metanarrative of the world at large. In continued search for alternative epistemologies, it is imperative for us to recover the pre-Western map of the world evident in the itinerary of these travelers we are examining here. It is therefore here that we can ask where exactly is "the global south?" Reimagining the global south begins by the most immediate question of where and when was the global south constituted? To come close to this global south we must altogether abandon the continental thinking of Europe or Asia or Africa, as we need to abandon the colonial and postcolonial formations of nation-states altogether. Countries such as Iran, Turkey, Egypt, or India now emerge as a mode of cosmopolitan worldliness, while the United States is seen as the paragon of imperial worldliness. This introduces an epistemic rupture into our critical thinking in between the South and the North, the East and the West. Here South is no longer a mere state of mind. Nations here emerge as discursive propositions, not territorial fixations. In my *Iran without Borders* I explored how beyond the territorial and bodily claims of the state, the nation is ipso facto a transnational proposition. On that transnational scale, these travelers have already, for more than a century, navigated a world and left us a body of literature far beyond the imaginative geography of a colonial project that continues to abuse and distort them – from British colonial officers of bygone ages down to the colonized mind of a younger generation of scholarship in our own time.

In this line of critical thinking, states are territorial because they are founded on force, as Trotsky said, and on "legitimate" violence, as Weber expanded and theorized the idea.[51] States claim a monopoly of violence that extends from territory to body, as I have explained in detail in my *Corpus Anarchicum*, where I argue suicidal violence is against the substitution of the body for territorial domain of state violence.[52] ISIS and Israel are total states, states without nations, while Palestinians are a stateless nation, a nation without a state, as Egypt, Iran, and Turkey are nations with parasitical states. In *Iran without Borders* (2016) I have sought theoretically to liberate the nation from its colonial entrapment inside the fictive frontiers of any state that lays a false claim on it, while in *Iran: Rebirth of a Nation* (2016) I have suspended the idea of the nation on its own *aesthetic intuition of transcendence*, forever liberated from the violent myth of the state.

---

[51] See Max Weber, "Politics as a Vocation," in Hans Gerth and C. Wright Mills (eds.), *From Max Weber: Essays in Sociology* (Oxford: Oxford University Press, 1946): 78.

[52] See Hamid Dabashi, *Corpus Anarchicum: Political Protest, Suicidal Violence, and the Making of the Posthuman Body* (New York: Palgrave, 2012).

The significance of this body of hitherto abused literature produced by traveling public intellectuals, becoming *public* on a transnational public sphere, is precisely in its overcoming that myth of the state before its full colonial constitution. The translation of the British colonial officer James Morier's *Hajji Baba* by Mirza Habib in Istanbul is the example *par excellence* of this transnational public sphere on the parapublic domain of an idea of the nation beyond any fictive frontiers.

So where do we go from here, where is the "global south" if we were to overcome the fictive frontiers of the postcolonial states – where the records of an alternative universe are forced into a false narrative? That "global south" is not on the imaginative "south" side of the rolling globe because the central engine of the globalized capital was planetary and environmental from the get-go. Weber's question in *Protestant Ethic and the Spirit of Capitalism* (1904–1905) of why capitalism emerged here and not there was a sort of Monday morning quarterbacking, asked after the fact. He asked a logical question to which he offered an ethical response. Capitalism emerged because of the "protestant ethic" of asceticism proposed. Even if so, as Fanon fully recognized a couple of generations after Weber, Europe and its capitalism was a creation of their "Third World." At this very moment the capital and the empire that seeks to sustain it are no longer merely global. They are planetary, inter-planetary, spread far and wide into the outer space, and even the cyberspace. They are interchangeable and totally amorphous. The "global south" therefore is not a place on any map, turned upside-down, or above all not a state of mind. "The global south" is the theoretical differential and the open-ended dialectic between what we know and what we don't know, and what we know ipso facto disables us to know what we don't know. It is the negative dialectic between two competing questions of "can non-Europeans think" and "can Europeans read," without assimilating backward to what they already know.[53] The answer to the latter question is of course a resounding "No!" They cannot. So, as I have now argued for about a decade, we need to change the interlocutor, we are no longer writing for Europeans to convince them of anything, so far as "Europeans" remain trapped inside their own metaphor.

---

[53] I have addressed this question in my *Can Non-Europeans Think?* (London: Verso, 2015).

We write for "non-Europeans," for the world at large, for the world at the receiving end of European moral, material, intellectual, and epistemic violence perpetrated on this planet at large. Europeans must exit the myth of Europe and join the world to understand it. That dialectic, however, is aided by the interface between the world we know and worlds that are unfolding in front of our eyes, but above all the worlds we have missed to see like the worlds of these travelers, hitherto violently compromised by disregarding their actual itinerary and privileging only the European portion of their sojourn. Alternative epistemologies at the root of "the global south" is a dialectic between the critical and the creative, it is an aesthetic intuition of self-transcendence rooted in what we know as we reach out for what we do not know.

Deterritorialized, Reterritorialized

These travelers are being systematically and consistently "deterritorialized," to borrow and extend Gilles Deleuze and Félix Guattari's rich and potent term, thereby marking the fluidity of the normative subjectivity they experience and narrate as they cross from one fictive frontier to another in a very amorphous colonial geography. The spatial location of the subject they constitute in their narratives is now consistently interpolated, extended from one territory to another, linking the expanding capital to the defiant colonial, the assertive imperial to its rebellious subjects. The intellectual interlocutor of the globalized subject is here liberated on the site of a "deterritorialized" subjectivity, categorically concealed if we falsely think they are going from Iran to Europe and back "to modernize" and liberate their people: a categorically flawed and abusive reading of who these travelers were and what they were doing. These acts of *deterritorialization* are never absolute, leading to any imminence, but always relative yielding to successive manners of *reterritorialization*. The structural link between culture and geography is hereby loosened and reconvened. The mobility of the cultural subject and his and her confrontation with alternative cultural settings destabilizes the fixed subjections forever. The term "liminality" is entirely flawed and misleading here, for the traveler does not link a point of origin to a point of destination to become bicultural. He or she effectively creates a tertiary space that transcends both these locations through the successive acts of de- and reterritorialization.

Deleuze and Guattari posit a capitalist threshold when this decoding and deterritorialization takes place, when "naked labor, independent capital become operative," and when in fact the very idea of "State" seems to be out of place. This is precisely the moment when these travelers have trespassed the geographical domains of these states and are navigating, literally, a *terra incognita*. Globalized economy, now framing their travels, here becomes a cosmopolitan force in and of itself.[54] Deleuze and Guattari insist, however, "Whatever dimensions or quantities this may have assumed today, capitalism has from the beginning mobilized a force of deterritorialization infinitely surpassing the deterritorialization proper to State."[55] On the colonial site, outside the French theorists' purviews, both capitalism and the states it forms and frames, condition fluidity of the colonial subject formation, which is never totally tabulated. Deleuze and Guattari rightly argue: "Capitalism . . . is not at all territorial, even in its beginnings: its power of deterritorialization consists in taking as its object, not the earth, but 'materialized labor,'" the commodity. I have put the same point differently: From the time Adam Smith wrote *The Wealth of Nations* (1776), wealth was not national. Capitalism was always transnational from the get-go (predicated on the Protestant Reformation, French Revolution, and Industrial Revolution). Nation for capitalism was always a bookkeeping proposition, as the invention of "Western Civilization" was a replacement for "Christendom," which was no longer of any conceptual use to the European bourgeoisie. In the production of the commodity that Deleuze and Guattari correctly mark, the colonial power offers capital and the colonial site cheap labor and raw material. But the expanded market between the capital and the colonial links them both together, so much so that the beneficiary of the capital are the native elite and the elite colonizers together, and those disenfranchised by it (the labor class) remain equally cross-cultural. From here Deleuze and Guattari move on to argue that a nation-state is "the State as model of realization."[56] True, but the nation from this very moment has a reality *sui generis*, irreducible to state on its colonial gestation. Deleuze and Guattari believe: "The constituents of the nation are a land and a people," from which point they suddenly make a bizarre

---

[54] Gilles Deleuze and Félix Guattari, *A Thousand Plateaus*. Translated and Foreword by Brian Massumi (Minneapolis: University of Minnesota Press, 1987): 453.
[55] Ibid.   [56] Ibid.: 456.

U-turn to a major Zionist slogan and propose: "The problem of the nation is aggravated in the two extreme cases of a land without a people and a people without a land."[57] This is their blind spot, where their Zionism prevents them from seeing Israel as a (garrison) state without a nation, and Palestinians as a (fragmented) nation without a state. Their conclusion is, however, definitive: "In short, the nation is the very operation of a collective subjectification, to which the modern State corresponds as a process of subjection ... State becomes the model of realization for the capitalist axiomatic."[58] True: But these travelers are navigating a space between two aggressive state formations: the imperial and the colonial. Mirza Habib's Persian translation of James Morier's *Hajji Baba* takes place on the borderline space where the will of the nation asserts itself beyond any state formations on the imperial or colonial site. Historically, Istanbul has been definitive to this remissive/transgressive space.

Here between the operation of capital and the axiomatic function of state, Deleuze and Guattari disregard the equally if not more important dis- and re-location of "the nation" entirely separate and adjacent to state – and here is precisely the enduring historical significance of Mirza Habib's translation for a conception of Iran as a nation beyond any state control. What is *Hajji Baba*? It is the noxious journey of a fictive "Iranian" who disguised himself as a trickster careerist to appeal to the racist fantasies of a British colonial officer and in return borrowed his English penmanship to write himself into the annals of his time on the European bourgeois public sphere, just to return to the Persian prose of his homeland through the ingenious craftsmanship of a translator who turned the English vessel upside-down to tease the spirit of that disguised Persian soul out of his fake English garb. What else could be more magnificent than this twisted pathway for a Persian purpose of a national revolt against domestic tyranny (colonized state) and foreign abuse (European imperialism) to baptize itself in the fire of an English prose that would take him into every European household. Entirely unbeknownst to himself, James Morier was the carrier of a Persian prose into the fertile soil of European bourgeois public sphere, from which the very idea of "Iran" as a postcolonial nation eventually

(ın H.B. Housı.)

---

[57] Ibid. It is perhaps not accidental that the Israeli army finds Deleuze and Guattari's theories quite useful to their military conquest of Palestine. See Eyal Weizman, "Lethal Theory," *LOG Magazine* 5 (April 2005): 53–78.

[58] Deleuze and Guattari, *A Thousand Plateaus*: 456.

emerges, as I have argued in detail in both *Persophilia and Iran without Borders*.

Morier thus inadvertently gave the cosmopolitan culture of Indo–Iranian encounters with colonial modernity an enduring metaphor of journey from one to another end of the earth. It was the miracle of Mirza Habib's translation that turned the sour lemons of colonial arrogance into the sweet lemonade of anticolonial uprising. Decentering Europe as the first and final destination of these journeys assumes a fascinating twist in James Morier's *Hajji Baba*, a decidedly Eurocentric fiction that becomes a positively anticolonial tract in its Persian rendition. As the original went one way, Orientalizing Persia and Persians, Orientals and the Orient, its Persian translation went precisely in the opposite direction and enabled, ennobled, and empowered resistance to Orientalism and colonialism alike. As Morier took *Hajji Baba* to Europe to Orientalize, mock, ridicule, and denigrate him, Mirza Habib Isfahani brought him back home to his people in Iran and India as a provocative piece of autocratic to mobilize and oppose and end British imperialism and domestic tyranny that had conditioned such an abusive relationship to begin with. James Morier was the product of the sick and sickening colonial encounters between Europe and the Indo–Persian world. Mirza Habib was the product of the rebellious public sphere in Istanbul where Arabs, Iranians, Turks, and all other nations gathered to rid themselves of the colonial bastardy of James Morier and his ilk. As an entire history of colonial Eurocentrism falsely imagined the world pivoting toward it, as its first and final destination, the very end of its Hegelian historical Geist, a simple interpretative appropriation of a typically nasty colonial piece of literature reversed that narrative delusion and placed the interpretive will to knowledge of a nation against that Hegelian fantasy.

5 | *A Shirazi Shares His Travelogues*

Mirza Saleh Shirazi

↳ This is what enables
the audience to
whom
M. Habib Isfahani
addresses himself

We must drink wine
And we must walk
In a youthful shade –
That's all!

Which way towards life?
How do I get to a hoopoe?
And listen how this very word
All through the journey
Kept disturbing
The window of our sleep –

What was it singing in your ears
All through the journey?
Think carefully:
Where is the hidden kernel
Of this mysterious melody?
What is it putting pressure
On your eyelids?
What a warm delightful weight!

        Sohrab Sepehri (Mosafer/Traveler, Babol, Spring 1966)

Sohrab Sepehri was the master metaphysician of the visible and the worldly, the poet of the evident and the manifest, the sojourner of a truth we lived. His poetry was at once powerfully presentist and mystically ancient. His poetic voice thrived on marking the obvious made unobvious by too much matter-of-fact-ness about things. He made us aware how numb we had become to our existence. He took us to a journey into and out of ourselves. He basked in a plain language of the apparent and the visible made invisible by too much exposure. He was and he remained the poet of the manifest, the aesthetician of the palpable, made improbable by our hysterical blind-ness. He gave new sight to his blinded readers. He made us put our

hands once again on the tangible, feel the physical, reconnect with the
tactile mystery of the world we lived – the entirety of the world, the
quintessence of it, a world liberated from our habitual geographies.
His poetic mystery had a long, sustained, and detailed historical consciousness – at once his and his alone, and yet collectively memorial.
His poetic genius notwithstanding, his emotive universe had a long and
sustained genealogy, rooted in the historical consciousness of his
homeland. In this book I am digging under the feet of his poetry,
excavating the hidden layers of his ahistorical consciousness, in the
historical record he had to repress to be able to sing his songs.

Parody as Subterfuge

Toward the end of his Persian rendition of James Morier's *Hajji Baba*,
Mirza Habib Isfahani takes leave of his readers by way of a tongue-in-
cheek parody: "Oh those who have heard my story of Hajji Baba, as
I have learned by experience from Iranian snake charmers and idle
orators I am going to stop my story right here. I am your most obedient
servant. My point is before you have measured the mettle of a precious
metal don't take it home."[1] Every phrase of Mirza Habib's exquisite
translation has a sarcastic twist to it, taking its nasty racist original for
a caring twist to make it speak a radically different tongue to his
Persian-speaking reading public. But who is that reading public, and
how was it formed, informed, and posited? Judging by Mirza Habib's
sarcastic tone, we can surmise he had a learned and critically self-
conscious audience in mind when he translated James Morier into
Persian. In covering these sojourners of the rising horizons around
the world, I went from Ilchi to Morier because the British colonial
officer was associated with the Qajar envoy in more than one way.
Onto his English-speaking reading public Morier projected an entirely
ignorant image of Iran, befitting the delusions of his colonial fantasies.
Right between Ilchi's travelogue and Morier's novel we have another
piece of extraordinary document in the form of Mirza Salah Shirazi's
travelogues, which inform us of the critical disposition to which Mirza
Habib was speaking, and to which I wish now to turn for its corresponding significance to our purpose here.

---

[1] Mirza Habib Isfahani's translation of James Morier's *Hajji Baba* as *Sargozasht-e
Hajji Baba Isfahani/The Life of Hajji Baba Isfahani*: 367. My translation.

What does it mean to say <u>Mirza Saleh Shirazi</u> was <u>perhaps the most</u> <u>influential public intellectual of his time</u>? We initially come to know him <u>as he was a rather high-ranking</u> courtier at the service of the reformist Qajar Prince Abbas Mirza (1789–1833), from where he conducted a number of crucial travels around his homeland and then around the world, from which he brought back to his people a globally informed critical consciousness, a simplified Persian prose befitting the urgencies of his time, and a printing machine with which he published the very first newspaper in Persian. The combined impact of his travelogues and newspaper was instrumental in the eventual formation of a *public con-* *sciousness*, upon which the very notions of *public space, public sphere,* *public reason*, and *public happiness* could now be articulated. The fact that Mirza Saleh Shirazi was equally instrumental in introducing ideas of liberal democracy and parliamentary rule of law in his homeland is entirely secondary to the far more crucial societal foregrounding of a *public persona* in his country. Let us retrace his history together.

A Caravan of Knowledge

In 1953, Motajaba Minovi, a preeminent Iranian literary scholar, published an essay in a leading academic journal, *Yaghma*, which he called "Avvalin Karevan Ma'refat/the First Caravan of Knowledge." In this seminal essay, Minovi told the story of the first group of Iranian students who 140 years before had gone to England and, in his words, "benefitted from the crop of Western civilization and knowledge and as soon as they returned to Iran they scattered the seeds of progress and modernity in the land of their ancestors."[2] Minovi then proceeds to quote from the Bible, "And when he sowed, some seeds fell by the way side, and the fowls came and devoured them up" (Matthew 13:4), from which passage he concludes that despite the fact that many such caravans of Iranians have traveled to Europe, we have not advanced because our land was not fertile enough. He compares Iran to India, Japan, Egypt, and Turkey, where he believes the land was far more fertile, and thus those seeds of European civilization have resulted in far better fruits. The rest of the essay is a learned and well-argued tribute to the first groups of

---

[2] Mojtaba Minovi, "Avvalin Karevan Ma'refat/The First Caravan of Knowledge" (*Yaghma*, 1953), Reprinted in Minovi, *Tarikh va Farhang/History and Culture* (Tehran: Khwarizmi Publications, 1973): 380–437.

Iranian students who were dispatched to Europe by the Qajar prince
Abbas Mirza, two in 1811 and five in 1815, and who came back to
inaugurate many institutional changes, ushering in, as Minovi puts it,
European civilization for Iranian people. Among this second group of
Iranian students Minovi picks the most learned, Mirza Saleh Shirazi,
and through the travel account he wrote, Minovi gives a full panoramic
view of the manner in which European modernity and civilization, as
our learned scholar suggests, was brought to Iran.

Two facts are paramount in this account offered by a seminal Iranian
literary scholar in the mid-twentieth century: the deeply learned and competent knowledge of its author and yet his astonishingly self-Orientalizing
colonized mind. Iranians, in his estimation, were a sleepy band of lazy
Orientals waiting for a goodhearted traveler to go to Europe and bring
them the good news of progress and civilization, and yet they were incompetent fools and did not much benefit from that gift of foreigners.

More than half a century later, in 2015, Nile Green, a professor of
history at the University of California at Los Angeles (UCLA), published a learned book, *The Love of Strangers: What Six Muslim
Students Learned in Jane Austen's London*, in which he told the story
of the selfsame Iranian students from exactly the opposite vantage
point. Nile Green too saw the "mission" of these students "to master
the modern sciences behind the rapid rise of Europe."[3] His account is
far more entertaining and far less somber and providential than Mojtaba Mondovi's. Green's learned account opts to entertain and amuse
his English-speaking audience. He throws in a bit of Jane Austin to
make these foreigners familiar to his readers by sharing their stories of
attending operas and enjoying other aspects of European culture. The
result is quite successful. His book reads like *Alice in Wonderland*. But
he also makes sure to attest to the fact that these foreigners were in
England to learn about advanced institutions of European modernity,
from visiting massive factories to getting acquainted with advanced
hospitals. Altogether, Nile Green's account is to offer a "story of
friendship" rather than the usual accounts of differences and hostility.

In the same year that Green published his book, another British
connoisseur of things Persian, Christopher de Bellaigue, published a
learned essay, "Stop Calling for a Muslim Enlightenment" (2015), in

[3] See Green, *The Love of Strangers*.

which he, too, paid detailed attention to Mirza Saleh Shirazi.[4] His point of contention in this essay is that, "after every terror attack the call rings out for the Muslim world to become modern. But ... Muslims have strenuously engaged with all that is new for hundreds of years." As one such example, Christopher de Bellaigue refers to Mirza Saleh Shirazi and his journey to England. "One of the earliest Middle Easterners to appreciate the unavoidable, tentacular qualities of modernity," he reports,

was the Iranian Mirza Muhammad Saleh Shirazi. He was one of five students who were sent to England by Crown Prince Abbas Mirza in 1815 to study useful things and bring them home. The travelogue that Mirza Saleh wrote is among the first books written in Persian about a Christian country. Reading it one gets the sense of a worldview that is changing; even Mirza Saleh's writing alters as he acclimatizes to Regency London, moving from stiltedness to fluency, directness and utility. Here, in real time, is the literary modernization of the Middle East.[5]

Christopher de Bellaigue here very much repeats the same standardized narrative, that Mirza Saleh was sent to England "to study useful things and bring them home," that he was a Muslim writing about "a Christian country," that his very prose is an indication of how this trip to London had occasioned "literary modernization of the Middle East." Christopher de Bellaigue's prose, as the title of his essay suggests, is a lovely tribute to "Muslim reformists," delivered kindly to tell his fellow British, Europeans, and North Americans to leave Muslims be. They are doing the best they can.

Absent from all these accounts, from Minovi's to Green's to Christopher de Bellaigue's, more than half a century apart, is any serious grasp of the colonial condition under which this group of Iranian students undertook a journey that eventually took them to London, and that before and after that city they had seen much more. The Russian imperial incursion into the Qajar territories was relentless and unyielding at the time. In two consecutive treaties the Qajars had eventually lost much of their claim to their northern territories. Hoping to challenge

[4] See Christopher de Bellaigue, "Stop Calling for a Muslim Enlightenment" (*The Guardian*, The Long Read, February 19, 2015). Available online here: www.theguardian.com/world/2015/feb/19/stop-calling-for-a-muslim-enlightenment. Accessed February 8, 2017.
[5] Ibid.

British imperial conquests from behind, Napoleon had approached the Qajar court offering to help advancing their military capacities in exchange for a right of passage to India. The British had sought to sabotage that arrangement by offering their own military assistance in exchange for not allowing Napoleon to create an inroad against their most prized colonial possession. It is in this context that Prince Abbas Mirza suggests dispatching a group of Iranian students to England to learn mostly military sciences in order to come back and help advance the military machinery of their homeland. The person in this group who matters to us most, namely Mirza Saleh Shirazi, who actually wrote an extensive travelogue in the course of his journeys, had no interest in the substance of this mission whatsoever. He had no knowledge or interest in military matters. He was not on this journey "to study useful things and bring them home" in any military sense of being "useful." He in fact says specifically early in his travelogue that he told Abbas Mirza he had no interest in practical sciences. His interest in this journey was entirely intellectual and his expenses being covered was the only reason he was part of the group. In other words, the fact of his travelogue is the single most significant testimony of where he went, what he saw, and what this journey outside Iran meant to him and his posterity.

The Traveler and His Travelogue

In 1968 a famous amateur historian, Ismail Ra'in, prepared the first critical edition of Mirza Saleh Shirazi's travelogue.[6] He called it *Safarnameh Mirza Saleh Shirazi*, and wrote an extensive introduction to it. Another Iranian scholar, Mohammad Shahrestani, revised Ra'in's edition and corrected some of its typographical mistakes for its subsequent editions. In his introduction, Ra'in refers to three extant copies of the travelogue he had obtained to prepare his critical edition. In one of these manuscripts we learn Mirza Saleh himself had said that one copy of his text was given to Henry Willock, the United Kingdom Chargé d'Affaires at the Qajar court (1815–1826), who had in turn asked the author for "superfluous passages be deleted from it." There are no such indications that this edition has deleted any passage. But Isma'il Ra'in's own introduction still entirely falls into the selfsame

---

[6] See Mirza Saleh Shirazi, *Safarnameh/Travelogue*. Edited with an Introduction by Isma'il Ra'in (Tehran: Rozan Publications, 1968).

trope of how Europeans came to Iran and Iranians went to Europe to learn from their superior ways and bring them back to Iran, and how Mirza Saleh's text was the evidence of such encounters. Ra'in, however, is much more fully aware of the corruption of the Qajar court and the colonial conditions in which these students were sent to England. He gives a detailed account of the lives of these Iranian students and their predicament in England. He is also very clear that the primary purpose of dispatching these students to England was for them to learn military related sciences. He is fully conscious of how abusive of these students the British authorities were once they were in England.

Ra'in, however, gives his readers a full biography of the author of this travelogue. From his research we learn Mirza Saleh Shirazi was born and raised in a learned family in Kazerun near Shiraz in south-central Iran. He eventually moved north to the court of the renowned Qajar reformist prince Abbas Mirza in Tabriz in a particularly tumultuous period in the history of his nation. In addition to a solid command of his native Persian and Arabic, Mirza Saleh seems to have had a comfortable familiarity with English, French, and perhaps even Latin even prior to his journeys, which included a short visit to England. What is significant about his life is his obvious commitment to political reform and an unflinching championing of liberal democracy in his homeland. The fact that throughout his travel narratives he insists on highlighting such new and progressive aspects of the places he visits is a clear indication that he was deeply concerned about the democratic future of his homeland even before he left Iran. His travelogue is the space in which he picks and choses issues he wants to underline for the democratic institutions of his country. He does not just report what he sees. He picks and chooses issues like Peter the Great's reforms in Russia, or the causes and consequences of the French Revolution against a corrupt aristocracy, or the rule of law and representative democracy in England, in order to underline their necessity for his own country. As we begin to read his travel narratives, it is perfectly evident that all these issues had concerned him before he set foot outside Iran.

In Abbas Mirza's court, Mirza Saleh eventually emerged as a prominent political figure who, because of his travels in and around Iran and as far as Russia and Europe, performed key tasks during the tumultuous years of Qajar entanglements with Russian, British, and French imperialism early in the nineteenth century. The text of the travelogue that has now reached us gives an account of his earliest travels to

Russia and England and back during the 1815–1816 timespan. In 1821–1822 he was dispatched on a diplomatic mission to England, and then in 1829 he was involved in the crucial negotiations between the Qajars and the Russians. In much of the delicate negotiations between the two Person-Russian wars (1804–1813 and 1826–1828), Mirza Saleh was present and active at the highest diplomatic levels. He was also among the top Qajar diplomats dispatched to St Petersburg when the Russian envoy Alexander Griboyedov (1795–1829) was murdered by a mob in Iran. We therefore need to make a distinction between his various diplomatic missions to Russia and England on behalf of Qajar court, and his personal narrative in his travelogues that speaks of an entirely different set of sensibilities.

All his diplomatic services to the Qajar court notwithstanding, the single most significant achievement of Mirza Saleh for posterity has been his travelogue, and in writing that text its singular significance is the text itself and its revolutionary and transformative role in the simplification of Persian prose, i.e., in coining words that correspond to "freedom," "the rule of law," "social justice," "parliament," "revolution," etc. He was chiefly responsible for bringing the craft of printing to Iran for decidedly public purposes, for personally bringing a printing machine back from England, and also for later dispatching another Iranian, named Mirza Asadollah, to St Petersburg to learn about printing machines.[7] It is with the machine he brought back from England that he published his newspaper in Persian. Two significant topics are paramount in the very first issue of the journal *Kaghaz e Akhbar:* first, that he addresses it to "sakenin-e mamalek-e mahruseh/ the residents of the royal realm," and second, that he says he will publish news of "the East and the West"; and then he identifies what he means by "the East" and mentions Arabia, Anatolia, Armenia, Iran, Khwarazm, Turan, Siberia, Mongolia, Tibet, China, Japan, India, Sind, Kabul, and Qandahar. As for "the West," he says that region includes Europe or Farangestan, Africa, America, or Yingi Dunya, and the islands connected to it. In other words, "the West" includes Africa![8] On another occasion, Mirza Saleh identifies "Western territories" as those of Europe and the Ottoman domains.[9] This contour of his imaginative geography, and where is "East" and where "West," is exceptionally important for our understanding of his journey, for the

<hr/>

[7] Ibid.: 20.   [8] Ibid.: 21–22.   [9] Ibid.: 28.

idiomaticity of his newspaper is very much the extension of his prose and politics evident in his travelogues.

A quick look at the outline of Mirza Saleh's travelogue in this first edition reveals the actual itinerary of his travels, which is much more than just going to England, as it has been habitually read. The text is divided into four chapters. The first, very short chapter is concerned with his preliminary remarks of getting ready to leave Tabriz after he receives an audience with Crown Prince Abbas Mirza. Mirza Saleh tells Abbas Mirza he wants to study French, English, Latin, and natural philosophy. Abbas Mirza asks him specifically what technology he wants to study, and he says he has no interest in any technology and his interests are language, culture, and philosophy.[10] The second chapter describes Mirza Saleh's journey from Tabriz to Russia, first to Moscow and then to St Petersburg.[11] Here he very much enjoys the journey, occasionally sitting by the Aras River and reciting Hafez's poetry. Everywhere he arrives he gives a full description of the landscape and the agricultural products of the region. He says specifically in this trip he wants to study religions and therefore visits churches and engages in discussions with priests.[12] In Tbilisi he enters into a deep discussion about trade in the region, and later he gives a full and detailed account of colleges and their curricula. While in Moscow, Mirza Saleh writes a full account of the Napoleonic invasion of Russia.[13] This section reads like a short historical treatise on Napoleon and his imperial conquests. Why should all these precious pages be ignored, diminished in significance, categorically compromised with the fictitious assumption that he was "going to England"? Yes, he was also going to England. But much more is happening on this journey.

From Moscow, Mirza Saleh goes to St. Petersburg and upon his arrival offers a detailed description of that city, too. He describes Peter the Great (among other Russian royal families) and the extent of his political and social reforms.[14] Mirza Saleh leaves Tabriz on April 19, 1815, and does not leave for England until September 10 of the same year.[15] It is not until the third chapter that Mirza Saleh starts writing about arriving in England, and his account of his visit there is an extension of his observations about Russia, and later about the Ottoman Empire.[16] The fourth chapter is the account of his journey from England to Tabriz, with full descriptions of his observations about the

---

[10] Ibid.: 44–48.   [11] Ibid.: 48.   [12] Ibid.: 59.   [13] Ibid.: 88.
[14] Ibid.: 142.   [15] Ibid.: 158.   [16] Ibid.: 162.   [17] Ibid.: 389.

Ottoman territories.[17] Of the total pages of the travelogue in this edition, he spends 7 pages on the preparatory stages of his journey while he is still in Iran, 114 pages from Tabriz to Russia, 227 pages on his visit to England, and 67 pages on his journey back from the United Kingdom to Iran. In other words, 188 pages in this edition are on his journey outside England and 227 pages in England; give or take a few pages, his travelogue is just short of 50 percent outside England and 50 percent in England. The obvious point is, why is he not considered for his trip to Russia and the Ottoman regions and simply assumed to have gone to England? Why are his observations about Iran, Russia, and then the Ottoman territories any less significant than what he writes about England, or conversely, why should his observations about England not be considered as integral as other things he writes about the rest of the world – for that is in fact what he does?

Figure 7 "Moscow, Russia in the Nineteenth Century." The Russian Empire was a principal point of contact between the travelers we are reading in this book and the rest of the world they visited. The Russian and Ottoman empires were contiguous and placed these travelers between the Indian subcontinent and Europe, beyond which they reached deeply into Africa and Latin America. The political cartography of that map completely disappears if we were to privilege Europe or any other part of their itinerary. Reprinted with permission from Classic Image/Alamy Stock Photo.

"To Ascertain My Faith"

A second edition of Mirza Saleh Shirazi's travelogue was prepared some sixteen years later by Homayoun Shahidi and published in the Fall of 1984. This edition is based on a couple more manuscripts that the editor had procured in addition to those available to Ra'in. Shahidi also mentions the previous edition had many "mistakes" he had corrected. This edition is, however, more or less the very same travelogue, divided into the selfsame four chapters, plus the addition of a very useful index. What distinguishes this edition is the fact that it was published in the aftermath of the 1979 revolution and as a result has a more blunt and open introduction, attending to the colonial context of its original publication. It denounces the Qajar dynasty and its repeated ignominious defeats at the hands of Russians. It gives a full description of the obscene wealth and corruption of the Qajar monarchs and princes. It gives a full account of the diplomatic relations between Iran and England during this critical period. It attends critically to the treaty signed between England and Qajars in March 1812. This is all as a preliminary account leading to the first group of Iranian students whom Abbas Mirza had sent to England, among whom was Mirza Saleh. Shahidi makes a point about Mirza Saleh having joined the Free Masons but seeks to exonerate him for having been a devout Muslim.[18] From Shahidi's introduction one still gets the sense of the primary purpose of Mirza Saleh's journey having been to go to England. All other aspects of his journeys in and around Iran are disregarded.

Early in the first chapter of his travelogue, when he describes his encounter with Abbas Mirza trying to convince the Qajar prince to finance his journey, Mirza Saleh shares with his readers an exchange regarding his rationale for wishing to go to this trip outside his homeland. Abbas Mirza tells him, what is the use of this journey, "you'll be in the company of illiterate people," he says, "what is the point?" Mirza Saleh politely disagrees and offers something of a theological explanation as to why he wishes to go. He says just seeing the trees, valleys, and prairies is good for him to see how the world is created by

---

[18] See Mirza Saleh Shirazi, *Gozaresh Safer/Account of a Journey*. Edited with an Introduction and Notes by Homayoun Shahidi (Tehran: Rah-e No Publications, 1984): 1–51.

just one creator, no matter everywhere we go. Then he says it is good for him to see how different people praise God in their own ways. In addition, he will have a chance to compare and contrast various religions and arrive at his own certitude. "I will get to know the world," he further adds, "return to Iran and perhaps I could be of some use to Muslims, which will ascertain my own salvation."[19] These initial pages of the travelogue are full of the anxieties of Mirza Saleh, first concerning whether the prince will allow him to leave; and once he tells him he can leave, whether he would allow him to study languages, cultures, and philosophy, rather than anything pragmatic; and when all of that is secured, he tries to hide this journey from his friends, for they were admonishing him for undertaking such a pointless (in their estimation) journey.

Halfway through the second chapter and while he is still in St Petersburg, Mirza Saleh gives a full geographical description of Russia that reveals a clear image of his geographical understanding of the globe. This is what he says:

Russia is one of the greatest countries in the world, and the most powerful European kingdom. Some of its territories are considered to be European, they call it "European." Some other parts in the north are part of the Yingi Dunya (USA), which is called Pacific Ocean, and much of these areas are in the East which is called Asia. From the north it is connected to the North Pole, and the Arctic Ocean. From another side it is connected to China, India, Constantinople, and Iran. From the East it is connected towards the northern part of the Pacific Ocean, or the Eastern part of the ocean. From the west it leads towards Austria, Prussia, and the Baltic Sea.[20]

What is important here are the porous boundaries of Asia, Europe, and the Americas, which are very much in a state of flux. Mirza Saleh is discovering this geography as he writes and maps it. These passages are crucial, for they are the clear indications that "Europe" is still very much a mysterious and vague proposition and therefore the very assumption of Mirza Saleh and his fellow travelers having traveled to "Europe" is a deeply flawed and anachronistic proposition. But all these passages will categorically elude us if we begin with the unexamined assumption that he went "to Europe." "Europe" emerged not as

[19] Ibid.: 54.   [20] Ibid.: 131. My translation.

continental designation but an emotive universe, and at the time of these travelers that universe was still very much in the making.

The occasion of Mirza Saleh being in England is spent far more in the crafting of a new character in the narrator of the travelogue than merely in sight-seeing. On these pages we are witness to how a new Persian persona is being formed, a learned man encountering a changing world and figuring himself out in its context. A crucial encounter between Mirza Saleh and Sir John Malcolm (1769–1833), a prominent colonial officer and Orientalist with a prolonged engagement in India and Iran, will be good to recall here. Upon his arrival in London, Mirza Saleh goes to pay a visit to Sir John Malcolm, who immediately admonishes his Iranian guest and warns him to stay away from too much partying in London and stick to his education. Here Mirza Saleh confesses to his journal that two mentors have been instrumental in building his character, one the prominent Qajar vizier Mirza Qaem Maqam in Tabriz, who told him to stay away from nonsensical poetry, and here Sir John, telling him to stick to his education and not waste time going to too many banquets.[21] It is in this light that we should read how much of the third chapter, which covers his sojourn in England, is devoted to a narrative on the history of England, which he may have either copied from an English source he was reading or else jotted down in his travelogue as he was learning.[22] The travelogue here really reads like a college notebook a student might take while reading a text. It is in this context that he then gives a full description of London and its major buildings and institutions,[23] just before he gives a detailed account of the nature of government in the United Kingdom, where he informs his readers of the division of governance among the king, the House of Lords, and the House of Commons.[24]

On Saturday, July 24, 1819, Mirza Saleh and his friends boarded a ship off Port Gravesend and sailed through Thames back toward his homeland. They crossed Gibraltar on August 11, and on September 1 they arrive in Malta.[25] While traveling through the Ottoman territories, Mirza Saleh gives a full account of the Turkic tribes from the middle of the ninth century forward – again the travelogue becomes

[21] Ibid.: 173–174.
[22] Ibid.: 205–278. This is more than one third of his entire chapter on his visit to England.
[23] Ibid.: 279–308.   [24] Ibid.: 309–321.   [25] Ibid.: 374–390.

the site of a self-taught history lesson as when he was in Russia or
England. Given the fact that he gives mostly Gregorian dates for this
quick history lecture, perhaps he was using an English source.[26] Mirza
Saleh's interest and curiosity about the Ottoman Empire are almost
identical to his interest in Russia or England, so he might as well have
considered undertaking this journey for those destinations. Just
because England was the farthest he traveled from his homeland does
not mean that that country was the sole purpose of his journey.
Textually that assumption cannot be corroborated. We would close
the factual evidence of a much wider set of horizons he visited if we
privileged any one destination over another. While in Istanbul he relies
on the oral account of an Iranian physician he met there and who had
evidently lived there for a long time.[27] But he also relies on the account
of a certain Dr. Russell, a British medical doctor, who had lived in the
region and written his observations.[28] Finally, on November 23, 1819,
Mirza Saleh departs from Erzurum for Tabriz.

More than One Journey

By far the most comprehensive critical edition of Mirza Saleh Shirazi's
travelogues appeared a year later in 1985.[29] The most significant
superiority of this edition over the two previous editions is the inclusion of two additional travelogues, of which there is not even a hint in
the previous two editions: a travelogue to Isfahan and a travelogue to
Russia, chronologically bracketing his trip to Russia, Ottoman territories, England, and back. There are any number of other improve-
ments in this most recent edition. The print is of a better quality, dates
have all been unified and standardized, Latin names carefully identified, and altogether a far superior set of annotations accompanies the
text. Curiously, though, the learned editor of this volume does not
mention anything about the previous two editions. His introduction is

---

[26] Ibid.: 390–412.   [27] Ibid.: 413.   [28] Ibid.: 417.
[29] See Mirza Saleh Shirazi, *Majmu'eh Safarnameh-ha-ye Mirza Saleh Shirazi/
Collection of Mirza Saleh Shirazi's Travelogues*. Edited and Annotated by
Gholamhossein Mirza Saleh (Tehran: Nashr-e Tarikh-e Iran Publications,
1985). A second, more handsome printing of this edition appeared by a
different publisher in 2008 as Mirza Saleh Shirazi, *Majmu'eh Safarnameh-ha/
Collection of Travelogues*. Edited by Gholamhossein Mirza Saleh (Tehran:
Nashr Negah Mo'aser, 2008).

more attentive to the history of travel writing in this period. The first travelogue, identified as destined toward Isfahan, is actually more than that and includes a journey from Tabriz through Kashan, Qom, and finally the Qajar capital Tehran. This journey took place some three years before Mirza Saleh's journey to Russia, the Ottoman Empire, and England. On this journey he accompanied Sir Gore Ouseley and his pregnant wife. His short travelogue to Russia is related to his diplomatic mission in 1827 to ensure a peace treaty between the Qajars and Russia.

This third edition of Mirza Saleh's travelogues contains an informed essay on his pioneering work in establishing a Persian newspaper.[30] In this essay, Mohammad Isma'il Rezvani informs us that the origin of Iranian attention to press and journalism ought to be traced back to India and not Europe. It was in India that Iranians for the first time encountered printed press and publication of newspapers. The significant community of Iranian expatriates in Istanbul was equally aware of Ottoman, Russian, and European press. We also know that Christian missionaries had already introduced press in Isfahan during the Safavid period. Equally important is the fact that Fath Ali Shah and Abbas Mirza were personally scared witless of foreign press, for until their time no one had dared questioning the king's power and authority, and now they suddenly began reading open and harshly critical accounts of their deeds (and the affairs of other monarchs and sultans in the region and faraway lands) in Russian, Ottoman, Central Asia, Indian, and European press. It is perfectly evident from Mirza Saleh's own account that he was fully aware of this environment and upon his arrival in London began thinking of learning the art of printing and bringing back to Iran a printing machine. During his subsequent trips to Russia, he remained equally eager to facilitate other printing machines brought to his homeland.

When we look at this most recent edition of Mirza Saleh's various journeys in and out of Iran, of paramount importance are these questions: How are we to read such travelogues, what do they signify, why have they all been reduced to a one-dimensional reading of his short visit to England? Generations of scholars have produced learned work

---

[30] See Mohammad Isma'il Rezvani, "Mirza Saleh Shirazi va Ruznameh-negari/ Mirza Saleh Shirazi and Journalism," in Mirza Saleh (ed.), *Majmu'eh Safarnameh-ha-ye Mirza Saleh Shirazi/Collection of Mirza Saleh Shirazi's Travelogues*: 13–33.

based exclusively on fishing out aspects of Mirza Saleh's encounter with "the West." More recently, for example, Nile Green has been keen to map out aspects of this encounter in very informative essays, emphasizing the evidence of the first printing machine that Mirza Saleh brought with him to Iran and thus underling aspects of "print and modernity." He points out:

> In the travelogue of Mirza Saleh Shirazi (d. after 1841) we have an incomparable firsthand account of the circumstances surrounding the transfer of printing to Iran that we lack for Egypt or India. However, there are also substantive reasons for this Iranian focus in that the development of Muslim printing in Tabriz preceded by several years that of Egypt's better-known pioneers at Bulaq and the less famous state press of Nasir al-Din Haydar at Lucknow.[31]

No doubt such positivist historiography has its uses and benefits. But is that all there is to such travelogues – that Mirza Saleh brought a printing machine to Iran? Could that fact be part and parcel and integral to a larger set of considerations as to what these travelers were doing beyond "going to the West," so that such printing machines and newspapers and books they were publishing could be understood in a different light, perhaps?

In another equally excellent essay, Nile Green has argued how "the modernizing initiatives of the crown prince 'Abbas Mirza ... [were contingent on] increasing Iranian interaction with Europe."[32] He further proposes:

> By reconstructing the evangelical character of the university encounters of the group of Iranian students sent to England in 1815 [among which was Mirza Saleh, he wishes to] emphasize the religious dimensions ... [of the] increasing interaction with Europe by demonstrating the degree to which British co-operation with the Iranian attempt to access European science was predicated on an evangelical agenda of winning Persophone Asia for Christ.[33]

---

[31] See Nile Green, "Journeymen, Middlemen: Travel, Transculture, and Technology in the Origins of Muslim Printing," *International Journal of Middle East Studies* 41:2 (May, 2009): 203–224.

[32] Nile Green, "The Madrasas of Oxford: Iranian Interactions with the English Universities in the Early Nineteenth Century," *Iranian Studies* 44:6 (2011): 807–829.

[33] Ibid.

The epistemic foregrounding of the encounters between "East and West" or "Muslims and Europe" ("evangelical" or otherwise) remains narratively constant, and ever more erudite details are added to it to make it even more robust and solid. The basic assumption, the binary opposition, that "Europe" was the center of the universe and that these backward lost souls went there to partake in its glories to the limits of their jaundiced abilities, remains constant. It is in the same cast of mind that in yet another typical essay representative of the dominant historiography of the Qajar period in English language, we see Mirza Saleh cast as an example of Iranian observers falling into the two opposing camps of "Anglophilia and Anglophobia,"[34] the totality and integrity of his travelogues that include Iran, Russia, and the Ottoman Empire categorically neglected and his short visit to England privileged as the sole purpose of his entire existence.

"Persian Image of Europe"

The best example of a sustained course of flawed historiography distorting the evidence of such historic documents as Mirza Saleh Shirazi's travelogue is evident in an entry in the highly authoritative *Encyclopedia Iranian* under the title of "Persian Image of Europe," in and of itself privileging Europe in a misreading of history of Iran over the last millennium.[35] The standard assumption about the relation between Iran (and the larger Muslim world) and Europe is summarized in this sentence: "Prior to the Mongol era, information available to Persians about Europe beyond the Byzantine frontier was scanty and consisted largely of fixed and formulaic wisdom." But the reason for that truism is here left out. There was neither a "Europe" in the contemporary sense of the term nor anything particularly noteworthy to know about it beyond the political and intellectual encounters of Persians and later Muslims with the Greeks and then the imperial encounters of the Sassanids with the Romans and the Byzantines.

[34] See Abbas Amanat, "Through the Persian Eye: Anglophilia and Anglophobia in Modern Iranian History," in Abbas Amanat and Farzin Vejdani (eds.), *Iran Facing Others: Identity Boundaries in a Historical Perspective* (New York: Palgrave Macmillan, 2012): 125–150.
[35] See "EUROPE, PERSIAN IMAGE OF" (*Encyclopedia Iranica*): Available online here: www.iranicaonline.org/articles/europe-persian-image-of. Accessed February 16, 2017.

In an astonishingly anachronistic presumption, the whole totality of "Europe" is assumed ahistorically constant, and then other people from China to India to Iran are interrogated as to whether they did or did not have any idea about this "Europe." Never is the question itself interrogated: Why or how should any people have any knowledge about this chimeric construction that would be generations and millennia in construction beyond Greek city-state and then Roman empire of which the larger Mediterranean world and the Persian and Muslim empires were of course aware of them.

Equally erroneous is the assertion that "it is only with the coming of the Crusaders to the Levant that the (Arab) Muslim view of Europe and Europeans began to transcend the fantastic and the bizarre."[36] The Crusades were an entirely tangential border skirmish in Anatolia, exceptionally important for the Christian fanatical zealotry of the time that had initiated them in Europe but utterly irrelevant to the course of Islamic history, the civilizational epicenter of which had by that time shifted much farther to the east under the Seljuqids. As for Iran ("Persia"), the Crusades were completely irrelevant to its political and cultural developments, and there was scarcely an awareness let alone a response to it. The reason that later during the Ilkhanids period Rashid al-Din Fazlollah paid a modicum of attention to "Europe" in his *Tarikh-e Afranj/History of the Franks* is not because "Europe" had anything to say or do to be of importance to the Ilkhanids but because as a domain of the Mongol empire they needed to have a minimum of information about the region they were now ruling. The rise of interest in "Europe" during the Safavid, the Mughals, and the Ottoman periods was in part because certain areas of the European continent was now the subject of the Ottoman Empire and also because commercial interactions between the rising European empires and Muslim empires were now leading to critical colonial encounters. Without keeping these specific historical developments in mind, much ahistorical questioning of what did Muslims or Iranians know about "Europe" is categorically ahistorical.

If "for all the frequency and seeming importance of the various Sherley [British travelers'] missions to Persia under Shah Abbas I, not one Persian chronicle so much as mentions the name of either of the two brothers,"[37] the answer is very simple: These visitors were not

---

[36] Ibid.   [37] Ibid.

important, noteworthy, or remarkable for any mention of them to be left for posterity. This ahistorical sense of wonder is a clear indication of a self-importance by a Eurocentric historiography that the whole world must have written with due pomp and ceremony that Europeans had gone to visit them. Indeed:

> Such aloofness was clearly instilled by the Safavid Weltanschauung, which was underpinned by unquestioned assumptions of religious and civilizational superiority. Safavid chronicles suggest a universe with Persia at its center and a realm ruled by a monarch who was seen as God's vicegerent and, as grandiosely, the exalted sovereign of the world. Europe hardly figured in such a worldview.[38]

Safavids were not alone in any such "aloofness." All empires and all the civilizations they stage think they are the center of the universe. Why should they not? It is only this strange Europocentric historiography that either demands attention or else accuses other civilizations of ignorance or of "aloofness" and arrogance if they simply had nothing to say about "Europe."

The Safavids were "poorly informed" about Europe because Europe did not have much to attract their attention. The proposition that "yet Persian society showed itself little inquisitive about the dynamics of European society and culture" must be modified to reflect the status of "Europe" at the time in global affairs. The problem with this kind of historiography begins right here: "the Napoleonic period, followed by British diplomatic and commercial overtures toward Persia, and the early 19th-century Russo-Persian military confrontation provide the backdrop to the beginning of a more intensive interaction between Persia and Europe and thus a more profound knowledge of Europe among Persians."[39] Just because the European age of imperialism begins to encroach upon the world (from Asia to Africa and Latin America) it does not mean the world rolled over and played dead and abandoned its own vision of the world at large. The "interaction" has always been between Iranians (and other non-Europeans) and the world at large and not just with Europe. The world, the globe, the planet, did not disappear into thin air just because "Europe" became politically self-conscious. I have already argued that when Fanon said "Europe" is the invention of the "Third World," the proposition was

[38] Ibid.   [39] Ibid.

not merely material but equally symbolic.[40] That historic invention is today at the other end of its categorical legitimacy. It had a short lifespan. We should not presume it quintessential in history.

Desire for the Invisible

Let me now shift gears and ask a philosophical question I am used to asking: Can non-Europeans think?[41] Could these travelogues be considered occasions in which people other than "Europeans," thus consolidated in the fiction of their own convictions, find reasons to think through their existence, who and what they are, to discover perhaps new horizons that include but are not limited to Europe, and such discoveries are mere moments to rediscover themselves. Let me turn to a text on the borderline of European and Hebraic thinking to ask this question more pointedly.

In a crucial section of his seminal text, *Totality and Infinity* (1961), which he calls "Desire for the Invisible," Emmanuel Levinas cites a line from the French poet Arthur Rimbaud (1854–1891), with a twist: "The true life is absent," Rimbaud says in that poem, and then adds, "We are not in this world." Levinas changes that second phrase to: "But we are in the world." What is that "world" in which we may or may not be? Let's see, what does Levinas's exquisite philosophical mind do with that phrase:

Metaphysics arises and is maintained in this alibi. It is turned toward the "elsewhere" and the "otherwise" and the "other." For in the most general form it has assumed in the history of thought it appears as a movement going forth from a world that is familiar to us, whatever be the yet unknown lands that bound it or that it hides from view, from an "at home" ["chez soi"] which we inhabit, toward an alien outside-of-oneself (hors-de-soi), toward a yonder.[42]

---

[40] See Hamid Dabashi, "Europe Is the Creation of the Third World" (*Aljazeera*, June 26, 2016). Available online here: www.aljazeera.com/indepth/opinion/ 2016/06/europe-creation-world-160613063926420.html. For a more extensive treatment of the subject, see my forthcoming book, *Europe and Its Shadows: Coloniality after the Empire* (London: Pluto Press, 2019).

[41] See Dabashi, *Can Non-Europeans Think?*

[42] Emmanuel Levinas, *Totality and Infinity*. Translated by Alphonso Lingis (Pittsburgh, PA: Duquesne University Press, 1969): 33–35.

What were Mirza Saleh and generations of his fellow travelers doing outside a world that was familiar to them moving toward "the yet unknown lands"? Could he or anyone of his generation of travelers be allowed the possibility of having asked similar questions as they moved from one horizon to another? Why privilege only one among myriad other places they visited and extract the evidence for the corroboration of a Eurocentric universe as if outside that universe no other world existed? Could theirs be considered the moment of "the elsewhere" in the life of a nation that was now discovering itself outside its imperial pedigree? The world outside was the "otherwise" of this emerging selfhood, and the world was its "other." What was familiar was becoming foreign, and what was foreign had to become familiar. In that dialectic Mirza Saleh Shirazi and his fellow travelers were not just discovering but in fact inventing themselves. Could we perhaps read them in that light? They were no longer "at home" at home. They needed to get "outside-of-oneself" to rediscover who they were, who they needed to be in the world that was dawning on them. Privileging "Europe" as their destination robs these travelers of their expanding moral imagination, easing itself outside their habitual home and reaching out with every stroke of their pen to who and what they were meant to be. Why not dwell on the moment when Mirza Saleh sits by a river and recites a poem of Hafez to himself? What was he thinking at that moment? Could he be allowed to think? He had said to Abbas Mirza he wanted to study philosophy. Could this travelogue be considered as a philosophical moment in the life of a traveler, perhaps?

Let us consider when Levinas insists: "The term of this movement, the elsewhere or the other, is called *other* in an eminent sense. No journey, no change of climate or of scenery could satisfy the desire bent toward it."[43] But that eminence is always already contingent on a journey, on a change of climate and scenery, for without it how else will we reach the very recognition of that enduring eminence? I do not wish to reduce the philosophical to the historical. Quite to the contrary, I wish to lend the historical to the philosophical, as I habitually do. The reading of these travelogues as if they were "bent toward" Europe has done them immeasurable violence and enduring damage, not just historically but, far more importantly, morally, ethically (Levinas's concern), imaginatively, epistemically: as if they were a lifeless

---

[43] Ibid.

cadaver waiting to be dissected for positivist historiography. Their
sense of wonder has been robbed from them, their measure of philosophical amazement denied them. An entire nation, an entire universe
of critical imagination and wonder, is robbed of its sense of self-
transcendence by thinking it unidirectional, from the East to the West,
from Tradition to Modernity, from backwardness to progress. This is
simply obscene.

Let us remember, again, Levinas's superior insight into when we exit
ourselves and become the other: "Their *alterity* is thereby reabsorbed
into my own identity as a thinker or a possessor. The metaphysical
desire towards *something else entirely*, toward the *absolute other*."[44]
This *absolute other* is not "Europe," it is not the "West" – though
those eventual abstractions will soon become integral to it. It is the
world outside the tightening habitat of Mirza Saleh and his fellow
travelers that is pushing them out toward the other to embrace it as
their own self. That dialectic is definitive to our global whereabouts
today. They were not moving toward "Europe," for "Europe" did not
even completely exist as a metaphor. They were moving toward the
world. "The metaphysical desire," of which Levinas speaks here, "does
not long to return, for it is desire for a land not of birth, for a land
foreign to every nature, which has not been our fatherland and to
which we shall never betake ourselves."[45] These travelers (Iranians,
Muslims, wonderers) are not even allowed into the world to discover
it, let alone seen returned to remain on that hinterland of ethically
rethinking the world anew. That desire for the invisible is there, in the
very letters of their travelogues, if we were to allow them to write what
they wrote and not assimilate it into a sad commentary of peripheral
nations on the centrality of the trope of "Europe," which evidently
cannot even trust its own existence on its own and always needs a
peripheral vision of itself from all its *others* in order to believe (in)
itself.

Put two sublime insights of Levinas together (one European the
other Biblical): "Desire is absolute if the desiring being is mortal and
the Desired invisible," and "to die for the invisible – this is metaphysics"[46] – and ask yourself if an Iranian, a Muslim, any non-European,
can ever be even mortal on this philosophical page, let alone desire the
invisible, let alone find a space in the metaphysical? A person must first

---

[44] Ibid.   [45] Ibid.   [46] Ibid.

be allowed to be, to be mortal, if the Muslim person is ever allowed to connect to the Invisible, to be immortal, to be able to be and to think outside the peripheral vision of "Europe."

Can non-Europeans harbor a desire for the invisible – long before and long after Levinas's philosophy? Not if everything they do, say, think, or wonder is twisted to mean something for the Europeans – for unless they went to Europe, they went nowhere at all. There is an epistemic arrogance in that very assumption. It is impossible to understand these travelers we are reading here together without, first, reading them cover to cover and, second, going through a whole constellation of them back to back – and then allowing them to breathe in their own narrative airs. That patience and perseverance has never before been afforded these travelers. These texts have been systematically abused by reading a few pages here and a chapter there, all taken out of their total contexts and put to some Eurocentric use or another. Once we actually read an entire collection of these travelogues back to back, cover to cover, in multiple editions, and spread over more than a century, an epic drama emerges from the pages we are reading. It is not accidental that the fact and phenomenon of these travel narratives eventually rose into the earliest works of fiction and ultimately the most sublime moments of Persian poetry of the last century. Without going through the trouble of having a gestalt view of each and every one of these travelogues, no single one of them, let alone a few pages of each, would make much sense. There was indeed not just a desire for the invisible. Long before Shahab al-Din Yaya Suhrawardi's visionary recitals in the twelfth century and now after Sohrab Sepehri's poetry in the twentieth, and then on every single page of these travelogues around the globe – there were sustained allegorical and poetic visions of the invisible, if we only had the grace and the patience to sit down politely and read, listen, and learn.

6 | *A Wandering Monarch*

Nasir al-Din Shah
(u journeys)

> Pass me the wine –
> we need to rush:
> I am returning from a journey
> Through an epic – and I know
> The story of Sohrab and the Elixir
> By heart –
>
> Sohrab Sepehri (Mosafer/Traveler, Babol, Spring 1966)

Sohrab Sepehri's poetry is material, in tune with the ligneous texture of the world he has seen, the world he maps out, the world he has discovered for us. In the midst of the most sublime he introduces the most anodyne, the most tangible, the very quintessence of things. The ordinary thus becomes strange, the sublimity it accompanies suddenly rubs on it to endear it to our senses in manners unknown before. The reference to the epic in the passage I just quoted is of course to Ferdowsi's *Shahnameh* (1010), and its story of Rostam the towering hero inadvertently killing his own son Sohrab and looking in vain for Nushdaru/Elixir to bring him back to life. Sepehri uses that tragic urgency in futility to mark a Khayyamesque moment in his worldly poetry. Life is urgent, the world is vast, the occasion vital, fleeting. The passage brings power and primacy to our personhood, to our presence as sojourners through a passage in this world, in this life. The phrase I have had to translate into the idiomatic "know by heart" in the original reads through the Persian idiomatic expression of "know like a running water," in which the image of water and a flowing river sustains the metaphor of the journey. The move is predicated on and thus reinforces the aesthetic intuition of transcendence that (flowing like a running river) in and of itself bestows sovereignty to the nation as a collective, knowing subject and enables the people it thus constitutes to say "We." No other agency, no other power commands any authority over this sovereignty. The poem does not begin to

154

be political. It overwhelms and overcomes and redefines the political. The poem is not an anticipation or a prescription of what is to come – political or otherwise. It is a culmination of things that have happened, events that have occasioned it, journeys that have been made, destinations in the offing. Kings and clerics who have historically ruled over us were delusional in thinking we were their subjects. Our subjections have always been in the making in the hands of our poets, tireless in the feet of those who traveled far and beyond, in and out of us.

The Monarch and His Musings

While visiting London, Mirza Saleh Shirazi is troubled one day by the sudden news that one of his companions, Ostad Mohammad Ali, has fallen in love with a British girl, and has gone to a church and, "based on British customs," married her. Panic-stricken by the prospect, Mirza Saleh does all he can to prevent this marriage from happening, for he thinks it inappropriate. He talks to people in positions of power and authority over their group, all to no avail.[1] The pages of Mirza Saleh's travelogue are indeed replete with such spontaneous events of an ordinary man trying to come to grips with a changing world in which cultures and climes, countries and their habitats, customs and religions, identities and alterities are all up for rethinking – not just in "Europe" or in "non-Europe," but indeed around the globe, in the very texture of human habitat. The imaginative geography of the world in the mind of Mirza Saleh and his contemporaries is changing, and these travel accounts we are reading are the bricks and mortar of how that world is being irretrievably recreated.

In this chapter, I wish to take a closer look at one of Naser al-Din Shah's many travel accounts, the very first trip he took outside his own homeland, *Safar-Nameh/Travelogue* (1873). Much had happened around the globe between Mirza Saleh's travels in 1815 and Naser al-Din Shah's journey in 1873. Three major events can be singled out for their enduring significance in the colonizing and colonized worlds. The defeat of Napoleon in the Battle of Waterloo in June 1815 for a while outmaneuvered the French as a major rival to British imperialism. Soon after that, the two Opium Wars – the First Opium War (1839–1842) and the Second Opium War (1856–1860) – significantly

---

[1] Shirazi, *Safarnameh/Travelogue*: 379.

fortified the British colonial control over the Asian trades. The French–British colonial rivalries, however, again flared up during the 1859–1869 period and the construction of the Suez Canal. Naser al-Din Shah, as a result, left his homeland fully conscious of the colonial rivalries within Europe, but equally aware of the Russian and Ottoman imperial contexts of his own realm in particular.

The Qajar monarch's personal accounts of his journeys in and out of his own royal realm are in many ways the prototype of the genre, except for all the pomp and ceremony that accompanies him when he travels, of course. It is fair to say that Naser al-Din Shah was an itinerant monarch. He loved to travel and while away from his royal palace he continued to manage his affairs via correspondences and emissaries, as he was deeply engaged in his daily observations about what he saw abroad, and attended official meetings with kings, queens, and heads of state. His four journeys abroad (which except the one to Iraq included Europe but were not limited to Europe), in 1873, 1878, and 1889, were part and parcel of his life as a peripatetic monarch. The reign of Naser al-Din Shah, as a result, is a unique and path-breaking example of how the reign of a monarch over a nation had become a transnational affair. Iran at his time is now the target of colonial intrigues, and he finances his trips outside Iran by selling off his nation's resources. His trips abroad and their published accounts in Iran and India (and some of their translations in European languages) were subjects of much later resentment and anger that fueled the preparatory stages of the Constitutional revolution of 1906–1911, in particular the Tobacco Revolt of 1890–1891, which was a rebellious reaction to a lucrative tobacco concession the Qajar monarch had granted Major G. F. Talbot, a British colonial merchant, during one of his European trips for a full monopoly over the production, sale, and export of tobacco for fifty years. But that singularly important event should not detract from the rich and significant body of travel narratives the Qajar king has left behind. In his own somber and sonorous way, His Majesty has much to teach us.

The Labyrinth of the Patriarch

Naser al-Din Shah Qajar (1831–1896) ruled Iran with an iron fist, a velvety glove, a wide-eyed demeanor, and a bewildered soul from September 5, 1848, to May 1, 1896, when he was assassinated just as he was getting prepared to celebrate his golden jubilee.[2] His long reign, the vast number of women he married, his love of photography, his insatiable appetite for traveling, his disarmingly simple prose, his relationship with reformist ministers like Amir Kabir and Sepahsalar, the rise of the revolutionary Babi movement during his reign, his fortuitous granting of commercial concessions to European colonial agents, one of which concerning tobacco, became his final undoing, and his momentous assassination are chief among the landmark events of his long and languorous rule. He saw his homeland from the last vestiges of its imperial past and delivered it to its postcolonial fate. No categorical judgment about his character or reign is possible, fair, or even necessary anymore. To the degree that he was amenable to structural changes in his kingdom initiated by capable and caring ministers such as Amir Kabir and Sepahsalar, he is remembered fondly and positively, and to the degree that he crushed the revolutionary uprising of the Babi movement or sold his country to colonial interests, or that he ordered the murder of perhaps the most capable minister in his court, of course he is judged harshly. He was a common man with an imperial pedigree and harbored more than a dram of evil in him. But the chief concern of this chapter is with his travelogues and not with how he met his creator and received the balance of his mis/deeds. Especially those trips he took outside his homeland are of importance in this chapter, for in them he shared the excitement of his fellow travelers discovering new horizons and unearthing hitherto unknown souls.

The prolonged monarchy of Naser al-Din Shah was marked by some extraordinarily significant events in Iranian history. Perhaps the single most important of such events was the premiership of Mirza Taghi Khan Farahani, known as Amir Kabir (1807–1852), whose groundbreaking reforms in civil administration and foreign affairs the Qajar patriarch initially supported and encouraged but whom he ultimately dismissed and ordered murdered when he realized those reforms destabilized his own reign. Among the towering achievements of Amir Kabir

---

[2] The best biography of Naser al-Din Shah available in English is Abbas Amanat's *The Pivot of the Universe: Nasir al-Din Shah and the Iranian Monarchy, 1831–1896* (London: I. B. Tauris; Revised edition, November 15, 2008). There is an abundance of sources in Persian, of course, the most recent of which is Behzad Karim, *Naser al-Din Shah Qajar: Panjah Sal Saltant/Naser al-Din Shah Qajar: Fifty Years of Rule* (Tehran: Bongah Tarjomeh va Nashr Ketab Parse, 1392/2013).

was the establishment of Dar al-Funun, the first ever institution of higher learning independent of the Shi'i clerical order – much to their anger and several objections. The second equally important event during Naser al-Din Shah's reign was the Shi'i millenarian Babi uprising (1844–1852), which shook the Qajar dynasty to its foundations. Before his dismissal, Amir Kabir was instrumental in suppressing the Babi and other rebellious movements challenging Naser al-Din Shah's reign. He was a loyal servant of the throne and wanted to save it from what he saw as the inclement winds of global changes. He failed – and he paid with his life for it. Meanwhile, the internecine territorial claims of the Qajars over Herat in Afghanistan were met with vehement opposition from the British, who in 1856 invaded Iran and forced the Qajar monarch to yield to the Paris Treaty of March 4, 1857, conceding that he would never again even think of challenging the British colonial interest in the region. The imperial imagination of Iranian dynasties was being cut to the colonial size of nation-states dictated by rising empires. The Herat campaign frightened the Qajar monarch out of his wits. He realized he was no match for either the Russians or the British or even for the Ottomans, for that matter. He therefore began to accommodate their power, facilitate their colonial interests in Iran, and in exchange procure for himself luxurious travels abroad. It is in these imperial and colonial contexts that Naser al-Din Shah's travels abroad into Russian, Ottoman, and European colonizing capitals ought to be understood. If we disregard these crucial contexts and have a psychopathological fixation on his "trips to Europe" we will miss the point. The end of Naser al-Din Shah's time in effect began in 1891 with the revolt against the tobacco concession he had given to a British colonial merchant – thus began the snowballing of a historical event that ultimately ended with his assassination in 1896. But let us not rush to that unfortunate end and instead join him in his happier times.

The Peripatetic Monarch

Naser al-Din Shah loved to travel, and he loved to write about his travels.[3] He personally wrote many of his own travel narratives, and

---

[3] For a very sympathetic reading of Naser al-Din Shah's travels in and out of Iran, see Sohrabi, *Taken for Wonder*: 73–103. In the established tradition of Qajar

the rest he initiated and then had his royal scribes traveling with him to finish it for him. It will distort the totality of his travels and the extent to which he recorded the details of his travels if we were solely to concentrate on his travels to Europe – for among other reasons "Europe" was and remains a floating signifier, and "Europe" became "Europe" in part by the manner in which travelers like Naser al-Din Shah wrote it down in their travelogues. Even when he says in a travelogue, "this is a travelogue (Safarnameh) to Europe (Farang)," when we actually read the text itself it usually begins with his observations about his own homeland and then about places like the Russian and Ottoman territories before he gets to Europe, and then after Europe he continues to write about other places outside Europe that he visits before he comes back to Iran. If these were only the travel accounts of his visits to Europe, as they have usually been abusively read, then why did he write about his observations before and after Europe – sometimes far more extensively in terms of page numbers and details than the sections about Europe? These texts narratively link Iran to its environs, which include Europe but are not limited to Europe. There are altogether twelve travelogues he wrote while traveling inside Iran, and only three travel accounts that are nominally about his travels to Europe, but still, about half of his observations even in these texts are about non-Europe, much of them about his own homeland. The overwhelming majority of his travels and travel accounts, as a result, are about non-Europe. And as soon as I call these "non-Europe," I have already privileged "Europe" as the deciding factor of these narratives. That is false and falsifying. It would be a gross misrepresentation of these facts if we were to privilege those European parts of his journeys under the false epistemic binary of an Iranian monarch going to Europe. His visits to Europe will have to be squarely located within the larger frame of his travels in and out of his homeland in general.

Naser al-Din Shah loved to hunt, and on many occasions his hunting expeditions and traveling were integral to each other.[4] We have an

---

period scholarship, Sohrabi, too, considers all Naser al-Din Shah's journeys outside his homeland categorically as "travels to Europe." She of course is not the first or the only one. This is the standard normative reading of these travelogues, against which I offer an alternative reading.

[4] Naghmeh Sohrabi falsely distinguishes Naser al-Din Shah's travels from his predecessors for not being for hunting (Sohrabi, *Taken for Wonder*: 77). This is

account of his hunting expeditions between 1862 and 1864. The
eminent Qajar historian Fatemeh Qaziha (the presence of her extraordinary work is conspicuously absent among Qajar historians who
write in English based in the US or UK) has done extensive work in
editing and introducing Naser al-Din Shah's travelogues.⁵ This book is
a detailed account of the Qajar monarch's hunting expeditions around
his own homeland. In another book, titled *Yad-dasht-ha ye Ruzaneh
Naser al-Din Shah/The Daily Diaries of Nasr al-Din Shah*, we read his
firsthand account of both internal affairs in his capital of Tehran as
well as his hunting and excursions around his country, covering three
years from 1883 to 1886.⁶ In another, similar account, *Ruznameh
Khaterat-e Naser al-Din Shah /Daily Diaries of Naser al-Din Shah*,
we read detailed accounts of his "anthropological" observations about
Ta'ziyeh performances in Tehran as well as short trips and hunting
expeditions around the country.⁷ When we put these accounts
together, what in effect we are witnessing is a firsthand report of the
Qajar monarch giving us detailed narratives of his own daily life,
travels, and hunting, and descriptions of Muslim practices and pilgrimages. Texts like these have nothing to do with Europe and yet frame his
journeys abroad in a much larger context otherwise lost under the false
epistemic framing of a "Muslim discovery of Europe."

Beyond these hunting expeditions around his capital of Tehran,
Naser al-Din Shah made two specific trips to Khorasan, for as a Shi'a
monarch he had a particular penchant for Shi'i pilgrimage sites. These
two trips occurred in 1867 and 1882, and their accounts were written
by His Majesty's own personal physician, Ali Naqi Hakim al-Molk,
and his own pen, respectively. The king's personal military guard,

directly contradicted by many references of Naser al-Din Shah himself to hunting,
both in Iran and even when traveling abroad, as well as by extensive
scholarship in Persian about the Qajar monarch's hunting expeditions. It is an
unfortunate fact that these scholars do not follow the vast and formidable body
of scholarship that is done in Persian in Iran or Afghanistan and mainly engage
with their own peers and professors writing in English.
⁵ See Fatemeh Qaziha (ed.), *Gozaresh Shekar-ha ya Naser al-Din Shah/An
Account of Naser al-Din Shah's Hunting* (Tehran: Sazeman Asnad Melli Iran,
1390/2011).
⁶ See Parviz Badi'i (ed.), *Yad-dasht-ha-ye Ruzaneh Naser al-Din Shah/Daily Diary
of Naser al-Din Shah* (Tehran: Sazeman Asnad Melli Iran, 1378/1999).
⁷ See Abdolhossein Nava'i and Elham Malekzadeh (eds.), *Ruznameh Khaterat-e
Naser al-Din Shah/The Daily Diaries of Naser al-Din Shah* (Tehran: Sazeman
Asnad Melli Iran, 1390/2011).

numbering 9,000, were keeping him company on this trip, which lasted six months. He offers exquisite details of his visit to the Eighth Shi'a Imam Reza's mausoleum, where he expresses his most obedient pieties. One of these two travelogues is also illustrated. What is obvious about these travelogues is the king's personal interest in detailing the particulars of his realm – cities and villages coming one after the other in his narratives – as he goes about offering his readers personal eyewitness accounts of what he sees and what he does. When we read these texts, it is impossible to miss the point that Naser al-Din Shah made these trips specifically to write about them. He enjoys writing in detail, or else dictating to his royal amanuensis.[8] In the same vein is Naser al-Din Shah's travelogue to South–Central regions of his country bordering with Iraq in the Ottoman territories. This text also shows the proximity of the regions in the Ottoman–Qajar territories welcoming the Persian king in his insatiable desire to travel. Naser al-Din Shah traveled North to Mazandaran province once during 1861–1862 and another time in 1875. On these trips his court, including his wives, traveled with him and he spends the journey north picnicking and hunting. On one of these trips he spends time visiting Russian ships on the Caspian Sea and he is officially received by Russian authorities and dignitaries.[9] In 1869, Naser al-Din Shah took another trip north toward Gilan on which he again gives his readers an account of his visiting the Russian navy in the Caspian Sea. In 1886 he took another trip to Gilan, which was not completed and was aborted because of a heavy snow fall. He returned to the capital. Even of this incomplete journey he makes and leaves an account.[10] As Fatemeh Qaziha puts it, "During his 50 years' reign, Naser al-Din Shah traveled to Qom seven times, four times during his other trips and three times specifically to Qom."[11] She has collected and edited all these trips in one volume, *Safar-ha-ye Naser al-Din Shah to Qom/Naser al-Din Shah's Trips to*

[8] For a brief account of these travelogues, see Fatemeh Qaziha, *Safarnameh ha va Khaterat-e Naser al-Din Shah dar Dakhel-e Keshvar/Travelogues and Memoirs of Naser al-Din Shah Inside Iran.* (Tehran: Markaz-e Da'irat al-Ma'aref Bozorg Islami). Available online here: https://cgie.org.ir/fa/news/128137. Accessed July 22, 2017.
[9] For more details, see ibid.   [10] Ibid.   [11] Ibid.

Qom.[12] During these trips, Naser al-Din Shah met with the religious authorities.

A particularly important note here is that during his third "trip to Europe," as it has been historically read, of the 621 pages of the original manuscript only 136 pages are actually about outside Iran and the rest is about Naser al-Din Shah's traveling inside his own homeland.[13] That is less than 22 percent of the total text about outside Iran. Now, how could this text possibly be considered an account of "the third trip of Naser al-Din Shah to Europe?" Taking the totality of his travelogues into consideration, Naser al-Din Shah was an ocular-centric monarch. He loved to see his realm and beyond to believe it. Instead of reconquering it by a wobbly sword as his ancestors did, he opted to write it with a solid pen. His love of photography and painting and his peripatetic, ocularcentric proclivities were integral to each other. He sought to do with his eyes and his pen what his ancestors did on their horseback and with their swords.

The King Leaves His Realm

Naser al-Din Shah traveled outside the boundaries of his own kingdom and discovered new horizons of his earthly abode four times altogether – for pilgrimage with his wives to sacred sites in Iraq once and to the capitals of three dominant empires – the Russians, the Ottomans, and the Europeans three times.[14] Three of these journeys have been categorically considered trips he took to "Farang/Europe." But even a casual examination of the actual content of his travelogues clearly shows they were in fact the records of an itinerary that began before and continued well after his visits to Europe. There is no textual or justification or contextual reason whatsoever to privilege those parts

[12] See Fatemeh Qaziha (ed.), *Safar-ha-ye Naser al-Din Shah to Qom/Naser al-Din Shah's Trips to Qom* (Tehran: Sazeman Asnad Melli Iran, 1381/2002).
[13] Qaziha, *Safarnameh ha va Khaterat-e Naser al-Din Shah dar Dakhel-e Keshvar/ Travelogues and Memoirs of Naser al-Din Shah Inside Iran.*
[14] Naghmeh Sohrabi offers an exquisite account of the rich texture of travel narratives both originally composed in Persian and those translated from other languages during the reign of Naser al-Din Shah (Sohrabi, *Taken for Wonder*: 79–87), thus enriching our understanding of these journeys abroad. She makes a very persuasive argument to place Naser al-Din Shah's travelogues (which, alas, she still persists in calling "travelogues to Europe") in these larger contexts.

of the journey he took in Europe, even though the author himself tells us at the beginning that this is the record of his trips to Farang/Europe – for what he wrote in his own text exceeds the known boundaries of that imaginative geography. Naser al-Din Shah was the reigning monarch of a kingdom now coveted by three encroaching imperial interests. He was drawn to power and attracted to royal ceremonies. The three dominant geopolitical powers in his world to which he was particularly attracted were the Russians, the Ottomans, and the British – and that is precisely the itinerary of three of his four journeys outside his homeland toward these empires. He moved from his capital first north to Russia, then west to the Ottoman Empire, and then even farther west to England via continental Europe. On his way back to Tehran he is invariably interested in Muslim pilgrimage sites he visits. The pattern is identical with all other travelers of this period. These journeys can therefore be equally called trips the king took to Russia or to the Ottoman Empire, if we were to disregard and violate their narrative totalities and cherry-pick only one segment of them. The cherry-picking of Europe is predicated on a false epistemological binary, superficially and ideologically imposed on the boldly resisting letter of the texts that clearly and in black and white (as it were) tell you otherwise. The source of this epistemic violence is the fundamentally flawed metanarrative of "European Modernity" in which the unexamined metaphor of "the West" was modern and "the Rest" was backwards and therefore "the Rest" (Asians, Africans, Latin Americans) went to Europe to be "modernized." Almost without a single exception, the entire field of Qajar scholarship (in English and Persian alike) has fallen into this theoretical trap. Iranians are not the only victims of this false binary. Arabs, Turks, all other Muslims – they all think this metanarrative is truth manifest and they go and read their sources with this false teleology flatly and falsely in their minds.

The first trip of Naser al-Din Shah abroad began on 21 Safar 1290 (April 20, 1873) and concluded on 14 Rajab of the same year (September 7, 1873). He wrote his travelogue himself, and it was repeatedly published both in Iran and in India – which means it has had a readership beyond the royal courts.[15] While traveling through Russia,

---

[15] See Fatemeh Qaziha (ed.), *Ruznameh Khaterat-e Naser al-Din Shah dar Safar Aval Farangestan/The Memoir of Naser al-Din Shah during His First Trip to Europe* (Tehran: Sazeman Asnad Melli Iran, 1371/1992).

the Ottoman Empire, and Europe, the Qajar monarch made many observations about what he saw as he paid close attention to the affairs of his own realm, including the dismissal of his reformist minister Mirza Hossain Khan Moshir al-Dowleh Sepahsalar (1828–1881) and the mourning for the passing of his mother Malek Jahan Khanum, Mahd-e Olia (1805–1873). Naser al-Din Shah's second trip abroad began at the end of Rabi' al-Awwal 1295 (April 2, 1878) and ended on 8 Sha'ban of the same year (August 7, 1878). During this trip he does not go to England and only visits Russia, Central Asia, and Ottoman territories and then continental Europe, particularly Germany and France. Again, while going through this journey he keeps his running of his kingdom apace from afar. It is during this trip that he makes detailed observations about the Paris exhibition as well as about the museums and factories he visits.[16] He begins to write the initial pages of this travelogue and then his attendants continue and finish his dictations. The third and final trip of Naser al-Din Shah abroad begins sometime in Sh'aban 1306 (April 1889) and ends on 24 Safar 1307 (October 20, 1889). Again, this trip is not just to Europe and includes much more, including hundreds of pages of his correspondence with his court back in Tehran as he attends to his royal duties. His is in effect a mobile court as he visits foreign lands and thus the boundaries of his kingdom are narratively extended in his text to places he visits. It is a gross misreading of these texts (hitherto made standard) to consider them solely for the purpose of going to Europe, though Europe of course is included in his itinerary.

The Wider Geographical Imagination

Instead of assimilating Naser al-Din Shah's travelogues and all other travel narratives of this period into the false and slanted "Islam and the West" (or "lo and behold an Oriental has been off to Europe") narrative, as it is habitually done by Iranian and non-Iranian scholars of the period alike, we need to place it where it belongs: in the more immediate geographical imagination of Iranians and Muslims and

---

[16] For more details, see Fatemeh Qaziha, *Safar-ha va Safar-nameh-ha-ye Farangestan Naser al-Din Shah Qajar/The Journeys and Travelogues of Naser al-Din Shah to Europe* (Tehran: Markaz-e Da'irat al-Ma'aref Bozorg Islami). Available online here: www.cgie.org.ir/fa/news/127238. Accessed July 23, 2017.

their own rich and diversified body of travel literature, both before and after this period. The further we go back in history, the more striking becomes the bizarre operation of power and knowledge that has manufactured this false binary between "the West and the Rest." As early as Ahmad ibn Fadlan (flourished 920s), or perhaps even earlier, Muslims have traveled far and wide exploring new cultures and climes. They have repeatedly and consistently remapped the world they had inherited from previous generations of geographers and cartographers. The memories of those travel narratives have now been completely overshadowed by the more immediate parallax colonially manufactured between "Islam and the West." Ibn Fadlan's account of his travels to the Volga Bulgars in his *Risalah/Treatise* remains one of the earliest sources of our knowledge about Muslims traveling into foreign lands and keeping a record of it. His *Risalah* gives a full account of Ibn Fadlan's observations, mostly of a geographical and anthropological nature, while traveling through Central Asia all the way to Moscow. Ibn Fadlan was sent to Central Asia by the ruling Abbasid Caliph al-Muqtadir bi-llah (895–932, reigned 908–932) to propagate Islam and extend his caliphal authority. The journey and its detailed account had obvious political implications, but it has also left for posterity a document of extraordinary significance about the imperial geography of a period furthest removed from the epistemically forced binary of "Islam and the West" superimposed on these literatures.[17] To overcome that falsifying epistemic trap we need to open the frame of our reference and look at Muslim, Chinese, Indian, and African travelers, geographers, and cartographers to place travelogues such as Naser Khosrow's into its own proper cultural and historical context.

Another case in point is of course the towering geographer Ibn Hawqal (flourished 943–969), a major Muslim traveler and cultural anthropologist who had a lasting influence on the genre. His *Surat al-Ard* (977) remains to this day a monumental achievement of Muslim intellectual history, itself expanding upon such earlier texts as Ibn

[17] For an excellent essay on Ibn Fadlan and his travelogue, see Mohammad Reza Barani, "Mo'arrefi v Naqd-e Safarnameh-ye Ibn Fadlan" (Fasl-nameh Tarikh dar A'ineh-ye Pazhuhesh, 1388/2009). Available online here: www.hawzah.net/fa/article/view/84002. Accessed July 24, 2017.

Khordadbeh *Masalik wa Mamalik* (844–848), Istakhri's *al-Masalik wa al-Mamalik* (951), and Ahmed ibn Sahl al-Balkhi's *Suwar al-Aqalim* (921). As he points out in his introduction to *Surat al-Ard*, Ibn Hawqal was attracted to geography from his youth, and by that he meant knowledge of people and their habits, habitats, and cultures. Muslims were not born the day before the British landed in India or the French in North Africa. When we read these classical texts, it is in fact difficult to distinguish between fields of geography, history, anthropology, sociology, travel narrative, and history. In his writings, Ibn Hawqal combines written sources and conversations with knowledgeable and traveled people plus his own personal travels around the world.[18] We now know Ibn Khordadbeh as the "author of the earliest surviving Arabic book of administrative geography. He was not, apparently, the first geographer to write in Arabic, but he is the first whose book has survived in anything like its original form."[19] He was an Iranian Zoroastrian originally who converted to Islam. We also know him as a theorist of music. The point here is not to give a full view of Muslim travel narratives, a vastly rich and potent body of literature in and of itself, but simply to point to the height of the Abbasid caliphate when the spectrum of knowledge production was from a position of imperial power and authority rather than a position of passive weakness that has endured in both colonizing and colonized minds to this day to the effect that everything is mis/read in terms of positing a false binary between "Islam and the West." I find it utterly astonishing for otherwise perfectly competent scholars to actually read the words on the pages of Naser al-Din Shah's travelogue, or any other traveler's account of his period, and then just cherry-pick the sections on "Europe" and disregard the rest.

Tehran Travels

Let us now take a closer and more detailed look at one of Naser al-Din Shah's travelogues abroad – the very first trip "to Europe" (as it is

---

[18] For a learned introduction to a critical edition and Persian translation of Ibn Hawqal's *Surat al-Ard*, see Ja'far Shu'ar' (ed. and tr.), *Surat al-Ard* (Tehran: Bonyad-e Farhang-Iran, 1345/1965).

[19] See the entry "EBN ḴORDĀḎBEH, ABU'L-QĀSEM ʿOBAYD-ALLĀH" in *Encyclopedia Iranica*. Available online here: www.iranicaonline.org/articles/ebn-kordadbeh. Accessed July 24, 2017.

(1st trip)

habitually called) he undertook in the year 1290/1873. Without a thick description of the total content of this travelogue, however tasking our patience, no full grasp of what the Persian monarch was up to in these journeys is possible. The Qajar monarch wrote this travel account himself, and it was published a year after he wrote it in a lithograph edition in Tehran. Two other subsequent editions were published in Mumbai in 1876. Other printed editions appeared until 1992 when the eminent Iranian Qajar historian Fatemeh Qaziha prepared a critical edition of this travelogue, comparing all its various versions with the original handwritten copy.[20] Numerous publications of the travelogue, from the time of Naser al-Din Shah to this day, in both Iran and India, are clear indications of its significance in the public sphere in which this was read and discussed, furthest removed from the confinements of royal courts.

Before his departure, Naser al-Din Shah entrusts the matter of state to his uncle and his crown prince, visits his army in a nearby garrison, and gives audience to foreign emissaries whose countries he will visit on this trip. His entourage includes top Qajar aristocracy plus his own personal physician. This entire trip was facilitated and encouraged by his reform-minded minister Mirza Hossain Khan Moshir al-Dowleh Sepahsalar, who kept him company on this journey, hoping His Majesty's personal visit to Russia, the Ottoman Empire, and Europe would open his mind to the necessary reforms in his own homeland. Sepahsalar (premier, 1871–1873) was influenced by the Ottoman reforms during his ambassadorial tour of duty in Istanbul. What his intentions were, and what such trips actually achieved, are of course two vastly different things.

The general itinerary of the trip begins in Bandar-e Anzali, a harbor town on the Iranian side of the Caspian Sea, from which the Qajar king sails to Xacitarxan (Hajji Tarkhan or Astrakhan) at the right bank of Volga on the Russian side of the Caspian Sea. From there he sails to Saratov, a major port on the Volga River, and from there he goes first to Moscow and then to St. Petersburg. From the Russian capital he travels to Warsaw and Germany, spending a few days in Berlin, before

---

[20] Qaziha, *Safar-ha va Safar-nameh-ha-ye Farangestan Naser al-Din Shah Qajar/ The Journeys and Travelogues of Naser al-Din Shah to Europe.*

he departs for Brussels in Belgium, and from there he sails to the port of
Dover where he embarks on his journey to London. From London he
goes back to Portsmouth, boarding a ship sailing to Cherbourg where
he takes a train to Paris. From Paris he goes to Geneva, and from there
he goes to Turin in Italy, before leaving for Milano and from there to
Vienna and Salzburg in Austria. From there he travels to Brindisi Port
in Italy, where he takes a ship to Istanbul. From there he sails
through the Black Sea back to Russia, visiting Tbilisi and Baku – after
which he returns to Bandar-e Anzali again in his own homeland. The
journey took about five months. As the outline of this itinerary
clearly shows, Naser al-Din Shah visits three (not one) major imperial
powers whose prolonged interests in his kingdom were encroaching
upon the very existence of the Qajar dynasty: the Russians, the Ottomans, and the Europeans. The Russians were far more militarily
threatening to his dynasty than were the Europeans, and the Tanzimat
(1839–1876) reforms in the Ottoman Empire were far more consequential than anything Europeans might offer. We must keep these
facts in mind as we travel with the Persian patriarch through his
journeys.

Naser al-Din Shah's journey begins in Tehran quite casually.[21] The
Qajar monarch reports that the news of his journey abroad has been in
circulation for about a year and, despite not feeling well, he solicits the
Almighty's protection and embarks on his journey on Saturday
21 Safar 1290 (April 20, 1873). He visits the cavalry regiments of his
army, pays his respects to his mother, and reports of windy weather in
Kan village near Tehran, where he has fun hunting and writing about
the beautiful prairies, gardens, and fresh flowers of the season. While
he is in Kan, the Ottoman ambassador comes to pay him a visit and
invite him to his capital Istanbul. Naser al-Din Shah is particular in
reporting how many of his courtiers are with him on this trip. From
Kan he dismisses the Crown Prince to go back to Tehran and proceeds
to Karaj in the company of the Russian ambassador. The repetitive
nature of his prose shows as if the king has separation anxiety from his
capital. He brings along some of his courtiers and keeps sending them

---

[21] The edition I use is Naser al-Din Shah Qajar, *Safarnameh Naser al-Din
Shah/The Travelogue of Naser al-Din Shah* (Isfahan: Mash'al Publications,
no date).

back while keeping others with him. He tells us he hunted a rabbit and saw a few British emissaries at the same time. Naser al-Din Shah has a sharp eye for the natural beauties of his realm, and is particular in telling us which tribe or person owns what part of the landscape he visits. Eventually the royal company reaches Rasht in Northern Iran and from there reaches Bandar-e Anzali, where the Russian royal navy and warships are awaiting him. One early morning the royal disposition is frightened out of his wits at the sight of fog, but it eventually clears, and he is happy to see the Russian ships are firing cannons in his honor.[22]

On Wednesday 16 Rabi' al-Awwal (May 14), Naser al-Din Shah and his entourage reach Hajji Tarkhan. He is as excited as a teenage boy on his first Walt Disney trip – wide-eyed, curious, observant, happy, and hurried. He gives a detailed account of how plentiful the Volga River is, how rich and cultivated its banks, how excited the inhabitants of those fishing communities were to see him arrive with his ship. He enters the city of Hajji Tarkhan, where he is received with all pomp and ceremony and is invited to watch a fire department drill, before taken to see an opera. During the following days he visits the Muslim communities in the region, especially a Shi'a mosque run by local Iranians. From Hajji Tarkhan he eventually finds his way to Moscow, where he is received by the local dignitaries, and invited to watch a ballet. In Moscow he visits the Kremlin, followed by a visit to an ethnographic museum, in which he reports realistic representations of various people who were on display.[23] Naser al-Din Shah seems to have read other travelogues of this period, for he very much follows the standard narratives of Iranians as they visit abroad – visiting institutions, noting aspects of the local and regional arts and sciences, industries and factories, military and political apparatus. He is nowhere near Europe yet, and he is fully in control of the prose of his consciousness, where he is, what he is doing, and what his visit in Russia means.

The Qajar monarch finally reaches the Russian capital St Petersburg where he and his entourage are royally welcomed by Alexander II (reigned 1855–1881). A few times during his Russian visit Naser

---

[22] Ibid.: 1–14.   [23] Ibid.: 14–24.

al-Din Shah writes about Russian royalties going to "Farangestan/ Europe," such as the Russian Empress going to "Farangestan" for treatment of her chest pains,[24] or that the Emperor and his wife and Crown Prince were going to "Farangestan."[25] This clearly indicates he has a conception of "Europe" quite independent of Russia, which means even in his own words what he writes about Russia (and perforce the Ottomans) is not about "Europe." In other words, we still see him traveling from one to another imperial setting – his own, Russian, Ottoman, and European. Meanwhile, in Russia the king is deeply impressed by how in Haji Tarkhan, Moscow, and St Petersburg he keeps seeing pigeons who do not run away when they see people.[26] While in St Petersburg, his love for photography takes him to the studio of a prominent Russian photographer who takes his royal portrait, something we will soon see him do also in Europe and in Ottoman territories.[27] Much of the Qajar King's attention in this travelogue is directed toward detailing the pomp and ceremony with which he was being received. There is an element of high expectation and assured satisfaction that his person is in fact treated royally, as an equal with the Russian emperor Alexander II. The fact that the Qajar royalty is treated equally by the Russian and European royalty deeply satisfies the Persian king.

Upon his arrival in Prussia, the Qajar patriarch is received by Emperor William I (1797–1888) and other dignitaries, including Otto von Bismarck (1815–1898), who was then at the top of his political power. But Naser al-Din Shah seems entirely oblivious or perhaps even ignorant of who these leading European royalties are, what they have achieved, and what sort of regional geopolitics is being redrawn by towering European statesmen like Bismarck. He is just mesmerized by the details of the royal welcome he is receiving, or by how far the emperor walked to see him off to his residence palace. He is all form and not an iota of substance, not a moment of reflection on what he actually sees, except an occasional reference to how handsome the soldiers giving him official welcome looked. While in Berlin, Naser al-Din Shah visits Potsdam, attends a ballet, goes to see an aquarium, travels to Wiesbaden, and then travels to Frankfurt. His itinerary here

---

[24] Ibid.: 28.   [25] Ibid.: 42.   [26] Ibid.: 34.   [27] Ibid.: 39–40.

in Germany is very much that of a tourist who might procure an all-inclusive round trip from Tehran for a couple of days and is taken by the tour guide to the most basic tourist attractions of the country. Most of his observations are casual, artificial, repetitive, reaching the point of inanity – not a single sparkle of intelligence about what he sees and what he writes. Page after endless page for thirty pages he sounds like a broken record, just like those one hears on double-decker red buses in London: pointing out the tourist attractions one after the other, though this time obsessively preoccupied with power and pomp and ceremonies.[28]

He eventually leaves Berlin and tells us the details of his sailing on the Rhone toward Coblenz and then Cologne before he reaches Belgium, where he travels to the city of Spa and gives us some description of the spring spas he visits, where he attends a magician's show. He visits the Belgian monarch Leopold II (1835–1909), though the Qajar king has no blasted clue who he is and what murderous carnage and thievery he is up to in Congo. Instead we read him tell us about his visit to the zoo.[29]

In England we hear more of the same broken record. On June 19, he crosses the English Channel, and he tells us the weather was lovely and the sea was as calm as a river.[30] He lands in Dover, where a massive crowd, he tells us, welcomes him with pomp and ceremony. Queen Victoria (reigned 1837–1901) had sent his children to welcome him. He is welcomed at Buckingham palace, where he meets various dignitaries. He visits Windsor palace where he meets Queen Victoria and they exchange royal insignia with each other. He tells us the queen had a book to be signed by all visitors, and he signs it too.[31] He visits factories, he goes to the zoo, he travels to Portsmouth, and he is invited to join the queen during official military parades. He travels to Manchester, and he spends time enjoying the Hyde Park.[32] He also visits Saint Paul Cathedral and Westminster Abbey. Alice in Wonderland: That is Naser al-Din Shah in England, minus of course the wit, the intelligence, the curiosity, and the adventurous spirit.

"Today we must go to Cherbourg Harbor in France," the Qajar king writes in his travelogue on Saturday 9th Jumada I 1290 (July 5, 1873).

[28] Ibid.: 42–72. [29] Ibid.: 82. [30] Ibid.: 84. [31] Ibid.: 93.
[32] Ibid.: 112.

We woke up very early in the morning. During these eighteen days in
London it was always cloudy. We did a lot of shopping in London too. At
any rate, the English Crown Prince … the Foreign Secretary … as well as
Prince Alfred and Prince Arthur and others all came and we boarded a royal
carriage and drove towards the train station. A large crowd had gathered
mournfully [on our way.] It was quite evident that all the people of England
were truly sad we were leaving.[33]

That very much sums up the texture of Naser al-Din Shah's travelogue – who among the top aristocracy and dignitaries of his host
countries welcomed him; how honorably he was treated; how happy
were people to see him arrive and how sad to bid him farewell; what
lovely places he saw; how handsome the soldiers looked; what precious
things he bought; whether he was feeling well or a bit under the
weather. He is welcomed in Cherbourg, and with all proper etiquette
and ceremony, sent off to Paris. In Paris he of course visits Champs-
Élysées and Place de la Concorde. But here in Paris he engages in a bit
of understating the French politics. The bed he is given to sleep in while
in Paris belongs to Napoleon I, he reports to us, the very bed on which
the French world conqueror had wedded Marie Louise, the Austrian
archduchess.[34] He finds the French a bit morose and forlorn, but they
still cry out their best wishes for him: "Vive the Persia King" he tells us
he heard them say. He reports that there are many monarchists in
France now. But they are all divided into multiple factions. There are
also "red republicans" and more moderate republicans. He says unless
they make up their minds, these French would be in trouble.[35] Mind
you, this is May 1873, just over two years after the monumental events
of the Paris Commune from March 8 to May 28, 1871, and the
publication of Karl Marx's *The Civil War in France* (1871). Naser
al-Din Shah eventually finds his way to the Arch de Triumph, from
there he reports how the ambassadorial dignitaries came to pay him a
visit. He of course visits Les Invalides: "When something great
happens, like a major military victory, or something like that, they fire
cannon balls from Les Invalides. They did so upon and in honor of our
arrival."[36] He visits a "panorama" screening, which he tells us was
invented by an American, and is quite flabbergasted by the 360-degree

[33] Ibid.: 128.   [34] Ibid.: 132.   [35] Ibid.: 132–133.   [36] Ibid.: 141.

spectacle he sees. He of course visits Notre Dame de Paris, and Jardin du Luxembourg, goes to see some factories, finds his way toward the Louvre, and of course the Paris zoo and botanical gardens are also on his itinerary. He is received at Élysée Palace for an official soiree. He attends a circus and is quite impressed by how a horse was sitting and eating at a table, while another horse was attending to it.[37] He finally leaves Paris for Dijon on the 20th of May, and from there he leaves France for Switzerland, arriving in Geneva.

Naser al-Din Shah and his entourage arrive in Geneva and are received by the local dignitaries. He goes to his hotel residence and reports how people had gathered to welcome him along the way. Soon he boards a ship and goes for the tour of Lake Geneva. They stop in Vevey and have lunch at Hotel Des Trois Couronnes (I have visited this hotel in Vevey). The Qajar king has a lovely time and finds the Swiss women quite pretty.[38] From Geneva he then travels to Turin in Italy, where he is received by Victor Emmanuel II (1820–1878). He spends Friday, July 25, in the company of the king of Italy, visiting a museum of armory. After sharing a discussion about a recent hunt with Victor Emanuel II, the Qajar king travels from Turin to Milan, where he goes for a visit to the city cathedral.[39] From Milan he goes to Salzburg in Austria and then to Vienna, where he visits an exposition in which Iran has a pavilion, and he expresses his satisfaction at the sight.[40] After some more hunting with the royalty and taking a few of his portraits at a local photography atelier, he eventually finds his way to Brindisi where the Ottoman authorities had prepared a ship for him sailing toward Istanbul.[41]

In Brindisi the Persian monarch notes how this port city was rich in olive production, and how it was a key strategic point for the link between England and its Indian colony.[42] Near Greece he is reminded of Plato and Aristotle and of the battles between the Ottomans, the Russians, and the British powers.[43] He finally approaches the capital of the Ottoman Empire where "almost three thousand of the Iranian residents of Istanbul sailing on five ships" are among the Ottoman and Iranian dignitaries coming to welcome the Qajar monarch.[44]

---

[37] Ibid.: 161–162. [38] Ibid.: 168. [39] Ibid.: 179. [40] Ibid.: 195.
[41] Ibid.: 211. [42] Ibid.: 213. [43] Ibid.: 215. [44] Ibid.: 219.

Of his host Sultan Abdülaziz (reigned 1861–1876), he writes, "The age of Sultan is forty-four – he is as old as I am." Indeed, Abdülaziz was born on February 9, 1830, and Naser al-Din Shah on July 16, 1831. He visits Abdülaziz at Dolmabahçe Palace and makes sure to tell us how the Sultan came down "to the bottom of the stairs" to welcome him.[45] Naser al-Din Shah spends Tuesday 24 Jumada II (August 19, 1873) receiving various ambassadors at his residence. During the rest of his Istanbul stay he has an official lunch with the Sultan, visits Hagia Sophia, receives representatives of the Jewish community, "who were wearing European suits," and attends a magician's show. From Istanbul he sails toward the east of the Black Sea, coming to the port city of Poti in Georgia, and from there travels through the Caucuses on the very last leg of his journey home.

Early in the morning of Wednesday 3 of Rajab (August 27), the Persian monarch gets up bright and ready, prays, recites from the Holy Quran, and goes back to sleep, then wakes up and receives the news from his kingdom that all is peaceful and prosperous.[46] Upon his arrival in Poti, Grand Duke Michael Nikolaevich (1832–1909), the Governor General of Caucasia, whom Naser al-Din Shah introduces to us as "the brother of the emperor,"[47] comes to welcome him. From Poti he soon boards a train toward Tbilisi, then to Baku, Ganja, Shaki, and eventually sails toward the Anzali port, but the Caspian Sea is quite stormy, and it takes His Majesty quite a commotion to land in his own homeland and go to a high tower and thank God Almighty for his safe return and well-being.[48]

At the end of the edition I have been reading, there is a note that Naser al-Din Shah's travelogue was printed in the official state printing house on 6 Safar 1291 (March 25, 1874), some seven months after it was completed by His Majesty on 13 Rajab 1290 (September 6, 1873).

An/Other Traveler

As the fates would have it, Naser al-Din Shah met a counter-narrator, a traveler of different sort, who was as enthusiastic about his travels as the Qajar monarch was and yet told a global history entirely different than the one the itinerant Shah was writing in his travelogues. Seyyed Jamal al-Din al-Afghani (1838–1897) was the antidote of Naser al-Din

---

[45] Ibid.: 222.   [46] Ibid.: 236.   [47] Ibid.: 238.   [48] Ibid.: 252.

Figure 8 "Approach to the Lake Geneva, Villeneuve, Switzerland. 19th century scene. After the engraving by E. Finden, after the drawing by C. S. Stanfield." The mental images that emerge in the writings of these travelers are markedly different from the European imageries of themselves or of others they encountered. If read closely and carefully, a whole new world emerges from the pages of these Persian travelogues, a world in which Europe is integral to the rest of the globe, not separated and fetishized as something strange and unusual, coveted or despised. There is no doubt a sense of wonder and amazement about these travelers' prose, but it is equally evident about anywhere they visit, in Asia, Africa, the Americas, or Europe. We would miss that sense of amazement and wonder if we were to just focus on and privilege the European segments of their travel accounts. Reprinted with permission from Lebrecht Music & Arts/Alamy Stock Photo.

Shah and his ultimate undoing. Seyyed Jamal was some seven years younger than the Qajar king and died within a year after one of his followers assassinated Naser al-Din Shah. Al-Afghani was a restless and adventurous Islamist who became instrumental in mobilizing multiple Muslim nations into a defiant political consciousness. He was the

political conscience of his anticolonial age. According to scholars who
have studied his life closely, "Although for much of his life he claimed
to be of Afghan origin, probably in order to present himself as a Sunni
Muslim and to escape oppression by the Iranian government, overwhelming documentation now proves that he was born and spent his
childhood in Iran."[49] His early life and education was first in his
hometown of Asadabad near Hamadan in Iran, followed by more
advanced studies in Qazvin, Tehran, and Najaf and Karbala in Iraq.
From his youth he was attracted to the radical teachings of the Sheikhi
school, the most widespread Shi'i millenarian philosophy of the time.

From the Iraqi sacred cities, in 1856 al-Afghani left for India where
the Indian uprising (what the British called "the Great Mutiny")
against the British colonialism had just commenced. "After India he
may have gone to Mecca, Baghdad, the shrine cities, and perhaps
Istanbul."[50] Thus commenced his lifelong peripatetic life traversing
the Qajar and Ottoman territories and then to British-occupied India
and back deep into Europe. He was both attracted to power and
repelled by it – had the illusion that it could influence power and the
audacity to break loose from it. Everywhere he went, he claimed he
was from somewhere else. In the Arab world he pretended he was an
Afghan. In India he pretended he was a Turk. The British suspected
him to be a Russian agent; Iranians thought he was an agent of the
British.[51] By 1870 we find him in Istanbul giving lectures at the newly
founded Darülfünun, "comparing philosophy to prophecy not wholly
to the advantage of the latter and implicitly calling prophecy a craft."[52]
The religious establishment in Istanbul had him expelled from the

---

[49] For a judicious study of al-Afghani, see Nikki R. Keddie, *An Islamic Response to
Imperialism: Political and Religious Writings of Sayyid Jamal ad-Din "al-
Afghani"* (Berkeley, CA: University of California Press, 1983). I have also
examined his significance in detail in my book *Shi'ism: A Religion of Protest*.
Nikki Keddie has also a good encyclopedic entry on him in *Encyclopedia
Iranica*, "AFḠĀNĪ, JAMĀL-AL-DĪN," available online here:
www.iranicaonline.org/articles/afgani-jamal-al-din. Accessed July 29, 2017.
My references are to this last source. I prefer Keddie's account precisely
because her Orientalist suspicions of all the primary Persian and Arabic sources
she uses result in a bland narrative that balances al-Afghani's revolutionary life.

[50] Ibid.

[51] In my book, *Shi'ism: A Religion of Protest*: chapter 6, I have a section on his
life and career in which I expand upon this unique ability of al-Afghani to
overcome identity politics.

[52] Nikki Keddie, "AFḠĀNĪ, JAMĀL-AL-DĪN," *Encyclopedia Iranica*.

capital of the Ottoman Empire.[53] He spent the next decade
(1871–1879) in Cairo, teaching philosophy, reconfiguring the intellectual disposition at the heart of the Muslim world. This decade of al-
Afghani's prolific life in Cairo coincided with two of Nasr al-Din
Shah's travels to Europe in 1873 and 1878. As the Qajar monarch
was enjoying the company of Russian, Ottoman, and European kings,
queens, and sultans, "from 1875 on Afghani entered directly into
Egyptian nationalist and anti-British politics in several ways."[54] The
towering Egyptian critical thinker and revolutionary activist Mohammad Abduh (1849–1905) was his principal disciple in this period.
Because of his agitations against the British and the French, he was
finally expelled from Cairo, "and he went back to India, where he
continued his anti-British activities and published a major treatise, 'The
Refutation of the Materialists,' which was directed rather against the
pro-British Sir Sayyed Ahmad Khan than against materialism."[55] After
the British arrested and expelled him from India he went to London, to
the very heart of empire, where he invited his disciple Mohammad
Abduh to join him and where together they published the groundbreaking newspaper *Urawa al-Wuthqa*, a revolutionary event in the
rise of Pan-Islamism in the Arab and Muslim world. In 1886 he went
back to Iran and spent more than a year agitating against the British,
which resulted in Naser al-Din Shah having him expelled to Russia. Al-
Afghani went to Russia and spent two years (1888–1889) trying to
provoke the Russians against the British.

Seyyed Jamal al-Din al-Afghani was the antidote of Naser al-Din
Shah of Qajar, his exact nemesis, his doppelgänger, his undoing. In a
different life, they could have swapped places. If conservative Qajar
historians writing in English (which with laudable exceptions very
much defines the normative historiography of the period) celebrate
Nasr al-Din Shah for his diplomatic skills and for stabilizing "Persia,"
we then need to mark Seyyed Jamal's revolutionary disposition to fight
against those very colonial designs the Qajar dynasty in general was
too weak to fight and was in fact complicit in accommodating. During
Naser al-Din Shah's third trip abroad (1889), he met with al-Afghani
and invited him to Iran. But upon his arrival in 1890, Seyyed Jamal
began his habitual agitations and the Shah ordered him arrested.
Al-Afghani took sanctuary in the Shah Abd al-Azim shrine, from

---

[53] Ibid.   [54] Ibid.   [55] Ibid.

where he continued to write against the Qajar's concessions to colonial powers, which now resulted in the Tobacco Revolt, at which point Naser al-Din Shah had him arrested and expelled to Iraq. From Iraq he was instrumental in mobilizing the public sentiment against the tobacco concession, which resulted in a famous fatwa that the leading Ayatollah Shirazi wrote forbidding the use of tobacco, which resulted in a major mobilization against the Qajars and forced them to cancel the colonial concession. Seyyed Jamal collaborated with Mirza Malkam Khan and published fiery essays in his reformist venue "Qanun." By 1892, al-Afghani found his way back to Istanbul, where he kept close company with revolutionary Iranian thinkers in exile, Mirza Agha Khan Kermani and Sheikh Ahmad Ruhi in particular. Among al-Afghani's disciples in Istanbul was one Mirza Reza Kermani, who eventually returned to Iran and assassinated Naser al-Din Shah. A year after the assassination of Naser al-Din Shah, al-Afghani died of cancer in Istanbul in 1897.

After a Close Reading

What is the significance of this and similar trips that Naser al-Din Shah and many other travelers like him took outside their own homeland? What were they looking for, what did they find, and upon publishing their observations, what difference did they make upon the unfolding history of their homeland? The standard answer to such questions, specifically when asked about Naser al-Din Shah's travels, is that his close advisors such as Mirza Malkam Khan and Sepahsalar (and before them Amir Kabir) were eager to take him to Europe so he would see the "progress" Europeans had made and to allow for such "progress" also to happen in their homeland too. This assumption is flawed for many reasons, two chiefly among them.[56] First, such Eurocentric readings

[56] Naghmeh Sohrabi (*Taken for Wonder*: 74–75, et passim) rightly criticizes the scholarly literature before her excellent book for its dismissal of Naser al-Din Shah's travelogues by limiting them to their literary significance (by which they mean their role in helping with the simplification of Persian prose), and their purported impact on Eurocentric reform. She also correctly draws attention to the *written* record of these travels and their impact beyond the Qajar king's own travels. She draws attention to their significance in the context of the geopolitics of the region (87) as well as "imperial narratives of stability" (89). But despite these crucial observations, she too falls squarely into the trap of reading these texts as travelogues to Europe and even calls the king's travels

reduce the travel account of the Qajar monarch (or anyone else for that matter) only to the segments about Europe and disregard the rest, and second, no such significant change because of the monarch's encounters with Europe actually happened, as in fact evident in the Constitutional revolution that soon after his death ripped the country apart. Even before that revolution took place, one principal outcome of these journeys was actually the opposite of reform and resulted in the colonial concessions the king made to European venture capitalists, which at the end caused him far more trouble than comfort. Europe for sure was integral to geopolitics of the region that included Russian and Ottoman powers as well. Iran was increasingly drawn to these spheres of imperial power. We will therefore not get anywhere even close to that emerging, volatile, shifting world if we privilege and fetishize (as it has been historically done) "Europe" as if it were the talisman of all cures or calamities. It was not. The privileging of Europe and assuming that Iranians went there to learn how to progress and better their lives are the deepest form of epistemological colonization of the minds of the historians of this period. The very cornerstone of this assumption, a uniquely reasonable and progressive Europe bracketing the classed, gendered, and colonial carnage it was causing in and out of its own imaginative geography, never enters the historians' analysis.

The significance of these trips abroad, instead, will need to be seen in the manner in which they eventually map the world anew for their authors and readers alike or differently, in multiple manners and upon an emerging transnational bourgeois public sphere, a mapping in which the very idea "Iran" and with it the idea of "Europe" are in fact being placed on the global map.[57] These travel narratives both confirm and complicate the Orientalist fantasies of "the Europeans" even or particularly for themselves, so far as that segment of the journeys is concerned. On these pages we are witness to the formation of postcolonial cosmopolitanism, a kind of cosmopolitanism that is

inside Iran as "non-European travelogues" (79)! But even in her concern for the narrative consequences of these travelogues, Sohrabi is entirely text-based and totally disregards the active formation of the transnational public sphere and readership upon which these texts were eventually read and which are the real significance of these narratives. She also shares, without a moment of hesitation or reflection, the assumption that this "Europe" is indeed the final measure of reason and progress, and that going there was the talisman of truth.

[57] I have detailed the active place of "Persia" on the global formation of this bourgeois public sphere in my *Persophilia: Persian Culture on the Global Scene*.

rooted in the colonial experience but transcends it, points beyond it. But what would such a "postcolonial cosmopolitanism" even mean? In about two hundred years after these initial travelers of varied walks of life went around the globe in search of identity and alterity, if we were to do a quick jump cut for heuristic purposes, European philosophers like Jacque Derrida began to think about "genuine innovation in the history of the right to asylum or the duty to hospitality."[58] But what "right to asylum," and what "duty to hospitality"? Who has the right and who the duty? Within the fluid domains of three concurrent empires – the Russians, the Ottomans, and the Europeans – the fate of post/colonial nations, fragments and remnants of older empires, were being drawn at the writing of these very travelogues – both the public spheres they helped shape and the historical agency they entailed. That matrix of power and authority, the active fusion of public sphere and agential autonomy, the "right to asylum," and the "duty to hospitality" are the paramount parameters of our historical consciousness today.

Montesqv· [handwritten margin note]

From the time that Montesquieu wrote his *Lettres persanes/Persian Letters* (1721) and imagined two fictive Persians coming to Europe for a visit to the time when these real Persians we are reading now actually did so, the porous boundaries of the fiction of the emerging nation-states were being both economically and epistemically violated. Montesquieu used the fictive ruse of two familiar foreigners coming to France far more to criticize his own European domain than to lampoon "the Oriental harem." The European politics in Montesquieu's binary is as intriguing as "the Oriental harem" – and the two sides of the simile become interchangeable. As I have already argued in some detail in my *Persophilia* (2015), the famous phrase "What does it mean to be a Persian" really means "What does it mean to be European?"[59] In *Persophilia*, I have already argued that the European receptions of various aspects of the Persian culture were instrumental in the active unfolding of the structural transformation of the European public sphere (Habermas's theory). Here my proposal is that the trans-national domain of that structural transformation requires a far more

[58] See Jacque Derrida, "On Cosmopolitanism" (2001), as reprinted in Garrett Wallace Brown and David Held (eds.), *The Cosmopolitanism Reader* , (Cambridge: Polity, 2010): 413.
[59] See the chapter on Montesquieu in my *Persophilia: Persian Culture on the Global Scene*.

comparative global understanding of the context of the already globalized capital and its circulations of labor, raw material, and market,
rather than this bizarre and distorting fixation on "Muslims going to
Europe" that has for so long plagued Qajar and Pahlavi scholarship,
and in fact the overall understanding of "Islam and modernity"
project.

From Cosmographic to Cartographic

In by far the most significant work of scholarship on Qajar geographical imagination, Firoozeh Kashan-Sabet has thoroughly documented
the manner in which, in this crucial period, the worldly place of Iran as
a nation-state was being reconfigured. In her *Frontier Fictions: Shaping
the Iranian Nation, 1804–1946* (1999), Kashani-Sabet revolutionized
our understanding of the manner in which our understanding of
"Iran" as a nation-state eventually emerged in the larger context of
cosmogonic, cartographic, normative, and narrative contestations. In
this groundbreaking work she has successfully marked the period in
which, as she puts it, "a transition from a cosmographic vision of the
earth (and the nation) [changed] to a cartographic one."[60] This is an
exceptionally important distinction, but we must be careful how to
read it. That transition was not sudden and as it happened it was at
once transnational and national, and in fact the very idea of "the
nation" was being formed on that very plane. "The world," Firoozeh
Kashani-Sabet points out, "was no longer divided into seven climes
centered around Iran, and new cartographic techniques supplanted the
cosmographic perception of Iranian centrality in the universe."[61] That
universe was now worldly and present, and through such travelogues
as Naser al-Din Shah's was being narratively constituted. The point at
this stage and beyond, though, was far less expansionist in territorial
claims than in narrative speculations. Every border and every frontier
has two sides, the one inside and the one outside. Every inclusion is
also an exclusion. "Iran" was formed as "Farang" was being bordered
out. Let me explain.

---

[60] See Firoozeh Kashani-Sabet, *Frontier Fictions: Shaping the Iranian Nation,
1804–1946* (Princeton: Princeton University Press, 1999): 73.
[61] Ibid.

In order not to read Kashani-Sabet too literally, but push her useful binary forward, it is important to recall that this vast transformation of a global conception of the world did not suddenly begin or end with the Qajar period. There has never been a period over the last 1,400 years of Islamic history that geographies have not been in a state of concurrent imperial flux. When Ibn Jubair (1145–1217) moved from Andalusia to the Arabian Peninsula and wrote a magnificent travelogue, was he also not moving from a "cosmographic" to a "cartographic" conception of the world? Did Ibn Battuta or Naser Khosrow not traverse the mapped-out world of their times? Muhammad al-Idrissi (1100–1165) was a geographer and a cartographer long (very long) before the Qajars in Iran. Was his mapping the world not "cartographic" enough? Why? How? The change is not a sudden shift from a "cosmographic" to a "cartographic" in the Qajar period. The shift is from an imperial to a colonial, from imagining the globe to being imagined by it. In between cosmographic and cartographic stands the far worldlier transformation from an imperial to a post/colonial geography. Not all those Muslim imperial mappings were cosmographic, and not all geography after European modernity was cartographic. The grandest of all cosmographic illusions was and still remains "the West" itself.

If we stop reading these travel narratives as those of "traveling to Europe," read them in close detail for where they actually go and what they actually observe, and thus to locate them into the two concurrent contexts of their own total narrative spontaneity and the new imaginative geography they were in/forming, a far more compelling account of their enduring (and still unfolding) significance will emerge.

Naghmeh Sohrabi makes an astute (but alas self-defeating) observation: "Due to the place of Europe in the formulation of Iranian modernity by later historians, there has been a reification of these travel accounts placing them exclusively in the discourse of Europe as opposed to the larger developments of the period such as the geographical interests."[62] This is based on a false premise resulting in a brilliant conclusion. Europe had no place in Iranian modernity. European colonial domination of Iran had a role in the formation of an

[62] Sohrabi, *Taken for Wonder*: 82.

anticolonial modernity.[63] These are two vastly different perspectives. But Sohrabi is absolutely correct that this false premise (which alas she shares) has had a distorting effect on overriding the European segments of Naser al-Din Shah's travels (which again she shares). Naser al-Din Shah's travel narratives while visiting countries and climes outside his own homeland and realm, as indeed all the other travelogues we are examining in this book, help in constituting the transnational public sphere on which the very idea of "the nation" is being constituted and upon which they are in turn read. There is a dialectic of reciprocity at work here. These travel narratives craft the public sphere in which they are in turn read. They create their own readership and in the process form a local and regional extension of the transnational public sphere. Naser al-Din Shah's travels themselves and what he saw and what he did are far less significant than the eventual reading public his travel-ogues generate and sustain. The royal court at the immediate vicinity of the Qajar king was initially integral but ultimately antithetical to the formation of this public sphere. In other words, we have to see the paradoxical fact that in these travelogues Naser al-Din Shah in fact helps in crafting the public sphere in which revolutionary rabble-rousers like al-Afghani were read and received and in the end culmin-ated in his own undoing. In these pages Naser al-Din Shah was in fact writing his own demise!

A sustained and enduring epistemic violence has been perpetrated on this rich and multifaceted body of literature (each travelogue teaching us a slightly different thing) by systemically ignoring the totality of their narrative, their beginning, middle, and end, and cherry-picking only the European component of the journey. It is not until the emer-gence of a younger generation of scholars (here best represented by Firoozeh Kashani-Sabet) that a far more critical attention has been paid to these travelers and what they write. While Firoozeh Kashani-Sabet has single-handedly turned the field of Qajar historiography upside-down by raising crucial questions of both a cartographic and historiographic nature never raised before her, Naghmeh Sohrabi has offered an exceptionally judicious reading of these travelogues, though she has not been able to dispense with the distortive consequences of

---

[63] I have detailed the idea of "anticolonial modernity" in my *Iran: A People Interrupted*.

the deeply flawed and falsifying Eurocentric epistemology that she has inherited from her previous generations.

These texts are not the evidence of "the Muslim discovery of Europe," or of "Europology," or of "Alice in Wonderland," or "Tradition versus Modernity," or "Islam and the West," or any other such abusive, flawed, and distorting binary. Quite the contrary: These texts are the narrative evidence of a liberated sense of geography transforming the imperial imagination of Muslim dynastic histories into first colonial and then postcolonial nation-states. The coupling of "the nations" and "the states" have in turn fetishized the fictive frontiers of the postcolonial map of the world, for while "states" have been confined to and entrapped within the contours of these postcolonial boundaries, "nations" are entirely and categorically liberated from them. What we are reading in these travelogues is in fact the textual evidence of the emergent public sphere on which each and every one of these nations has been imagined and formed. The amorphous idea of "Europe" was colonially coterminous with the formations of these nations and their narrations on these transnational public spheres. Naser al-Din Shah among other travelers was not going to a fixed destination called "Europe" simply because his and other travel narratives like it were in fact instrumental in making the imaginative geography of that designation possible. He made "Europe" read like "Europe" by writing it. As such, "Europe" was not the telos of these trips, as has been hitherto assumed and trusted. De-Europeanizing our reading of these texts, and thus decentering Europe epistemically, liberates the postcolonial critical thinking in a manner that enables a renewed significance in our reading of these precious texts and with them the public sphere and postcolonial agency they had enabled. If the imaginative geography of nations has been hitherto trapped inside the territorial boundaries of colonial cartography, the corporeal mobility of these travelers into and out of those fictive frontiers is the surest evidence of the fluidity and permeability of worlds now presumed to be impermeable and transfixed.

7 | *Hajj Sayyah Leads a Peripatetic Life*

The journey took me to a garden
I knew in my early youth –
And I stood there for a while
For my heartbeat to calm down –
I heard a palpitating sound
And when the gate opened
I suddenly fell on the ground
When Truth rushed out –

> Sohrab Sepehri (Mosafer/Traveler, Babol, Spring 1966)

How did we get here from there? It never ceases to amaze me how from the lumbering lunacies of those royal visits around the world we eventually reached the point where truth mattered, when a robust poetic voice could stand up and look around the world and wonder with Sepehri's piercing gaze – reversing the colonial gaze against its own banalities and evil. We were lost souls, forgotten to ourselves, in the full grip of nasty colonial conquests, our selves lost to others, and here there was a band of travelers gently and haphazardly finding their way around the globe, mastering a fresh prose to write it, remapping it, allowing themselves to reimagine it, cultivating in themselves the triumphant courage to look back – not at "Europe," but at the world. They learned the new world by walking its earth, breathing its air, feeling its fire, sailing its winds and tasting its waters. It took some two hundred years for Iranian travelers to produce a poet like Sepehri and draw a global map on which his "Traveler" could walk to the garden of his early youth and prostrate to truth rushing out.

Luxurious Buffooneries Undone

While traveling through Austria, on Monday 9 Jumada II (August 4, 1873), Naser al-Din Shah was invited to join a hunting expedition with the Austrian emperor, after which to go for an official dinner to his palace. The following day the Qajar patriarch wakes up and has his picture taken by an official photographer. He loved photography, especially having his own pictures taken by professional photographer. In the evening, His Royal Majesty goes to watch a ballet at the Vienna Opera House and he notes in his travelogue how much he loved it: "Despite the fact that we had not had dinner yet, we did not wish it to end. It finally ended and we left and the emperor accompanied us all the way down to the carriage. We arrived at the train station, came home, had dinner, and went to bed late."[1]

About five years after such luxurious ambiance surrounding a Persian royalty traveling through the world, a different traveler embarked on a different itinerary to discover a vastly different vision of the planet he shared with the selfsame Naser al-Din Shah. In this chapter, I wish to dwell on the extraordinary character of Hajj Muhammad Ali Sayyah (1836–1925) and his *Khaterat/Memoirs* (1878) and *Safarnameh/Travelogue*. In his early twenties, Hajj Sayyah ("Mr. Traveler," if we were to get the Persian humor of his nickname) embarked upon a journey around the globe that would last almost two decades and take him from Iran to Central Asia, to Europe, to the United States – where he lived for about a decade, became a US citizen, and met with the eighteenth US president, Ulysses S. Grant (in office 1869–1877) – before he traveled to Japan and China. What is particular about Hajj Sayyah's travels is that they are decidedly global in their expanse, and thus we might measure their contributions to the active formation of what today we might call a non-unitary "nomadic subject." While still in Iran, he tells us, he was being cajoled to marry his cousin and forced into a domestic life when he decided to run away from it all and see the world. He faked his own death while still traveling in Iran in a gesture of supreme symbolic significance in anticipation of new lives he would discover in these journeys, before he embarked upon his peripatetic life around the planet. What prompted this journey around the globe, whence the wanderlust, wherefore the return?

Restored to their textual totality, the travel narratives we are reading together here, whether by a monarch like Naser al-Din Shah or a poor man like Hajj Sayyah, dismantle the false binary opposition presumed between "the West and the Rest." Disabused from their misreading,

---

[1] Naser al-Din Shah Qajar, *Safarnameh Naser al-Din Shah/The Travelogue of Naser al-Din Shah*: 197–201.

they in fact do precisely the opposite of what they are forced and manhandled to do: to cross-authenticate "the West" and its metaphysical primacy of meaning. The act of re-reading these texts in the totality of their planetary map is as much liberating for "the Rest" as it is for "the West." The exaggerated metaphysics of Reason and Progress attributed to "the West" have already ended up in the death camps of Auschwitz and Dachau, and in the post-Holocaust crisis of meaning it has dismantled the project of European modernity. The colonized minds operating on the colonial edges of "area studies" (in which Qajar historiography squarely belongs with minor but important exceptions) has been subservient to this false celebration of "the West" by documenting its own marginality. The task of the postcolonial critical thinking is to bring together the postmodern critique of the European Reason within the project to the postcolonial critique of progress from without to rethink the very colonial underpinning of colonial modernity anew. No articulation of the postcolonial subject is possible without this overdue critique.

Dying before Your Death

Hajj Mohammad Ali Sayyah Mahallati (1836–1925) was a revolutionary blessing to his own age, and today he is a nightmare for any Eurocentric attempt to read his life and travels – for his meanderings around the world cannot be pinned down to Europe, though because of his travels through the United States he has been labeled with yet another outlandish anachronistic term: "Iranian-American" and a champion of "human rights"!

Mirza Mohammad Ali Mahallati, known as Hajj Sayyah, was born to a prominent Shi'i clerical family and raised in Mahallat in central Iran.[2] After his early education, his father Molla Mohammad Reza

---

[2] For an introduction to Hajj Sayyah's life and thoughts, see the excellent essay in *Encyclopedia Iranica*, ḤĀJJ SAYYĀḤ, available online here: www.iranicaonline.org/articles/hajj-sayyah. Accessed August 8, 2017. There is an even more detailed and up-to-date essay on him available in Persian, "Haj Sayyah Mirza Mohammad Mahallati," *Danesh-nameh Jahan-e Islam*, available online here: http://rch.ac.ir/article/Details/9295. Accessed August 8, 2017. The best source of biographical information about Hajj Sayyah is of course his own book, *Khaterat-e Hajj Sayyah: Doreh-ye Khof va Vahshat/Memoirs of Hajj Sayyad: The Period of Fear and Terror*. Edited by Hamid Sayyah and Seifollah Golkar (Tehran: Sepehr Publications, 1967). For an excellent

Mahallati sent him to Tehran to further his scholastic learning. In Tehran, at this time the cosmopolitan capital of the Qajar dynasty, his paternal uncle Molla Mohammad Sadegh Mahallati took control of his nephew's education and soon sent him off to Iraqi seminaries in Karbala and Najaf for more advanced studies. Right here it is important to keep in mind that the young seminarians attending these schools in Najaf and Karbala came from all over the Muslim world, and their campuses and dormitories were the hotbed of political discussions and critical thinking about the past, present, and future of their homelands in the Muslim world. The first cosmopolitan environments in which Hajj Sayyah becomes regionally and globally conscious is right here in the Shi'i and by extension Muslim scholastic contexts of Iran and Iraq. After he completes the initial stages of his scholastic learning, Hajj Sayyah returns from Iraq to Iran where his uncle Molla Mohammad Sadegh wants him to marry his daughter, Hajj Sayyah's cousin.[3]

comparative reading of Hajj Sayyah's travelogue (though alas, still in the false framing of travels "to Europe") see Kamran Rastegar's *Literary Modernity between the Middle East and Europe: Textual Transactions in 19th Century Arabic, English and Persian Literatures* (London: Routledge, 2007) – particularly part 3 on "Literary Modernity between the Middle East and Europe": 75–144. The section includes a pioneering comparative assessment of Persian, Arabic, and European travel narratives.

[3] Naghmeh Sohrabi abuses this reference to a potential marriage to his cousin by sarcastically remarking about Hajj Sayyah, "who left Iran in the early 1860s to escape marriage to his cousin" (See Sohrabi, *Taken for Wonder*: 106). Writing this phrase in English carries the negative connotation of marrying one's cousin, which is a perfectly normal practice in Iran and many other cultures and has no negative connotations. The phrase also makes a mockery of Hajj Sayyah's lifetime of traveling and political engagements as all caused by "escaping marriage to his cousin." In the *Encyclopedia Iranica* entry on Haj Sayyah, the more responsible scholar, Ali Ferdowsi, contextualizes that phrase by references to Hajj Sayyah's own writing about the cause of his travels. Ferdowsi suggests: "But the *Memoirs* and his other published works, particularly his *European Travelogue* strongly suggest that he left Persia ultimately because of the rising national awakening. 'Indeed the cause of my departure from Iran,' he writes later, 'was having witnessed these undeserved hardships and atrocities which were beyond the endurance of beasts, let alone men, inflicted upon poor, hapless and ignorant Persian subjects like myself.'" (*Iranica*). Ferdowsi, though, has a tendency to over-politicize Sayyah's travels. What is certain, Hajj Sayyah did not wish to be trapped inside domestic life and family responsibilities in Tehran or anywhere else for that matter – marrying his cousin or the Queen of Sheba were irrelevant in this matter. In Iraq he was already exposed to significant global events happening in his time. So "escaping marriage to his cousin" was most certainly not the reason for his travels, but nor was he a full-fledged revolutionary determined to change the world when he embarked on these travels. Somewhere

He runs away from a domestic life, travels north to the Caucuses and thus commences an eighteen-year sojourn that took Hajj Sayyah around the globe before he returned home to his family and friends to become a key player in the course of the Constitutional Revolution in Iran (1906–1911).

Upon his arrival in Tabriz and before he leaves his homeland, Hajj Sayyah arranges for a message to be sent home to his family in Mahallat that he has died, so they would give up on him. He in effect opts to die to a domesticated life and is resurrected to a worldly awareness that defines his restless, tumultuous, and morally rich and satisfying life. Here we need not have a necessarily Christian notion of being "born again": "Jesus answered and said to him, 'Truly, truly, I say to you, unless one is born again he cannot see the kingdom of God'" (John 3:3) – for we have a similar wisdom in Islam as best offered by Rumi in a poem based on a Prophetic tradition that says: "Go and die before your death/So you will not suffer the pain of dying/ A kind of death that you will enter a Light/Not a death that you will enter a grave!" At the young age of only twenty-three, perhaps a bit precocious, perhaps a product of his family's learned environment, or perhaps already politically conscious, Hajj Sayyah now realizes there are larger fish to fry outside the confinements of a domesticated life in his own homeland. It is now the late 1850s and the Shi'i millenarian Babi movement (1844–1852) has wreaked havoc on the Qajar dynasty. The revolutionary ideas of Shaykh Ahmad Ahasa'i (1753–1826) and his followers' formation of the Shaykhi school of Shi'ism are turning into potent political uprisings. In his early twenties, Hajj Sayyah could not have been totally immune to all these tumultuous events among all the social and intellectual events of his homeland. From Mahallat to Tehran, from Iran to Iraq, Hajj Sayyah had already shifted gears in his worldly consciousness enough, long and formative years before he "left for Europe" and beyond, to realize something significant was happening around the globe and he wanted to be part of it. Before he went to see the world, the world had come to see him. It is imperative to keep in mind that by the middle of the nineteenth century Iran was in the eye of the storm in much that was happening in

in between these two exaggerations is where Hajj Sayyah's temperament would lie. Marriage, as he says specifically in his own words, would have trapped him in a domesticated life in his homeland.

the world – regionally and globally. So, the image of a wide-eyed "Alice in Wonderland" leaving a closed society for an open "West" is a prototypical colonial concoction (shared by the colonized minds of later scholarship) we need to discard when reading these travelogues.

In the Caucuses commences Hajj Sayyah's next cosmopolitan education, where he learns Turkish, Armenian, and Russian in addition to the native Persian and scholastic Arabic he already knew by that time. This is the heyday of Russian revolutionaries and their political agitations against the czarist empire in the region, in which Hajj Sayyah is a participant observer. The Iranian, Iraqi, and now Russian political environments are being actively transfused into a multilingual and multicultural consciousness entirely independent and long before he spent a relatively short time in Europe. A key question is how did Hajj Sayyah pay for his living costs and finance his trips. Here again the multilingual context of these environments is crucial, for we know that while in the Caucuses he gained "employment as an instructor in Arabic and Persian in a school in Tbilisi."[4] From the Caucuses, Hajj Sayyah went to Istanbul, where he learned Turkish and began his study of European languages, and from Istanbul he traveled to Europe, where he learned some French, German, and English, and met with some European and Russian dignitaries. How did he know about such towering European leaders like Garibaldi and Bismarck? Where had he learned about European politics? Certainly not upon his arrival in Europe. From Europe he sails to the United States, and from there he travels to Japan, China, and India. In India he visits Agha Khan Mahallati, the revered leader of the Isma'ili community, and his fellow Mahallatis recognize him and inform his family back in Mahallat that he is alive and well. His mother writes a letter to Agha Khan and asks him to send his son home. Thus, he returns home after eighteen years of traveling literally around the globe, without any one of the regions he visited ever being his destination. His destiny and his destination were always his own homeland, which he now morally and imaginatively connected to a renewed conception of the world.

Much has been made of Hajj Sayyah's travels to and in the United States. According to one scholar who has studied this particular aspect of his travels closely, Hajj Sayyah "entered the United States at New York and spent nearly ten years traveling around the country.

---

[4] *Iranica.*

He repeatedly met with Ulysses Grant, the U.S. president from 1868 to
1876 ... He eventually found his way to San Francisco and there,
according to the decree issued by the District Court of the 12th Judicial
District of the State of California, became a naturalized U.S. citizen on
May 26, 1875."[5] Hajj Sayyah's own son, however, in his introduction
to his father's *Memoirs* downplays the significance of any such official
citizenship and tells us that his father obtained certain "traveling
documents" (*Tasdiq-nameh*) sufficient only for his travels to China
and Japan, "for China and Japan did not have diplomatic relations
with Iran and therefore did not recognize an Iranian passport."[6] On
another occasion in the course of his *Memoirs*, Hajj Sayyah himself
refers to having asked his family in Mahallat to send him his "Tazkireh" that he had obtained from the United States to travel to China
and Japan.[7] This Tazkireh could also be a mere visa, or traveling
document. In his *Memoirs*, Hajj Sayyah also refers to this whole
incident of seeking refuge in the US embassy as a "Vaqe'eh-ye Asaf-
nak/A Sad Incident."[8] He in fact corroborates his son's report that he
only obtained this Tazkireh to ease his travel to China and Japan.[9] He
also says he has given a detailed account of this in his travelogue
"Abroad/Kharejeh." Here Hajj Sayyah mentions specifically that he
was reluctant to tell the US ambassador in Iran the circumstances of his
arrest and incarceration out of "a sense of nationalism/gheyrat-e
vatanparasti," and then he adds, "because in Iran to be subject to
tyranny is the cause of admonition and to be a tyrant is a source of
pride."[10] Could it be that Hajj Sayyah had indeed become a US citizen,
but his son was downplaying the fact lest his having "become an
American" might compromise his father's reputation as a prominent
Iranian patriot? It is equally possible that his having become a

[5] Ibid.
[6] See Hamid Sayyah's Introduction to his father's book, *Khaterat-e Hajj Sayyah/
Memoirs*: 2, document.
[7] Ibid.: 433.   [8] Ibid.
[9] Other scholars also specifically indicate that Hajj Sayyah's travel documents
issued by the US were only limited to grant him entry into Japan and China.
See Bert G. Fragner, *Persische Memoirenliteratur als Quelle zur neueren
Geschichte Irans* (Wiesbaden: Steiner, 1979): 43. But the date of this study
(1979) is much earlier than further work reflected in the *Iranica* entry, which is
dated 2012.
[10] Ibid.: 434–435.

naturalized US citizen is later exaggerated by later "Iranian-Americans," as they call themselves, to generate a legitimate genealogy for themselves?

Be that as it may, Hajj Sayyah eventually leaves the United States for Japan, and from there he travels to China, Singapore, Burma, and India. According to the same scholar preoccupied with Hajj Sayyah's US visit, "Very little is known about the details of his travels and activities in the U.S., as the journal of travels in North America which he claims to have kept, and which probably formed the remainder of his published *Book of Travels in Europe*, has not yet been found."[11] In absence of any evidence, it is hard to say what exactly is the significance of his sojourn in the United States. The enthusiasm of this one particular scholar, who himself is US-based, about Hajj Sayyah's visit to the United States must be curbed for now until such time that we have more evidence of what he did actually do or say about the United States.[12] We do of course know that during the heyday of his troubles in Iran he did once seek refuge in the US legation in Tehran. Nevertheless, as we gather a more complete knowledge of Hajj Sayyah's traveling around the globe and in his own homeland, a completely different image of him emerges, apart from any particular significance being attributed to any part of his journeys – except his overwhelming concern about and consequences of these travels for his own homeland.

Remapping the World

The most extraordinary aspect of Hajj Sayyah's *Memoirs* is the fact that he began writing it in India toward the end of his globetrotting and just before he arrived in Iran, and that the entirety of it is almost exclusively about his travels inside Iran and his observations about the foregrounding of the Constitutional Revolution of 1906–1911. Only a few pages of the long book are devoted to short descriptions

[11] *Iranica.*

[12] For the Persian translation of an interview that Hajj Sayyah purportedly did while in the US, see Ali Ferdowsi, "Goftogu ba Hajj Sayyah/Conversation with Hajj Sayyah" (*Bokhara*, Tir 1389/June–July 2010). Available online here: http://bukharamag.com/1389.04.2107.html. Accessed August 9, 2017. The interview, if authentic, is replete with silly Orientalist clichés by both the interviewer and the responses he attributes to Hajj Sayyah himself. Even the translator of this "interview" himself is suspicious of some of the outlandish remarks that the interviewer attributes to Hajj Sayyah.

of multiple tours he took abroad, both before he arrived in Iran and during his stay in his homeland. He of course constantly refers to the travelogue he has written while traveling abroad.[13] Benefiting from his command of multiple languages and cultures, close to two decades of traveling around the globe, and a deeply committed and principled mind, his primary concern is to write about his own homeland. His observations are therefore informed by a sharp set of critical eyes and consistent and systematic criticism of what he sees in Iran. This gives Hajj Sayyah's observations a very peculiar reflective character – looking at his own homeland as if from afar while close up and personal. Here in his *Memoirs,* he is not telling us what he sees abroad. But what he has seen abroad is informing his observations about Iran. He was worldly before he left and he returned even more worldly than he was. His prose, as a result, is a richly dense and informed prose, a worldly prose, composed by the cosmopolitan cast of his character. His *Memoirs,* as a result, is the site of the emplotment of Iran into a global context as he had seen and experienced it.[14]

(rel.
beтω.
worldly
&
cosmopoli-
tan?)

[13] Naghmeh Sohrabi altogether dismisses Hajj Sayyah as having written a travelogue! She writes, "Hajj Sayyah, who undoubtedly defined himself as a traveler (thus the moniker of *Sayyah*, or well-traveled), did not necessarily produce what constituted a travelogue in the 1860s when he traveled" (Sohrabi, *Taken for Wonder*: 106). This unfortunately is a bad joke. Within his *Memoirs,* Hajj Sayyah repeatedly, with detailed dates, tells us of his multiple travels all over the world, in Asia, Africa, the Muslim world, and Europe, and is proud to have traveled to "seventy-five cities" around the world during these journeys! (See Sayyah, *Memoirs*: 214). Sohrabi, however, has a legitimate point about how much later after Hajj Sayyah's death, another editor, Ali Dehbashi, published a portion of Hajj Sayyah's travelogues as "travel to Europe" because it fit the genre. But alas, again, Sohrabi herself is squarely blindsided within the selfsame trap when she says the "destination" of Hajj Sayyah's travels was Europe, which it most certainly was not.

[14] The only serious scholar who to the best of my knowledge has taken the entirety of Hajj Sayyah's travels into account and specifically written of his travelogues as his observations about the world is Roxane Haag-Higuchi in her excellent essay "Touring the World, Classifying the World: The Iranian Hajj Sayyah and His Travel-Writing" in Roxane Haag-Higuchi and Christian Szyska (eds.), *Erzählter Raum in Literaturen der islamischen Welt/Narrated Space in the Literature of Islamic World* (Wiesbaden: Harrassowitz Verlag, 2001): 149–160. But that global perspective still does not prevent her from the Eurocentric reading of this literature and considering Hajj Sayyah as an example of those who traveled to Europe and recorded their observations regarding "modernization and progress, which was encroaching on their native countries" (ibid.: 149). Astonishing, indeed, is this plague of Eurocentrism when a scholar actually cares to read the entirety of a travelogue and writes so

Equally extraordinary is the fact that almost halfway through his *Memoirs*, Hajj Sayyah crosses the Iranian border and travels to Russia and from there commences yet another tour of the world before he comes back to Iran and resumes his narrative. In other words, there is no pomp and ceremony about his traveling abroad. He comes to Iran after almost two decades, travels through his homeland, exits his country and travels around the world, comes back and resumes telling his stories, and then deeply plunges back into the thicket of Iranian revolutionary politics. In the course of his *Memoirs*, as a result, he maps out an entirely different topography of his homeland in and out of Iran. "Iran," in other words, has no border here, for his geography is borderless. There is no indication that when he leaves Tehran and eventually enters Bandar Anzali he had intended to go to Russia, or when in Russia he had intended to go as far as England. He is just on a different emotive universe, traveling on a different map than the one presumed between "Islam and the West," or between "Iran and Europe."

From Bandar Abbas, Bandar Langeh, and Bushehr where he lands on the northern coasts of the Persian Gulf in his homeland on July 25, 1877, Hajj Sayyah travels north to Shiraz and from there to Isfahan, Kashan, and soon meets with his family in Mahallat, before he travels to and arrives in Tehran on December 9, 1877, where the ruling monarch Naser al-Din Shah summons him to his court and has a conversation with him about his travels and also has his command of French, English, and Russian tested. The Qajar monarch invites Hajj Sayyah to join his court, but he politely refuses. In these major Iranian cities, Hajj Sayyah writes about his encounters with political and clerical authorities and his disappointment at their corruption, cowardice, and opportunism. He continues to travel through Iran, write his *Memoirs*, and criticize what he

---

well on the global space he was navigating, yet still categorizes the text as an example of "19th century travel writers from the Islamic world to Europe"! Be that as it is, this short essay is by far the best close and critical analysis of Hajj Sayyah's *Travelogue* and *Memoirs* available in English – though some of the author's observations about the bifurcations Hajj Sayyah presumably makes between his "fatherland" and the world are actually reversed. He never denies his identity. He is giving Iran a new identity written in his travelogues and lived through his many travels. Toward the end of her essay, Roxane Haag-Higuchi cites Edward Said and accuses Hajj Sayyah of creating a binary opposition between the world and Iran. She of course completely misread the auto-criticism of an author who is determined to alter the course of history in his country.

sees. He holds the Qajar aristocracy and the ruling clergy chiefly responsible for the backward state of his homeland. He has seen the world (not
just "Europe") and he wants to see the best for his homeland. At this
stage and in these pages, Hajj Sayyah is chiefly responsible for articulating the notion of *vatan/homeland* and of the struggle to advance it. His
Memoirs reads like a detailed set of critical observations about his travels
inside Iran. What we have in his case is not a travelogue outside Iran, but
a traveled person traveling through Iran with sharp and informed eyes
and writing about Iran, with his trained gaze. From Tehran he eventually
travels to Mashhad, and from there to Sistan, Kerman, before returning
to Shiraz, from there moving on to Yazd, coming back to Isfahan,
Mahallat and Sultanabad, before returning to Tehran. From Tehran he
travels north to Rasht and arrives at Bandar-e Anzali. He is restless,
mobile, agitated in his prose. He has seen much. He wants to see more.

From Bandar-e Anzali, Hajj Sayyah's wanderlust intensifies and he
sails toward Astrakhan in Russia. At this point in his *Memoirs* he says:
"I have explained these areas in the volume of my travels abroad/
Siyahat-e Kharejeh."[15] He does not use the phrase "Farang" or "Farangestan," or "Europe," which means he has already a far more global
conception of his travels, as he most naturally should. In this journey,
he tells us, he eventually arrives in Moscow, visiting his brother who he
says teaches Persian in Moscow. After a few days he goes to St Petersburg, and from there to Warsaw, Berlin, Brussels, Paris, and London.
He then turns around and goes to visit Vienna, Italy; altogether, he
visits "seventy-five cities," he tells us, before he returns to Istanbul. At
this point again he mentions: "a short summary of what I have seen in
my travels abroad" is written in his "Safarnameh-ye Kharejeh"/Travelogue Abroad" (again no mention of "Europe.") He also says how
Iranians become sad upon visiting "Abroad/Kharejeh."[16] From Istanbul he sails to Jeddah, and from there he goes to Mecca and then to
Medina, and then to Alexandria, Aleppo, and moves to Iraq to Kazimayn and Basra, and from here he returns to Iran. Without interrupting his narrative, he continues to tell us how from Basra he goes to visit
Shushtar and Dezful, and from there Poshtkuh and Khorramabad –
then he comes back to his hometown of Mahallat and from there to
Tehran. From the Qajar capital he continues his travels to Isfahan and
Kurdistan, and then to Sanandaj, Salmas, Maku, Khoi, Tabriz, back to

[15] Sayyah, *Memoirs*: 213.   [16] Ibid.: 214.

Tehran, from there to Zanjan, Qazvin, back to Tehran, off to Isfahan, right before he travels back to Mecca and immediately to India, back to Mecca, turning around to come down to Iraqi sacred cities, and then again back to Tehran. It is crucial here to keep in mind that Sayyah is traveling from one city to another city – countries, climes, nation-states, borders, and boundaries mean very little or nothing to him.

Seyyed Jamal Comes to Visit

On 22 Dhu'l-Qa'dah 1303 (August 31, 1886), Hajj Sayyah informs us that none other than Seyyed Jamal al-Din al-Afghani is visiting Iran. Hajj Sayyah becomes instrumental in inviting him to Isfahan to meet with Zell al-Sultan, Naser al-Din Shah's son and the powerful governor of that significant city. But pressures mount on the visiting revolutionary and Seyyed Jamal leaves for Russia, and Hajj Sayyah becomes an immediate suspect. His affiliation with al-Afghani costs him dearly and antagonizes the Qajar court against him[17] – and this would be just the beginning of his troubles back in his own homeland.

In the course of this segment of his *Memoirs*, Hajj Sayyah gives us a precious firsthand account of Seyyed Jamal al-Din al-Afghani – who he was and what he was up to, defines him as exceedingly charismatic and persuasive, consistently refers to him with the honorific title "Agha/Sir," and places him on the top of any ten leading Muslim leaders of his age.[18] This first account of the towering Muslim revolutionary of his age is priceless in terms of its authenticity and power, accuracy, and first person eyewitness to a momentous period in Iranian and Muslim history. Hajj Sayyah tells us that although Seyyed Jamal is a Shi'a and a Seyyed in honorific descent from the Prophet, he changes his turban from white to black depending on where he is and whether he conceals or flaunts his Iranian Shi'i identity. Hajj Sayyah reports how there were those who believed Seyyed Jamal was the Promised Mahdi, but al-Afghani dismissed all these as superstitions. While in Isfahan, Seyyed Jamal visits the Safavid architectural buildings and is angered by their dire circumstances and complains to those among the Qajar authorities he meets about their silence on such calamities befallen their historical heritage. When he meets with the governor of Isfahan Zell al-Sultan privately, Seyyed Jamal admonishes him about how in "Europe,

---

[17] *Iranica.*   [18] Sayyah, *Memoirs*: 286.

China, India, and other countries, old buildings are kept in good conditions but not in Iran."[19] In other words, the point of reference for Seyyed Jamal is not solely "Europe" but "Europe, China, India and other countries." Seyyed Jamal proves to be a divisive presence in Iran for some members of the Qajar aristocracy, and the clerical class likes and admires him while others dislike and fear him. He finally leaves Iran for Russia and Europe, and Hajj Sayyah tells us he wrote and asked his brother in Moscow to welcome and host him. His brother soon sends him a picture of himself in the company of Seyyed Jamal and another mutual friend.[20] Hajj Sayyah's eyewitness account during these pivotal days in Iran is deeply informed by his global perspective, comparative assessment of politics, and deeply caring and worldly intellect.

In part because of his close affiliations with Seyyed Jamal, by September 1888 Hajj Sayyah was forced into exile to the northeastern city of Mashhad. While in Khorasan he of course continues with his travels in the surrounding areas and quite frivolously writes of a man who had pretended to be a woman and a Seyyed at that (a descendent of the Prophet) and worked as a masseuse in a women's public bath until he is discovered to be a man, and Hajj Sayyah is entrusted with the naughty news and delicate task of rectifying the issue. He does his best, he tells us, tongue in cheek, to resolve the matter, but it becomes quite a scandal.[21] While still in Khorasan, Hajj Sayyah informs us on 17 Moharram 1307 (September 13, 1889) that Naser al-Din Shah has met with Seyyed Jamal in Europe and has invited him to come to Iran. Seyyed Jamal had written to a mutual friend and informed Hajj Sayyah of his pending arrival and solicited his help and guidance.[22] Seyyed Jamal's second journey back to Iran, this time by royal invitation, is not any more successful than his first. Both the corrupt courtiers and even more corrupt members of the Shi'i clergy fear and loathe him for he exposes their cowardice and corruption. "Agha Seyyed Jamal," as Hajj Sayyah habitually calls him, does win a lot of supporters and admirers from all walks of life. But even that adds fuel to the fire of his enemies and makes them even more determined to get rid of him. Here we have a sense that Hajj Sayyah uses his penchant for traveling to get out of troubling spots. For example, soon after he realizes Seyyed Jamal is not willing to speak softly to the king and continues with his

---

[19] Ibid.: 292.   [20] Ibid.: 295.   [21] Ibid.: 309.   [22] Ibid.: 321.

agitations, Hajj Sayyah says he had to go to his hometown of Mahallat and attend to some business, and from there he commences yet another journey outside Iran to Iraq and visits Kazimayn, Baghdad, Samara, Karbala, and Najaf before returning to Iran. Such spontaneous journeys are both typical of his routines, and yet there is a rescue purpose to them too. When he realizes the kitchen is getting too hot, as it were, he opts to travel.

The bromance between the perpetually bewildered Qajar Shah and the incorrigible al-Afghani did not last, and the revolutionary rabble-rouser was kicked out of Iran again after he was suspected of fomenting revolt against the tobacco concession the Persian patriarch had given to a British colonial merchant. This was the beginning stage of the Tobacco Revolt, and the agitation against the Qajar monarch ultimately led to his assassination on May 1, 1896, by Mirza Reza Kermani, who was among the acquaintances of Hajj Sayyah, and about whom Hajj Sayyah had repeatedly warned the Qajar authorities. Hajj Sayyah gives us one of the most detailed accounts of the manner in which Seyyed Jamal had sought refuge (bast) in Shah Abd al-Azim shrine near the capital and how on the order of the Shah he was dragged out of his refuge and disrespectfully kicked out of the country. He describes the manner in which Seyyed Jamal was dragged into mud and snow, his clothing items falling off his body and his genitalia exposed as he was mounted on a mule. Later Hajj Sayyah reports how pro-Shah clergy were making fun of this scene and telling each other they had seen Seyyed Jamal's genitalia and he was not circumcised. As one of his devoted followers, Mirza Reza was going around the shrine trying to mobilize people against this indignity. Hajj Sayyah tries to portray himself as a principled follower of Seyyed Jamal, and yet he tells us his first recommendation to his mutual friends was to find Seyyed Jamal's briefcase and make sure his friend's letters to him did not end up with the security forces of the monarch. He is obviously concerned, and rightly so, that he would soon be identified with the revolutionary Seyyed Jamal and get into trouble with the authorities.[23]

---

[23] Ibid.: 331.

Traveling toward Rasht and Russia

By April 1891, Hajj Sayyah is deeply drawn to a series of public letters he and his comrades write to Qajar elite and widely circulate around the country agitating for political reform. He credits himself with the idea. But by this time in his *Memoirs* we realize he is not as courageous as he wishes his readers to read him. Yes, he is involved with these momentous events, but he carefully tries his best to stay out of trouble – to the point of collaborating with Qajar security authorities. Be that as it may, these activities ultimately result in the arrest and imprisonment of Hajj Sayyah from April 1891 to about January 1893. On April 25, 1891, Hajj Sayyah reports of his arrest and incarceration in Tehran. Among his charges was the fact that he was receiving and reading *Qanun*, a periodical published by Mirza Malkam Khan in London about which Qajar authorities were particularly fearful. What we are witnessing here is a close symbiosis in the body of these travel narratives between inside and outside the homeland, categorically blurring the porous boundaries of the emerging nation-states. While in jail, Hajj Sayyah is a cellmate with Mirza Reza Kermani, the future assassin of Naser al-Din Shah, from whom he constantly dissociates himself. Upon his release from prison he fully realized the hostile environment against him, and in February 1893 he sought refuge in the US legation in Tehran, invoking his US citizenship, where he spent about six months under their diplomatic protection.[24] He became a suspect upon the assassination of Naser al-Din Shah in 1896, but because he had warned of its possibility in writing to Qajar authorities he was left unharmed. Based on his own writings, we can conclude that Hajj Sayyah is essentially a mild-mannered reformist in the company of a leading revolutionary of his time and lays a claim on him more than he actually deserves. But on specific circumstances he does help Seyyed Jamal's message get milder and come across to Qajar tyrants' attention. Be that as it may, the letters that he and his friends write to the king, to the Qajar aristocracy, and to the clerical establishment were clearly critical of the status quo. He was a worldly-wise man; his *Memoirs* is the extension of his travels and embedded in them. He was integral to a generation of critical thinkers and activists trying to effect institutional changes.

[24] *Iranica.*

In the summer of 1901, Hajj Sayyah "embarked on yet another journey that took him to Europe, North Africa, Russia, Mecca and Central Asia. In this trip, like his earlier ones, he met with many prominent figures of the time."[25] His *Khaterat/Memoirs* is the place to look for these travelogues. You need not see a book with the word "Safarnameh/Travelogue" written on it for you to recognize it as indeed a travelogue! In fact, the significance of Hajj Sayyah's travel narratives is precisely in its crossing the borders in and out of Qajar territories and mixing his acute observations about both sides of the porous borders without much pomp and ceremony. In this case, Hajj Sayyah traveled through Iran until he reached the Persian Gulf and then from Bushehr he sailed to Djibouti and Arabia, and repeatedly performed his Hajj pilgrimage and more than once earned the title of Hajji and Sayyah! From Egypt he went to Europe, from Europe to Russia and the Ottoman territories, returning a year later in 1902 – all the while making a mockery of all subsequent scholars who disregard the actual itinerary of his travels and laser-beam only on his European journeys. He continued with his critical thinking and political activism apace and in the heyday of the Constitutional Revolution remained a crucial force in the fate of his homeland. In 1907, he traveled back to Russia, where he remained actively involved throughout the course of the Constitutional revolution for the rest of his life.[26] In his notes dating from 1905, Hajj Sayyah talks critically of the ruling Qajar monarch's repeated and useless travels to Europe, obviously comparing them with his own and other reformist and revolutionary activists' travels. He tells us all Ottomans and Europeans and Russians know that the trips Qajar ruling elite made abroad are categorically useless.[27]

The Russians and the British were particular in encouraging such useless trips to weaken the government, he tells us, and people in these countries did not pay much attention to these royal travelers except as the luxurious journeys similar to any other wealthy person. He laments

---

[25] Ibid. I cite another serious scholar who has actually read the book to corroborate my own assertions here. Compare the fact of these trips and their accounts here in *Memoirs* with Naghmeh Sohrabi's outlandish remark that what Hajj Sayyah published "did not necessarily produce what constituted a travelogue in the 1860s when he travelled" (Sohrabi, *Taken for Wonder*: 107). Hajj Sayyah's *Memoirs* contains his travelogues abroad – and not just to Europe – if someone cared actually to read it cover to cover.
[26] *Iranica.*   [27] Sayyah, *Memoirs*: 542.

the progress other countries have made and the affliction of Iran with corruption and backwardness. His point of reference is global, not "European." Both for him and for Seyyed Jamal al-Din, his hero, the frames of critical consciousness are decidedly worldly – China, Japan, India, the Russians, the Ottomans, and of course Europe (but never exclusively Europe). In his discussion of the reign of Muzaffar al-Din Shah and the Constitutional Revolution, Hajj Sayyah offers a solid geostrategic assessment of all the powers around Iran and their vested interests. He then offers a detailed, deeply informed, and nuanced reading of the causes and consequences of the Constitutional revolution.[28] Without his repeated travels in and out of Iran, all referenced with dates and details in his *Memoirs*, without his impeccably trained eye and sharp critical intelligence, none of these observations would have been possible. The epithet "Sayyah" that he was given, was just, was right, was appropriate, and he had richly earned and deserved it.

I leave Hajj Sayyah's *Memoirs* with one of his last phrases that defines his entire existence: "On 27 Safar 1325 (April 11, 1907), I travelled towards Rasht and Russia."[29] Rasht (today inside Iran) and Russia (an entirely different country) were almost interchangeable in his prose and purpose. Both sides of the Caspian Sea were his home – and with it, the rest of the world he so lovingly traveled and meticulously narrated. Hajj Sayyah was the eye of the world on Iran, wide open, critical, conscious, caring, competent, self-aware, worldly-wise. He went around the world and came to Iran to teach his homeland what it was and where in the world it was located. Toward the end of his life, his son Hamid Sayyah tells us, he (Sayyah's son) had an ambassadorial function in Russia, and had come home to visit and spent some time with his ailing father. Seeing how ill he was, Hamid Sayyah wanted to spend more time with his father. But Hajj Sayyah insists that he should go back to his duties in Russia. He is away in Russia when he hears his father had passed away. "Later I learned why he so insisted that I go back to Russia, for he had said: 'My father died missing his son, and I too must die missing my children.'"[30] All his life he had carried the guilt of having left his homeland, declaring himself dead to his parents, from which pain his father had died – and now in his own final hours he too wanted to pay homage to his own father, whom he had wronged by declaring himself dead to a homeland to

[28] Ibid.: 560–565.   [29] Ibid.: 573.   [30] Ibid.: 634.

which he had returned to resurrect the collective consciousness of an entire nation.

The Prequel

[handwritten annotation: editor invents the title]

I am now holding in my hands the book titled *Safarnameh Hajj Sayyah beh Farang/Hajj Sayyah's Travelogue to Europe* (published in Tehran in 1363/1984).[31] I have been reading it closely over the last few days, carrying it with me as I have traveled for lecture and research from New York to Ocho Rios in Jamaica and Mexico City, Tehuixtla, and Taxco de Alarcón in Mexico. The volume I am holding in my hand is a complete and unmitigated travesty of irresponsible scholarship. It is based on one single incomplete manuscript whose scribe is unknown, and no effort has been made to find out who he or she might have been. A person by the name of Habibollah has a poem of Hafez on one of its margins. Was he the scribe? Habibollah who? The manuscript was found in the library of a prominent literary figure, Mahmoud Farrokh, and subsequently entrusted to Tehran University Library. How did it end up there? Hamid Sayyah, Hajj Sayyah's son, has verified that the handwriting on the few marginalia is indeed his father's. That is a necessary but not sufficient reason to trust the handwriting. There is, however, no reason to be unduly suspicious. The book certainly reads in style and compares in prose to Hajj Sayyah's *Memoirs*, and the timing of the travels it relates corresponds to Hajj Sayyah's journeys. Then comes the real travesty: Nowhere in the text is there any indication that Hajj Sayyah actually called this book *Safarnameh Hajj Sayyah beh Farang*, or anything else remotely similar to that fictitious and delusional title. The title is entirely the figment of the editor of this volume's deeply colonized and Eurocentric imagination. While traveling in Dublin, Hajj Sayyah specifically refers to this volume simply as "Seyahat-nameh," which means "Travelogue," with no indication that he called it "Seyahat-nameh" or "Safar-nameh-ye Farang."[32] He had started writing it long before and long after he visited what today we call "Europe." The title the irresponsible editor has ahistorically, inaccurately, and erroneously given it is, as a result, an entirely false

---

[31] See Hajj Sayyah, *Safarnameh Hajj Sayyah beh Farang/The Travelogue of Hajj Sayyah to Europe* (Tehran: Nashr-e Nasher, 1363/1984).
[32] Ibid.: 509.

attribution. This title simply cannot be found anywhere in this book. In this chapter, I will refer to this book as Hajj Sayyah himself did and call it *"Seyahat-nameh/Travelogue."*

By what authority should an editor take such egregious liberty to give a book a title it simply does not have? To make the matter even more ludicrous, the very same editor spends the first few pages of the book writing an utterly inane introduction, defending the Islamic Republic and condemning colonialism! The very title he falsely attributes to the book is itself the supreme sign of a colonized mind. All roads must end up in Rome, as it were. The whole exercise is a calamity in print. Just to make the matter even worse, the copy I have obtained through Columbia University library, for which my research assistant and my librarian colleagues have spent inordinate time and effort, is a travesty of printing: Pages 17 through 32 are repeated twice, and appear right between pages 128 and 145, and there are no signs of those missing pages anywhere else in this copy of the book. The bookbinding is yet another travesty – as soon as you open the book to actually read it, the hardcover comes off and the pages begin to be at the mercy of God Almighty to stay together. More than forty years ago, when I left Iran under the Pahlavis, this very calamity was the state of bookbinding in Iran, and more than thirty years into the Islamic Republic nothing has changed – the same incompetence carried over from one dynasty to another "republic." The depth of incompetence in the current state of scholarship and critical editions in Iran could not be better staged than in this ridiculous volume of a book exceedingly important, by all accounts, in the history of Iranian encounters with its surrounding world in a crucially transformative period.

Be that as it may, and if we were to disregard all such irresponsible clumsiness in handling a precious text, the volume itself is of extraordinary significance. Hajj Sayyah's *Travelogue* begins and ends as a mixture of a memoir and a travelogue, very much on the model of his *Memoirs*. The author clearly identifies himself on the very first page: "This poor humble Mohammad Ali Sayyah on 5th of Safar 1276" [September 3, 1859]. He is precisely twenty-three years old as he writes this line, and the date corresponds with the commencement of Hajj Sayyah's travels abroad, which the editor has irresponsibly misread as "travels to Europe."[33] The author tells us that his father, Molla

---

[33] Based on this original Persian text, Hajj Sayyah's granddaughter has prepared an English translation again under the false title of "An Iranian in Nineteenth

Mohammad Reza, had commanded him to go to Mohajeran, which he tells us is a village of the Kazzaz municipality today in Central Province of Iran. His wealthy uncle receives him and he soon discovers that he intends to marry his daughter to him. There is no name or description of this poor girl, of whom we only know that she was meant to marry Hajj Sayyah, and Hajj Sayyah opted out of this marriage. What happened up to here, who did she marry if anyone, how many children did she have, if any? Nothing – she only appears as a prop in Hajj Sayyah's story. Hajj Sayyah says that they decided to delay the wedding, for it was winter and doing something haram/forbidden was difficult. There is no explanation; what in the world could this mean? Marrying one's cousin is perfectly normal and not a forbidden act. At any rate, the marriage is delayed, giving Hajj Sayyah ample time to think about the whole idea of marriage and his own future.

decision not to marry

At this point Hajj Sayyah shares with his diary and for posterity to know that if he were to marry his cousin, he would have to spend the rest of his life in this remote village "and know nothing about nothing and nobody."[34] The prospect of a domesticated life frightens him, and he decides quietly to slip out of his habitat and map out a different future for himself. Thus, he spends a sleepless night on May 13, 1860, wakes his brother Molla Mohammad Baqer up, and tells him he needs to go somewhere nearby for a visit. This part of the *Travelogue* reads a little bit dramatic: His brother follows him for a while, before Hajj Sayyah asks him to go back, exchanges his robe with that of his brother, for his brother's robe was older, then, with a pair of *giveh* (a handwoven sneaker) with no socks, a piece of cloth he used both as a table spread and a belt and his turban, three pieces of bread, and 1,000 dinars cash, he leaves the village.[35] This fusion of fact and fantasy,

escape from family

Century Europe." There is no such title in the original and by the author himself. Both the editor of the Persian original and this translator have made these titles up out of their colonized and Eurocentric imagination. See Muhammad Ali Sayyah, *An Iranian in Nineteenth Century Europe: The Travel Diaries of Haj Sayyah 1859–1877*. Translated by Mehrbanoo Nasser Deyhim. Foreword by Peter Avery (Bethesda, MD: Ibex Publishers, 1999). For a laudatory appreciation of this English translation, see Roxane Haag-Higuchi's review in *Iranian Studies* 33:1/2 (Winter–Spring, 2000): 259–261. All my citations are from the Persian original.

[34] Hajj Sayyah, *Safarnameh Hajj Sayyah beh Farang/The Travelogue of Hajj Sayyah to Europe*: 25. In deference to Hajj Sayyah's own text, I will refer to this book as he did, "Seyahat-Nameh," which is Persian for "Travelogue."

[35] Sayyah, *Travelogue*: 25–26.

drama and truth, in Hajj Sayyah's *Travelogue* is evident right here in the initial pages of the book and is sustained throughout the rest of the narrative. What we are reading therefore is a dramatization of facts by a writer who obviously enjoys both traveling and writing about his travels. He does not appear to lie. But he thrives at the prose of his own adventures.

Hajj Sayyah continues to write dramatically of traveling on foot, of fearing for losing his ability to walk, until he eventually reaches Hamadan, where he begins to practice a judicious decision not to tell strangers too much about himself. He spends the night at local mosques, speaks of arrogant mollas and of simple and hospitable mollas, takes care of his *giveh*, and eventually leaves for Bijar, where he buys a few samples of poisons in case at some point in his travels he may opt to end his life.[36] There is a straight matter-of-fact simplicity to his prose at this point when he shares this piece of rather morbid information with us. Half of his cloak is his mattress, he confides in his *Travelogue*, the other half his blanket, and his hand his pillow.[37] He travels and moves forward with various means until he reaches Maragheh. On his way, when he hears Kurdish and Turkish languages that he does not understand, he speaks of the calamity of ignorance and wishes he knew more languages than he did. Later when we read him struggle with the Italian or German language, it would be good to remember these passages when his curiosities are as much alerted while traveling in his homeland as when he is in Europe or elsewhere. He intentionally declines to accept the hospitality of strangers, for he is determined to recast his character as he travels around the world – though later on during his travels we will see him more confident and willing to accept the kindness of strangers. His *Travelogue*, however, remains his solitary confinement for his wits and whereabouts. It sustains his sense of purpose. It is therapeutic and it builds confidence in him as he progresses around the world apace – familiarizing himself with foreign lands.

"Like a Piece of Broken Wood Floating on a Sea"

In this particular narrative, Hajj Sayyah does not give us a precise date of his travels, which could be an indication that the date of writing his

---

[36] Ibid.: 30.   [37] Ibid.: 30–31.

Travelogue is sometime after the time of his actual travels, though
while still traveling. He gives us phrases like "the next day," "after
three days," "the following morning," "after a few days," and so
forth.[38] Based on these indications, it is quite possible that he is writing
at least parts off this travelogue from memory and not on a daily basis,
though there are times he tells us he sat in a café and wrote in his
Travelogue. Be that as it may, he eventually finds his way to Tabriz,
Yerevan, and from there to Tbilisi. Traveling through Echmiadzin in
Armenia, his *giveh* finally gives at just about the time that a stranger
offers him a pair of boots.[39] What is crucial to remember here is the
ease with which Hajj Sayyah travels from one city to the next without
any formal declaration of moving from one country to the next in his
Travelogue, but simply traveling from one urban setting to the next,
while he makes acute observations about the differences he sees in one
place as opposed to another. His detailed description of how for days
he had nothing to eat and was getting ready to die[40] leaves little doubt
that this entire *Travelogue* is both a concurrent and a postpartum
exercise in dramatic narrative, based on facts and truth no doubt but
also mixed with his active and excited imagination. He has an audience
in mind, and he wishes to impress upon that audience with his steadfast
determinations, his defiance of all odds, the strangeness of his circumstances. He is not lying, or does not appear to tell lies, but he does
dramatize the facts.

Eventually, Hajj Sayyah reaches Istanbul. While in Istanbul he eventually decides to travel to Paris, where we are about eighty pages into
his *Travelogue*. But his first major destination is Belgrade,[41] and from
there he eventually travels to Vienna, which he admires for its multicultural and multi-religious polity.[42] In Trieste he is fascinated by
public spaces, open markets, and tells us how he attended theaters
and visited factories.[43] He then goes to Venice and visits St. Marco
Cathedral. While in Venice his attention is drawn to young women's
education and the existence of all-female schools. Here he tells us he
had learned some Polish and French, and yet both these languages were
useless to him, for people in Venice spoke only Italian.[44] Speaking the
native languages of countries he visits remains a key concern throughout his travels. He is always modest as to how much of these languages

---

[38] See, for example, ibid.: 36, 45, 46, and 48.   [39] Ibid.: 48.   [40] Ibid.: 51–53.
[41] Ibid.: 86.   [42] Ibid.: 93.   [43] Ibid.: 105.   [44] Ibid.: 109.

he has managed to learn, as indeed very circumspect he is about his knowledge of the world in general. He is intellectually open, emotionally naked, altogether exposed and vulnerable – and these are precisely the attributes that make his authorial voice real and appealing. He is an Iranian abroad. He is becoming more and more an Iranian as he travels abroad. His identity is fortified in his encounters with the world – a worldly character, a self-knowing person, is eventually emerging in him.

Hajj Sayyah meets an Armenian person in Venice who tells him he wants to go to Paris but does not understand French, and Hajj Sayyah agrees to help him as his translator and companion on this journey – only on one condition: that they travel "sayyahaneh" (meaning casually like tourists or travelers).[45] Along with his traveling companion, Hajj Sayyah now goes to Padua, Verona, and Milan, where he even visits a prison and is deeply impressed by the humanity of the treatment of its inmates.[46] In Turin he visits a botanical garden, and notices the extraordinary respect people showed toward the picture of the Italian nationalist hero Giuseppe Garibaldi (1807–1882). People loved and admired him, Hajj Sayyah tells us, because "we were slaves to the Pope, and dominated by all other countries. This man gave us a name, and made us known among nations, and brought us together, without expecting anything from anyone."[47]

He eventually reaches Lyons and Dijon, soon to arrive in Paris, where he is flabbergasted by the spectacle of what he sees are its decidedly public spaces in which men, women, and children go for

---

[45] Ibid.: 111–112.

[46] Ibid: 121. As I was reading this copy of the book, I could not tell what happens between Turin and Valence, for this section of the copy of the book I have obtained with much difficulty (pages 129–144) is missing, and instead we have a repeat of pages 17–32 – the gift of the unsurpassed incompetence of printing houses in my beloved homeland. I am reading this part of Hajj Sayyah's book while giving a keynote in Mexico City where I have just been given a copy of a magnificent catalogue of Universidad Nacional Autónoma de México (UNAM) and am struck by the stark difference between these two volumes lying on the small desk in my hotel room: one literally coming to pieces with loose pages scarcely kept inside its ugly cover, and the other beautifully printed, bound, and illustrated. From the English translation of the book I checked, he travels through Genoa, Monaco, Nice, Toulon, Marseilles, Avignon, and reaches Valence. Upon my return to New York, I obtained another copy of the Persian original from Harvard University, thanks to my resourceful research assistant Sumaya Akkas, and double checked these missing pages from that copy.

[47] Ibid.: 127.

casual walking. Upon his arrival in Paris his pen becomes like a
camera, absorbing everything from the police stations to carriages to
the white cloth on the tables of restaurants. Along with his Armenian
companion, he finds his way to a small inexpensive hotel called
"Europa" on Boulevard Magenta. He goes out, and with his eyes
and pen swallows everything he sees. His companion says Paris is
better than paradise, to which he says we don't know about paradise
yet, so we'd better avoid comparison. But still, there is no doubting his
excitement about seeing Paris. While in Paris, he sees the arrival of
Sultan Abdülaziz to visit Napoleon III. He visits a panorama and says
the cities they showed were quite similar to what he had seen himself in
person.[48]

   The most potent part of Hajj Sayyah's observations in Paris is when
he encounters a group of French laborers cursing Napoleon III as he
passes by and wishing to see him executed just like Louis XVI.[49] Hajj
Sayyah is surprised they are doing so and engages in a conversation
with them. They educate him about French colonial conquest in
Mexico and imperial alliances with Russia, none of which is of any
benefit to his subjects. He is surprised by such observations and goes to
his hotel and asks the hotel manager if what he heard is a minority
opinion or has a more widespread presence among the French. He is
assured that this is a widespread opinion in France.[50] At this point he
becomes homesick. The hotel manager is surprised by this sudden
sentiment for his homeland. He says I thought you considered everywhere to be your home. Hajj Sayyah says he wishes people in his
homeland cared for their vatan/country as the French did.

   Hajj Sayyah continues his journey by visiting Versailles as well as the
Bibliothèque Nationale de France. A good 35 pages of this edition of
the *Travelogue* is devoted to Paris, followed by 26 pages of a detailed
description of his visit to London. He arrives in London via the
Thames River and the first thing he notices are the ships going to
America and India. Upon his arrival in London, he starts learning
English. His preoccupation with learning new languages begins while
he is still traveling in Iran and continues throughout his journeys. He
blames himself for not knowing German while in Vienna and Italian
while in Italy and expresses his happiness of knowing French while in
France.[51] He goes through the routine of visiting various sights,

---

[48] Ibid.: 163.   [49] Ibid.: 163–164.   [50] Ibid.: 164.   [51] Ibid.: 195.

including a brewery (though he does not share with his readers if he tried drinking!), the Royal Albert Hall and the British Museum, the Courthouse, and Madame Tussaud's. Again and again we read him lament the fact that he does not know English, though he tells us he is doing his best to learn it with the limited means at his disposal. We see him class conscious and dismissing the achievement of those who have inherited wealth.[52] Through the hurdle of his inability to communicate with people in their own languages, Hajj Sayyah is reaching a critical level of self-consciousness about class divisions and the privileges and disadvantages they entail.

In London Hajj Sayyah sadly bids farewell to his kind and generous Armenian friend who had kept him company from Venice and covered his expenses for that part of the journey. Hajj Sayyah spends another month in London after his friend leaves, wondering where to go next – whether to go back to France or travel to Russia. He opts instead to go to Belgium.[53] At this point he strikes up a conversation with a fellow passenger, in the course of which we learn that upon his arrival in Belgium he has spent five years away from Iran.[54] Although at least parts of this *Travelogue* may have been written from memory, it follows a chronological order. These are notes he was taking while traveling, though he may not have dated them on a daily basis. Omissions of precise dates may also have to do with his habitually practicing *Taqiyyeh* (dissimulation) and opting not to give detailed chronology of his whereabouts. He has left a tyrannical dynasty behind and ventured into unknown worlds. This consistent pattern of opting for anonymity is perfectly understandable.

He finally enters Antwerp, for which he gives its French name of "Anvers," where he relies on the kindness and generosity of strangers to proceed with his travels.[55] In part, we may surmise here, people are impressed by this stranger traveling the world empty-handed, and some do what they can to help him out. Upon his arrival in Antwerp, he learns the Belgian King is a magnificent and generous man named "Leopold II" (1835–1909). He makes no comment about this particularly illustrious, mass-murdering European monarch, which is a clear indication he is entirely clueless about what a monstrous colonialist was this Belgian king. Hajj Sayyah finally meets with a certain Swedish man named Alexander Petermann, who knows Arabic and says he had

[52] Ibid.: 202.   [53] Ibid.: 218.   [54] Ibid.: 219.   [55] Ibid.: 220.

learned it in Jerusalem as a diplomat. Through this person he actually meets with King Leopold, who tells him "everything European is better than Asian," with which sentiment Hajj Sayyah readily agrees and sarcastically adds, especially in weapons of murdering people. In Asia we are trying to get rid of swords, he tells the Belgian king, and you in Europe have invented far more murderous weapons.[56] The king and his Arabic-speaking diplomat both think Hajj Sayyah is an official in disguise and comes from a high-ranking family. His insistence that he is an ordinary person they do not buy.[57]

He eventually travels to Liege, Luxembourg, reaches Nancy, and in Strasburg he finds his way to a library where he asks for books from the East. He is given an anthology of poetry in which he spontaneously composes a poem in Persian and Turkish.[58] Finally he reaches Switzerland, enters Basil, from there he goes to Zurich, Lucerne, Bern, Freiburg, Lausanne, and Geneva, doing mostly sight-seeing. He then travels to Italy, visits Turin, Parma, Bologna, and enters Florence, where he stays for some time before moving to Rome, on his way visiting Pisa and Livorno, goes to Vatican, moves down to Genova and Naples, attends a theater, then goes to Pompeii, eventually to Brindisi, and finally Athens, where he visits a hospital for blind people.[59] In Athens, he has a discussion with a person he meets who asks his opinion of Athens, and he says he has seen more garrisons and churches than schools.[60] He says he was robbed in Rome but was met with generous hospitality in Athens.[61] He now has comparative assessments of his travels, peoples he has met, cultures and languages to which he has been exposed. His prose is increasingly worldly, richly written with his own personal experience.

He moves from city to city without any pomp and ceremony or making a fuss that he has traveled from Iran to Russia, Ottoman territories, or above all from "the West" to "Europe." He enters or leaves Europe with much of his attention directed toward natural beauties and urban life, with rare and only occasional discussions of politics. He mostly conceals his identity, not that he has much to say about who he is. He comes from a learned but very humble background. Sometimes people confuse him with a high-ranking diplomat. But he never pretends to be anyone important. In Gallipoli he notes how people speak both

[56] Ibid.: 226.   [57] Ibid.: 226.   [58] Ibid.: 236.   [59] Ibid.: 317.
[60] Ibid.: 323.   [61] Ibid.: 325.

Turkish and Greek and that they are part of the Ottoman Empire but are constantly critical of the government.[62] He finally reaches Istanbul, where he stays for twenty days and decides to travel to Moscow. He goes to Odessa where his detailed description of social life in that Russian city is almost identical to that of Paris and London – without making much distinction between Europe or non-Europe. In Odessa he decides to improve his knowledge of Russian. He meets with Emperor Alexander III.[63] In a brief conversation he has with the Russia Emperor, he is asked how did he learn Russian, to which he responds, his body is Iranian but his soul from His Majesty's state. He is given a monthly stipend by the Russian Emperor. From here he goes to Sebastopol, a major military port in Russia. He thus aimlessly travels from one Russian city to another. When he visits the New Nakhichevan, he makes a point that it is on the European side and is not to be confused with another Nakhichevan that is in Asia.[64] Finally he comes to Astrakhan, from there he moves on to Shaki and Ganja. He is aimless, flippant, curious, restless, making his plans up as he goes. Hajj Sayyah is by now born again as a traveler. He is at home nowhere and everywhere.

In Ganja he gets entangled with a local dignitary called Iskandar Khan, who is offended by Hajj Sayyah, and they start insulting each other, which results in a satirical poem being composed by one of Iskandar Khan's own retinue and widely publicized in the city. They end up in court, and Hajj Sayyah is finally exonerated and released.[65] At the end of this story, he says the details of this story are written separately as part of "Qazaya/Incidents." What are these "incidents" we do not know. He eventually gets to Tbilisi. He gets to Grozny, and from there he finally returns to Odessa again, where he reports he has run out of money. Here he is again suspected of being highborn, but he insists he is just a poor man. He reaches Kiev, and eventually goes back to Moscow.[66] His twenty-day stay in Moscow is spent doing similar things – walking, writing, visiting theaters, and making observations about people he meets there and the number of theaters and newspapers he has counted.[67] He proceeds toward Nizhni Nóvgorod and

---

[62] Ibid.: 327.   [63] Ibid.: 339.   [64] Ibid.: 358.

[65] Ibid.: 373–379. On page 388 of this edition we have a footnote that the scribe could not read the name of a city, and Hajj Sayyah in his own handwriting writes Orajonikidz (also spelled Ordzhonikidze). This means Hajj Sayyah had some sort of editorial control over the production of this manuscript.

[66] Ibid.: 428.   [67] Ibid.: 428–434.

comes back to Moscow.[68] The purpose of these trips is solely to write about them and to have a written record that Hajj Sayyah has actually been there and done that. By this part of the travels, all dramas and cliffhangers are wiped out of the narrative. He just obsessively moves from one city to another simply to make a record of it in his *Travelogue*.

From Moscow he goes to St. Petersburg; from there with his fellow traveler Monsieur Jean he travels toward Germany again, entering Warsaw where he spends seven days.[69] This turnaround, going in a circle, is the clearest indication that Hajj Sayyah has absolutely no "destination" in mind – anywhere at all, let alone to "Farang/Europe." He is just chasing after his own tail. He eventually moves toward Berlin, observing how beautiful the roads are. He writes of beautiful churches and synagogues – from there he travels toward Bayreuth, spends time in Munich, Stuttgart, and Karlsruhe, where he goes to a library and engages in a conversation with a curator and reads a few coins they had in their possessions.[70] He visits schools and factories, and while in Karlsruhe he has a ring that a fellow traveler had given him, and he thinks of selling it to provide for himself. In the course of a conversation with a head of a museum, he likens himself to a broken piece of wood (*takhteh pareh*) floating on a stormy sea: "Where the waves will carry me I have no clue, only God knows if I will ever reach any safe shores. The days I began my travels I considered my existence completely annihilated before I took my first steps."[71] A traveling mystic is born in him, the world giving him a new spectrum of metaphors with which to understand himself.

From here to Heidelberg, Manheim, Wiesbaden, Frankfurt, Gottingen, Hanover, Hamburg, and Lubick – and from there to Copenhagen, where he visits museums and universities, comes back to London, and travels to Birmingham, Manchester, where he visits the condition of prisoners.[72] Aimless, itinerant, high on the wonder of the world, Hajj Sayyah moves on and visits Ireland and Dublin – while in Dublin he challenges the famous phrase "jahan-dideh besyar guyad dorough/ the world traveler tells much lies."[73] In Dublin he also hints at the idea that he hopes to publish his travelogue, specifically calling it "Seyahat-nameh/Travelogue."[74] It is right there, in black and white,

---

[68] Ibid.: 448.   [69] Ibid.: 456.   [70] Ibid.: 471.   [71] Ibid.: 473.
[72] Ibid.: 500.   [73] Ibid.: 506.   [74] Ibid.: 509.

that he calls his book a "travelogue" – just to make sure how he thought of his own work – if future graduate students would kindly consider it a "travelogue," and not impose their own definition of the genre on it. He moves to Belfast and spends three days there before moving toward Glasgow for five days – then off to Edinburgh, where he attends a court proceeding regarding a marital infidelity case.[75] Then off he goes to Liverpool and Hover for a week. While in Rhone he tells us that he goes to a cafe and sits at a corner writing in his travelogue,[76] referring to it as "this meaningless Siyahat-nameh" again.[77] Here someone asks him who he is and what script he is writing, to which he responds he is writing these to remember them and, God willing, will take his travelogue back to his people as a gift.[78] Soon he returns to Paris, and from there travels to Orleans and from there to Tours, where the travelogue abruptly ends.[79]

Although Hajj Sayyah's *Travelogue* is incomplete, it offers a perfectly complete picture of his worldly disposition, his global perspective, and his comparative assessments of the cultures and climes he has seen and experienced in person. In these pages we keep company with a wandering soul, a restless spirit, never standing still anywhere for more than a passing moment for his eyes to see and his pen to register the wonders he witnesses. Hajj Sayyah's mission becomes clearer as he moves on: to see the world, to be an eyewitness to the changing universe in which his homeland is now located. That is the quintessence of his *Travelogue*. His visits to Europe are entirely incidental to that much more important task. He writes the world in Persian upon a global scene. The purpose of his travels and *Travelogue* was not to go to Europe or to any other particular destination. His readers have hitherto been far more Eurocentric in their reading of his *Travelogue* than he ever was when writing it. His insatiable desire was *to see* the world in its entirety and map it out in his own mind and soul. There is an ocular-centrism to Hajj Sayyah's narrative, a determined will *to see* for himself and to record for his compatriots what it means to be in this new world.

Chicago, Chicago

What happened to Hajj Sayyah and what did he see and say about his journey through the United States and beyond we do not

[75] Ibid.: 517.   [76] Ibid.: 523.   [77] Ibid.   [78] Ibid.   [79] Ibid.: 529.

Figure 9 "Broadway, New York, from the Western Union Telegraph Building Looking North; Color lithograph, color printing inks; Currier & Ives (Nathaniel Currier (1813–1888); 1875; PR20.1875.1." The navigational trajectory of these travelers finally reaches New York, and from there deeply into the United States, all the way to the West Coast and from there to "the Far East" of Europeans and the very Asian neighborhood of Iranians and Indians themselves. The far-reaching arc of these travels alters the self-consciousness of the Indo–Iranian weltanschauung and reclaims the world far beyond the European colonial and colonizing imagination. The entry of New York into the itinerary of these travelers opens up an entirely new horizon of imaginative geography unforeseen before. Reprinted with permission from New York Historical Society.

know yet – but that he did travel through the United States and obtained at least a traveling document and perhaps even became a full-fledged US citizen we know for fact. But a contemporary of Hajj Sayyah, a certain Haj Mirza Mohammad Ali Mo'in al-Saltaneh, has a nearly contemporary travelogue abroad that includes a good portion on the United States that might be useful here to examine.[80]

---

[80] See Homayoun Shahidi (ed.), *Safarnameh-ye Chicago: Khaterat-e Hajj Mirza Mohammad Ali Mo'in al-Saltaneh beh Orupa va America, 1410 Hijri Qamari/ Chicago Travelogue: The Memoirs of Hajj Mirza Mohammad Ali Mo'in*

The original copy of this travelogue was first published in Paris. Its author is originally from Isfahan, but at the time of his trip abroad (1310/1892) he was a resident of Rasht. The primary purpose of his trip, as he says in the introduction, was to attend the World's Columbian Exposition, aka the Chicago World's Fair held in Chicago in 1893 to celebrate the 400th anniversary of Christopher Columbus's arrival in the New World in 1492. He leaves Rasht on April 20, 1892. From Rasht, Mo'in al-Saltaneh travels to Russia, and from there to Poland and Austria and eventually to France, England, and Ireland. He finally sails toward the United States and arrives in New York on Saturday, June 17, 1893. In the United States, he visits New York, Philadelphia, Washington, DC, Chicago, Colorado, Iowa, San Francisco, back to Chicago, and up to Niagara Falls. He then returns to Europe, back through the Ottoman territories and Russia, and ultimately to Rasht on August 1, 1894.

In the introduction to his travelogue, Mo'in al-Saltaneh tells us that he intended to go to Chicago to attend the opening of Chicago World's Fair of 1893. He obviously knew about the Exposition before he left his homeland. Initially he takes his father along to Vienna for an eye surgery and then proceeds to travel to the United States. What is remarkable about this travelogue is the author's fixation on the surface of things he sees, filmicly describing them with a brainless camera. In the company of a fellow merchant named Hajj Mohammad Baqer, who evidently lived in Vienna, and later this man's son Aqa Mohammad Ali, and finally with a certain Mr. Morad, "who knew six languages," as his translator, he travels from Iran to Russian and Ottoman territories and from there to Europe and the United States, scarcely talking to anyone and simply reporting what he sees. It is in Chicago, as he tells us, and what he sees at the Chicago Exposition, that the spectacle of that event becomes definitive to his travelogue. Just like the exposition he had gone to visit, everything about this travelogue is visual, filmic, there to be seen, not to be comprehended. Reading this almost simultaneous travelogue with Hajj Sayyah's

al-Saltaneh to Europe and United States, 1892 (Tehran: Elmi Publications, 1363/1984). Neither the scribe of the manuscript on which this edition is based nor the author himself refer to this book as "Chicago Travelogue." Again, this is a figment of the editor's imagination. In his own Introduction to Mo'in al-Saltaneh, the author says: "For a long time I had intended to visit North America especially on the occasion of Chicago Exposition" (ibid.: 204).

writings is a lesson in appreciating the latter's moral imagination and intellectual superiority.

Mo'in al-Saltaneh's first visit to the actual site of the Chicago Exposition is on Tuesday, July 4, 1893, and the first spectacle he notices is an exhibition of Arabs in the Exposition, singing and dancing with camels and horses.[81] Then comes a Hungarian concert, then a spectacle of Buffalos, followed by people from Lapland, followed by an exhibition of the African Kingdom of Dahomey, which was enjoying its last year of existence, for by 1894 it was incorporated into the French African empire. From here Mo'in al-Saltaneh goes to see the Chinese Exhibition, where we see him in a rare short exchange with a human being when he asks a waiter who serves him lemonade to write him something in Chinese, and he writes the length of a dragon featured in the show for him.[82] For days on end he just wakes up in the morning, says has prayers, has breakfast, or "tea" as he says, gets on a train, and attends an exhibition in the Exposition. That is all he does, scarcely talking to anyone or attributing any significance to what he sees, until finally one day he leaves for Nebraska. It is a bizarre "travelogue." We are in the presence of a mindless camera, with some sort of obsessive-compulsive disorder, that keeps repeating what he does and what he sees, without as much of an iota of intelligence evident in recording what he does or what he sees. There is, however, a profound significance to his ocularcentricism – the evidence of the visual dimension of this and many other similar travelogues. These travelers just wanted to *eyewitness* the world outside their homeland, to have a written record of where they had been and what they had seen. Mo'in al-Saltaneh's travelogue makes us more conscious of this visual dimension of Hajj Sayyah's travel narratives. Hajj Sayyah is of course infinitely more verbose, talkative, argumentative, and contemplative. But still, he too wants to see and make a record of what he sees. Their prose, both Mo'in al-Saltaneh's and Hajj Sayyah's and most others, at times reads like a drone shot – mindless and senseless, and yet panoramic and embracing.

[margin handwriting: traveles like Moin]

Colonial Modernity versus Worldliness

Hajj Sayyah's is a restless soul, having narrated himself into something of an obsessive traveler. His intuitive impulses are to run away from a

---

[81] Ibid.: 356–357.   [82] Ibid.: 360.

Sιγγαɦ

domesticated life. He wants to see what has already been heard and generically known in his own homeland. His single most important encounter in his short stay in Paris is not with European modernity but with the spirit of rebellion he detects among a handful of French laborers against tyranny. The seeds of regicide are planted in his mind in Paris when he hears French workers wishing Louis Napoleon is put under the guillotine the way Louis XVI was executed. Decades later he would be a cellmate and a close friend of the man who would do precisely that and assassinate Naser al-Din Shah. But because of his constant traveling and a sense of survival, he was circumspect and judicious in sharing his thoughts or divulging his identity. He did not have much of an identity when he left his homeland. He has a thirst for seeing and learning and confines himself to his *Seyahat-nameh*. He was intuitively reluctant to publish his travelogue, for he was afraid of its consequences for himself and his family. The part pertinent to Iran he reluctantly published toward the end of his life, and the other part he did not at all until they were published posthumously. But from the vantage point of our own time when we read these travel narratives by Hajj Sayyah and his fellow travelers, they were the narrators of a cosmopolitan worldliness far beyond the limited confinements of what later Eurocentric historiography would falsely call their attention to "European modernity."

Predicated on Hajj Sayyah's sojourn to Europe and the United States, the tired old hobby horse of "modernity" is therefore dragged out, and poor Hajj Sayyah is charged with having brought "the modern subject" to his homeland. He did no such thing – and this sort of uncritical encounter with "European modernity" is typical of a generation of scholarship (in and out of Iran) beholden to "Western modernity." This is a common motif that runs through much of the scholarship on the significance of these travelogues – that Iran was backward, Europe was advanced, and these travelers went to "the West" and brought "modernity" to their homeland. The proposition that these travelers traveled to Europe, and in the case of Hajj Sayyah to the United States, and they brought with them "the modern subject" and with it the whole project of modernity is categorically false – and even worse it covers up and camouflages the extraordinary fact of these travelers going around the globe and thereby expanding the trans-national public space upon which the very idea of a homeland/vatan would soon emerge, and within that space the eventual making of a postcolonial subject. This entire spectrum is buried and hidden under the cliché-ridden banality of "Western modernity."

This by now very old and very tired cliché is predicated on the blind spot of categorically disregarding the totality of these travelers' itineraries and then the world that these travels engendered and sustained. The rise of Iran as a postcolonial nation-state is predicated on the active formation of that world and not on an "encounter" with European modernity, the colonial disposition of which these scholars systematically ignore. Travelers like Hajj Sayyah lived a worldly life – literally. They lived in and out of Iran. When they were out, they carried their homeland with them, and when they were in, they brought the world (not "the West") back to Iran with them. They saw the world with Iranian eyes and they saw Iran through their experienced worldly perspectives. Hajj Sayyah in particular linked his homeland to the global space as it was being reconfigured. He crossed all borders and recognized none. Any attempt at pinning him down to "the West" (Europe or US) fails to recognize the totality of his worldly being. It made little difference to him if he went from Bushehr to Shiraz and from Shiraz to Isfahan and from there to Tehran and Mashhad, or he went from Astrakhan to St Petersburg, Berlin, London, and New York and San Francisco. Some scholars have emphasized his Iranian origin and destination, others his European, and still others his US journeys. Very little to no attention is given to his journeys through Asia, Africa, or the Arab and Muslim world. But in and out of Iran, he was a worldly wanderer. He was restless at home and he was restless abroad. He deeply cared for his homeland and yet the depth of its monarchical and clerical corruption deeply troubled, frustrated, and paralyzed him. He endured exile and imprisonment. He suffered the political consequences of his hopes and aspirations for his homeland. Like his hero Seyyed Jamal al-Din al-Afghani, he was both attracted to and repelled by power.

There is no understanding of "Modernity" without a simultaneous awareness that this specifically European modernity was a by-product of capitalism, that it was white, and that it was masculinist, and that it was savagely colonizing the world. Without a recognition of this dynamic of modernity, the world and all its dynamics are divided between a progressed "West" and a "backward East." People from this East then travel to that West and learn about modernity and go back to their homeland to make it modern. What bizarre, contorted,

and convoluted perception of world history is this? "Hajj Sayyah –
First Persian to Become an American," in the words of one such
abusive reading of his life, "he later returns to Persia to work against
ignorance."[83] This racist conception of history is itself the product of a
colonized mind already slanted toward a delusional blind spot called
"the West." There would be no capitalist modernity without its colonial foregrounding. Travelers like Hajj Sayyah were going from the
colonial edges of European capitalist modernity around the globe,
including Europe and the United States, not to learn how to modernize
but to see the global spectrum of that particular power-relation that
called itself "modernity." Without the slightest exaggeration, generations of Iranian scholarship are predicated on this delusional
historiography.

Chief among my concerns in this book is to argue against the
established cliché in reading these travelogues as the textual evidence
of their authors' exclusive interest in and traveling toward the destination of Europe. This is simply wrong and based on textual evidence of
these travel narratives that is fundamentally flawed and misleading. An
entire academic industry is built on this manufactured Eurocentrism.
Singling out "Europe" as the sole "destination" of these journeys,
which is untrue, totally distorts the complete picture of the maps they
traveled. *The world* was the ultimate destination of these travelers, not
"Europe." These journeys certainly included Europe but were not by
any means limited to Europe. Europe is neither the first, nor the last,
nor indeed the sole destination of these journeys. The travel itinerary of
these journeys began long before Europe and continued long after
Europe into North and South America, into Africa, Asia, and particularly into the hearts of the Arab and Muslim world. China and India
and Japan, and occasionally Latin America were on these travelers'
itinerary. Why should they be ignored, short-shrifted, and concealed,
and Europe privileged? The Eurocentric imagination and colonized
mind of those who have abused and misread these travelogues have
imposed on them a gridlock against the very letter of their texts, the
very prose of their narrative. Even when Naser al-Din Shah tells us he
is going to Europe, he tells us much more in the text of his travelogue.

---

[83] See Steve Holgate, "Hajj Sayyah – First Persian to Become an American"
(*Pars Times, The Washington File*, no date). Available online here:
www.parstimes.com/news/archive/2003/washfile020.html. Accessed August
10, 2017.

When it comes to travelers like Hajj Sayyah, he most certainly and decidedly travels around the globe, and his frames of reference are consciously global and regional and not "European."

In order to make my points even clearer, I have also indicated that since the earliest of these travels began late in the eighteenth century, "Europe" itself is still very much a floating signifier and is being written, among other places, in these very pages. Geographies are in a state of fluidity, the borders of nation-states are in a colonial state of flux, and the Indo–Persian world, rooted in the Safavid and Mughal eras, is very much interwoven and part and parcel of a unified cultural heritage and consciousness. Neither "Iran" is completely "Iran" as we understand it today, nor "India" is "India" as in its postcolonial designation we understand it today, nor, a fortiori, "Europe" is still completely "Europe." All these distant and adjacent geographies are being colonially re-conceptualized. So "Europe" was not a reality *sui generis* to which these travelers decided, as Alice did into that rabbit hole, to plunge and come back. This is not to suggest they did not go to Europe, or Europe was any less significant an aspect of their travels, or most certainly, the colonial power of European empires was irrelevant to these travelers. This is simply to suggest in these pages we are witness to a remapping of the world and not readers of a tour guide to Europe to civilize the colored people. In that remapping, Iran and its environs, from India to North Africa, are being actively rewritten into world history. Thinking of Europe as the destination of these journeys has systematically distorted that fact. The construction of the false and falsifying binary between "Islam and the West," or "the West and the Rest," or "Tradition and Modernity," and perforce that of "Iran and Europe" are all predicated precisely (but partially) on this aggressively abusive misreading of the very literature we are examining here.

Iranians are not, of course, the only ones systematically misreading these texts. In such texts as Ibrahim Abu Lughod's classic *The Arab Rediscovery of Europe: A Study in Cultural Encounters* (1963), anticipating Bernard Lewis's *The Muslim Discovery of Europe* (1982), traces of such privileging of Europe is already evident. Restoring these travel narratives to their factual open-endedness is tantamount to retrieving the liberating moment of the emancipatory geography upon which they were actually written. These texts are in fact crafting a new, open-ended world of their own, a liberating geography of their own devising. They are as much excited about visiting Europe as they are about their sojourn through their own homeland, or else in India, the Ottoman or Russian territories, or when they get as far as South Africa, North, Central, and South America, and especially the Arab and Muslim world. Scholars have done the world a fundamental disservice, denying them and us that joy, when they have imposed their own deeply colonized Eurocentric minds on their travel records. This book is an attempt at retrieving those worlds hitherto hidden to their prejudiced eyes.

8 | *In the Company of a Refined Prince*

'Abd al-Samad Mirza

On my travel roads
Devout Christian monks
Were pointing towards the silent portrait
Of Prophet Jeremiah –
While I was reciting out-loud
From the Book of Ecclesiastes –
As a few Lebanese farmers
Were sitting under an old cedar tree
Counting the oranges on their branches
In their minds –

By the roadside as I was traveling
I could see blind Iraqi children
Looking at the script
Of the Code of Hammurabi –
As I was catching up
With the latest newspapers
From around the world.

Sohrab Sepehri (Mosafer/Traveler, Babol, Spring 1966)

From Prophet Jeremiah to the Book of Ecclesiastes, from the Code of Hammurabi to the latest newspapers from around the world, all gathered on the mobile memories of the traveler moving from Iran to Iraq to Lebanon, and then from there, beyond. Sepehri's poetry breathes in the world. The collage he paints as he paces the footsteps of his travels brings lives and livelihoods, religions and convictions, terrors and the troublesome, the sacred and the mundane, all together. He is both present and absent in these scenes. He tells us what he sees and what he does and what he thinks and what he feels, but no one notices him. He just thinks and talks to himself – as we follow him and see and listen with and to him. There is a sublime solitude in Sepehri's poetry, the solitude of a solitary traveler. Thriving, basking in that solitude, he seems to be talking to himself, but he is talking to an implied reader he must have known he was creating as he traveled and wrote. From what he saw and from what he wrote, he gazed at a posterity he imagined gazing back at him – as he brought forth a priority into the interiority of his poetry. There is a luxurious elegance about his confidence – we colonial folks did not know we deserved. He is the prince of his own poetry, the captain of his own destiny, the guide of his own sojourn – and we, his readers, become the princely author of our own destiny.

The Notion of the Nation

In my previous work, I have already argued and demonstrated in some historical detail how the very idea of "nation" (vatan) is narratively formed on a *transnational public sphere* formed beyond the colonially conditioned frontier fictions on which postcolonial nation-states now actively imagine and understand themselves.[1] What this body of travel narrative I now closely examine here in this book offers us is a far more elaborate and detailed tapestry of textual evidence of how that notion of "homeland" was dialectically composed on a transnational public sphere these travelers helped to form and make politically effective. As Jürgen Habermas had originally theorized early in the 1960s, the idea of "public sphere" was predicated on the Renaissance and early modern phases of European bourgeois societies in which, above all, the merchant class needed reliable information about far away countries with which they were now actively trading.[2] Neither universities nor governmental agencies were the sufficient, reliable, or economically feasible intelligence resources these emerging companies and corporations needed before risking to invest and endanger their capital. Let us remember that the earliest generation of British Orientalists were primarily employed by the East India Company and not by any university. Such British scholars and literary figures as Henry Thomas Colebrooke (1765–1837) and Charles Lamb (1775–1834) were

---

[1] Most recently I have made this argument in my *Persophilia: Persian Culture on the Global Scene* and *Iran without Borders: Towards a Critique of the Postcolonial Nation.*

[2] See Jürgen Habermas, *The Structural Transformation of the Public Sphere: An Inquiry into a Category of Bourgeois Society* (Boston, MA: MIT Press, 1962/1989).

"writers" in East India Company. This is the clearest indication of the colonial origin of the rise and transnational expansion of the European public sphere and its bourgeois disposition. These European bourgeois "public spheres" therefore had a decidedly colonial character, and in turn expanded globally to include colonial sites too.

As evident in the travelogues we are reading here, such public spaces as coffee houses and restaurants, concert halls and opera houses, trains and ships, railway stations and boulevards were the physical locations of such gatherings of the emerging colonial interests of the bourgeoisie and eventually the press and by extension the literary public sphere in the form of travelogues, novels, and poetry; and of course anthropological accounts of faraway lands and "cultures" helped the nascent European bourgeoisie do two things at one and the same time: gather intelligence on far away countries and create a public sphere in which they articulated their collective (now dubbed "democratic") interests and which at the same time was in support or at odds with the interest of their ruling classes. This I believe is the way in which we need to re-read Edward Said's *Culture and Imperialism* (1993), though as a literary critic he was far more concerned with a close reading of European fictions such as those of Austen or Dickens and theorizing their imperial pedigree than with the public sphere upon which these Europeans were reading these texts as the literary background widely consequential to their commercial interests. When Said in his *Culture and Imperialism* says he is after describing "a more general pattern of relationships between the modern metropolitan west and its overseas territories,"[3] he is in effect mapping out the literary public sphere upon which these travelers roam around the globe, though not in the fixed binary polar opposites Said implies. That public sphere, as I have documented in detail, was ipso facto transnational.[4]

A key element in the formation of this colonially anchored European public sphere was of course European travel narratives to the East plus the eventual rise of anthropology as an academic discipline, a discipline that emerged from those very traveling narratives. As perhaps best evident in Claude Levi-Strauss's classic text, *Tristes Tropiques* (1955), as both a travelogue and an anthropological treatise, we can see how the two narratives eventually come together. The body of the Persian travelogues

---

[3] See Edward Said, *Culture and Imperialism* (New York: Vintage Books, Random House, 1993): xi.
[4] See Dabashi, *Persophilia: Persian Culture on the Global Scene*.

I am examining in this book, and that has been hitherto used and abused as evidence of Iranian or Muslim encounters with "Europe," or "the West," or even worse, "Modernity," is in fact nothing of the sort. This literature is the veritable evidence of the corroborative texts produced on the selfsame colonially anchored public sphere from the vantage point of the worldly colonized. But because these travelogues were written in Persian, or else in Arabic, or Turkish, etc., they never entered the European or Europeanized consciousness of that public sphere except as satirical lampoons on the model of James Morier's *The Adventures of Hajji Baba of Ispahan* (1824). Generations later, irresponsible and colonially compromised Qajar historiography began reading these priceless texts not as integral to that transnational public sphere occasioned by the global capitalism but as evidence of the encounters of the backward barbarians from the East with the civilized West. Among my reasons for writing this book is to right this terrible wrong.

A Prince and His Shadows

Let me now move on in this chapter, as I promised, and examine Prince Abd al-Samad Mirza 'Izz al-Dowleh Salur's two *Safar-Namehs* (1873 and 1883), the written records of his two trips abroad. Abd al-Samad Mirza (1843–1929) was a Qajar prince, the fifth son of Muhammad Shah Qajar (1808–1848) and his wife Aghul Beikeh Khanom, a lady of Turkmen origin, and the younger brother (from a different mother) of Naser al-Din Shah the ruling monarch. He became an orphan in childhood and ever since at the mercy of his older and more powerful brother, the king. From a very young age, Abd al-Samad Mirza, who attended the prestigious Dar al-Fonun School, was given a royal title and appointed as the nominal governor of a number of cities and provinces, basically to keep him away from the capital. At a very young age, he was appointed governor of Qazvin and soon after that of Borujerd, Hamadan, Malayer, Toyserkan, and Nahavand during the subsequent years, and then the governor of Zanjan for two years, 1901–1902. He would be repeatedly appointed and dismissed as governor of various provinces away from the capital to keep him on the close leash of the royal court. He would also be appointed the minister of justice for a brief time. Abd al-Samad Mirza was also dispatched by his king brother, Naser al-Din Shah as a royal emissary to Russia to congratulate Alexander III on his accession to the throne. But more importantly for our purpose here, Abd al-Samad Mirza accompanied his brother Naser al-Din Shah during his travel abroad and kept a written record of this trip.

What is important, therefore, to remember is that Prince Abd al-Samad Mirza was a learned and cultivated man, commanded a number of languages (Persian, Arabic, and French), led a luxurious princely life in his palatial houses, was occasionally dispatched on cere-monial diplomatic missions, and was an avid follower of global news. He was a poet and a painter, a man of letters, a learned, cultivated, luxurious man who loved hunting more than the trappings of a diplomatic life. His appointment and dismissal as a governor of various states continued after the assassination of his brother, Naser al-Din Shah, and during the reign of the last three monarchs of the Qajar dynasty. He survived the collapse of the Qajars and toward the end of his life assumed a newly mandated "family name" under Reza Shah Pahlavi, for which he chose his maternal tribal name of "Salur." His entire character and culture were somewhere "in-between," linking the dying days of the Qajars to the triumphant but doomed rise of the Pahlavis. A kind of hypnotic somnambulism defined his age. He was sleepwalking through it.

I am interested in Prince 'Izz al-Dowleh because he represents a strata of Qajar aristocracy exuding a class-based princely sense of patriotism with which they traveled the world around their homeland and helped reminding it of its dying past for its emerging posterity. The love of their homeland, no doubt, was actively fused with their fear for their own dynasty. But they did offer observations as they traveled the world that helped constitute a transnational public sphere upon which the idea of "Iran" as a nation-state would soon coalesce. Their dynasty in effect meant their homeland. But they had also traveled the world and seen it from their own vantage point. Despite his aristocratic birth, he led a comparatively secluded life, for he was intentionally kept away from the capital, forced effectively into internal exile lest he and his ilk might pose a threat to the reigning monarch. That fact had given Prince 'Izz al-Dowleh a sense of quiet bitterness and repressed resentment, and yet he could not altogether abandon the privileges of his birth. The princely disposition, the aristocratic aloofness, the cultivated manner-isms and poetic and aesthetic disposition of the Prince are what gives his travelogue a pointed interest for posterity. The world was his oyster – though he lacked the sword to open it.

The Traveling Amanuenses

More specifically, two aspects of Prince Abd al-Samad Mirza's travels and travelogues are of particular interest to me in this chapter. First is the fact that its author had a rather distanced, princely disposition and was neither in any significant position of power nor indeed in opposition, and as such represented a stratum of Qajar royalty that was relatively educated, socially alert, politically acute, and, from his far-flung aristocratic vantage point, deeply concerned about the location of his homeland in the larger regional and global context. It is precisely this removed aristocratic detachment of Prince Abd al-Samad Mirza that makes his travelogue of interest to our story. He was there and he was not there. He traveled and he observed and he left a record as if for a posterity he could not quite envision.

The prototype of this character trait among Qajar princes is the most erudite among them all, Jalal al-Din Mirza (1827–1872), who was a pioneering figure paving the way toward Iranian bourgeois nationalism from the heart of Qajar aristocracy. Despite his aristocratic lineage, he joined Mirza Fath Ali Akhondzadeh and Mirza Malkam Khan, two towering intellectual figures of his time, in their pioneering efforts in critical thinking and political reform. Written in "pure Persian" (meaning artificially avoiding any word with Arabic roots), Prince Jalal al-Din Mirza's book, *Nameh-ye Khosrovan/The Royal Book*, became a staple of Persian nationalism at the expense of racially profiling Arabs and Muslims. The desire of this generation of Qajar reformists for reform, however, was deeply infested with racist and xenophobic and particularly anti-Arab sentiments. Many of the subsequent racist traits in Persian nationalism can in fact be traced to Jalal al-Din Mirza and his ilk. His desire to write "pure Persian," as evident in his correspondences with Mirza Fath Ali Akhondzadeh, were rooted in this calamitous Persian jingoism. At a time that Arabs, like all other colonized nations, were equally engaged in their own battles against European colonialism, Jalal al-Din Mirza seeks and cultivates a kind of Persian nationalism that is predicated on the violent racialization and demonization of Arabs, in effect partaking freely in the racist European Orientalism of his time. Be that as it is, his generation of Qajar princes had an active role to play, for better or for worse, in cultivating the very constitution of the Iranian public sphere. Though, alas, such critical considerations are almost totally absent in the existing state of scholarship in Qajar historiography.[5]

Predicated on the prototype of an aloof Qajar prince, what is specific to Abd al-Samad Mirza is how his princely disposition translates into a lazily luxurious traveling habit that gives his travelogues their most distinct and important characteristics: the fact that he did not write them himself – which brings us to the second reason for the significance of these texts. Prince 'Izz al had a personal assistant, Mirza Ali Khan Farrashbashi, a servant whom he had now charged as his amanuensis, who wrote the first of his two travelogues for him. His second travelogue, ostensibly based on a diplomatic mission to Russia on the occasion of Alexander III ascending to the Russian throne, is even more intriguing, for the Prince began writing the first few sentences himself and then entrusted it to yet another personal assistant, Mirza Taqi Monshi, to continue writing it. This fusion and ambiguity of authorship, this narrative gathering of a prince and his servants, his hands, as it were, is what makes these travelogues of extraordinary significance here. It is the question of authorship of these pages that poses an extraordinary literary twist to their narratives. Even more intriguing is the fact that during his second trip to Russia, Abd al-Samad Mirza had asked two other companions to write their own respective accounts of the journey. Again, these two other narratives, Mirza Hasan Khan Monshi's and Taher Khan Iftekhar-e Nezam's, add further twists to this one journey. What further complicates these narratives is the fact that the entire enterprise is a reflection on Naser al-Din Shah's own account of these travels. So, in effect one trip abroad has multiple narratives: one by the monarch, one by his half-brother, and then both given further spins by effectively three other accounts by their servants. We have a palimpsestic succession of narratives that both describe and re-inscribe a single journey. The kaleidoscopic picture that emerges sculpts the travel experiences of these and other travelers.

Who are these characters writing these travelogues, for what purpose, and who was to read them? Naser al-Din Shah, who had ordered this diplomatic journey to his brother, was very much fond

[5] For a typical treatment of Jalal al-Din Mirza in the current context of Qajar scholarship, see the "JALĀL-AL-DIN MIRZĀ" entry in *Encyclopedia Iranica*. Available online here: www.iranicaonline.org/articles/jalal-al-din-mirza. Accessed August 16, 2017.

of reading and writing travelogues. Were these additional two accounts also ordered by the Qajar monarch to check on his brother for what he was doing in Russia? Speculative questions add further intrigue to these multiple travel narratives of a single journey. Page after page of these travelogues do indeed read like intelligence reports for a security apparatus headed by the king himself to find out how this crucial diplomatic mission had been performed in the minutest detail. Had the king asked his brother to write his own account as well? We have a set of multiple narrators gathering around these journeys, perhaps for immediate pragmatic reasons, to gather sufficient intelligence for further examination upon return to the capital – but at the same, time leaving posterity a wealth of narratives to consider in this crucial period in the history of an emerging post-imperial nation.

The question of a shadow writer, a ghost writer, though knowingly a ghost writer, raises the issue of authorship of these travel accounts to an entirely literary significance, beyond their immediate historical record. But this is not in merely literary abstraction. We know for a fact that Prince 'Izz al-Dowleh did travel abroad. We also know of his aristocratic, princely, deeply erudite and cultivated character. It is the fusion of these two aspects of the authorship – one a deeply learned prince, and the other a domestic servant rising in the ranks, that is significant here. The two commingle on these pages. We don't know much about this shadow writer. But we know much about the prince who had employed him. So, what we are going to see, what we are reading, is from the mind and perspective of the prince but from the hand of his amanuensis. The two, as we shall soon see, communicate on these pages. The word "amanuensis" that I am using here is obviously English, and its Latin origins in "servus a manu/hand (writing) secretary" and "ensis/belonging to" clearly show its function as someone recruited to write something for his/her employer. The word that is used by both the prince and his amanuensis, however, is "Farrashbashi." Farrashbashi is far more generic, and it simply means a servant, with its roots in the word "farsh," literally the servant in charge of sitting arrangements of his/her master. The Qajar prince had more than one such amanuensis. He had others too. They all wrote for him and with him and instead of him. The multiple narratives of one event that result give the traveling narratives their "Rashomon effect."

As in Akira Kurosawa's classic film, *Rashomon* (1950), where we are witness to a murder and rape incident from four different perspectives, here too the fact of a travel abroad is recorded from varying perspectives. As in "Rashomon," the point here is not to

Figure 10 "Portrait of Jalal al-Din Mirza (ca. 1827–1872), son of Fath-Ali Shah; attributed to Abu'l-Hasan Ghaffari, Sani' al-Mulk (ca. 1814–1866); Iran, probably Tehran, dated Shawwal AH 1275 (May 1859); oil on canvas; Purchase – Friends of the Freer and Sackler Galleries; Arthur M. Sackler Gallery, S2016.9a–b." [Public domain] – A key component of these travelers venturing outside their homeland and roaming the globe was members of the Qajar aristocracy, including Naser al-Din Shah Qajar, himself, who was exceedingly fond of traveling and writing about his travels. These travelers came from all walks of life, but mostly from the aristocratic, clerical, and merchant classes. The writing of these travelogues in effect crafted a new type of Persian prose narrative and with it countercrafted a traveling knowing subject beyond their class origins or privileges. The intention of the texts here overcame the intention of the authors.

search for the "truth" of what happened, but to observe the sculpted perspective that emerges from all of them together.

Travelogue to "Europe"?

Abd al-Samad Mirza 'Izz al-Dowleh Salur wa do Safar-nameh Ou beh Orupa, 1290 and 1300/Abd al-Samad Mirza 'Izz al-Dowleh Salur and His Two Travelogues to Europe 1873 and 1883: I have managed to procure a pdf copy of the complete book and am now reading it in Geneva where I am attending a conference. The first thing that strikes me in this volume is again the fabricated title privileging the European part of the travelogue. The journey begins in Tehran and the entourage of the royal trip moves to Bandar-e Anzali in Northern Iran; from there they sail through the Caspian Sea and through the Volga River and eventually arrive in Moscow, where Naser al-Din Shah meets with the Russian emperor. From Moscow, the royal company takes the train to St. Petersburg and from their they travel to Poland, Germany, and then arrive in Belgium. From Belgium, they go to England and meet with Queen Victoria. The itinerary of Abd al-Samad Mirza is of course identical with Naser al-Din Shah's travels – he simply offers an alternative point of view to the monarch's perspective. From England they go to France, Italy, Austria, and spend much time and ink in the Ottoman Empire, which along with the Russian Empire is the first and the last non-European part of this engineered "European" journey of the Qajar monarch and his brother and others to "the West." From there they eventually come back to Bandar-e Anzali and return to Tehran.

The second travelogue in this book is an account of Prince 'Izz al-Dowleh's diplomatic mission as an envoy extraordinaire to the Russian court on the occasion of the coronation of Alexander III. This account is then corroborated by two additional travelogues written by two of his fellow travelers. The multiple narratives we read here had an obvious functional aspect to them. The ruling monarch, Naser al-Din Shah, loved to travel, and loved to read and write about travels. But the accounts also read as a kind of intelligence gathering for the Qajar court and the emerging Iranian diplomatic culture with modern nation-states, thereby becoming a nation-state of its own. The journey has absolutely nothing to do with Europe and is entirely within the domain of Qajar and Russian empires. The mission in fact arrives in Moscow a day after the official ceremonies! The reason for this is explained as 'Izz al-Dowleh not having been permitted by his royal brother to take off his hat in the church where the ceremony was taking place.[6]

In the same volume, we also read a few letters from Naser al-Din Shah and other Iranian officials to their Russian counterparts. There are also some additional letters that 'Izz al-Dowleh writes to his brother, the king, further elaborating the details of his journey to the Russian court. These letters add lovely reads to the volume but also further expose the bizarre insistence to call the whole book a "travelogue to Europe." "Traveling to Europe" as the new *qiblah* for Muslims replacing their own by now had become an overwhelming narrative trope and sold to a market already sold on the idea of Iranians (or Arabs or Muslims, etc.) going to Europe and being exposed to "modernity," or becoming "civilized." This level of self-conscious anxiety for multiple nations across the globe to see themselves beholden to "Europe" is a pathology borne out of an inferiority complex incurable for generations past and into the future. It did not matter, it does not matter, if these travelers traveled far and wide. The few stops they made in a European capital made their worldly wandering a "journey to Europe." This pathology is far less evident in the actual travel narratives they wrote and far more evident in the editorial apparatus of the subsequent generations that dug out, published, and read these travelogues.

A closer look at the composition of this volume, sold as "Abd al-Samad Mirza 'Izz al-Dowleh Salur's travelogues to Europe," will expose the travesty of this entire genre of literature on which so much time and energy have been wasted without actually reading and seeing through what is the substance of these texts. When you start reading this book, you realize that the first 174 pages of a volume of 414 pages are a detailed introduction about 'Izz al-Dowleh Salur's life and various governmental responsibilities. These pages could very well have been part of a short biographical entry or even monograph about a rather minor figure in Qajar history. After this lengthy introduction, we have another five pages as an introduction to the first travelogue printed in this volume, before finally the travelogue "to Europe" begins on page 180 and ends on page 253. This is the total of 73 pages

[handwritten margin note: ie not just a travelogue]

---

[6] Abd al-Samad Mirza 'Izz al-Dowleh Salur, *Do Safar-nameh Ou beh Orupa, 1290 and 1300/Two of His Travelogues to Europe 1873 and 1883*. Edited by Mas'ud Salur (Tehran: Nashr-e Namak, 1374/1995): 288–289.

dedicated to a traveling itinerary that begins in Iran, goes through Russia, includes a few stops in a handful of European cities, and then concludes with a passage to Iran through the Ottoman Empire. Then begins the Russian diplomatic mission to the court of Alexander III, which has absolutely nothing to do with "Europe." Here again we have 4 pages of introduction by the editor, from page 263 to page 266, and the rest of it, from page 267 to page 356, is the account of the same journey to Russia by his companions. In other words, in a book of 414 pages, only 73 pages are on a trip that included a few pages, from page 190 to page 230 (when they leave the Port of Brindisi for Istanbul), on Europe, which is to say only 40 pages of a massive 414-page volume (only 1 percent of the total number of pages) is about what today we call "Europe" – and yet the whole thing is branded and ticketed as a travelogue to "Europe." If this is not the most blatant, the most egregious privileging of Europe over the rest of the world then I don't know what is. Let me emphasize, this travesty of scholarship has nothing to do with the actual content of the travelogue that 'Izz al-Dowleh Salur and his amanuenses wrote. They travel from Iran to Russia, from there to Europe, come back to Ottoman territories, and return to Iran and make moderately intelligent observations about what they see. It is this bizarre, twisted, pathologically Eurocentric Qajar scholarship that insists on privileging Europe as the point of destination for all these travelogues. A mind could not be more warped, a critical intelligence more twisted, than evident in this psychotic Eurocentrism.

This is not to say that Europe is not part of this travelogue, or even an important part of 'Izz al-Dowleh's narrative, or that he is not thoroughly impressed by Europe. This is simply to draw attention to the much and egregiously neglected totality of a narrative and what it entails by giving equal significance to the other parts of his journey and observations. The running leitmotif of Salur in his travelogue is how some cities or sights he visited were like "paradise." In opting for this metaphor, it makes no difference whether he is still in Iran, Russia, or Europe. "The paradise of Iran is Gilan," he says early in his travelogue.[7] In a similar vein, "Moscow is paradise."[8] Upon his arrival in Europe: "The banks of the river Rhone are the paradise of Europe, and

---

[7] 'Izz al-Dowleh Salur, *Two of His Travelogues to Europe*: 187.   [8] Ibid.: 188.

Europe is the paradise of the world."[9] Later he has occasions to
emphasize how Paris is the most beautiful city ever,[10] for "Paris is
the envy of paradise,"[11] and even more emphatically, "Europe is
paradise."[12] While making such observations, his mind is always on
Iran and Muslims. While in Russia, he visits mosques on the Volga
banks,[13] and upon his arrival in Europe he compares children greeting
him in Germany with children throwing stones at strangers in Iran.[14]
Europe is therefore as much an occasion of 'Izz al-Dowleh's reflections
on his homeland as is the Ottoman Empire. He, like many other
travelers of his time, was remapping the world around his homeland.
His or others was not a binary symmetry (or asymmetry) between Iran
and Europe, or even worse, between "the West and the East." He is re-
worlding the global map, all around his own homeland. Europe is part
of that world, not the origin or its destination.

There is, however, another symmetrical (or asymmetrical) binary at
work in this travelogue that is of much more enduring significance for
us here – and that is the parallel narratives that animate its prose. This
particular travelogue is bivocal – it speaks with two voices: the voice of
the author and the voice of his amanuensis, a certain Mirza Ali Khan
Farrashbashi, who accompanied 'Izz al-Dowleh in this journey and
actually wrote the travelogue on behalf of his employer. While traveling and writing his travelogue, we eventually realize, 'Izz al-Dowleh
has a peculiarly dialogical relationship with his chosen amanuensis.
The master and the servant have a symbiotic relationship – they
complement each other's voices and perspectives. They reverberate
each other's prose. As we read through the travelogue, we eventually
realize that the author and his amanuensis have a running dialogue in
the text, a division of labor, a bivocal perspective.[15] The servant
corroborates his master's opinion of London being really a great city.[16]
They both love London and Paris. The amanuensis occasionally takes
liberty of paraphrasing famous poems in a silly way, such as when he
abuses Rumi's famous opening line in his *Masnavi* by composing the
following line: "Listen to me when I tell you a story/When I complain
of Europe."[17] When revising his amanuensis's prose and poetry, 'Izz
al-Dowleh criticizes him for having composed such silly poems.[18]

[9] Ibid.: 193.   [10] Ibid.: 207.   [11] Ibid.: 210.   [12] Ibid.: 201.
[13] Ibid.: 187.   [14] Ibid.: 192.   [15] Ibid.: 194.   [16] Ibid.: 197.
[17] Ibid.: 202.   [18] Ibid.: 189.

There is no doubt a relation of power between the author and his amanuensis. But the result is not merely asymmetrical. The result is a bivocal, polyphonic voice that informs, agitate, animates, excites.

This polyphonic bivocality of that narrative voice adds a hermeneutic twist to our reading of the text. The author and his amanuensis come from two different social classes – an aristocrat and his servant. The servant amanuensis is there to appease his master author, while the master is there to use and abuse his amanuensis – to say things that he would otherwise hesitate from saying. There is therefore a running dialogue in the text. We are as a result witness to a well-trodden travel narrative that consolidates the prose of these passages into an *institution* of collective reflection on a changing world. We are no longer reading a *personal* account of a royal travel. We are at the moment when through the dialectic of its two opposing classes a *nation* is dialogically reflecting on itself and its place in the world. An entire nation is being born through this dialogical narrative.

The dialogical narrative of 'Izz al-Dowleh's text yields it to the enduring insights of the Russian literary theorist Mikhail Bakhtin and his work on *The Dialogic Imagination*.[19] The two unequal partners in this travelogue posit two dialogical phrasings, or "utterances" as Bakhtin calls them, which in turn move toward the heteroglossia of the travel narrative we are reading. The "active participation of every utterance in living heteroglossia," Bakhtin remarked, "determines the linguistic profile and style of the utterance to no less a degree than its inclusion in any normative-centralizing system of a unitary language."[20] The unitary language was stabilizing and conservative. This heteroglossia was pathbreaking and opened onto new horizons. If all other travelogues before and after 'Izz al-Dowleh's are decidedly monologic, his is positively dialogic in the sense that it carries within itself, and through itself with the entire genre, a sustained dialogue with the whole idea of travel writing. As a result, in light of this travelogue we will read all others differently. In their running dialogues, 'Izz al-Dowleh and his amanuensis perform a contrapuntal reciprocity that reflects the whole genre of travel writing – and not just their own. When 'Izz al-Dowleh dictates a point, he is conscious of his amanuensis's presence, and when his amanuensis writes something, he is

[19] See Mikhail Bakhtin, *Dialogical Imagination: Four Essays*. Edited by Michael Holquist. Translated by Caryl Emerson and Michael Holquist (Austin, TX: University of Texas Press, 1981).
[20] Ibid.: 272.

conscious of 'Izz al-Dowleh's shadow over his shoulder. The result is a dialogical travelogue that reflects and refracts back on everything else written before or after it. Travel narrative thus becomes institutional to the Iranian dialogical encounter with European colonial modernity with a decidedly global perspective. If we disregard the worldly, the global framing of these narratives (as Qajar historiography has hitherto systematically done), that colonial encounter completely loses its emancipatory dialogical power.

In the same way that these travelogues and the institution they represented were dialogical, so was their worldly disposition against the grain of European colonial claims on the world – even if they did not know it, even if they were still too much in the sun to see it. This makes the position of Iranian encounters with European colonial modernity dialogical and not submissive and reactive, as it has been habitually framed under the false binary of "tradition versus modernity." It entails and posits agency, not denying the postcolonial subject its historic formation. This gives us an entirely different point of view on the colonial encounter with the very idea of "Europe." The reactionary reading of these travel narratives as fascination with "the West" or single-footedly moving to see and love and admire "Europe" (now consolidated in the Qajar historiography) was very much a product of the Pahlavi modernization project, later leading to the Islamist nativism of the Islamic republic. Evident in this bivocal prose we read in this travelogue is the fact that neither the author nor his shadow is writing in a vacuum. They are both rewriting the world in the plot of a travel prose that is now mapping the globe anew, their polyvocality definitive to the sculpted disposition of the emerging echoes the world hears from one end to another. The polyvocal prose is in and of itself subversive of any and all totalitarian regimes of knowledge production. So much of the rich and powerful aspects of these travelogues have been flattened out and disregarded by blindfolded Qajar historiography. My entire project in this book might be considered simply opening the world to see what has been missing beyond that dead-end *cul de sac* of "Islam and the West," "the West and the Rest," "Tradition versus Modernity."

Over-Correcting Orientalism

The travel narratives gathered under the name of Prince Salur and misidentified as his travelogues to "Europe" offer us a vastly different and far more important body of literature than such a false title suggests. Because of Naser al-Din Shah's fascination with traveling and travel narratives and also because of his dynasty being caught in a crucial period of world history when things were changing too fast for a slumbering dynasty to realize, multiple narratives of a single trip have reached us from a period when *authorship* was itself in a state of flux. Prince Abd al-Samad Mirza 'Izz al-Dowleh was a member of Qajar aristocracy, a learned, poised, and respectable man. The task of writing his travel diary was delegated to his servants and entourage. What has reached us under his name is therefore not a single-authored narrative but a multi-authored document. This ambiguous authorship elevates the very discourse of travel writing into an institution of gathering intelligence and mapping a global awareness. These writers, both individually and collectively, were writing back to the world, claiming the world, trying to reconfigure themselves in it.

Partially responsible for the distorted reading of these travelogues as travels to "Europe" is a paradoxical consequence of Edward Said's *Orientalism* (1978). Though the abusive reading of these travelogues began long before Edward Said published his *Orientalism*, because of a terrible misreading of that seminal book by disregarding the colonial relations of power underlying its argument, mostly apologetic scholars opposing (or else seeking to "balance") Said have written books about "Occidentalism," or "Europology" or else work through such metaphors as "the Persian Mirror" upon which "the West" was reflected. The result of this twisted reading of *Orientalism* has been a historic abuse of these texts and much more by disregarding their totality and singling out only their European part. Even before Edward Said's *Orientalism* (1978), Jalal Al-e Ahmad's *Gharbzadegi/Occidentosis* (1962) had a similar effect in causing reactionary moves to argue that the Orientals had also misread "the West." This, again, is not to argue that these travel narratives are entirely innocent themselves and cannot yield to such abusive readings – or that their authors themselves do not occasionally imply their narratives were to "Europe/Farang." This is simply to point out that there is a totality to these travelogues, their actual text and itinerary, that has been systemically ignored, abused, and manhandled.

But Said's *Orientalism* itself can be used to correct this flawed vision. What Edward Said and after him others have called "imagined geographies" were colonially conditioned not just due to European

Orientalism but because Arabs, Iranians, and other Muslims had joined them in manufacturing that compromised space. It took two to tango. Muslims and Arabs self-Orientalized themselves too. They bought into the binary. Whether they embraced it or opposed it, whether they taught they should all become Westernized or picked up arms to fight it, they fetishized and authenticated an illusion, a colonial chimera that was there to facilitate the imperial pedigree of a whole global order. Not just "the Orient" but in fact its doppelgänger, the "Occident," too, was co-created together in decidedly colonial terms. From Edward Said's "imagined geography" to Benedict Anderson's concept of "imagined communities," critical thinkers of their generation have drawn our attention to the manner in which the colonial and subsequent national boundaries of realms and continents were mapped out in overwhelmingly political terms. That there has been a relation of power and domination to these imaginative geographies is the clearest indication that the textual evidence of entire national and transnational archives has been fed into their dominant ideological force. This is the reason why so many extraordinary travel narratives from Iran and the rest of the Muslim world have been so consistently abused and misread, butchered and fed into this colonial geography.

The "Western" imaginary informed and sustained the discourse of European global domination. Who gets to describe whom and by what authority – that was the epistemic logic of European imaginative domination of the globe. European travel narratives and the entire discipline of anthropology were and remain at the roots of the power of Europe to describe (not the Arab and Muslim or the Orient alone) the entirety of the world. Edward Said's *Orientalism* revealed part of this fact and concealed the rest. By privileging the "Oriental" part of the "Western imaginary," he perforce left out Africa and Latin America, which are not part of that "Orient" but integral to the European colonial fantasies. Global capitalism was planetary and soon will become extraterrestrial. In his *Orientalism*, Edward Said privileged the European description of the Arab and Muslim world, but disregarded the rest. This had certain strategic advantages but a terrible theoretical consequence. It correctly used part of the larger picture, but its insights blinded us to the total picture. The travel narratives we are examining here are not describing Europe. They are mapping the world. This was a battle narratively to claim the world. The fact that only the European part of their itinerary is privileged by later scholars is the clearest indication that the global south at the mercy of the European imperialism has failed to connect the dots of their common destiny and mark the writing back that was claiming the world – not merely knee-jerking against Europe. The response to Orientalism was not Occidentalism, a nonsensical term. Orientalism was only a fragment of a much more comprehensive total picture of claiming, calling, and writing the world. European imperialism was not merely writing the Arab, Muslim, or the Oriental world. It was writing the world, including the Orient. Muslim, Arab, Chinese, African, or Latin American travelers, diplomats, merchants, scholars, and journalists did not write back to Europe. They claimed the world.

9 | *A Wandering Mystic*

[handwritten:] Hajj Pirzadeh

[handwritten:] 1. Ottom. –Arab world - Euro
↓
incl·hajj

[handwritten:] 2. India - Egypt -Europe -Ottom

The journey took me
To Equatorial climes where
In the shade of that
Green that mighty Banyan:
How well do I remember
The phrase that descended
Upon the summer site
Of my mind:

Be vast, be solitary,
Be humble, be unbending.

Sohrab Sepehri (Mosafer/Traveler, Babol, Spring 1966)

In Sepehri's poem "Mosafer/Traveler," the factual and the fantastic fuse together – the real and the imagined commingle, the matter-of-fact and the mystical meet. We know for a fact he traveled far and away, and we know for a fact those travels were awakened to the sublimity of his poetry, where he was the captain of his own ship, the sailor of seas uncharted on any map. Throughout his poetic journeys he was a mystic wanderer, at once solitary and yet conscious of the society around and about him, the history that moved the world, the geography that defied any one mapping of the planet. But the planet, this particular abode, was only the surface of his journeys – upon which surface he taught and guided us how to live, how to be. On that surface he had discovered an inner palpitating force. He was after the discovery of the mystery of that surface.

The West as the Measure of Everything

Early in the 1990s, the publication of M. R. Ghanoonparvar's learned study, *In a Persian Mirror: Images of the West and Westerners in Iranian Fiction* (1993), brought to a solid scholarly summit a crescendo of thinking and writing about the manner in which "the West" was reportedly perceived and reflected in "the East," in this case in Iran.[1] In the publisher's note to this landmark study we read, "The extreme anti-Western actions and attitudes of Iranians in the past decade have astonished and dismayed the West, which has character-ized the Iranian positions as irrational and inexplicable. In this ground-breaking study of images of the West in Iranian literature, however, M. R. Ghanoonparvar reveals that these attitudes did not develop suddenly or inexplicably but rather evolved over more than two cen-turies of Persian-Western contact." Once we actually get to read the book, we see that the distinguished scholar of modern Persian litera-ture does indeed deliver on that promise. "This survey," again according to its publisher's note, "significantly illuminates the sources of Iranian attitudes toward the West and offers many surprising dis-coveries for Western readers, not least of which is the fact that Iranians have often found Westerners to be as enigmatic and incomprehensible as we have believed them to be." This "we" here of course refers to those "Westerners" on whose behalf the publisher's note reads the contemporary Iranian history, and that "them" to the object of this literary curiosity. In praising the study, Roger M. Savory, Professor Emeritus of Middle Eastern and Islamic Studies at the University of Toronto, had further added: "I do not know of any other work which surveys the whole range of 19th- and 20th-century Persian prose writing in this way – from the travel accounts (Safarnameh) of the 19th century down to the present day. Of special interest and import-ance to Western readers is the author's analysis of post-revolutionary writing." All in all, we the readers were informed, as we opened the book to read it, that we were about to find out how "the West" was reflected in "the East" (Iran).

This historically anachronistic, analytically flawed, and textually abusive confusion of post-revolutionary Iran in the 1980s and post-colonial nation-formation during the nineteenth and the early twenti-eth century is at the root of the fateful distortion of the body of literature I am examining here in this book. This false emplotment of a vast, rich, and increasingly significant body of travel narratives in a clumsy and ill-informed analytic is a singular source of epistemic

---

[1] See M. R. Ghanoonparvar, *In a Persian Mirror: Images of the West and Westerners in Iranian Fiction* (Austin, TX: University of Texas Press, 1993).

violence against a healthy and robust understanding of countries and climes like Iran at the threshold of their encounters with European colonial modernity. Entire fields of scholarship and with it the post-colonial fate of nation-states have been sent off on a wild-goose chase of "Islam and the West," or "Tradition versus Modernity," precisely because of this flawed and abusive reading of these sources. If only our distinguished colleagues were simply patient enough actually to read these texts cover to cover!

In his preface, Ghanoonparvar tells us how the seeds of his study "germinated" during the heyday of the Iranian revolution of 1977–1979, when, in his estimation, it had assumed an "anti-Western turn."[2] The study then proceeds with an astonishingly haphazard and ahistorical compilation of any reference the author could find to the term "Farang" in classical poets like Sa'di or Attar as conceptual precursors to its current use as "Europe." He then moves to Iranian travelers of the nineteenth century such as Mirza Saleh, Ilchi, and Hajj Sayyah, etc., cherry-picking a few passages from their vast compendium in which they have made some observations about "the West," particularly when they say something either pejorative or admiring, highlighting them and thus distorting the much larger picture of these travel narratives.[3] This section, titled "Understanding the Unknown,"[4] in which the author pays particular attention to the travelogues of the nineteenth century, is a prime example of a vertiginously Eurocentric and abusive reading of the genre, categorically and completely ignoring the totality of these travelogues and fishing for one scattered observation or another these travelers had made about Europe, taking it out of context and blowing it out of proportion as if they knew and cared for nothing except for this "Farang/Europe." They are given a false and nonexistent fascination and obsession with "Europe" or "the West," at the heavy expense of ignoring the rest of their stories. The author's own fixation with the delusion of "the West," centuries after those texts were written, is here projected backward to these travelers. Textual abuse confounds epistemic violence and results in a deeply flawed and ahistorical reading of these texts.

The key problem with the entire trajectory of scholarship Ghanoon-parvar's otherwise fine study of "the modernist" Persian literature represents is the systematic suppression of the totality of a traveling

---

[2] Ibid.: xi.   [3] Ibid.: 1–10.   [4] Ibid.: 11–37.

narrative now anachronistically foregrounded as the precursor to the animus of the postcolonial revolutionary mobilizations that have been completely sold to the idea of "the West versus the East." Evident in the pages of these travelogues themselves, if anyone cared to read them cover to cover and page after page, is the fact that they are not a precursor of any animus between two delusional categories code-named "the West" and "the East." They in fact do exactly the opposite and narratively subvert the colonial gaze by circumambulating the imaginative geography of "the West" and depicting a whole different map of the world. Colonialism was not just a matter of military conquest and economic plundering of nations. Colonialism was contingent on a form of symbolic representation of the world, predicated on an imaginative geography in which "Europe" was manufactured on top and the world at the bottom; "Europe" was the destination, the world moving toward it. Varied forms of aesthetic representations and cultural technologies of domination were integral to the colonial gaze, and who had the power to cast it. With every twist to emerging technologies – painting, printing, photography, film, fiction, etc. – "the West" was set against "The Rest," and its geography elevated to the normative spatial contours of its global presence. What these Persian travelers we are examining here did was not to follow that geography but in fact to subvert it. Simply by starting to make a record of their journey from the heart of their own homeland to anywhere else (including Europe) they traveled, they remapped the world decidedly against the grain of that colonial Eurocentrism. This inclusion of Europe in this itinerary was in fact the most powerful, the most symbolic, the most "democratic" indication that Europe was part of a much larger, much more familiar world. They neither privileged nor dismissed Europe. They incorporated it into *their* world, defying the European (colonizing) world. The state of scholarship that Ghanoon-parvar's otherwise excellent summary and argument represents is the distance between that vastly more enabling imaginative geography and the time that the mind of the scholar had become thoroughly colonized.

A Traveling Dervish

Among the travelers Ghanoonparvar mentions early in his book is Haji Pirzadeh, whom he believes, because of advanced age and a mystical disposition, was far less critical and far more admiring of "the West."[5] Such characterizations, however, are symptomatic of the entire genre of scholarship this prominent literary critique represents and unfortunately furthest removed from the factual evidence of the total text in its organic entirety that requires a whole different mode of serious reading.

Let's first get to know the traveler: Haji Mohammad Ali Pirzadeh (ca. 1835–1904) was a Sufi mystic, with a profound predilection for purposeful traveling. He was born and raised in a prominent Sufi family from Na'in in central Iran.[6] His maternal grandfather was a certain Haj Abd al-Wahab ibn Abd al-Qayyum, who was a prominent and deeply loved and admired Sufi master in Na'in. Haji Mohammad Ali Pirzadeh spent the first twenty years or so of his life (1835–1855) in his birthplace of Na'in. His early youth was spent in Tehran (1855–1858), where he was much loved and admired by members of the Qajar aristocracy, who sought his gracious company and solicited his blessings. As we will soon see, he too very much enjoyed the company of the royalty, of the rich, and of the powerful. But still he did so with an unmissable sense of self-dignity and moral decorum. There is a decree dated April 1905 in which Mozaffar al-Din Shah Qajar, the reigning monarch, orders the transfer of Haji Mohammad Ali Pirzadeh's regular salary from the Qajar court to his descendants – which means our mystic master was quite close to the Qajar monarchy.[7] But we also know that his residence in Tehran was a way station for mystics from all over the Muslim world, and that Mirza Abu al-Hasan Khan Jelveh the leading Muslim philosopher of the time, was a close friend and confidant of Haji Mohammad Ali Pirzadeh, as was Ma'sum Ali Shah, a prominent Sufi master and hagiographer of the time, with whom Haji Mohammad Ali Pirzadeh exchanged poems praising each other's spiritual qualities. In these figures, the Qajar aristocracy had secured for itself an entourage of mystics, philosophers, and theologians, who in turn presented them with an aura of

---

[5] Ibid.: 26 ff.

[6] I take much of this short biographical sketch from the introduction of Iraj Afshar to Hafez Farmanfarma'ian's critical edition of Haji Mohammad Ali Pirzadeh's travelogue, *Safarnameh-ye Haji Pirzadeh* (Tehran: Tehran University Press, 1963): I: One-sixty-three.

[7] For the original text of this decree, see Afshar in *Safarnameh-ye Haji Pirzadeh*: I: Eleven–Twelve.

legitimacy. It is crucial for us to keep this environment of aristocratic elegance and intellectual effervescence as the context in which Haji Pirzadeh will soon commence his travels.

His presence in Tehran did not last too long (1855–1858). After his short residence in Tehran, Haji Pirzadeh spent more than a decade (1858–1870) in Istanbul, from which city he traveled throughout the Ottoman Empire, the Arab and Muslim world, and Europe. The Qajar ambassador to the Ottoman court, Mirza Hossein Sepahsalar Moshir al-Dowleh Qazvini, was a devotee of Haji Pirzadeh and had facilitated his sojourn to Istanbul. At the conclusion of his long residence in Istanbul, Haji Pirzadeh performed his Hajj pilgrimage to Mecca. When a superior Sufi mystic by the name of Haji Mirza Safa passed away, the same Mirza Hossein Sepahsalar Moshir al-Dowleh Qazvini had him buried in a beautiful garden and secured the permission of the reigning monarch, Naser al-Din Shah Qajar, to transfer the ownership and operation of that garden to Haji Pirzadeh, who had the custody of that sacred precinct for the rest of his life. In this garden, Haji Pirzadeh had planted all kinds of fruit trees, and from these fruits he regularly sent baskets full of gifts to the members of Qajar aristocracy, including the reigning monarch. There are letters in the handwriting of Mozaffar al-Din Shah Qajar thanking Haji Pirzadeh for the fruits he had sent him. It is also reported that the day that Naser al-Din Shah Qajar was assassinated in Shah Abd al-Azim shrine, he had intended to spend some time with Haji Pirzadeh in this garden. Haji Pirzadeh had named various passageways and corners of this garden after a phase and a stage in Sufi path: *Safar*/Travel, *Towhid*/The Unity of God, *Halqeh-ye Mohabbat*/The Circle of Love, *Bab al-Arefin*/The Gate of the Mystics, *Tekyeh Foqara*/The Corner of the Poor, etc. He had turned this garden into a way station for Sufis passing through Qajar territories. After his return from a second trip abroad, he is reported to have predicted to a friend that soon men and women will sit down in this very garden and under the very same trees and there will be no barrier between them. Was this garden, thus designed and designated, a blueprint of his map of a world, both real and parabolic, over which he would travel as far and as wide as he could?

Haji Pirzadeh traveled twice outside his homeland.[8] He did not keep a written record of his first trip, which took place sometime around 1868.

---

[8] Under the influence of European Orientalism, even the eminent historian Iraj Afshar, in his short biography of Haji Mohammad Ali Pirzadeh, describes

His second trip, in which he wrote his extensive travelogue, began on Thursday, May 19, 1886, and concluded on Monday, February 26, 1889, and it took him to India, Egypt, France, United Kingdom, Germany, Austria (and other parts of the Austro-Hungarian empire), and the Ottoman Empire, including Syria, Palestine, and Iraq. None of these "non-European" aspects of his travels ever get any except a passing attention by those who generations later care to refer to this travelogue. As a devout Muslim, he performed his Hajj Pilgrimage in Arabia, recording the details of performing his religious duties. As a Shi'a, he performed his pilgrimage to Shi'i sacred sites in Iraq, all with devotion and humility. As a curious and conscious human being, he visited India, the Ottoman Empire, and the Arab world. But none of that has mattered or figured in understanding who he was and what he was up to in making such journeys. All that has mattered to the colonized minds who have cared to read a few pages of his travelogue is that he went to "Europe." In these journeys, he met with some of the most prominent intellectuals and statesmen of his time, including Mirza Habib Isfahani, Edward G. Brown, Mirza Mirza Malkam Khan, Muhammad Abduh, and Mirza Shirazi. Here too the only person he met and has been worthy of cherry-picking is the British Orientalist E. G. Browne.

After his first trip and before his second, Haji Pirzadeh married and had two sons, Nur al-Din (d. 1918) and Nayyer al-Din (he was born in 1897, and at the writing of Iraj Afshar's biography of Haji Pirzadeh in 1963, he was still alive). Haji Pirzadeh died on Saturday, March 12, 1904, and was buried in his garden. He had a rich and fulfilling life and he helped his nation remap the world for their posterity.

A Persian Mystic Abroad (the second trip)

Let us now take a quick look at Pirzadeh's itinerary and see where did he actually go, what did he do, and what was the outline of his

---

these two trips as "twice he went to Europe" (see Afshar in *Safarnameh-ye Haji Pirzadeh*: I: Twenty-four). Whereas, he has seen it right in front of his eyes that Europe was as much a part of his trips as were Central Asia, North Africa, the Arab and Muslim world, and the Ottoman territories. Much to his credit, the editor of the volume, Hafez Farmanfarma'ian, never refers to the volume as a travelogue to Europe, but only as a text in understanding the Iranian history of the nineteenth century. (ibid.: I: 1–4).

travelogue. He leaves Tehran for Shah Abd al-Azim Shrine and from there he goes to Qom, from where he goes to Mahallat and visits with Hajj Sayyah, before leaving for Isfahan and Shiraz and their environs. He gives detailed accounts of these movements within his own homeland. Then he goes to Bushehr and travels by sea to Karachi and Mumbai; from here he sails for Cairo and Alexandria, before he sails for Paris. At this point, before he sails for Paris, we are 180 pages into his travelogue, of the 320 total pages in the first volume of the travelogue. That is almost 60 percent of the total pages having nothing to do with Europe. He has not even reached Europe at this stage. This part of the travelogue is as much integral to his happily casual observations as the rest. This, in short, is NOT a travelogue to Europe, though Europe is part of this travelogue. Considering this text as a travelogue to Europe is not just misreading it. It is simply not to read it at all.

The second volume of Haji Pirzadeh's travelogue begins in Paris and continues with his trip to Berlin, Vienna, and Bucharest, before he leaves for Istanbul. He devotes altogether 68 pages of this second volume to his observations about Europe – that's all. From Istanbul, he goes to Izmir and from there back to Alexandria in Egypt, and then to Cairo, back to Alexandria and Port Said, and then off to Beirut, Syria, Baghdad, Kazimayn, Karbala, Najaf, Samara, and then back to Iran. In short, of the 457 pages of the second volume, only 68 pages are devoted to "Europe" – just over 1 percent of the travelogue is about Europe! How in the name of decency is this a travelogue to Europe? What sane person who has actually read this book cover to cover, page after page, can ever call this a "travelogue to Europe?" The absurdity of the proposition simply boggles the mind. Only a deeply colonized mind would call these sorts of travelogues evidence of trips to Europe, or documents in the encounters of "Islam and the West," or any other such nonsense.

According to Iraj Afshar, who wrote a learned introduction to this volume, Pirzadeh made two major travels abroad – and not to "Farang/Europe," as he falsely says. The first one was in 1285/1868, and the second from 1303/1885 to 1305/1887. Of the first trip we have no record, and his surviving travelogue is about his second trip, which as we saw is much wider than his short visit to Europe, and most of the text is in fact about India, the Arab and Muslim world, and the Ottoman territories. What is paramount in these travels is not a linear progression from Iran to Europe and back. These travels are in fact

circular, with Iran as their epicenter with India, Russia, the Arab and
Muslim world, Ottoman territories, and of course a bit of Europe too.
In his preference for and privileging the European part of Haji Pirzadeh's travelogue, Afshar gives an inordinate amount of attention to his
meeting with the prominent British Orientalist E. G. Brown, and
details their letter exchanges and friendly relationship. A significant
part of Afshar's biography of Pirzadeh is entirely devoted to his correspondence with Browne. This is unfortunate and disappointing. The
late Iraj Afshar was a towering figure in Iranian scholarship, and yet,
alas, his mind was as thoroughly Eurocentric as anyone else in his
subsequent generations.

Such privileging of a single Orientalist Haji Pirzadeh had met is in
sharp contrast with the letter and spirit of the travelogue itself. The first
thing that strikes the reader of the travelogue is Pirzadeh's friendly
disposition toward everyone he meets. He has lots of friends and loves
to talk about them. He constantly mentions the names of his close
friends with whom he is traveling or whom he visits upon arrival in a
new city. But this does not extend to his family. He tells us he left
Tehran for Shah Abd al-Azim without telling his wife where he was
going,[9] but then plunges into barrages of bromance with his close
friends, leaving first for Shiraz with his buddy Moayyed al-Molk,
while a prominent philosopher of the time, Mirza Abu al-Hasan
Khan Jelveh, we learn, was also accompanying him for part of the
way. He knows Hajj Sayyah and stops by to say hello to him.[10] So
when he meets with Browne and makes a record of this visit, there is
nothing unusual about the encounter. It is only the later historians such
as Afshar who privilege that meeting over others.

Another major concern for Haji Pirzadeh is his preoccupation with
major cities he visits in the course of his journeys. It is important to see
how he begins his major observations about Isfahan and its historical
sites long before he gets to Paris or London. He spends pages and
describes in exquisite detail his observations about Isfahan and its
historical sites. The same is true about his detailed description of
Shiraz and its suburbs,[11] in which he mixes his observations about
political issues and the climate of the city, as well as additional details
about the prominent figures of the city, interrupted by his feeling
depressed and forlorn at a key moment when he goes to a corner

---

[9] Ibid.: I: 3–4.   [10] Ibid.: I: 8.   [11] Ibid.: I: 33 ff.

and, in solitude, cries.[12] He then moves on to talk about a couple of wedding ceremonies that were taking place in Shiraz among his acquaintances, before he turns to a description of the major monuments of the city: Masjid Vakil, Hammam Karim Khan, Bazar Vakil, plus full descriptions of mosques and madrasas.[13] He spends pages after pages giving the details of Shirazi dignitaries, before turning his attention to beautiful gardens of the city, and then an even more detailed anthropological description of people's clothing habits. In short, page 13 of this edition to page 91 (almost 80 pages) of this travelogue to "Europe" is all about Shiraz and its environment. To be sure, here on page 92 he says he intends to travel to "Farangestan/ Europe" for some medical treatment, but he does not fly to London, or disappear into thin air and resurface in Paris. First, he has to go to Bushehr. On his way to Bushehr, he is kicked by a mule and his leg is broken,[14] which continues to bother him for pages and miles. He again spends a good amount of time describing Bushehr, including his observation that a US warship had landed there.[15] From Bushehr he eventually goes to Bandar Abbas and sails toward Karachi, and from there to Mumbai, which draws a serious amount of attention from him. So far, Isfahan, Shiraz, and Mumbai draw most of his detailed attentions. In Mumbai, he spends considerable time and ink and detailed attention to its economic and social fabric, describing factories, the social demography of its population,[16] its dresses, a thick description of Hinduism, the condition of Zoroastrians, Jewish and Muslim communities, as well as the Ismailis. It is simply insane to disregard these passages and jump to what he says about Europe. He has a complete fascination with major cities, where he basks in telling his readers what he sees and what is the significance of what he sees.

From Mumbai he sails toward Aden.[17] He reaches Cairo, which again draws much of his detailed attention. Mosques, schools, mausoleums, Al-Azhar mosque, the Bektashi Sufis – he is meticulous in his descriptions of that city. He offers a detailed account of the urban setting, and the British colonial occupation of Egypt. He then goes to Alexandria. He is with seven Iranian merchants wherever he goes, including Alexandria.[18] From Alexandria he finally sails toward Brindisi in Italy, where he eventually travels to Turin.[19] By the time he takes

---

[12] Ibid.: I: 63.   [13] Ibid.: I: 70 ff.   [14] Ibid.: I: 103.   [15] Ibid.: I: 109.
[16] Ibid.: I: 127.   [17] Ibid.: I: 140.   [18] Ibid.: I: 171.   [19] Ibid.: I: 178.

a train from Turin to Paris,[20] we know that given his experiences of Isfahan, Shiraz, Mumbai, and Cairo, he would be fascinated by Paris too. Upon his arrival in Paris he gives a full description of the Iranian diplomatic corps as well as the Iranian merchants living there. Then he plunges into a thick description of Paris. Altogether he spends an inordinate amount of time about Paris, more specifically from page 182 to page 290, more than 100 pages. No doubt Paris for him is Europe and Europe is Paris – but we will not understand his fascination with Paris if we skip his descriptions of all the major cities he has visited and described on this trip. He dwells on Paris extensively, but not much more than he did on Shiraz or Mumbai or Cairo. In fact, without his accounts of Shiraz, Mumbai, or Cairo, his description of Paris would be out of place.

The same happens when Haji Pirzadeh travels from Paris to London.[21] His arrival in London coincides with the Golden Jubilee of Queen Victoria in June 1887, of which he makes a note. While in London, he and his companion Moayyed al-Molk are warmly hosted by Mirza Malkam Khan, who introduces them to a number of British dignitaries and foreign diplomats, including Sir Henry Creswicke Rawlinson (1810–1895), the renowned British colonial army officer and Orientalist, famous for having deciphered the Old Persian portion of the trilingual cuneiform inscription of Darius the Great at Bisitun, Iran. When Rawlinson finds out Haji Pirzadeh is a Sufi, he asks him how come the Sufi order in Sudan is fighting the British – are they not supposed to be peaceful – to which Pirzadeh responds, no sir, not all dervishes are peaceful.[22] From his conversations with Rawlinson we gather he is a politically astute but socially polite and gentle man. He is not abrasive or confrontational. But he is not sheepish either.

Haji Pirzadeh spends some time sight-seeing in London, including the Post Office, offering a full discussion of the British press and visiting an asylum house, orphanage, the Hyde Park, Prince Albert Memorial, Thames River, British Museum, Madame Tussauds, etc. He also meets with E. G. Browne in London. He is happy and impressed to see him but makes nothing like the big fuss later historians have made

---

[20] Ibid.: I: 183.

[21] As he sails through the English Channel, Haji Pirzadeh tells us how the sea was calm, contrary to when he crossed it on a previous occasion in 1280/1863 when it was very stormy. See ibid.: Volume I: 291.

[22] Ibid.: I: 295.

of the encounter. He ends his observations about London with a long poem praising the splendor of the British capital.[23]

Figure 11 "A view of Beirut and the Lebanon in the 19th century." Terms such as "the Middle East," "the Near East," or "the Far East," all manufactured by and for the benefits of the Eurocentrism of European colonialism, are nowhere to be found in these nineteenth century travelogues. The Arab and Muslim world is here integral to the larger Mediterranean and global map these travelers are re-imagining for their Persian-speaking readership. Falsely privileging Europe as the sole destination of these travelers ascribes a Eurocentrism to the project of colonial modernity that the fuller picture of their travels decidedly dismantles. Reprinted with permission from Classic Image/Alamy Stock Photo.

Bringing Home the World

The second volume of the travelogue begins on Thursday 22 Shawwal 1304/July 14, 1887, when Haj Pirzadeh and his companion leave London for Paris. On his return visit to Paris he continues his observations about the French capital and begins with a discussion of how a republic works, while reporting on how many in France were still monarchists. He spends a good amount of time writing about the irrigation system of Paris and its fruits and vegetables and also includes

---

[23] Ibid.: I: 318–321.

a full discussion of Parisian dogs and cats.[24] But not everything he writes while traveling through Paris is about Paris. There are a considerable number of pages devoted to Iranian politics, Persian diplomats, and impromptu poems he composes on such occasions. He does compose a long poem in praise of Paris too, to be sure.[25] But a few pages later he also composes another poem complaining of his woes in Paris. All it took was nine months of living in Paris to turn that "clean, lovely, and magnificent" city into "a prison full of snakes and scorpions."[26] We will miss these nuances, these narrative meanderings, in the prose of the observant traveler if we just pick and choose a few passages of the thick and foreboding volume.

Haji Pirzadeh is finally happy to board a train with his companions and leave Paris via Belgium and arrive in Berlin, where he immediately commences his sight-seeing by visiting its zoo.[27] He is as impressed with Berlin as he was with Paris or any other major city he visits, from Isfahan to Mumbai to Cairo. He visits the Prussian arms manufacturing factory in Berlin; he goes for an outing in the Berlin park; he attends a banquet the Qajar envoy gives in his honor, with other dignitaries accompanying him. The wife of a Jewish merchant does a portrait of Haji Pirzadeh in Berlin.[28] He eventually leaves Berlin for Vienna – again deeply impressed with the city, as he is with every other major city he visits. He gives full descriptions of the buildings, churches, places, spas, opera house, theaters, photography house, garrisons, medical physicians. From Vienna he bids Moayyed al-Molk farewell, receives some money from him for the rest of his trip, boards a train and travels to Bucharest, where again he spends some time exploring. He eventually travels toward Bulgaria, before he arrives in Istanbul.

Upon his arrival in Istanbul, he immediately visits the Iranian embassy and gets ready to explore the city. First the diplomatic corps of the Iranian embassy and then the Iranian merchants living there grab his immediate attention. In Istanbul, he has a severe backache and spends some time treating it. In Istanbul, he visits Mirza Habib Isfahani, the towering intellectual figure among the Iranian expats whom we know primarily as the translator of that nasty colonial tract, *The Adventures of Hajji Baba of Ispahan*, by the British colonial officer James Justinian Morier. Mirza Habib's worldly and cosmopolitan

---

[24] Ibid.: II:14–17.   [25] Ibid.: II:33–37.   [26] Ibid.: II:41.   [27] Ibid.: II:43.
[28] Ibid.: II:48.

disposition rubs Haji Pirzadeh the wrong way. He considers him too frivolous. He wishes Mirza Habib was more proper, polite, and less playful. Nevertheless, he praises Mirza Habib for his knowledge and his love for his homeland.[29] He spends a good amount of time discovering Istanbul, including its non-Muslim communities. He spends pages decrying the reigning Sultan Abd al-Hamid. Haji Pirzadeh devotes detailed pages on describing the political and military apparatus of the Ottoman Empire. He is particularly drawn to the fact that the Shi'i community lives in peace in Istanbul and even performs their ritual devotions to their Imams without any hesitations.[30] Page after page of the travelogue reads like anthropological report on the people of Istanbul and their customs and habits. He pays particular attention to the Sufi gatherings in Istanbul.[31] These pages are imperative to correct our understanding of Haji Pirzadeh's travels abroad, which are most defiantly not to "Europe" but to major cities around his homeland that include Europe but are not limited to Europe.

On 24 Jumadi al-Thani 1305/March 3, 1888, Haji Pirzadeh leaves Istanbul and sails toward Alexandria. On his way he visits Izmir and spends some time exploring and describing it.[32] Upon his arrival in Alexandria, he attends a wedding. He spends a good amount of time describing this wedding and its lavish banquets and receptions for a variety of classes in Alexandria. From Alexandria he eventually goes to Cairo, where he continues his previous observations and sight-seeing. He and his companions meet with Egyptian dignitaries, celebrate Nowruz, and feel at home. Haji Pirzadeh spends a good number of pages describing how Egyptians were so respectful of Shi'is and their beliefs.[33] From his descriptions we learn that there is a prominent Iranian community living in Egypt, all of them happy to receive Haji Pirzadeh and his dignitary friends. His descriptions of Cairo in exquisite detail are not any less enthusiastic than those of Paris. This travelogue might as well be describing a journey to Egypt if these details were to be compared. But neither Cairo nor Paris are the exclusive destiny of his journey, so far as the actual text of his travelogue is concerned. They both are – and Cairo and Istanbul are not in "Europe." They are major Muslim cosmopolitan cities. His descriptions of Cairo are in fact much more detailed than anywhere else. Again, page after page of the

---

[29] Ibid.: II: 95–97.   [30] Ibid.: II: 113.   [31] Ibid.: II: 120.   [32] Ibid.: II: 130.
[33] Ibid.: II: 156.

travelogue reads like an anthropological survey of the culture and habits of the people of Egypt. He is particularly impressed by men and women who had mastered the art of Qur'anic recitation.[34]

After spending some two months in Cairo, finally their hosts get fed up with them and they hurriedly leave for Alexandria, and from there they go to Port Said, where he spends some time exploring the region in some detail. While in Port Said, Haji Pirzadeh witnesses the Italian navy sailing toward Somalia in the heat of their colonial conquest of Africa, in what would be called "Italian Somaliland." Haji Pirzadeh shares with his readers the poor and defeated spirit of the Italian soldiers who were returning to Italy, and via a local report compares it with the high-spirited colonial arrogance they had when they were going to Africa. Why do no such parts of the travelogue ever make it to the learned scholarship on these travel narratives? From Port Said he sails to the port of Haifa and Acre, where his contemporary Babis had gathered. From there he moves to Beirut, where we read his detailed impressions of the city and of Mount Lebanon. Like anywhere else he travels, he first pays visits to the prominent Iranians in the city. But he also meets with Sheikh Muhammad Abduh, who at this time was living in Beirut. He eventually leaves Beirut for Syria and arrives in Baalbek and marvels at the historical sites he visits. He is eventually drawn to Damascus, where he spends a good amount of time exploring, and writing about its major mosques and other significant sites. His fascination with Damascus is no less than it was with Cairo or Istanbul or Paris, with the most detailed attention paid to its urban and rural lives.

He eventually leaves Damascus for Baghdad and Kazimayn. On his way, he stops for visits at many villages and their historical Roman sites. Particular, however, he is in performing his ritual pilgrimages to Shi'i sacred sites, paying his respects to prominent Shi'i notables who reside in Iraq, giving a full description of Kazimayn, offering detailed accounts of the Shi'i shrines in the city, and making a note of the distance between Kazimayn and Baghdad. In Baghdad he habitually visits the Iranian residence of the city, before he offers his readers a detailed account of the ancient cosmopolis. He then moves on to Karbala and performs his pilgrimage at the site of the Third Shia Imam Hussein.[35] While giving a fuller description of Karbala, he is critical of the Ottoman authorities for having abandoned Iraq to its nonexistent

[34] Ibid.: II: 186.   [35] Ibid.: II: 316 ff.

means and not attending to its well-being. From Karbala he travels to Najaf, continuing with his pious pilgrimage to the most sacred sites in a Shi'i geography. It is impossible to imagine any serious person reading Haji Pirzadeh's pious, respectful, devoted passages upon his visit to the first Shi'i Imam's mausoleum[36] and still calling this a travelogue "to Europe." How, by what authority, and for what purpose should we disregard these crucial parts of a Muslim's travels around the world and only privilege one part of it? It makes no sense. He gives a full description of how paying respect to Shi'a sites is performed. He gives a detailed account of the seminaries in Najaf. He reports of his meeting with a prominent Shi'is figure, Mirza Habibollah Rashti. He details the physical setting of Imam Ali's mausoleum before moving on to give us a fuller description of Najaf's architectural landscape and urban design. He returns to Karbala and continues with his observations of the Iranian and other Shi'a pilgrims, paying attention to the Bektashi Sufis, offering more detailed descriptions of the Imam Hossein's mausoleum and other equally significant sites, and giving a full description of prominent Shi'is clerics residing in Karbala. A very strange "travelogue to Europe" indeed!

In Karbala, Haj Pirzadeh's backache returns to bother him.[37] But it does not prevent him from noting and celebrating Naser al-Din Shah's birthday while in Iraq. From Karbala he moves to Samara, gets lost on the way, but finally gets there and continues with his pious pilgrimage. From Samara he returns to Kazimayn, before returning to Baghdad and getting ready for his return to Iran. This whole section of the second volume of the travelogue is the most detailed, patient, poised, and prominent part of the travelogue, and it has nothing to do with Europe, let alone the inanity called "the West." On his way back he visits Taq-e Kisra at Ctesiphon, visits the mausoleum of Salman the Persian, and finally reaches the port of Basra, from which he again gives a full physical description of the city and its environs, before he finally sails from Basra to Bushehr.

The ship he boards to leave Basra for Bushehr is an utter disaster, filled to the brim with horses with no room left for Pirzadeh and other passengers even to stand, let alone to sit or rest.[38] It is a ship owned by a British company, manned by particularly nasty British sailors. There is a kind and caring Zoroastrian physician on the ship who tells

[36] Ibid.: II: 328 ff.   [37] Ibid.: II: 368.   [38] Ibid.: II: 402 ff.

Pirzadeh that both the captain and all his lieutenants on the ship are in fact children born out of wedlock in British bordello houses. This incident gives Pirzadeh the occasion to write critically about Europe and its social malaise, with people no longer living in houses but in hotels, eating in restaurants and not at homes, having sex with prostitutes rather than having lawful wives, all of which having led to a decline in population in some European countries such as France.[39] So yes, he is a mystic alright: but a mystic with a critical bone to his intelligence.

Pirzadeh gives a detailed description of Bushehr as if he were still traveling abroad. He is impressed by the British, Indian, Dutch, and Ottoman political and commercial presence in the port city. He is equally impressed by the presence of an Iranian ship at the port, called "Persepolis," and emphasizes the significance of even more such ships to be present in the Persian Gulf. There is a tone of urgency in his prose here, for having traveled extensively around the world he now looks at his homeland and its political security differently. He criticizes the poor condition of the port and its lack of facilities compared with other ports he has seen. He gives detailed recommendations as to how to build proper commercial ports.

From Bushehr he eventually moves toward Borazjan and Shiraz. He makes apt observations about all the small cities and villages he sees on his way, until he reaches Kazerun and uses the occasion to talk about that city in some detail. He talks about the landscape, population, gardens, architecture, and climate of Kazerun as if he were writing about any other city in India, Egypt, Europe, or the Ottoman Empire. Early in the morning of Friday, December 14, 1888, he and his fellow travelers arrive in Shiraz. Significant crowds of well-wishers come to welcome Moayyed al-Molk and his entourage, including Haji Pirzadeh. He tells us the duration of his travels abroad from the time he left Shiraz until his return was two years, two months and ten days. He eventually leaves Shiraz for Isfahan and Tehran, continuing with his observations about everything he sees on his way. Upon his arrival in Isfahan he spends the last few pages of his travelogue mostly talking about his friends and other dignitaries who had come forward to welcome and host him back to his homeland with open arms and generous greetings.

[39] Ibid.: II: 405 ff.

Intention of the Text

Let me now challenge my own theory: that these travel narratives are not to Europe but in fact are to the world at large, and that these travelers are in direct opposition to the colonial mapping of the world and are in fact producing a vastly different and ipso facto liberating geography. I have had many occasions in this book in which I have pointed out how these travelogues have been falsely cast as travel narratives "to Europe" when there is no textual evidence to that effect, when the author himself does not say so. What about when an author, such as Haji Pirzadeh, or before him Abu Talib Isfahani, actually says that his text is indeed a travelogue to Europe, what then?

Toward the end of his book, when he gives the duration of his journey abroad, Haji Pirzadeh calls his book the record of his "Safar-e Farangestan/European journey."[40] Is this self-designation by Pirzadeh an indication that he, too, privileged the European part of his trip, or simply an indication of the fact that the farthest point to which he has traveled from Shiraz, upon his return to Shiraz, was Europe? Either way, and however he meant it, the textual evidence of his travelogue, the text itself, points to a truth beyond either of these two readings of the intention of the author himself. The fact of his travels, and where he went and what he saw and what he wrote, are all indications of a circular and mostly urban-based itinerary beyond the furthest reach of his travels. He traveled from Iran to India and from there to Egypt, and then to Europe, back through the Ottoman territories, and finally back to Iran. This is not a journey to Europe, though Europe was the farthest he traveled. This itinerary is marked, more than anything else, by Pirzadeh's fascination with cities, all cities, and every major city he visits. But still, he says his trip was a "European journey." What then?

Here, the authorial reference to Europe must be placed within a larger hermeneutic context. To follow Umberto Eco's extraordinarily precise hermeneutics, the intention of the text here overrides even the intention of the author, or what we actually read trumps what the author announces at the end of his travel book. Let me explain: In his pioneering work on hermeneutics, *The Open Work* (1962), Umberto Eco placed the active reader at the center of the hermeneutic encounter with any text. It is the reader, he argued, who teases out of the text

[40] Ibid.: II: 429.

what is merely latent, or hidden, even to the author.[41] There is an active entanglement among the author, the text she writes, and the reader that has come to this text across time and space. Shortly after Eco, Derrida published his own subversive text, *Of Grammatology* (1967), in which he completely subverted the very idea of the coherent text and even suspended the reader in its meandering matrix.[42] For Derrida, even the text did not have any enduring claim on a coherence, let alone on the intention of the author or the intention of the reader, which had by now become entirely moot. In a subsequent essay, *Lector in Fabula* (1979), Eco continued to meditate on the role of the reader in making the text speak its hidden languages. Eco was never as radical in his subversive hermeneutics as Derrida was. The Italian hermeneutician remained loyal to a civil discourse and a sensible expectation from the text compared to his French counterpart. In his "The Death of the Author" (1967), Roland Barthes too completely abandoned any significance to the intention of the author in a text. But in *The Limits of Interpretation* (1990), Eco defied all such French speculations and developed his full-fledged triangulated theory of three intentions at work when we read a text: *Intention of the author, Intention of the reader, and the Intention of the text.*[43]

What I wish to add to Eco's triangulation is the *condition of readability* that sustains the impossibilities of reading as time unfolds. These texts have been *produced* at the cusp of coloniality and *interpreted* at the depth of anticolonial fixations on the metaphors of "the West," and are today in dire need of being *reread* and *restored* at the concluding end of postcoloniality, when minds are decolonized. These three successive moments give the condition of readability of the text its living organicity, an unfolding matrix of meaning, evident in the intention of the text even if contradicted by the intention of the author. None of these authors privileged Europe as the sole purpose of their journeys, and even if they occasionally did, their text recorded a far

---

41 See Umberto Eco, *The Open Work*. Translated by Anna Cancogni. Introduction by David Robey (Cambridge, MA: Harvard University Press, 1989).
42 See Jacques Derrida, *Of Grammatology*. Fortieth Anniversary Edition. Translated by Gayatri Chakravorty Spivak. Introduction by Judith Butler (Baltimore, MD: Johns Hopkins University Press, 2016).
43 Umberto Eco, *The Limits of Interpretation* (Indianapolis, IN: Indiana University Press, 1991).

richer and more detailed encounter with the world, which they were remapping as they traveled and wrote. Subsequent generations of readers entered these texts with their colonially compromised minds and read things that were not there and failed to read things that were there. It is long overdue we overcame that condition of coloniality and read these texts afresh for what they were doing before those colonized minds began reading and compromising their significance. These texts, ipso facto and in the body of their textuality, were the subversion of the colonial gaze – the undoing of the colonial map – not despite Europe being part of their itinerary but in fact precisely because Europe was part of their itinerary.

10 | *In and out of a Homeland*
Yahya Dawlatabadi

A commotion can be heard:
I am the solitary interlocutor
Of the winds blowing all over the world
And all the rivers of the world
Are teaching me the pure secret
Of disappearance –
Just to me!

I am the interpreter of the sparrows of the Ganges Valley –
And right by the road leading to Sarnath –
I have interpreted
The Tibetan earrings –
Studded with mysticism –
For the ears of the girls of Banaras –
Lacking in any adornment.

Sohrab Sepehri (Mosafer/Traveler, Babol, Spring 1966)

The "I" of Sepehri is the "I" of a world, the "eye" of the world, the consciousness of a cosmic order, the defiant agency of an entire history now coming to full awareness of itself. With that "I", and with that "eye," a postcolonial person could claim a history, a geography, an agency. That "I" was forever in the making, and that "eye" was all-seeing. Only a few of Sepehri's contemporaries had achieved that "I" – even fewer could see what he saw: Nima Yushij, Forough Farrokhzad, Ahmad Shamlou, and Mehdi Akhavan Sales chief among them. That "I" was worldly, that "eye" was all-seeing, knowing the world, walking it forward and backward, traveling it with full consciousness of itself, and coming home confident of what it had seen and where it had to go. That "I" had not been "to Europe" and back, that "eye" had seen far deeper and farther in the world. That "I" was the cosmogonic universe of the worlds past and the worlds present and the worlds to come. Sepehri's poem "The Traveler" is the single most solid

260

evidence that the Iranian travelers who had come before him had also
seen the world but lacked his poetic gift to rise above themselves.
Generations of colonized minds then began to heap their own contorted views of the world upon those travelers and thus severed the link
between them and the sublime poet they had anticipated in long
journeys and detailed writings. In this book I bring them together –
travelers and poets, sojourners of truth beyond the reach of Europe
and Eurocentrism.

reason for incl. Sepehri

Rel to 3. p. 258 (how to re-read)

Conceiting the Colonial Gaze

European colonialism was predicated on and sustained by varied forms
and dictions, modalities and conceits, narratives and normativities of
power and domination. It was predicated on guns and bayonets pushing the economic logic of capitalism around the globe, but it also
flourished into art, ideology, and literature, into music and opera,
poetry and social sciences, and the humanities. From the Renaissance
to the Industrial Revolution to the Enlightenment Modernity, the
European cultural hegemony was coterminous with the constitution
of the non-European sites of exploitation, discovery, and domination.
From the discipline of anthropology to the invention of photography,
from literary imagination to travel narratives, from projects of "World
Literature" to "World History," from Orientalist opera and paintings
to exotic romances, no major European bourgeois preoccupation was
ever launched without a colonial dimension to its logic and rhetoric.
The very idea of "knowledge" and the technologies of its production in
the aftermath of European capitalist modernity were geared toward
non-Europeans as the object of their desires and fantasies, investigations and dissections. Dominating and knowing their colonial possessions went hand in hand.

European travel narratives in particular were instrumental in
describing, inscribing, and possessing the lands they thus described.
European popular imagination and anthropological investigation went
hand in hand, from Marco Polo to Bronislaw Malinowski; in both
imagining and codifying foreign cultures, they fathomed, described,
codified, and occupied – mentally and physically – the lands they
studied. As social sciences and the humanities began imitating hard
sciences, positivistic methodologies lent further credibility to the necessity of observing, reporting, coding, and owning foreign colonies.

[Isn't the essentializ Europe here? Had is Marco Polo "Europ"?]

Bartolomé de las Casas's *A Short Account of the Destruction of the Indies* (1542–1552) is both the first travelogue and the first anthropology of cruel conquest and domination of "the New World." These travel narratives, from de las Casas and Marco Polo forward, were definitive to the European sense of superiority, entitlement, and the very constitution of the racialized notion of their "whiteness." The National Geographic magazine of today is the legacy of those bygone ages. World exhibitions in London, Paris, and Chicago eventually began to bring these exotic places to life, making them even more exotic, and place the European and now US colonialists in a position of power and observation, of knowing and owing. By now "the West" thought it owned the world, staged it, conquered it, claimed it. We were the limit of their imagination. They made us legible to themselves, and alas also to ourselves. We read ourselves with their language and script. But under the nose of their arrogance, we had started to think otherwise. They were too ignorant, too illiterate of our world to know, notice, or care to see it.

Returning the colonial gaze cast widely upon the globe at large required a critical consciousness fully aware of the intensity and longevity of that colonial gaze. Yahya Dowlatabadi had cultivated a deeply insightful awareness of the global disposition of colonialism. He has left behind monumental evidence of how he returned that colonial gaze. Let us read him closely.

Returning the Colonial Gaze

Everything that had happened before Yahya Dowlatabadi put pen to paper to write his long and illustrious life and extraordinary travels abroad culminated in Yahya Dowlatabadi. He was the summation of an entire history of travel writing. Yahya Dolatabadi's *Hayat-e Yahiya/ The Life of Yahiya* (1893–1939) achieves a density of prose and a clarity of purpose that could have only happened when an Iranian finally brought home an entire genre of critical thinking cultivated in the voluminous spaces of these travelogues. As a poet, calligrapher, social activist, detailed autobiographer, and tireless traveler of the Constitutional period, his posthumously published text *Hayat-e Yahya* is monumental evidence of a lifetime of revolutionary activism, in and out of Iran. Yahya Dowlatabadi came from a prominent revolutionary background, a highly respected family of learned scholars, and his commitment to educational reforms was steady and deeply rooted in both his Iranian upbringing and in his widely traveled consciousness of the significance of educating a new generation of Iranians for responsible citizenship. His frequent travels in and out of Iran had enriched his prose in a manner such that it no longer mattered if he was in Tehran, Moscow, Istanbul, Lausanne, Paris, Berlin, or Stockholm. He lived and breathed his homeland while traveling abroad, and he was fully aware and conscious of the worldly context of a new conception of his homeland.

Yahya Dowlatabadi was a vigilant eyewitness and a participant observer of perhaps the most vital events of his homeland at the turn of the twentieth century, linking the dying days of the Qajar dynasty to the rising fortunes of the Pahlavi monarchy under the tutelage of British and Russian imperialism. In his politics and in his historic significance, he was the promise and the delivery of a postcolonial subject for more than a century in the making, and he performed his task in defining the expanded transnational public sphere that became the normative underpinning of the foundations of his homeland as a postcolonial nation. In two hefty volumes that will take you some serious time and undivided attention to read cover to cover, Dowlatabadi helped in reversing the colonial gaze and mapped out a new world map for his homeland. The best way to know him is to read him closely, follow the tumultuous course of his homeland as he describes it, trace his footsteps through his travels, and come back home with him when the promise of an entire century of travel narratives finally came to fruition in the pages of his singularly important memoir and travelogue. I intend to read Dowlatabadi's memoir/travelogue closely in this chapter, for I believe it is in the pages of this book that everything that had happened before he put pen to paper comes to a crescendo and is brought back home to his homeland.

Remapping the World

I am holding the two hefty volumes of *Hayat-e Yahya* by Yahya Dowlatabadi in my hands – they are so thick you would need a small handbag to carry them around.[1] I am reading the volumes in New York in my study, for they are too heavy to carry around, and I could

---

[1] Yahya Dowlatabadi, *Hayat-e Yahya/The Life of Yahya* (Tehran: Ferdowsi and Attar Publishers, 1954).

not find a handy PDF copy of it. It is beautifully printed, nicely edited into two handsome volumes, with a picture of an old-fashioned pistol on the cover – I have no clue why. On the dust jacket we have a bizarre note by two publishers (Ferdowsi and Attar) in which we read how a reputable publisher had agreed to prepare this handsome copy, evidently improving on previous editions that were in miserable condition. The first volume begins with a handsome portrait of Yahya Dowlatabadi; on the title page, we learn this edition was published in 1362/1983. We then learn that the first edition was published in 1336/1954. Ms. Hamideh Dowlatabadi has a brief introduction to this volume, introducing the book by her father. The introduction is dated Ordibehesht 1336/April 1957. Then we have a brief introduction by the author himself, who starts by praising the significance of history and then tells us how since he was thirty years old in 1310 AH/1893 he had decided to write his memoirs in order to teach the future generations the true nature of things that had happened.[2]

The most remarkable aspect of this text is evident right from its table of contents,[3] where we see Dowlatabadi's multiple and extended travels abroad are not isolated from the rest of his life but in fact integrated with it. That this fact does not gel well with the idea of "travelogue" as it is defined by Europeans is of course their problem, not Dowlatabadi's. For us this text brings the saga of the nineteenth century Persian travelers abroad home by incorporating the trope of traveling right into the heart of the homeland, where the consequences of these travels ultimately mattered. In Dowlatabadi's book, the personal, the political, the regional, and the global are all interwoven seamlessly. The historical agency of the person who writes this book, Yahya Dowlatabadi, has been in the process of formation for over a century – so in one breath he can talk about his marriage, about the political turmoil of his homeland, and about global affairs, without the slightest sense of confusion or chaos in his narrative. From the earliest travelers we have read together to Dowlatabadi, every line any traveler has ever written comes here to culminate in the authorial voice of the narrator when he says "I".

Hayat-e Yahya begins with a brief autobiographical account of the author and his earliest travels to Iraq for his scholastic studies, his return to Iran when a plague breaks in Iraq, and his subsequent return to Iran before he gains his travels to Iraq, Arabia, and Egypt. All the

---

[2] Ibid.: I: 10.   [3] Ibid.: I: 8–9.

while, Dowlatabadi is deeply concerned about the internal and international developments affecting his homeland. Crucial events such as
the assassination of Naser al-Din Shah on May 1, 1896, and the
establishment of the modern schooling system are all affecting the
contours of his thinking in this text, and it does not matter any longer
whether he is traveling abroad or residing in Iran. Iran and its environs
in this text have become integral to an extended transnational public
sphere.

In the introductory autobiographical chapter,[4] we learn that Dowlatabadi comes from a learned clerical family that had moved from
Shushtar to a suburb of Isfahan called Dowlatabad. His father, Hadi
Dowlatabadi, becomes a member of the landed gentry and a prominent
cleric in Isfahan and its surrounding areas. He tells us he was born on
Thursday, January 8, 1863, and that he began writing this book when
he was thirty years old, meaning in 1893. He says until the age of five he
was under the care of mostly illiterate babysitters, though he tells us even
proper schools at this time were in fact in miserable condition. He is very
particular in the very first chapter to tell us of the miserable condition of
early education in Iran. His first teacher was a secretary to his father and
was more concerned about doing a business on the side than teaching
when he was not busy with his chief hobby, which was alchemy. His
second teacher came all the way from Isfahan, missed his wife and
children dearly, and could not wait to go back and spend the weekend
with them. This teacher finally convinces Yahya's father to send Yahya
and his brother to a seminary in Isfahan, which he does. The condition
of education in these seminaries is even more miserable. The only book
he loved was Obeid Zakani's *Cat and Mouse*, a classical satire; the rest
were torture. He studies the Quran, and has no clue what he is reading
and hates the difficult pronunciations. This critical attitude toward early
childhood education is entirely informed by Yahya Dowlatabadi's
lifelong preoccupation with reforming the education system in his
homeland, a commitment, as we soon learn when reading the rest of
his book, rooted in his extensive research while traveling abroad.

The remarkable aspect of Yahya's first trip abroad is that he and his
mother and siblings accompany his father to Iraq. He tells us his father
loved traveling, especially to sacred sites of Shi'i saints in Iraq, where
he also took his wife and children. This was in 1872, when Yahya was

[4] Ibid.: I: 11–17.

ten years old. Thus, his traveling life begins at the age of ten in the company of his parents, and the first cities he sees outside his homeland are Baghdad and al-Kazimayn, which is an exceptionally significant city for Shi'a Muslims. Dowlatabadi here gives a detailed account of how the center of Shi'a scholastic learning that was in Isfahan under the Safavids eventually moved to Iraq in Najaf because of the decline of the Safavid capital and the rise of prominent Shi'a leaders in the Ottoman territories.[5] Dowlatabadi's detailing of the manner of early education in Iraq is replete with his critical observations when he was thirty years old and writing these pages. He is detailed in his denunciations of the scholastic methods, wherein they spend lots of time mastering old texts in Arabic but are incapable of putting one Arabic sentence together.[6] He and his classmates move from one "teacher" to another, who are more babysitters than teachers. Dowlatabadi brings his mature pedagogical criticism in his thirties to reflect on these earlier parts of his education. What we are reading is a deeply informed, critically aware, and well-traveled pedagogue thinking about education in and about his homeland.

After a period of five years, Dowlatabadi and his family return to Iran in 1877, and his father decides to stay in Isfahan and does not return to Dowlatabad. In Isfahan his father becomes a prominent clerical figure.[7] He reports of internecine tribal warfare in Najaf among Arab tribes and of the significance of the Iranian community in that holy city. He also speaks of an outbreak of a plague while they were there. In Isfahan there is also a fierce competition among the Shi'i clerics, some of whom he charges with accumulating wealth rather than caring for their followers. Dowlatabadi's father becomes a prominent cleric in Isfahan and soon attracts the enmity of Zell al-Sultan, Naser al-Din Shah's corrupt brother, who was the governor of Isfahan. In 1880, when Dowlatabadi is seventeen years old, he accompanies his father to Khorasan, where the father becomes a leading cleric. Soon they return to Tehran as Dowlatabadi's father's fame and fortune increases, and Zell al-Sultan eventually becomes friendly with him.[8] Dowlatabadi places these observations within two consecutive chapters on the nature of governance in Iran, which he says consists of two modes of governance: one, the state apparatus ruled by Naser al-Din Shah and the other, the clerical establishment ruled by leading Shia

[5] Ibid.: I: 23–28.   [6] Ibid.: I: 28–32.   [7] Ibid.: I: 34–39.   [8] Ibid.: I: 39–44.

clerics from Najaf, Karbala, and Samarra.[9] He gives a detailed account of the two parallel modes of rulership in Iran, one from the royal palace and the other from the seats of clerical learning in southern Iraq and in effect in the Ottoman Empire. These two chapters are crucial to keep in mind about the nature and function of "nation-state" in this nascent period when old imperial orders are yielding to the colonial concoction of "the nation-state," for the second most important seat of power in Iran is, in effect, outside Iran.

Dowlatabadi gives two detailed descriptions of two major cities in Iran – Tehran and Isfahan. He introduces these two major cosmopolitan seats of power and knowledge as two competing epicenters of attraction for new ideas and provocative movements. He is very proud of his rising interests in Persian literary humanism and delighted that his father had allowed him to study calligraphy with a master in Tehran.[10] But in 1882 he is sent to Isfahan, where he is initially saddened to be away from Tehran but subsequently happy to make the acquaintances of two towering Iranian intellectuals, Mirza Agha Khan Kerman and Sheikh Ahmad Ruhi, who had come there from Kerman and were on their way to Tehran.[11] Dowlatabadi is very much impressed by both of them and gives us a firsthand account of their rising significance in the tumultuous events of the late Qajar period. His descriptions of Tehran and Isfahan and their respective intellectual atmospheres places these two Iranian cities on a platform along with Delhi, Cairo, Istanbul, and Moscow before Dowlatabadi sets his eye on any "European" city. This fact is crucial to our understanding of his global vision of his homeland.

In 1886, at the age of twenty-four, Dowlatabadi tells us in the company of his father he once again travels to Iraq for yet another visit to the Shi'a holy sites, as his father travels to Arabia to perform his Haj pilgrimage. On his way to Iraq, he tells us how fond of solitude he has become. In Iraq, his father entrusts his education to the prominent Shi'a cleric Mirza Shirazi and returns to Iran.[12] His time in Samara is lonesome and forlorn. He misses his family and homeland. But he plunges into his scholastic studies and gives us detailed reports of the nasty rivalries between various factions, marked by both intra- and inter-sectarian strife. From his reports we learn how Karbala, Najaf,

---

[9] Ibid.: I: 44–49 and I: 50–56.   [10] Ibid.: I: 56–62.   [11] Ibid.: I: 62–69.
[12] Ibid.: I: 69–75.

and Samara are wealthy cities with deep connections to the rest of the Muslim world.[13] In 1886 he travels from Iraq to Egypt, and from there to Arabia, and then through the Persian Gulf he sails to Yemen and back to Iran. He is mesmerized by his visit to the Pyramids in Egypt and spends time visiting museums and mosques in Cairo.[14] In Jeddah he meets a certain Haji Ali Tabrizi, who tells him he was a close friend of Jamal al-Din Al-Afghani, and that the revolutionary Muslim reformist was in fact from Asadabad of Hamadan.[15] Upon his return to Iran, Dowlatabadi continues with his visits to Bushehr, Isfahan, Qom, and Mashhad. In Isfahan he notices Russians have become very powerful in the city and can compete with the British colonial interests. He then spends an entire chapter on al-Afghani, describing his popularity and the enmity that this has caused among powerful people against him.[16] By this time in his combined memoir and travelogue we are witness to a deeply cultivated man, with periods of solitude strengthening his moral fabric and political commitments. But to see this character developing, one must read every single page of his travelogue patiently and with respect for the man who spent recording these exceptionally important years in the life of a nation.

Dowlatabadi spends an entire chapter on the deep corruption of Nasser al-Shah Qajar's governance, with a full regional and global knowledge of the world informing his poignant criticism.[17] He concludes this chapter by praising top public intellectuals and periodicals that expose the Qajar corruption – chief among them the Akhtar periodical, the writings of Mirza Aqa Khan Kermani, the treatise of *Yek Kalameh/One Word* by Mostashar al-Dowleh, the writings of Seyyed Jamal al Din al-Afghani, and the periodical Qanun, published by the leading Armenian-Iranian reformist Mirza Malkam Khan. The remarkable aspect of this book is that Dowlatabadi is an eyewitness to these groundbreaking historical events. He devotes a full chapter to the Tobacco Revolt of 1892 and attributes it to the corruption of the Qajar court that had sought to create a balance between colonial concessions it gives to the British and the Russian interests. Dowlatabadi details the manner in which the Tobacco Revolt was led by Ayatollah Ashtiani in Iran and Ayatollah Shirazi in Najaf.[18] He gives details of his father's troubles with Zell al-Sultan, the governor of Isfahan, and informs us that his father was accused of being a

[13] Ibid.: I: 75–81. [14] Ibid.: I: 82. [15] Ibid.: I: 84. [16] Ibid.: I: 91–100. [17] Ibid.: I: 100–105. [18] Ibid.: I: 105–111.

Babi.[19] He tells us he attended classes of Mirza Abu al-Hasan Khan Jelveh, a leading philosopher of the time – but his father objects and through a leading cleric warns him not to abandon his juridical studies. Dowlatabadi at this point has a midlife crisis and does not know what to do with himself when there is a cholera epidemic in Tehran in Muharram of 1310/July–August 1892, and he is stricken by it and almost dies. When he survives he decides to devote his life to his fellow human beings.[20] It is impossible to imagine the power of this simple prose and these simple pages to give us the most extensive details possible of how the seeds of a postcolonial subject, a deeply cultivated intellectual, have been cultivated in the heat of these colonial encounters.

The enmity between Dowlatabadi's father and the governor of Isfahan Zell al-Sultan intensifies, and finally his father writes to Naser al-Din Shah, soliciting his support. Meanwhile, Dowlatabadi is forced to marry a thirteen-year old girl against his own wishes.[21] At this time, the year 1894, he is thirty-two years old. Dowlatabadi's firsthand knowledge of the circumstances leading to Nasser al Din Shah's assassination is deeply informed and constitutes some of the most reliable information we have from this tumultuous period. He gives details of how Naser al-Din Shah's assassin, Mirza Reza Kermani, travels to Istanbul and meets with Jamal al Din al-Afghani and comes back to Iran to assassinate the Qajar monarch. He tells us how the revolutionary publications from abroad were sent to Iran in fact through diplomatic couriers with the British embassy, evidently unbeknownst to the British authorities.[22] He tells us how women of Naser al-Din Shah's Harem were used as spies. On the occasion of the death of Mirza Hasan Shirazi, he gives us details of the rivalries among the clerical class in political matters, and then he warns his readers that the political intervention of Mirza Shirazi in politics in the course of the Tobacco Revolt may have dire consequences in the future, for he believes the religious authorities must do their business and the political authorities theirs.[23] There are very few other such reliable sources about the critical events of this period. But that is not the central issue here. The question is how these historic events are, page after page, transforming the critical consciousness of a leading public

---

[19] Ibid.: I: 112.   [20] Ibid.: I: 117.   [21] Ibid.: I: 122.   [22] Ibid.: I: 124.
[23] Ibid.: I: 137.

intellectual – a young man in the prime of his life, fully conscious of his worldly surroundings.

In the course of his chapter on the assassination of Naser al-Din Shah, Dowlatabadi tells us that he actually saw the assassin Mirza Reza Kermani at the mausoleum Shah Abd al-Azim the night before the incident, on Friday, May 1, 1896, and he also shares with us the details of some conspiracy theories claiming that the monarch's court-iers and harem wives may in fact have had a role in the plot. He describes the circumstances of the succession of Mozaffar and gives a full description of the corrupt state of affairs at the Qajar court. He reports how the official propaganda of the court was branding Mirza Reza as a Babi. And he tells us how he composed a poem from the point of view of the assassin in which he confesses to be a twelve Imami Shi'a Muslim.[24] On August 12, 1896, he reports how Mirza Reza was publicly and ceremoniously hanged.[25]

Dowlatabadi gives a full description of the intellectual environment of Istanbul around the figure of Mirza Agha Khan Kermani.[26] The incurably corrupt Qajar court continues to be dysfunctional as before with the Shah's retinues' greed running amok, but reformist and revo-lutionary activists continue to mobilize for radical changes. Dowlata-badi sees himself among these reformists and informs us his particular interest is in the education of young boys and girls. He is full of praise for premier Amin al-Dowleh and his hopes for structural reform, particularly in education and more specifically reforming the manner in which the Persian alphabet is taught to children. He is a great advocate of public education and spends pages praising Mirza Hasan Rushdiyeh and his education reform schools.[27] What is crucial here is to see how Dowlatabadi's prose is at once informed by the travel narrative and yet writing the emerging historiography of the nation. He is exceptionally concerned about the backward condition of the schooling systems in Iran and positively reports on those who are advancing the cause of reform in the educational system.[28] His con-cerns about reforming the early education are definitive to his vision of a future free of tyranny and ignorance.

In May 1898 Dowlatabadi is asked to write and deliver a report on modern education for high-ranking Qajar authorities. He reports that

[24] Ibid.: I: 153.   [25] Ibid.: I: 158.   [26] Ibid.: I: 159–171.
[27] Ibid.: I: 178–185.   [28] Ibid.: I: 186.

parents of young children are very happy with such educational reforms, however the clerical establishment and the religious seminaries, who were the beneficiaries of the old school system, actively opposed such pioneering efforts.[29] He also reports of these high-ranking authorities' attention to the freedom of the press and he praises them for their consideration of this seminal aspect of a democracy. Dowlatabadi then proceeds to give us reports of such newspapers, periodicals, and publication houses as they were published in Egypt, by way of comparison.[30] Dowlatabadi's point of comparison here with Egyptian (and decidedly not the European) examples is a key element in our reading of his frame of mind that (as we will see in more detail) is decidedly anticolonial.

The democratic aspirations of the time, as Dowlatabadi reports them, were evident in higher ranking authorities who were more inclined toward British democracy than to Russian absolutism.[31] He speaks particularly of the reactionary power of the clerical establishment, whose interests are in the status quo and categorically opposed to reform. The course of such reforms, however, he reports, is very much at the mercy of one good-hearted and progressive high-ranking official leaving office and another hostile to such reforms coming to power. He also reports to us that in a short time he wrote a book on education and ethics for young children which he called "Ali."[32] The idea of establishing a National Library and an institution for translation and publication of new books as well as education for older people is also broached at this time.[33] He informs us of the formation of voluntary associations as an indication of the public sphere, such as Anjoman-e Ma'aref. Dowlatabadi reports that he had decided to establish a boarding school for orphan children.[34] He gives a detailed account of why the presence of periodicals like *Habl al-Matin,* published in Kolkata, and *Parvaresh,* in Egypt, were important for promotion of democratic ideas.[35] Whatever he says and whatever he does uncovers the details of a deeply engaged and committed public intellectual fully conscious of the unfolding world around him.

It is from the pages of his book that we find out Iran is effectively colonized by Russian and British imperialism. The north of the Qajar territories in particular is in full control of Russia by virtue of multiple

[handwritten margin note: dem. spread thru non-Euro means)]

---

[29] Ibid.: I: 193–198.   [30] Ibid.: I: 199–205.   [31] Ibid.: I: 206.
[32] Ibid.: I: 214.   [33] Ibid.: I: 221.   [34] Ibid.: I: 245.   [35] Ibid.: I: 280.

loans that it gives to the Qajar monarch. The British on the other hand are not particular in controlling the internal politics so far as they prevent the Russians creating any troubles for them in India. Iran therefore by and large remains a battlefield between Russian and British imperialism. The accusation of being a Babi is a principal way of silencing or eliminating opposition to the corrupt Qajar court and to the British and Russian Imperial interests.[36] Dowlatabadi devotes a complete chapter to the origin and the ultimate establishment of Dar al-Funun, on the model of European universities.[37] But by that time he has also spent a considerable number of pages talking about his own reformist ideals and aspirations about educational reform.

Particularly hostile to modern education and the new schooling system were the clerical establishments best represented by a certain Aqa Najafi from Esfahan, who considered modern education detrimental to their class interests and political power.[38] The picture that emerges from these pages is the active hostility and yet collaboration between powerful figures in the clerical establishment and those of the Qajar dynasty against modern education – against which vested interest there is a group of dedicated reformists with whom Dowlatabadi identifies. Meanwhile he is fully conscious of the emergence of the war between Russia and Japan at this point, and how the British take advantage of this situation to expand the domain of their influence in Iran.[39]

By the completion of the first of the four volumes of his memoir/travelogue we get to know Yahya Dowlatabad as a deeply learned and principled revolutionary activist, rooted in a prominent Iranian family, well-traveled in the region, fully aware of the global context of his troubled homeland, and seriously critical of both the ruling tyranny and the colonial intrusions into his country and beyond. The critical seeds of a fresh and defiant mind putting up valiant resistance to the colonial mapping of the world are in full view in these precious pages. He has full command of Persian and Arabic, through which two languages he is rooted in his own culture and has full access to the world around him. We finish this first volume eager to see what happens to our narrator.

---

[36] Ibid.: I: 324.   [37] Ibid.: I: 325.   [38] Ibid.: I: 338.   [39] Ibid.: I: 352.

The Home and the World

On November 28, 1905, Yahya Dowlatabadi completes the first volume of his memoir and starts the second volume – and paramount on his mind at this point is the victorious position of Japan during the Russo-Japanese War (1904–1905), which he tells us has given Iranian revolutionaries and reformists hope for progressive changes in the world.[40] The imperial Russian interventions in Iran have made Iranian revolutionaries hopeful and rooting for the Japanese victory. His narrative at this point is charged with domestic, regional, and global awareness. Globally, the Russian-Japanese war is casting a long shadow around the world. Regionally there is sectarian violence in Central Asia because of the Russian involvement in the Japanese war. Domestically the Qajar court is petrified by the threat of losing their Russian benefactor while the retrograde political establishment is seeking its own interests, as the reformists like him are excited by the prospects of some serious changes in the world. Dowlatabadi begins to pay attention to how foreign affairs have domestic consequences; for example, as the Russian political circumstances are agitated, the price of sugar goes up in Iran and causes riots.[41] We are now at the beginning of the Constitutional Revolution (1906–1911). Dowlatabadi's pages here read like a firsthand account of a participant observer of that momentous event.

Dowlatabadi provides perhaps the most detailed, sometimes hour by hour, account of the historic events of the Constitutional Revolution.[42] He tells us he has divided loyalties – because of the governmental subsidies and protection of his schools, he does not want openly to support the revolutionaries, while his sentiments are with the revolutionaries. He gives details of how some of the revolutionaries sought refuge with the British Embassy – a crucial turning point in the course of the constitutional uprising. His interpretation of why the British were supporting the revolution is very important. He believes the British were suspicious of Mohammad Ali Shah (reigned January 3, 1907–July 16, 1909) because he was very close to the Russians and as a result the British were concerned that if he were to come to power without any constitutional limitations, it would be contrary to their interests. That is the reason, Dowlatabadi tells us, the British supported

[40] Ibid.: II: 1.   [41] Ibid.: II: 10–12.   [42] Ibid.: II: 52–64.

the Constitutional revolution.[43] What is astonishing about his prose here is the strange feeling we get, as if, after more than a century, we are there during the unfolding drama of the Constitutional Revolution, as Dowlatabadi describes the events in precisely the language we understand today. This is how deep was the postcolonial agency the travel narratives of the period had invested in him and through him for the posterity of political consciousness in his homeland.

As Dowlatabadi gives us a full description of the process of writing the constitution, he informs us that the constitutions of other countries were considered as sources of inspiration for what was being written at the time. He also tells us that as the constitution was being drafted, he thought of establishing a periodical which he says he decided to call "Majles" in order to inform the newly elected representative of the parliament to be aware of their historic duties.[44] The ruling monarch, Mozaffar al-Din Shah (May 1, 1896–January 3, 1907), finally grants the constitution and soon after that, dies. His son, Mohammad Ali Shah, succeeds him and he has no intention of maintaining his father's promises or honoring the newly minted constitution. Dowlatabadi gives us the dull details of the Treaty of 1907, according to which Iran was divided into three sections, with Russia in control of the north, the British in the south, and a neutral area in between – in effect, however, he tells us there is no neutral area, and even the nominally "neutral area" was divided between the Russians and the British colonial powers in Iran. This is the first challenge that the new majlis had to confront. He is particularly critical of the notorious Shi'a cleric Sheikh Fazlollah Nuri, who appears in his account as an opportunistic charlatan who was playing in between both the revolutionaries and the reactionaries and finally sides with the reactionaries.[45] What is crucial in his account is the fact he is neither pro-clericals nor against them. He comes from that class, but because of his progressive political views, he is critical of anyone who is an impediment to the cause of the Constitutional revolution, the rule of law, and the cause of democracy. Keep in mind at this point he has not yet set foot in Europe, but he is fully aware of the colonial domination of the globe by European powers.

Much disagreement and consternation are evident in Dowlatabadi's prose as he tells us of the animosity among various factions around the constitutional uprising. What is evident, however, is the fact that there

---

[43] Ibid.: II: 81.   [44] Ibid.: II: 91.   [45] Ibid.: II: 107–108.

are progressive and reactionary forces among all factions of this period – from the Qajar court to the religious establishment and even among the revolutionaries, where there are both those who care about the future of the nation and those who only care about their own personal gains.[46] Among the important things that Dowlatabadi describes at this point is the establishment of a station in a major square in Tehran where people could telegraph their complaints to the royal court. His prose here is telegraphic and precise, informative and critical.

By February 1907, the reactionary forces have paved the way to replace the constitutionalist premier Moshir al Dowleh with the reactionary premier Amin al Sultan. "I the Author say," Dowlatabadi interjects, "our country hitherto had two heads – one was the king and the prime minister that were the heads of the state and the other the religious leaders who were considered the head of the nation. Today the nation has opened its eyes and tongue and is telling those two heads whatever you do must be to my benefit not to your own benefit ... and if you were to do as you were before I would chop you both off and I will grow a new righteous head – therefor your responsibility today is to be the true head of your nation so you won't suffer the consequences."[47] Dowlatabadi then gives details of how Sheikh Fazlollah Nuri was chief among the treacherous members of the clergy who had mobilized the reactionaries to go to the Shah Abd al-Azim shrine and stage a veritable force against the Constitutionalists.[48] At this point in his text, his prose speaks with the authoritative voice of a nation in the making.

Dowlatabadi gives a detailed account of the assassination of Mirza Ali Asghar Khan (1858–1907), also known by his honorific titles of Amin al Sultan and Atabak, the last prime minister of Iran under Naser al-Din Shah Qajar, in front of the Iranian Parliament on August 31, 1907. The assassination of Amin al Sultan creates havoc among the revolutionaries and the reactionaries alike. Dowlatabadi provides a close eyewitness account of these historic developments.[49] At one point he informs us that the reactionary forces who were against the constitution had mobilized prostitutes in the month of Ramadan to come out demonstrating, without veils, demanding their

---

[46] Ibid.: II: 110–117.   [47] Ibid.: II: 123.   [48] Ibid.: II: 129–141.
[49] Ibid.: II: 142–150.

freedom, as a pretext to the claim that with constitution comes women's liberation. In this report Dowlatabadi obviously has his sentiments with the constitutionalists; however, the prose of his report is such that those who were protesting were identified as "prostitutes" and "demanding freedom" – meaning equating women's liberation with prostitution.[50] This particular prose, no doubt, betrays the limits of Dowlatabadi's own critical imagination. Was this really a plot to discredit the constitutionalists – or was it a perfectly legitimate demonstration by women for their civil liberties? Dowlatabadi cannot make any distinction between these two vastly different readings.

Dowlatabadi is an eyewitness to the bombardment of the Majlis, which took place on June 23, 1908, in Tehran, when the Persian Cossack forces, under the command of the Russian officer, Vladimir, bombarded the Majles.[51] He also gives us details of how the revolutionaries were getting ready for an armed uprising. Much personal rivalry and animosity is evident in his prose here. What is evident is that Mohammad Ali Shah is not happy with the constitution and wants to renege on his father's promises, and in this he has the active support of his courtiers as well as a significant component of the clergy and some of the high-ranking officials of the Qajar elite. Dowlatabadi knows the full range of the revolutionary activists, the reactionary elements, and gives his readers a panoramic and a thick description of who's who at the momentous occasions.

Dowlatabadi has left for posterity a detailed account of the assassination attempt against Mohammad Ali Shah on Friday, February 28, 1908.[52] In the midst of all these revolutionary upheavals, armed uprisings, and assassination plots, Dowlatabadi's concern remains steadfast about education. He reports to his readers that one particularly prominent Qajar official, Ihtisham al-Saltaneh, had arranged with German authorities to establish a German elementary school for children in the capital. Dowlatabadi is excited by the idea but proposes to the official to start the German school from the fifth grade so the students have had a chance to master their mother tongue first, but this idea is dismissed and in this particular German school students are to learn both German and Persian simultaneously. His sense of linguistic nationalism is seriously offended by the proposition.[53] These detailed

---

[50] Ibid.: II: 160.   [51] Ibid.: II: 167–179.   [52] Ibid.: II: 199–206.
[53] Ibid.: II: 208–211.

descriptions of the revolutionary circumstance interrupted by his concern for early public education leave his readers, those who have cared to read him closely, with a far richer understanding of Iran in these vital days.

What in effect we are reading in these pages are the testimonies of a participant observer in the emergence of parliamentary democracy in a new nation-state. Iran is emerging as a nation-state, and there is extensive politicking happening between the ruling monarchy and the parliament and its various factions, and Dowlatabadi is telling us how these factions are interacting, mobilizing, and making coalitions.[54] The prose of Dowlatabadi's politics at this point is deeply informed by the condition of Iranians outside their homeland – for example, in chapter 23 of the second volume he shares with us the account of an Iranian telling the newly founded Majlis deputies how Iranians are treated terribly abroad, as in how one particular young Iranian was killed in Russia because of the lack of protection of his rights in a foreign land.[55] There is both an urgency and a detailed attention to these historic events that are happening and to which he is an eyewitness. Some of the most significant events of the time are taking place and he has the urge to write them – but for what, we might ask? Dowlatabadi has a sense that he is witness to some extraordinary events in the life of his homeland. It is the historical consciousness of the prose that is most evident in what he writes.[56]

Paramount among his concerns is the interference of both the Russians and the British in the internal affairs of his homeland. It is quite evident that the Russians are siding with the tyrannical monarch while the British are agitating for their own interests, not to the advantage of Iranian people but in opposition to the Russian interests.[57] The conspiracy of Mohammad Ali Shah and some of his reactionary courtiers plus the support of the Russian Empire all come together to deny Iranians the political fruits of their constitutional struggles. It is important to note that at this point Dowlatabadi informs us that the royal decree to dismantle the Majlis (The date of this decree is June 9, 1908) was the Persian translation of the Russian original decree when dismantling the Russian parliament Duma.[58] In other words, what we are reading here is the common feature of both Russians and Iranians

[54] Ibid.: II: 219–227.   [55] Ibid.: II: 228.   [56] Ibid.: II: 236–243.
[57] Ibid.: II: 253–2661.   [58] Ibid.: II: 264.

against the respective monarchies denying them their constitutional rights.

Who is Dowlatabadi writing this account of the Constitutional Revolution for, we may wonder. There is a thickness to his description and a purpose to his narrative. He seems to be aware and conscious of the historical significance of both the events that he is witnessing and the detailed accounts that he is giving. Chapter after chapter he turns to detailed accounts of what is happening. He is personally involved in many of the crucial issues. The ultimate result of his narrative is that there are basically two factions – those who are revolutionary and those who are reactionaries. The ruling monarch is chief among the reactionaries – and he has supporters in the court, among the clerical establishment, and among the merchant class. Opposing them are various revolutionary forces both within and outside the Majlis.[59] The language with which Dowlatabadi describes and analyzes these events is deeply informed by his enduring concerns for parliamentary democracy, his understanding of which is now deeply informed by closely following the events from India to Japan to Egypt to Ottoman territories, all the way to Europe and the United States. There is no privileging of any of these sites over the other.

As we read through his daily and regular reflections on the unfolding of the Constitutional Revolution and the interplay between the monarch's courts and the parliamentary politics in the Majlis, it becomes clear that the writing of this narrative actually helps him map out the emerging politics of the revolution. Dowlatabadi gives us some extraordinarily detailed accounts of how the revolutionaries were actually all armed and spread throughout the capital city, ready to fight against the Qajar military.[60] "Early in the afternoon I went to Majlis to see what's happening."[61] Phrases like this abound in the book, giving us a sense of how the daily lives of revolutionaries are organized around the crucial historic events. It also becomes clear, at these crucial days and nights of the revolution, that all the revolutionaries have decided to spend the nights on the site of the Majlis and not to go home – first because they have a lot to do, and second because they are afraid for their lives, and they do not have enough security forces to guard them at their residences, so they are asked to gather at the site of the

---

[59] Ibid.: II: 270–277.   [60] Ibid.: II: 290.   [61] Ibid.: II: 292.

Majlis.[62] As for feeding the revolutionaries, he tells us that some
merchants were sympathetic to the cause of the revolution and pro-
vided food for them, but he tells us that he too had some food brought
to the revolutionaries from his own household.[63]

Given the details of various revolutionary cells he identifies by name
and description, there is no doubt that he has a sense of posterity in
mind when writing these pages. An atlas of revolutionary Tehran
emerges from his prose, where the theater of revolutionary actors and
reactionaries is staged with a sense of drama, and he writes with a sense
of full awareness that he is giving an account for posterity. He gives the
gruesome details of the murder of two leading revolutionaries, Malek al-
Motekallemin and Mirza Jahangir Khan Sur Esrafil, in front of Mohammad Ali Shah.[64] He spends one full chapter on the political conditions in
the provinces,[65] followed by another chapter on the regional repercus-
sions of the constitutional revolution in Iran.[66] This is a particularly
significant move because he is writing in Tehran, but he wants to make
sure that there is both internal and external consciousness of his political
observations. He informs us that after Mohammed Ali Shah bombarded
the newly established parliament and physically eliminated the leaders of
the constitutional revolution, the capital was in a state of panic. The
monarch, now, thought all was well and his dynastic cruelty was under
his full command. Dowlatabadi writes specifically of three neighbors –
the Russians, the British, and the Ottomans, and he makes a distinction
between nations and the states. He believes Russian people are in
support of the freedom movement in Iran, while their state is not only
happy with the defeat of the constitutional movement but with their
own role in quelling the uprising. The same is with the British and the
Ottomans.[67] After Mohammad Ali Shah's bombardment of the Parliament and killing his political opponents, Dowlatabadi tells us that the
monarch remained particularly scared of two forces – one, the revolutionaries from Azerbaijan province and two, the Shi'a clerical establishment from Najaf, who wrote public letters back to Iran denouncing his
dictatorship.[68]

The summer following the bombardment of the Majlis on June 23,
1908, Dowlatabadi spends in fear and hiding, and by the end of that

---

[62] Ibid.: II: 300.   [63] Ibid.: II: 308.   [64] Ibid.: II: 335–345.
[65] Ibid.: II: chapter 37.   [66] Ibid.: II: chapter 38.   [67] Ibid.: II: 335–363.
[68] Ibid.: II: 364–373.

summer in August 1908 he obtains a visa for the United Kingdom and he leaves his homeland. He considers his journey outside his homeland as exile, as he brings the second volume of his travelogue/memoirs to a closure.[69] The first two volumes are therefore mostly about his early life, which culminates in the Constitutional Revolution, and the last two volumes, which I am about to read, about his travels outside his homeland. The four volumes are seamlessly interwoven, written with one consistent prose, the product of a single and singularly probing, caring intellect. Dowlatabadi loves his homeland, deeply cares for its future, is committed to new education, and is critical of the ruling monarchy and the clerical establishment in equal measures. He is critically aware of the colonial powers of the British and Russia. His towering concern is the independence and freedom for his homeland, civil liberties for its citizens.

Figure 12 Ivan Konstantinovich Aivazovsky (1817–1900), "View of Constantinople and the Bosphorus" (1856) [Public Domain] – Cities like Istanbul, Cairo, Mumbai, St Petersburg, Rio de Janeiro, or Cape Town become integral to a cosmopolitan worldliness that includes Paris and London but is not reducible to them. These travelers are systematically, consistently, and repeatedly remapping the world without privileging any country or clime or dividing the globe on any false binary. The transnational public sphere they map, narrate, and populate is the site of a postcolonial subjectivity generations in the making.

[69] Ibid.: II: 385.

A Man of the World

I am now holding volumes three and four of Dowlatabadi's travelogue/memoir, *Hayat-e Yahya/The Life of Yahya* in my hands. They are as heavy and imposing as the first two volumes. These two imposing volumes have been sitting on my little writing desk in New York for months – too heavy to carry to my office or to the little café near where I live and like to do my writing. Traveling with these books is also an impossibility. I can only read them right here at my desk – page after page, volume after volume, getting to know one of the finest critical minds of Iranian history in its fateful encounter with colonial modernity. His travels so far are mostly in the Arab and Muslim world, and through his own homeland. But he is about to venture to new horizons.

In the short introduction to these last two volumes, Dowlatabadi's daughter tells us how her father wished for his book to be published during his lifetime, but that was not to be. A quick look at the table of contents of the third volume shows the trajectory of Dowlatabadi's travels and his concerns about his homeland. He discusses whether this trip abroad is just for travel, or is it exile. He talks about his travels to Tbilisi and Constantinople. He writes about the revolution of the Young Turks. But at the same time, he also continues to reflect about his homeland. The third volume as a result complements the first two volumes, in the sense that Dowlatabadi continues to write about Iran in terms that indicate his awareness of the transnational public sphere and international politics that frame his life as an Iranian deeply committed to the democratic aspirations of his homeland.

The third volume reads like a travelogue proper. He leaves his homeland on Saturday, September 4, 1908, and asks one of his older students – his name is Mirza Taghi Khan Madhat – to accompany him on this journey. Dowlatabadi is particular to remind us that he is actually on the run from the Qajar king, for he is afraid for his life and he tells us that the monarch actually hates him, and he uses this occasion to indicate that he's leaving for exile. The rest of his first chapter reads like a travelogue. He moves from Tehran toward the Anzali port on the Caspian Sea and thus commences his journey into Russian territories and beyond.[70] While in Tbilisi in the Caucasus, Dowlatabadi visits with Iranians there and speaks of forming various

---

[70] Ibid.: III: 9–16.

revolutionary cells in the neighboring countries in order to assist with
the democratic mobilizations in their homeland.[71]

Upon his arrival in Istanbul, Dowlatabadi seeks the company of the
Young Turks whom he praises highly as harbingers of progress and
democracy in their homeland. He suggests that the Constitutional
Revolution in Iran has had a strong impact on the Young Turks in
their democratic aspirations.[72] While in Istanbul he continues to follow
the news of the revolutionary developments in his homeland, as if he
had not left it. While in Istanbul he tells us one of his major concerns
was to establish a center for collaboration with the revolutionary
causes in Iran. He also tells us that a network of such centers that
would extend all the way to as far as Paris and London, and as near as
Istanbul, would be very important to advance the cause of democracy
in his homeland.[73] He mentions the prominent Iranian writer (whom
we will meet in detail in the next and final chapter) Zain al-Abedin
Maragheh'i by name.[74] In Istanbul Dowlatabadi tells us there was a
meeting in which he participates and in which Ottoman, Iranian,
Armenian, Kurdish as well as European representatives were present
to express their support and solidarity for the Constitutional Revolution in Iran.[75] He is also invited to deliver a speech at this gathering,
and he gives us the text of this speech. While he is in Istanbul he
receives the news that his father has passed away in Iran.[76] The sense
we have at this point is, despite the fact he has crossed the borders of
the Qajar domain into Russian and Ottoman territories, he is very
much among Iranian and non-Iranian friends – in the company of
Russian, Turkish, and European revolutionaries.

An important development when Dowlatabadi is in Istanbul is a
prominent religious authority asking him to write a treatise about the
social circumstances in Iran – particularly the geopolitics of the region.
He obliged and writes an essay in Arabic for him, and in chapter 7 of
the third volume he gives us a draft of that treatise. He tells us that the
Arabic text of his essay was subsequently translated into Turkish and
given to Ottoman authorities. The gist of this essay is that Iranian
politics is divided by the imperial interests of the Russians in the North
and the colonial interests of the British in the South. He also gives a
description of the revolutionary mobilization in Iran and defends the

[71] Ibid.: III: 19.   [72] Ibid.: III: 26.   [73] Ibid.: III: 34.   [74] Ibid.: III: 34.
[75] Ibid.: III: 38.   [76] Ibid.: III: 50.

cause of the Constitutional Revolution.[77] Dowlatabadi is not very
happy with the nature of political activism of the Iranian community
in Istanbul and begins to form his own organization. What is important in these passages is the fact that he is deeply informed by the
developments inside Iran and that he is engaged with his like-minded
comrades in the Ottoman territories, as he is conscious of other Iranian
activists in London and Paris. In his prose, particularly evident in
chapter 8 of the third volume, is the manner in which he is following
the events inside Iran and placing them next to those in Asia and
Europe, all of which informing much of his commentary about what
needs to be done.[78]

Crucial in his reports from Istanbul is the fact that he is a witness to
the revolutionary uprising against the Ottoman sultans. He tells us the
uprising commences on April 13, 1909 – and it is highly significant to
see him so deeply involved in the details of these important events in
the history of late Ottoman and the rise of the Young Turks, for he sees
a solid solidarity between the Iranian and Turkish revolutionary aspirations.[79] He tells us that on Tuesday, April 28, 1909, he goes for an
outing on a boat on the Bosporus and sees the boats taking Abdul
Hamid II (Reign, August 31, 1876–April 27, 1909) away from the
capital. The collapse of the Ottoman Empire while Dowlatabadi is in
Istanbul gives a boost to his morale for revolutionary aspirations in his
own homeland. He reports that Mohammad Ali Shah is petrified by
the collapse of the Ottoman dynasty and the victory of the revolutionaries – because the two tyrannical dynasties were feeding on each
other. But he also reports that the Russians were not happy with the
success of the Young Turk revolutionaries. The events in Istanbul while
Dowlatabadi is there place him in a crucial location to reflect comparatively on the catalytic effect of the two countries on each other and also
on the colonial interests of the Russians and the British in the region.[80]
None of that is of course news to him, and he had these ideas before he
left Iran – but here he has firsthand experience of the events in the
neighboring Ottoman and Russian empires.

Encouraged by the revolutionary successes he witnesses in Istanbul,
Dowlatabadi resumes his political activism, is elected as the head of the
revolutionary cell in the Ottoman capital, and follows the news of his

[77] Ibid.: III: 57–64.   [78] Ibid.: III: 65–76.   [79] Ibid.: III: 77–84.
[80] Ibid.: III: 92–99.

homeland closely. He discredits Mohammad Ali Shah of his plots
against the Constitutionalists and denounces the Russians for their
conspiracies against the Iranian revolution, and the pages of his travelogue at this point are a space where he mobilizes, strategizes, and
theorizes the Constitutional Revolution he is witnessing and in which
he is actively participating.[81] While he is in Istanbul, Tehran falls to the
revolutionaries, and he is tempted to go back to Iran. But he does not
do so and gives us some explanation as to why: number one, he says,
he is busy reviving an old school in Istanbul – the one in which the
prominent revolutionaries Mirza Habib Isfahani and Mirza Agha
Khan Kermani used to teach. He also says it is too early to go back
to Iran, for he wishes to go to Berlin and Paris in order to collaborate
with the revolutionaries outside Iran. He in effect has become a link
between progressive revolutionaries inside and outside his homeland –
those who live in Istanbul and those who live in Paris and Berlin in
regular contact with each other. Not all of these revolutionaries are
even Iranians. There are Turks, Kurds, Arabs among them. This transnational geography of revolutionary mobilization is crucial to keep
in mind.

Finally, on August 18, 1909, Dowlatabadi leaves Istanbul for
Vienna via Budapest. He travels to Paris and praises its achievements.
While in Paris he meets with Iranian dignitaries in the French capital
before traveling to London to meet with E. G. Browne, the prominent
British Iranist. He then goes to Berlin and meets with Iranian activists
in the German capital and finally off to Warsaw and back to Baku
where he meets with Mirza Abd al-Rahim Talebof Tabrizi, the prominent literary figure of the period.[82] But he is eager to go back to
Tehran and join the revolutionaries. This is a quick trip abroad, much
of it in Istanbul, with only a quick few days in Europe, and only to
meet with Iranian revolutionary activists. His trip to Istanbul is far
more significant and consequential.

He returns to Tehran on October 22, 1909. He had been away since
August 18, 1909, so he had not been out of his homeland for more
than a couple of months. As soon as he arrives in Tehran he plunges
deeply into the politics of parliamentary democracy, for which he had
devoted the entirety of his life. He is deeply saddened by the factional-
ism that had emerged between the radicals and the more moderates in

---

[81] Ibid.: III: 100–107.   [82] Ibid.: III: 112–113.

the parliamentary politics of his homeland. He gives a full report of who is who and where things stand in this early experiment with parliamentary democracy.[83] The advantage of his observations about the tumultuous state of early parliamentary democracy in Iran is that he is fully aware of at least three other players – not just Russians and the British as we have always known, but the emerging interest of the Germans in the internal politics of Iran in order to manipulate the Iranians to their advantage.[84]

He spends about eighteen months between 1910 and 1911 in Iran, but he is not very happy with the consequences of the Constitutional Revolution. He thinks that despite his qualifications, nobody is paying much attention to him or taking advantage of his experience. He thinks particularly that because of his experiences in the Ottoman capital in association with the Young Turks, the younger generation of revolutionaries could have taken advantage of him, but they are not. Nevertheless, he publishes an essay he calls "The Gift of Yahya" and distributes it for free.[85] As much as he can, he encourages the revolutionaries to be in contact with reporters and scholars in England, France, Germany, Russia, and the Ottoman territories in order to promote the interests of the revolution. It is at this time that a major international conference on race is taking place in England, and he is invited to attend. This invitation, in and of itself, is a clear indication that by this time Yahya Dowlatabadi had established himself as a towering public intellectual of his time.

The conference in London to which Dowlatabadi is invited was billed as "the First Universal Races Congress, which met in 1911 for four days at the University of London and was dedicated to the cause of investigating racism around the globe. Speakers from a number of countries were invited to discuss racism and how to confront it. The conference reportedly had hundreds of participants. The idea of the conference was conceived as early as 1906 by leading authorities such as the American philosopher Felix Adler, Hungarian ethicist Gustav Spiller, and the British philanthropist Philip Stanhope. This is what we know about this conference outside Dowlatabadi's reports:

One hundred years ago, the First Universal Races Congress was held at the University of London. The Congress met July 26–29, 1911, and was called to

---

[83] Ibid.: III: 119–130.   [84] Ibid.: III: 131.   [85] Ibid.: III: 145.

focus attention on the problems of relations between nations and races of the world. The Congress had about 2,100 members, including official representatives from at least 17 governments, including Brazil, China, England, France, Germany, Haiti, Persia, South Africa, and the USA, as well as officials of colonial possessions (including present-day India). Dr. Felix Adler served as the US delegate, officially representing the United States Bureau of Education. While Leader of the New York Society for Ethical Culture, Adler was also a professor of Social Ethics at Columbia University and was recognized for his innovations in education. The Congress grew out of a proposal he advanced in 1906 at the meeting of the International Union of Ethical Societies in Eisenach, Germany.[86]

On February 1, 1910, Dowlatabadi tells us he is invited to this conference. He is delighted to receive this letter of invitation and gives us the further detail that in September 1910 he has to submit the draft of a paper to be read at the conference. Evidently, some other Iranians were also invited to this Congress but he is not sure if they will respond properly. He is particularly intent on attending this conference because he says representatives from India, China, and Japan have also been invited, and it is imperative for a person from Iran to attend this conference as well. He writes back to the Congress and informs them that he would be happy to attend and starts drafting a paper to submit to the organizers. He shares the draft of this paper with some of his friends. He writes the paper in Persian, and an Iranian who had been living in France for ten years, Yahya Khan Qaraguzlu, translates it into French. Dowlatabadi says he intends to take his ten-year-old son with him because he worries about his education. He is told there will be a photography exhibition in conjunction with the Congress and he should bring some pictures with him, too. He prepares a whole collection of photographs to take along with him to this exhibition in London.[87]

On Thursday, June 1, 1911, Dowlatabadi and a couple of other luminaries of the revolutionary elite leave Iran toward London, first by ship toward Baku and eventually reaching Vienna – from there he goes to Lausanne in Switzerland, where he meets a number of Iranian

---

[86] See Baltimore Ethical Society, citing "The following article written by Emil Volcheck, BES Secretary, has been reprinted from the Fall 2011 AEU Dialogue." Available online here: http://bmorethical.org/the-first-universal-races-congress-of-1911/. Accessed July 21, 2018.

[87] Dowlatabadi, *Hayat-e Yahya/The Life of Yahya*: III: 153–159.

students, particularly Mohammad Jamalzadeh (1892–1997), the
future founder of modern Persian literature, who was the son of Jamal
al-Dina Vaez Isfahani (1862–1908), who was a close friend of the
author before he was killed. (Decades later, I (Hamid Dabashi) visited
Jamalzadeh in Geneva, when he was in his nineties.) Dowlatabadi
leaves his young son in Vevey in Switzerland, and he tells us after his
daughter dies at a young age that he had promised himself not to get
close to his children, but then in the course of this journey, he had
become very attached to his son, and it was difficult for him to leave
him in Switzerland and go to London to attend the race conference but
also in time for the coronation of George V (reigned May 6, 1910–
January 20, 1936).[88]

Upon his arrival in London, Dowlatabadi gives us a detailed account
of the race Congress. The first session of the gathering is on Monday,
July 10, 1911, in which he participates, and he is much excited to
report of the presence of people from Africa and North America. Some
members of the delegation object to the very name of this conference
being "race conference." The second session is on Friday, July 14,
1911, in which Dowlatabadi speaks and proposes that the Congress
be repeated every three to four years, and that it must be held in
various continents. The first to be held in Europe was fine, but it should
be also held in Asia, the Americas, Africa, and Australia. He also
proposes the word "race" in the title be changed, for it is inappropriate. There are detailed discussions about language at the conference,
and about script, about religion, about politics, and about sectarianism.[89] The single most important aspect of this conference in London is
the fact that Dowlatabadi and other delegates get to meet people from
other colonized countries and continents. The trip is not as much "to
Europe" as it is to a conference in which Asians, Africans, and Latin
Americans get to see and meet each other and discuss their common
fate, their similar experiences with the very racist foundation of European (including and particularly British) colonialism.

While he is in London, he tells us that he is following the news of the
developments in Iran through the foreign press. The circumstances of
the ruling monarch, Mohammad Ali Shah, and the plots against him
and the developments within the newly established Majlis are the issues
that he is following through what the British press is reporting. At the

[88] Ibid.: III: 160–167.   [89] Ibid.: III: 168–175.

same time, between July 26 and 29 he attends eight sessions of the
Congress on race held at the convention hall, and he gives a full
description of the venue.[90] He tells us that initially he was the only
one who attended the meeting of the Congress in his habitual dress
from Iran, and that everybody else, despite the fact of coming from all
over the world, were wearing European clothes. But when they see him
appear with his national costumes, representatives from the Ottoman
Empire, from Egypt, India, and African countries, all go back and
return to the meetings with their national dresses. He also informs us
that in one of the meetings of the Congress there is a courageous British
woman who stands up demanding and exacting attention from the
chair of the sessions and delivers a devastating attack on British
colonialism, particularly in India, and tells the representatives of various countries not to be fooled by the British in their appearance of
humanitarian gestures toward other races. She tells them, if you really
want to know how we care about other nations and races, you have to
go to India and see the terror we have visited upon the Indian people.[91]
A few pages later, we learn this courageous woman was none other
than Annie Besant (née Wood, 1847–1933), the prominent British
socialist and women's rights activist who had fought valiantly for Irish
and Indian self-rule.[92]

Now imagine for a moment this scene. A top Iranian public intellectual goes to London to attend a conference on race, and while enjoying
the company of other people having come from other colonized
nations, from Asia, Africa, and the Americas, an English woman
stands up and blasts the entire conference and reminds them of the
terror of colonialism. The event is so memorable, and Dowlatabadi is
so receptive to the significance of this event, that he gives a full description of it in his travelogue – the same travelogue that generations of
readers have pretended to have read. Is this a man who went "to
Europe" to learn how to "Westernize" his homeland? The sheer
absurdity of the manner in which these travelogues have been abused
simply defies reason and sanity.

[90] Ibid.: III: 176–179.   [91] Ibid.: III: 181–182.
[92] Ibid.: III: 188. This of course requires some detective work deciphering from
Dowlatabadi's Persian script what the actual name of this woman was – for the
miserable condition of editing these seminal books does not benefit from any
careful reading or annotating.

Dowlatabadi is initially tempted to deliver his own speech in Persian. He is reluctant to do so but then he hears that the representative of Japan has said that he will deliver his speech in Japanese, so he, too, deliveries his talk in his native Persian but asks for a student who knew English to translate for him as he speaks. He gives us a synopsis of his speech in this Congress in which he defends the national liberation movement in his homeland and denounces the colonial rule of the British since 1907 both directly and indirectly by allowing for the Russian interference in the affairs of his homeland.[93] In other words, he has gone to London to join forces with other colonized nations to denounce British imperialism, not to learn how to "modernize" his country.

Dowlatabadi also informs us that this particular Congress was the place where European Zionists were actively trying to convince the world of the necessity of the formation of a Zionist state. He is not impressed by their propaganda. He mentions Felix Adler having told him that the idea of this Congress was actually his. Dowlatabadi discusses his conversations with Adler in the context of Zionist mobilization of global sentiments for the establishment of the state of Israel.[94] Adler puts him on the defensive by publicly asking him to comment on the condition of the Jewish community in Iran, to which he also publicly responds and defends the condition of Jewish Iranians and how they are integral to the rest of the society.

On August 12, 1911, Dowlatabadi leaves London for Paris. He says Paris is very warm at this time, and he soon leaves for Switzerland, where he stays in Lausanne. He spends his time bringing Iranian students together, and he also studies French. He follows the news from Iran closely and decides to go to Montreux and spend some time there during the hot summer months, and he continues to follow the news in Iran closely and is very enthused about the presence of Americans in the course of the Iranian Constitutional Revolution, who he thinks under Morgan Schuster (1877–1960 – an American lawyer who served the first Iranian parliament as its treasurer–general) are far more helpful to the revolutionaries and prevent the British and the Russian interventions.[95]

While he is still in Switzerland, he hears the news that the Russian military has perpetrated atrocities in Tabriz. He gives a detailed

[93] Ibid.: III: 183–184.   [94] Ibid.: III: 185.   [95] Ibid.: III: 194–195.

account of those atrocities. He also offers a detailed account of the rivalry between the British and the Russians, and he discusses the issue of a national Railroad because the Germans have just finished a railroad in Iraq, all the way to the border with Iran.[96] Despite the fact that the Russians had the right to do so, they had not yet implemented that promise, and the British were not happy that Germans had advanced all the way to the Iraqi borders. Meanwhile in London, he tells us, E. G. Browne, the prominent Orientalist, is defending the cause of Iranian national sovereignty and revolution.[97] He speaks very highly of E. G. Browne as well as of Morgan Schuster, both of whom he considers true friends of Iran. He received an invitation from the same Race Congress he had just attended to be appointed as one of the six delegates "from the East" that they wanted to include in their executive committee of the Congress. They have decided to appoint an Iranian, they tell him, only on the condition that he would be that person. On March 24, 1912, he writes a very detailed letter from Switzerland to the Race Congress in which he details his hopes and aspirations for this gathering in eliminating racism, but at the same time he refers to the power of capitalism in creating hostility among races and nations, and he doubts whether this Congress can address that issue.[98] By this time in his life in Iran and travels abroad, Dowlatabadi is a key public intellectual of unprecedented authority for his generation and before to speak on global issues.

While in Switzerland he notices the presence of representatives of Iranian tribal forces, such as the Bakhtiaris, in European capitals in order to procure the British (in particular) support for their political ambitions.[99] While he is still living in Lausanne he hears that a high-ranking member of the Qajar nobility, Naser Al-Molk, has come to Evian in France across from Lake Geneva for vacation. He takes a boat and goes to Evian, and he visits with him and discusses various aspects of politics in their homeland. Naser al-Molk recommends him to become a supervisor to Iranian students in Europe, but the officials in Iran do not agree, which causes much consternation in Dowlatabadi – for he is in financial need of such official appointments. Be that as it was, he decides to bring his family abroad, and he writes extensively about the significance of Iranian women and girls traveling abroad and

---

[96] Ibid.: III: 204.   [97] Ibid.: III: 206.   [98] Ibid.: III: 211–213.
[99] Ibid.: III: 221–222.

expanding their educations. He has a wife and two daughters in Iran, and he goes to Baku in order to bring them out.[100] What he had witnessed in the Race Congress in London had obviously made a deep impact on him, and he is now thinking of his own immediate family as integral to this global awareness of the surrounding world.

He does not get along with Iranian students in Switzerland, and in May 1914 he decides to go to London, and upon his arrival in London he is attracted to the woman-suffragists who are active in England, and he mentions Emmaline Pankhurst (1858–1928) in particular as a leader of the militant suffragists at this time. Dowlatabadi spends some time in London, meets with E. G. Brown and other scholars of Iran, and ultimately decides to go back to Iran for a number of reasons – first and foremost is of course financial, but in addition he says his wife is afflicted with tuberculosis and needs his help, and also he says that the next Congress of race is being organized, to which he is invited, but Iran has not done anything in preparation, and he has to go back to do something based on his commitments from the first Race Congress.

On his way to Iran he is stranded in a small town in Russia while waiting for his entry visa, where he sees a sizable Jewish community, among whom, he tells us, Zionists are actively hoping to mobilize resources to settle in Palestine. He speaks openly of the prejudices against Jews in Iran but also tells us how, in the course of educational reform, the Iranian Jewish communities were active in sending their children, particularly young girls, to modern schools.[101] He spends a whole chapter on the condition of education of young Iranian students abroad, which he divides into three categories: first, those who are too young to learn anything serious, second, those who have roots in their own country and are abroad to be educated and perhaps go back and be of some service to their homeland, and third, those who are wasting their time learning the worst things about the culture of their host countries and are of no use but in fact are corrupting the politics of their homeland. He also tells us that he established a small library while he was in Lausanne, but that there was disagreement and com-petition and hostility among the students who came to that library. Once in Lausanne, near the train station he sees a group of Bulgarian students celebrating and welcoming with all pomp and ceremony a literary figure who had come to Switzerland from Bulgaria, and he

---

[100] Ibid.: III: 231.   [101] Ibid.: III: 235.

spends pages lamenting why this is not the case with respect to Iranian students.[102] As we read Dowlatabadi page after page, we realize he is a walking body of feeling intellect deeply concerned about every aspect of his homeland. Whatever he does, whatever he sees, he turns into moments of reflection about advancing the lot of his homeland.

On July 1, 1914, Dowlatabadi returns to Iran and he tells us he is very depressed with the circumstances in his homeland. He has his three-year-old daughter with him, whose name is Fakhr al-Zaman, who had spent a year in Switzerland with him and had learned French and forgotten her Persian. Dowlatabadi spends a few pages seeing his homeland through the eyes of this young child and sympathizes with her regarding her disappointment with the circumstances of their homeland.[103] Chapter 30 of the third volume is an excellent example of what has happened to this generation of Iranian critical thinkers by virtue of their travels abroad. This chapter is a detailed analysis of the colonial condition in which countries like Iran find themselves early in the twentieth century. Dowlatabadi goes all the way back to the middle of the nineteenth century, describing the various rivalries and hostilities among England, France, and Germany in order to map out the political circumstances into which Russia and the Ottoman Empire also enter in the aftermath of which countries like Iran find themselves entrapped. This chapter is an excellent example of how traveling abroad exposes this generation to a far more global understanding of the geopolitics of the region. Toward the end of this chapter he also tells us that because of the pending war in Europe, which would later become known as the First World War, he has decided not to go to Paris to attend the second conference on race and instead stay home and try to be helpful to his homeland.[104]

In August 1915, he receives the sad news that his fourteen-year-old son has died in Switzerland while studying at a boarding school where he had left him. His son evidently had an accident while playing sports and subsequently contracted tetanus after what had been a minor injury.[105] He is devastated by the news and tries to distract himself by work. He says he is interested in establishing a scientific institution for the promotion of sciences. The news of World War I is now emerging in Iran, and he says he and his wife find solace in the fact

[102] Ibid.: III: 249–251.   [103] Ibid.: III: 260–264.   [104] Ibid.: III: 268–274.
[105] Ibid.: III: 279.

that it is not just their son but thousands of European children who have also perished in the course of this war.

Dowlatabadi's attentions are now drawn inside Iran where the ruling Qajar monarch, Ahmad Shah, had just ascended the throne at the age of seventeen and was in no position to run the country. There is a democratic parliament, but there are no competent parliamentarians. Russia and England are still very much in charge of the internal affairs of the country – placing Iran effectively under their respective imperial controls. World War I has now started, and because of the Iranian concerns against the Russians and the British, there is an understandable pro-German sentiment in the country, as Dowlatabadi reports to us. Meanwhile the Belgians are in charge of the finances and the Swedes in charge of the rural police, as the Germans are exploring their possibility of an inroad into Iranian politics. The sympathy even with the Ottomans is high because of their siding with the Germans during the war. Dowlatabadi gives us a full picture of the country at the commencement of the war – his prose crystal clear and purposeful after so much he has seen around the world.[106]

Russian forces finally enter the capital on November 9, 1915, under the pretext of protecting their interests against Ottoman, German, and Australian forces.[107] At this point, Iran from one end to another is under the colonial domination of Russia and England, with Ottoman, German, and Austrian forces in between, juggling for space and influence. Much of Dowlatabadi's prose at this point is a critical analysis of European colonialism in his homeland.[108] Many other nationalists like him at this point are particularly hopeful that the Germans might be sympathetic to the cause of the Iranian national interests, and Dowlatabadi spends much of his time traveling throughout Iran in anticipation of such help. What is particularly important at this point is to see how the transnational colonial rivalries among the Russians, the British, and the Germans are infiltrating deep into various Iranian provinces and small towns – from Tehran deep into northern and southern provinces. These are the most fascinating accounts of Iranian territories under the complete control of the occupying forces of not just the Russians and the British but in fact the Germans too – fighting their European battlers here on Iranian territories.[109] These are the defining

---

[106] Ibid.: III: 281–290.   [107] Ibid.: III: 291.   [108] Ibid.: III: 300–310.
[109] Ibid.: III: 310–345.

days, and Dowlatabadi's prose the defining narrative, of Iranian colonial experiences.

The alliance that emerges here during World War I while Iran is under the occupation of the Allied Forces – Dowlatabadi tells us there is a tacit alliance between Iran, Germany, and the Ottomans – will remain important in political configuration of colonial powers in his homeland for decades to come. But such political maneuvering in alliance with the Germans, the Ottomans, and the Austrians against the Russians and the British should not lead us to believe that all Iranians were fooled by such rivalries among European imperial powers. Dowlatabadi reprints an utterly brilliant "Shabnameh" (nightly pamphlet) in which a revolutionary thinker shares with his audience the fact that those who had allied themselves with the Germans and the Ottomans and the Austrians, etc., were actually fooled into such alliances, that these wars among the European powers were for their own interests, and the colonized countries were being manipulated into taking sides fighting for Europeans in their own internal wars. This Shabnameh is a remarkable historical document.[110] In it, here on the last few pages of the third volume of Dowlatabadi's book, we are witness to an acute anticolonial intelligence at work. He opts to end his third volume with this text as a summation of his own critical thinking about the matter – European colonial powers were plundering the world, dividing it into fragments to steal its resources and abuse its inhabitants more effectively. Written more than a hundred years ago, this Shahnameh could have been an opinion piece on Aljazeera today.

He Was at Home in the World

I have finally reached the fourth and final volume of Dowlatabadi's *Hayat-e Yahya*, which was published in Iran in 1983. It has forty-three chapters and some final concluding material. I am looking at the first chapter and it is quite disappointing. It reminds me of my teenage years when I used to buy books in Iran and in the middle of reading them I would suddenly discover that some pages were blank! That incompetent way of publishing books without checking that they actually have all the pages continues apace in the Islamic Republic of Iran. Be that as

[110] Ibid.: III: 366–369.

it may, I will continue to read this final volume in as many pages as the publisher has actually cared to print. To be fair, in four massive volumes, these are the first few pages I see missing early in the fourth volume.

On the first of May, 1916, Dowlatabadi leaves Iran for Iraq, because the circumstances of the Allied occupation of his homeland are no longer safe or tolerable. Such journeys abroad, no matter how important their consequences, are ordinarily left out of the scholarship on "the Muslim discovery of Europe" because they are not *to* Europe. Including these crucial journeys in our reading of these travelogues, as we must, opens up an entirely different horizon of understanding them, one in which Europe is neither privileged nor ignored, but placed within the larger frame of these travelers discovering a new world for themselves and their posterities. After a short stay in Baghdad and other Iraqi cities, in mid-June 1916 Dowlatabadi leaves for Istanbul via Aleppo.[111] On his way from Baghdad to Istanbul, he gives us an eyewitness account of the terrible condition of the Armenians in Ottoman territories. As Dowlatabadi puts it, the Armenian community had been manipulated by the Russians and by the British, who promised them independence of their own country, by virtue of which they had resisted Ottoman authority over their communities; in response, they were treated terribly by the Ottoman military and in the second chapter of the fourth volume of Dowlatabadi's book we have an account of the conditions of destitution and despair under which the Armenian communities lived between Aleppo and Istanbul. Upon his arrival in Istanbul, he tells us how improved the capital now looked compared to eight years ago when he had seen it. He praises the work that the Young Turks had done in bringing their country forward.[112]

While in Istanbul he gives us a full report of how the Germans in the Ottoman military have drawn an agreement, based on which the Ottomans are fighting the Russians on Iranian soil, with some help from the Iranian side. Dowlatabadi is particular about the achievements of the Young Turks and how they are crafting a new national identity for themselves in the construction of which they are using some Ottoman, some Iranian, and some European elements.[113] In Istanbul he meets with high-ranking Ottoman officials, and based on his own reports he particularly warns them about the predicament of

---

[111] Ibid.: IV: 9–16.   [112] Ibid.: IV: 17–25.   [113] Ibid.: IV: 26–31.

the Armenians as he saw them between Aleppo and Istanbul. He also insists that the Sunni-Shia sectarianism should not be exacerbated between the Ottomans and Iranians.[114]

On August 9, 1917, Dowlatabadi leaves Constantinople toward Scandinavia. He says he is very happy traveling north, and gives us details of his passage through the Balkans. He is full of admiration for Bulgarians and full of criticism toward the Turks. He admires the industriousness of the Bulgarians and Serbians until he reaches Austria. With respect to Hungary, as well, he is full of admiration and respect. He enters Vienna and gives us an account of how dilapidated and destroyed the Austrian capital looks compared to the last time he was there. He says this is the fourth time that he has visited Vienna. He finally leaves Vienna and travels toward Berlin. A particular issue that is deeply troubling him as he is traveling through European countries during the war is that he cannot carry any writing material with him, and, as a result, it is quite obvious he is writing this part of his travel narrative from his memories. A particular conversation that he has with a young Austrian person on August 31, 1917, in the train station deeply concerns him, and that is when this young Austrian asks him where the borders of Iran are. He initially wanted to give an answer of surprise, but then he pauses for a minute and realizes that the question comes from the fact that Iran is under military occupation by the Russians and the British, and as a result its boundaries and are not very clear. He enters Berlin and is taken aback by how devastated it is by virtue of having endured three years of war. He gives us details of how coupons and rationing are done in Berlin during the war and is full of admiration for the German administration in this period and also the patience of the Germans themselves.

On September 5, 1917, Dowlatabadi tells us he finally leaves Germany toward Sweden and sails through the Baltic Sea. He tells us that for the first time now he has pen, paper, and pencil, that he can write – and he summarizes his journey from Tehran under revolutionary and war circumstances toward Baghdad then from there to Constantinople and then through the Balkans toward Austria and Germany and then from there to Sweden as he is sailing through the Baltic toward Stockholm. At the German port of Sassnitz he says he reflects on the situation of war and peace in the world as he sails toward

---

[114] Ibid.: IV: 32–40.

Stockholm.[115] He enters Sweden and is full of admiration for how peaceful the country is, but he talks about the rivalries between the British and the Germans there while Sweden remains neutral. He speaks of the leader of the socialists in Sweden, to whom he refers (in Persian script) as "Branti." He is referring to Karl Hjalmar Branting (1860–1925), the prominent leader of the Swedish Social Democratic Party (1907–1925) and Prime Minister during three separate periods (1920, 1921–1923, and 1924–1925).

While he is in Sweden, Dowlatabadi tells us on page 48 of the fourth volume of his book that he writes an article titled "Aristocracy and Democracy," but the Swedish papers refuse to publish it because they considered it too radical, but he says that he publishes a French translation of it in the 31st issue of a newspaper called *La Nation*, published in Lausanne in Switzerland. He tells us this article was also published in *Journal de Geneva* on the same day and at the same page with an article that Lenin had just written. He gives us a Persian translation of Lenin's article. He now tells us that the reason for his presence in Sweden was to participate in a conference that the Social Democratic Party had organized, but the conference does not take place because the British and the French had not agreed for their representative from their socialist parties to come to Sweden. He now decides not to go back to Iran and spends some more time in Sweden He applies for permission to reside during the war in Sweden and is granted that permission.[116] So just as in the case of his attending the Race Congress in London, here in Stockholm, too, Dowlatabadi is not "in Europe" to learn how to civilize his people. He is in Europe to participate in a socialist conference and converse with his fellow socialist comrades. These are two vastly different readings of his travel "to Europe." He even publishes pioneering essays sharing his perspectives on democracy and socialism. As an Iranian public intellectual, he is joining his fellow socialists to think of a better world. The dastardly Orientalist reading of these travelogues, now carried out by Iranian scholars, perpetrates a systematic violence on these seminal texts by categorically disregarding such crucial details.

Dowlatabadi is in Sweden when the Russian revolution of 1917 happens, and he spent some time in his travelogue explaining various causes. But at the same time, he talks about the geopolitics of the

---

[115] Ibid.: IV: 41–47.   [116] Ibid.: IV: 48–54.

region extending from Russia to Finland and Ukraine. He commands an acute understanding of the geopolitics of the region and by extension the world. In his understanding of global politics, he is conscious of the fact that the US President Wilson has entered the European scene with certain imperial objectives. It is also in Stockholm that he meets with the other prominent Iranian revolutionary, Seyyed Hassan Taghizadeh (1878–1970), who had come there from Berlin in order to participate in the same socialist conference. At this point we read some of the most remarkable passages of the travelogue, in which Dowlatabadi discusses different socialist forces that had come to Sweden from around the world, particularly from the Arab world, from the Ottoman world, and from the Islamic world. He is particularly impressed to meet Mohammad Farid (1868–1919), the influential Egyptian revolutionary leader of Turkish ancestry, who had also come from Egypt in search of solidarity and support.

Dowlatabadi talks about similar revolutionaries from Tunisia, from Algeria, from the Ottoman territories, from the Caucuses, from India – all having come here to Sweden to join this conference. It is here in Sweden that all these socialist revolutionaries gather and discuss their common interest – not how to imitate the West and become Westerners, but how to put their forces together to overcome economic injustice. Dowlatabadi travels to Uppsala where he meets with the Archbishop, who seems to be a learned person with knowledge of Avesta. Anywhere he goes, particularly now in Sweden, he looks for learned scholars to discuss Iran with them. He finally decides to leave Sweden and go to Russia. That does not happen, and he has to go back through Denmark initially and then Germany. In Denmark he meets with the prominent Iranist and philologist Arthur Emanuel Christensen (1875–1945) in Copenhagen. Finally, on April 13, 1918, he leaves Denmark, traveling to Berlin on his way to Iran.[117]

Dowlatabadi returns to Berlin during the war. He gives a detailed account of what preoccupies the Germans in this period. Number one, he says, is the Russian revolution and the fact that Germans are divided between the working class, who are pro-revolution, and the capitalists, who are deeply troubled by its prospects. The second concern in Germany at this point is the increasing power of the United States. Their third concern is the fact that their own supporters, namely

[117] Ibid.: IV: 55–65.

Austria and the Ottoman Empire, are falling apart. On September 14, Dowlatabadi leaves Berlin toward Kiev, the capital of Ukraine.[118] He tells us that he is robbed in Warsaw of all his money and all his papers. He is desperate – until he finds one of his former students from Switzerland. He speaks of a Polish Jewish student who helps him until he sorts out his papers and resumes his journey.[119] From Kiev he goes to Odessa, where on September 26, 1918, he meets Isa Sedigh (1894–1978), the prominent Iranian educator and the first president of Tehran University. Finally, on October 10, 1918, three lunar years after he had left Iran, he returns to his homeland, crossing the Aras River and entering Azerbaijan.[120]

Here Dowlatabadi tells us he had left Tbilisi on October 6, 1918, for Tabriz. While he is in the area, he writes extensively about the Ottoman imperial interest in the Azerbaijani province of northwest Iran and gives a short treatise on the geopolitics of the region and the fragmentation of various nations in the aftermath of the collapse of various Muslim empires. He also tells us while in Azerbaijan he meets with Mohammad Hasan Mirza, the crown prince of the last Qatar monarch.[121] He finally leaves Tabriz and goes to Tehran. While in Tehran he is deeply saddened by the condition of poverty he witnesses. Most of his attention at this, as in other, times is devoted to various colonial interests in his homeland – the Russian and the British in particular. He is encouraged by the collapse of the Russian Empire and the rise of the Russian revolution. He talks admiringly of the revolutionary leader Mirza Kuchak Khan Jangali's (1880–1921) uprisings in Gilan. He welcomes the Russian acknowledgment of the atrocities of the Russian Empire. What is paramount in his mind as he returns to his homeland is a consistently regional and global consciousness of the imperial and colonial interests in his homeland. The single most important gift that he has brought for his country is this extraordinary awareness of the global circumstances of multiple empires and the fate of smaller nations like his homeland in this context.

Upon his return to Tehran he tells us that during the three years that he has been away from his homeland, he and his family have endured much financial hardship. He tells us that he used to receive a monthly salary from the Ministry of Education, but his salary was stopped upon his departure from Iran because of political hostility toward his

[118] Ibid.: IV: 70.   [119] Ibid.   [120] Ibid.: IV: 76.   [121] Ibid.: IV: 81.

principled positions. He spends quite some time at this stage explaining to us that because of his politics he is under severe financial pressure.[122] He tells us that he has some family property in Isfahan and that he goes there to perhaps sell that land in order to provide financial resources for his family; but for the rest of the chapter, usually when he talks about his personal financial issues, it is no longer personal but entirely devoted to understanding the circumstances of Iran, which is now under the Allied occupation. Traveling between Tehran and Isfahan and through various provinces gives Dowlatabadi an opportunity to talk about how the country is in utter chaos and despair.[123]

Dowlatabadi writes bitterly about Hassan Vosough (1868–1951), a prominent late Qajar statesman, and his notorious colonial treaty with the British, effectively handing over the administrative apparatus of Iran to British control.[124] Vosough played a leading role, evidently for a handsome bribe, in the negotiations with the British authorities, which resulted in the infamous Anglo-Persian Agreement of 1919. While deeply concerned about the internal affairs of his homeland, however, Dowlatabadi takes time to talk about the situation around the globe. He begins with the Russian revolution of 1917 and gives his readers pages of detailed accounts of how the British were trying to subvert that historic event. What is important in these pages is how he brings together his analysis of the internal affairs of his own country and those of the geopolitics of the region and the global condition at large.[125]

Meanwhile Dowlatabadi is in touch with Mirza Kuchak Khan Jangali, the revolutionary leader in Northern Iran, and is considered a trustworthy advisor to the Jangali uprising.[126] Much of his sympathy at this point is obviously with the revolutionary nationalists, his anger with the British and those Iranians who are siding with them. At this point his house is the epicenter of revolutionary activities against the British colonial interference in Iran. Meanwhile he continues with his cultural activities that supersede his concerns with the politics of his homeland. Among his concerns is changing the Persian alphabet, about which the religious establishments are in deep disagreement. We also read that it is at this time that the Europeans are trying to convince Americans to help them with the establishment of the League of

---

[122] Ibid.: IV: 103–104.   [123] Ibid.: IV: 116–122.   [124] Ibid.: IV: 123–132.
[125] Ibid.: IV: 133–140.   [126] Ibid.: IV: 141–149.

Nations. World War I is coming to an end and the Allied Forces, he tells us, would like to use the opportunity to establish a League of Nations in a manner that safeguards their interests.[127] This degree of critical consciousness about world affairs is emblematic of the wisdom acquired after a lifetime of traveling around the world.

Dowlatabadi tells us had a private audience with Ahmad Shah, the last Qajar monarch. What is important about his conversation with the monarch is the fact that Dowlatabadi had seen Europe during the war and as a result has no illusions about the particular superiority of their culture. What in effect we are reading in these pages are the final days of the Qajar dynasty. Ahmad Shah meets with the constitutional revolutionaries as well as the clergy, plus those who were drawn toward the British. Dowlatabadi is increasingly drawn to the internal politics of his homeland, in which he detects three major forces: the royal court and its supporters, the revolutionaries and their various factions, and those who are actively engaged on behalf of the British colonial interests.[128]

Dowlatabadi's critical assessment of the British colonial interests in effect shows that any assumption of a false fascination with Europe or "the West" is categorically flawed. Chapter 23 of the fourth volume is perhaps the best indication that at this stage of his memoir and travelogue and life there are absolutely no illusions about the thing called "Europe" or "the West." In this chapter he offers us a detailed account of the treacheries of British colonialism in Iran, and he explains in detail why it is that Iranians are drawn toward Russia in the aftermath of the Russian revolution. He says Iranians have suffered as much from czarist Russia as they have from colonial Britain, but in the aftermath of the Russian revolution things have changed, and a class consciousness has entered their political culture, which, impacted by the revolutionary uprisings, now recognizes who their international and internal enemies are.[129] In the same chapter he gives us the itemized content of the treaty between Russia and Iran, signed on December 14, 1920, in which all the colonial and imperial treaties between Iran and Russia are canceled, and the territorial integrity and the economic and political interests of Iran are mapped out in detail, and Russia commits itself to honoring them.

---

[127] Ibid.: IV: 171.   [128] Ibid.: IV: 190–203.   [129] Ibid.: IV: 197–206.

Dowlatabadi was destined to be a close eyewitness to the change of the Qajar to the Pahlavi dynasty. In his conversations with the Qatar nobility and other major actors in the course of these critical moments, Dowlatabadi warns them that in his words "a flood" is coming toward their homeland and is going to wash away many things, and they are to keep the best interest of the country at heart.[130] He has no inside scoop on the coup that is about to happen. But his critical awareness of the British colonial designs is highly alerted. Chapter 25 of this fourth volume is full of scorn for British colonialism for the coup they are plotting as their next move. Dowlatabadi detests the British and their Iranian collaborators for staging the 1921 coup that eventually led to the establishment of the Pahlavi dynasty. The coup was engineered by the British and executed by the Cossack Brigade headed by Reza Khan, planting Zia al-Din Tabataba'i as a decoy prime minister. The Qajar king put up no resistance. Reza Khan was then fully assisted by the British to overcome any political resistance or potential separatist movement.

Dowlatabadi specifically names Zia al-Din Tabataba'i as the political agent and Reza Khan as the military agent for the execution of the coup against the Qajar initiated by the British.[131] Later historical investigations revealed that a certain Major-General Sir Edmund Ironside, Lieutenant-Colonel Henry Smyth, and Walter Smart were the chief British colonial officers in charge of the coup that overthrew the Qajars and installed the Pahlavis. At this point Dowlatabadi tells us the military coup engineered by the British and executed by Zia al-Din Tabataba'i and Reza Khan was meant to bring Iran under the control of the heavy-handed Reza Khan in order to protect their economic and strategic interests in Iran and India and prevent the spread of socialist ideas from Russia in the region.[132] He gives us an eyewitness account of the transition of power from the Qajars to the Pahlavis as Reza Shah manages the coup and becomes the first monarch of the Pahlavi dynasty, all under the patronage of a British empire fearful of the Russian revolution.[133] Meanwhile, Dowlatabadi is increasingly wary of the prospect of US engagement in Iran and takes time to write about the murder of an American envoy, Robert W. Imbrie, from the United States Consul in Tehran – killed by a

---

[130] Ibid.: IV: 212.   [131] Ibid.: IV: 227.   [132] Ibid.: IV: 250.
[133] Ibid.: IV: 252–253.

mob.[134] So much political precision in the writing of a contemporary Iranian observer is crucial to keep in mind when we assess the significance of these travelogues in our reading of modern Iranian and world history.

Dowlatabadi spends a full chapter on Colonel Pesyan and Mirza Kucha Khan Jangali as two national heroes of his time in whom he has much trust and hope, and whom he knew personally and had deep admiration for.[135] This however does not prevent him from meeting with the future Reza Shah, who in the course of a meeting with Dowlatabadi gets very emotional in expressions of his nationalism. This meeting compromises his prose noticeably, and he begins to speak in a very reverential manner about Reza Khan. He also speaks in detail about Reza Shah's disdain for the clergy. In the course of their conversations, he tells us Reza Shah has a cozy relationship with the Shi'a establishment in Qom, for it helps the military junta fight communism.[136] But the power of the clergy is altogether reduced at this time – they mostly either side with Reza Shah or else keep to themselves. Reza Shah forces Ahmad Shah to make him prime minister. The weakling Qajar monarch, of course, agrees, on the condition the Pahlavi monarch would facilitate his trip abroad. Ahmad Shah knew the British had written him out of the Iranian scene. We are now close witness to the collapse of the Qatar dynasty in these precious pages of Dowlatabadi's book.[137]

Dowlatabadi gives us a detailed account of the composition of the first Majlis after the coup – and it is basically of three categories: the secular nationalists, the religious establishment, and the socialists. Reza Shah, though, tries to manipulate them all, securing dictatorial power for himself.[138] This very Majlis eventually legalizes the British coup, disempowers the last Qajar monarch, and declares Reza Khan the new king. Dowlatabadi at this point is closely collaborating with Reza Shah – giving him names of prominent leaders of the revolution to meet and implicate in his emerging power. Among them are the young Mohammad Mossadegh and Seyyed Hassan Taghizadeh – and of course himself. Dowlatabadi is also an eyewitness to the uprising of Sheikh Khaz'al in the south and gives details of how Reza Shah, through the intermediary of the British, manages to quell his separatist

---

[134] Ibid.: IV: 265.   [135] Ibid.: IV: 267–279.   [136] Ibid.: IV: 289.
[137] Ibid.: IV: 300–301.   [138] Ibid.: IV: 310–323.

In and out of a Homeland

movement.[139] He is therefore an eyewitness to the crucial period when
the British, under the direct micromanaging authority of their agent
Ironside, staged a coup to bring down the Qajar, pacify internal
dissent, and bring Reza Shah to the throne. Dowlatabadi was fully
aware and in fact collaborated with Reza Shah in this coup.[140]

There is much talk of Reza Shah preferring a republic to a monarchy. But as an eyewitness participant, Dowlatabadi tells us the idea
of a republic was actually a ploy by Reza Khan and the British and
their co-conspirators to dismantle the constitution and follow the
French model of Napoleon. The plot succeeds only to the point that
the Qajars are overthrown, and Reza Shah is appointed a king with the
active support of corrupt clergy fully on his side.[141] Dowlatabadi gives
us a detailed account in which revolutionary leaders spoke against this
transition from the Qajar to the Pahlavi dynasty – chief among them
was Mohammad Mossadegh, while the leading cleric Seyyed Hassan
Modarres had secretly agreed, according to Dowlatabadi, to help Reza
Shah become king.[142] It is quite clear here that Dowlatabadi's prose at
this crucial point is severely compromised by his own precarious
position in this transition. He is fully aware and critical of British
colonialism. He knows Reza Khan is their stooge. But still he collabor-
ates with him, while remaining committed to the Constitution, though
only a formal version of it as a new dictator is succeeding an absolutist
monarchy.

After the change of dynasty, Dowlatabadi eventually abandons
politics but continues to reflect on the domestic and foreign policies
of the new king which are basically keeping the British happy and the
Russians at bay.[143] Dowlatabadi decides to leave for Brussels and send
his family there, too. He also decides to get rid of his clerical robe.
Finally, on Saturday, October 26, 1929, he takes advantage of Reza
Shah's trip to Azerbaijan and swiftly leaves the county for Moscow,
and from there to Berlin and Brussels. Despite the fact that he had
helped Reza Shah in ascending to power, he remained suspicious of all
tyrants, and when push came to shove he opted out of politics. He
settles in Brussels with his family and goes to Paris to see his friends.
While in Paris, he tells us, he finishes the third and fourth volumes of
his Memoir/Travelogue.[144]

---

[139] Ibid.: IV: 324–334.   [140] Ibid.: IV: 335–344.   [141] Ibid.: IV: 345–361.
[142] Ibid.: IV: 383–385.   [143] Ibid.: IV: 406.   [144] Ibid.: IV: 413–414.

Dowlatabadi spends the last chapter of his fourth and final volume with a realistic assessment of Reza Shah and the commencement of his Pahlavi monarchy. What is left of the parliament, he says, is merely ceremonial and a political stratagem by Reza Shah in order to prevent members of the parliament from making trouble for him if they did not have anything to do. But the independence of the parliament, he tells us, is completely destroyed. This realistic assessment, however, does not prevent him from noting some of the achievements of Reza Shah. First and foremost, he celebrates the unveiling of women as a state policy that he considers a positive development. He refers to the disarming the various tribes as an important development also. He is instrumental in organizing the first millennial celebration of Ferdowsi as a national poet for the newly established monarchy. He is of course cantankerous, since despite the fact that this was initially his idea, he was not much appreciated. He refers to the renewal of the oil contract with the British, which he assures us is in the best interest of the British – regardless of how it was renegotiated. He refers to the mandatory changing of clothes – to which some of the clergy had put a up a resistance in Mashhad – in the context of the continued tensions between the newly minted monarchy and the clerical establishment.[145]

At the end of his book, Dowlatabadi gives us the details of some of the crucial dates of his departure from Iran. He moved to Brussels in November 1929 and he lived there for almost nine years until May 1938 and was more or less distant from the internal politics of his homeland – preoccupying himself with translating some European sources on Iran into Persian. He also receives a modest salary from Iran. He brings his fourth and final volume to conclusion, dating it June 2, 1938.[146] His daughter Forough writes an epilogue to the book, in which she tells us that after he put his memoirs in a safe deposit box in a bank in Brussels, Dowlatabadi moved back to Iran and spent the last year and four months of his life in his paternal home in Gholhak in Northern Tehran, visiting his friends, attending to a school he had established for poor students, and starting to write a biography of Ali ibn Abi Taleb, the First Shi'a Imam. Dowlatabadi dies on Friday, October 27, 1939.[147] In his last will and testament he considers himself

---

[145] Ibid.: IV: 417–436.   [146] Ibid.: IV: 442.   [147] Ibid.: IV: 444.

a citizen of the world but devoted to his homeland – and he remembers his 14-year-old son who had died in Switzerland.[148] At the very end of the book, the publisher adds a note in which he tries to explain and exonerate Dowlatabadi for having identified Modarres as a traitor and having advocated the unveiling of women.[149]

(didn't his daughter die too?)

The Devil in the Detail

I have opted for a detailed book report as the narrative texture of this chapter (with only occasional asides), for this is the only way I think it is possible to convey the rich texture of this particular text. Dowlatabadi was in many significant and enduring ways the summation of all the previous travelers in, through, and beyond his homeland. He was already a highly alert, critical observer when he left his homeland, and his critical consciousness was only intensified with the passage of time and through his extensive travels in and out of Iran. By and large Dowlatabadi is a fairly reliable and trustworthy chronicler of his homeland during his lifetime. When he is compromised by his proximity to power, he reports it and left to his own choices he immediately leaves Iran to protect his autonomous voice. More than any other Iranian traveler, he completely dismantles the Orientalist delusion that Iranians or Muslims "went to Europe" and "discovered the West" and came back to modernize and advance their country. He did no such thing. He went around the world with open eyes and critical mind, and he placed and saw Europe for and where it was – as a vastly colonizing project, and yet he was not Europhobic either. In Europe he found solid comrades – both from Europe and from other continents.

Dowlatabadi was integral to the most critical and progressive events of his time – anti-racist conferences, socialist gatherings, non-European nations from Asia, Africa, and Latin America coming together to think their present and future. He thought of Iran in the context of the world at large, and he brought the geopolitics of the *fin de siècle* and the Russian Revolution and World War I to bear on the fate of his homeland. He saw firsthand the Constitutional Revolution of 1906–1911 and the transition of power from the Qajar to the Pahlavis

---

[148] Ibid.   [149] Ibid.: IV: 449.

in the 1920s. He was totally aware and entirely critical of the colonial domination of the British and the Russians in his country. Through the thick and thin of these colossal events he managed to produce a prose that forever cast an anticolonial gaze back at the colonizing world and help remap the world anew.

11 | *The Fact and Fiction of a Homeland*

[handwritten: Zayn ol-Abedin Maraghe'ei]

[handwritten: Ibrahim Beg]

How lucky are the plants
In love as they are with light!
See how the expansive hand of light
Is cast upon their shoulders:
No, it is impossible to reach –
For there will always remain a distance ....
One must be afflicted –
Otherwise the whisper of wonder
In between two spoken words would be wasted.

Sohrab Sepehri (Mosafer/Traveler, Babol, Spring 1966)

Throughout his lyrical oeuvre, Sepehri had made of traveling a poetic metaphor of organic growth and gnostic enlightenment. Like plants, we gravitate toward light, guided by its caring hand, as travelers moving toward an unknown destination. But the journey is never complete, for there will always remain a distance that cannot be traversed, that the traveler cannot overcome. "Dochar bayad bud," he insists, one must be afflicted with the urge of traveling toward this unreachable light, just as the whisper of wonder moving in between two spoken words, the known origins and the intended destination, will be otherwise wasted. This poetic sublimation of the moment and momentum of traveling abandonment in the middle of the twentieth century would not have been possible without the sustained course of Persian travel writings having come to a significant literary height in the writing of one landmark work of fiction that had brought it to literary conclusion. I wish to devote this penultimate chapter of my book to this literary figure, for in his magnum opus we read the earliest account of how traveling had finally emerged from an actual into an allegorical metaphor, from a factual into a figurative allusion – not decades later but right at the time that these travelogues were being written and read. In this chapter, I will not discuss a journey that actually took place, but a journey that sublated all the other real

308

[handwritten: (but this is already present – eg Naqshbandi سیر در وطن)]

journeys into an abiding metaphor – for all the other actual travels abroad had to be become allegorical in a work of fiction before they transcended even higher into a poetic intuition of a nation – upon which the entire proposition of a people as a nation is contingent.

The Fictive Fact of Traveling

Zeyn al-Abedin Maragheh'i (1840–1910) was a pioneering Iranian novelist and a towering intellectual figure during the Constitutional Revolution of 1906–1911. He is today best remembered for his magnum opus, *Siyahat-nameh-ye Ibrahim Beg/Ibrahim Beg's Travelogue*, a scathing denunciation of the Qajar dynasty and its rampant incompetence and corruption, cast in the fictional narrative of a travelogue. The significance of Maragheh'i, however, predates and outlasts that singular achievement. We may indeed consider Maragheh'i as a transformative force in recasting the Persian literary imagination in the aftermath of its encounter with colonial modernity. But we must also remember that this text played a pivotal role in the social and political history of its time. Maragheh'i came of age in a particularly tumultuous period in the history of his homeland. In his political character and work of fiction, he brought a century of groundbreaking changes to fictive fruition. Simplification of Persian prose, introduction of printing machines, and eventual rise of a free and critical press outside the censorial control of the Qajar court and beyond its borders were chief among the factors that had facilitated the provocative formation of a public sphere upon which Maragheh'i had written and published his pioneering novel. Who was he, and how did his novel come about?

Born and raised in the Azerbaijan province in Northwestern Iran, Zeyn al-Abedin Maragheh'i hailed from a family of traveling merchants based in Maragheh. At a very young age he joined his father's profession, traveled in the region, and, finally, in the company of his brother he left his homeland for Tbilisi, where he was stationed as a merchant, and for a time even assumed some consular responsibilities at the Iranian mission. Maragheh'i eventually moved to Crimea, where his business success endeared him to the Russian royal family, which led to his obtaining Russian citizenship, a traumatic decision for him which he later regretted and renounced, reclaiming his Iranian identity. He soon married and settled in the resort city of Yalta, and the couple had three children. From here he finally moved to and settled in

Istanbul, where he published his pioneering work of fiction and wrote extensively on current affairs for the leading progressive journals of his time – published in London, Istanbul, or Calcutta. It was here in Istanbul that he emerged as a leading Iranian intellectual dissident, passionately fighting for the cause of democracy in his homeland. Maragheh'i's *Siyahat-nameh-ye Ibrahim Beg/Ibrahim Beg's Travelogue* is his most significant published work, having exercised an extraordinary impact on the course of the Constitutional Revolution in Iran. What sort of a book was this, from the pen of a professional merchant with a deep and enduring love for his homeland?

In world literature, Jonathan Swift's classic *Gulliver's Travels* (1726) is today the most commonly known and memorable example of fictional travel that is used as a satire for the current political conditions of the author's time. The origin of such traveling fiction traverses East and West of the globe and throughout various literary traditions and is not limited to any language or literature. What we are reading in Maragheh'i's *Siyahat-nameh-ye Ibrahim Beg/Ibrahim Beg's Travelogue* too is not the account of an actual travel, but a fictional narrative describing the journey of a protagonist back to his ancestral homeland. In this respect, we may have to go all the way back to Avicenna's (ca. 980–1037), or to Ibn Tufayl's (ca. 1105–1185) philosophical treatise *Hay ibn Yaghdhan*, or to Farid al-Din Attar's (ca. 1145–1221) *Conference of the Birds*, or to Shahab al-Din Suhrawardi's (1154–1191) *Ghorbat al-Gharbiyah*, or to Nur al-Din Abd al-Rahman Jami's (1414–1492) *Salaman and Absal*, or to Mulla Sadra's philosophical treatise *al-Asfar al-Arba'ah*, or before all of them to the Mi'raj account of the Prophet's nocturnal journey to heavens in the Qur'an as narrative antecedents of such allegorical journeys. It was, however, with Dante's (ca. 1265–1321) *Divine Comedy* that this genre of "spiritual journey" came to its European poetic climax. That seminal Italian event, however, is most probably, as many scholars have argued, rooted in a scant familiarity of the Italian poet with Islamic and/or Iranian sources, particularly with Prophet Muhammad's Mi'raj and/or the *Book of Arda-Viraf* ("Artay Virap Namak"), a Zoroastrian text written in Pahlavi describing the journey of a pious priest to heavens.[1] None of these indications proves that Dante was in

---

[1] For a pioneering essay arguing for the Islamic origin of *Divine Comedy*, see Miguel Asin Palacios, *Islam and the Divine Comedy* (London: Routledge Library Edition, 1926).

fact influenced by such prior examples of the genre. But they do point out a familiar theme in world classics. Dante's book in turn influenced many other subsequent examples of the genre, including Allamah Muhammad Iqbal's *Javid Nama* (1932). As we will see in the case of Maragheh'i's *Seyahat-Nameh-ye Ibrahim Beg,* his book too must be placed in the general landscape of such allegorical journeys in search of truth and all its consequences.

Maragheh'i's *Seyahat-Nameh-ye Ibrahim Beg Ya Bala-ye Ta'ssob-e Ou/Ibrahim Beg Travelogue or the Calamity of his Prejudice* (1903) was written at the borderline of fact and fiction at a crucial moment when the fact of Iranian colonial encounters with European colonialism was giving rise to a new language of liberation – a language that needed a crucial literary sublation. The significance of *Seyahat-Nameh-ye Ibrahim Beik* is in its protagonist being an Iranian who lives in Cairo and decides to travel to his homeland, and that plot twist gives Maragheh'i the subtext to write his book as a travelogue that raises the whole genre to a new literary height. Here in reversing the colonial gaze, when juxtaposed against countless European travelers traveling to Iran and casting an alienating look at it, Maragheh'i in effect brings the foreign eyes of a native to witness the familiar trouble spots of a homeland for which he only has an affectionate attachment and no realistic understanding. The author uses this narrative plot to bring his lead character to visit his homeland with the fresh eyes of a familiar foreigner – whereby its predicaments become more pronounced. The narrative plot works effectively. The significance of this book is therefore not just in being one of the most highly influential documents of the Constitutional period, but in the fact that the genre of travelogue had become so widely popular that it informed the writing of one of the earliest works of fiction in Persian. The narrative thus effectively reverses the gaze and the angle of vision back on Iran from the perspective of someone who has a highly romantic, entirely unrealistic, and therefore jarring conception of his homeland. It is no longer an Iranian who travels abroad, but an Iranian who travels home with the eye of a caring expat. This narrative, therefore, completes the cycle and brings the genre to a symbolic closure.

As the chief protagonist of the novel, Ibrahim Beg is a projection of Maragheh'i onto a fictional realm – emerging from a romantic delusion about his homeland facing a ferocious reality. The protagonist, just like the author, lives outside his homeland but yearns for it and is deeply troubled by its political predicament. The protagonist of the novel is born and raised in Egypt, to a merchant father. From his childhood, he inherits a deep love for his homeland, from which he inherits and cultivates a cherished sanctity. Following his father's wishes, Ibrahim Beg decides to travel and learn more about the world, particularly about his homeland, his image of which would be crushed by the reality of the conditions of Iran upon his arrival. People live in misery, the country is deprived of the most basic services, the religious authorities are ignorant and deceitful, and the political elite are corrupt and despotic, with the European powers preying on all such misery to rob the nation of its wealth and dignity.

A key motif in *Seyahat-Nameh-ye Ibrahim Beg* reflects a common theme among the travelers we have studied in this book: how the protagonist abandons his love for a woman whom he was supposed to marry (or to whom he was married) in order to travel abroad, or in this case, back to his homeland. The narrative, however, reverses the common pattern of these travelers starting with their homeland and traveling abroad by the protagonist having a nostalgic and romantic view of his homeland while living abroad and then coming home to a miserable country. In a way, Ibrahim Beg traces the itinerary of all the other travelers backward toward Iran, both reversing and complementing all their itineraries. From Egypt, he first travels to Istanbul, where he visits with the author of the book, Maragheh'i himself, who gives him a copy of the *Book of Ahmad*, a famous revolutionary tract by the prominent Constitutionalist Abd al-Rahim Talebof (1834–1911), to read to disabuse him of his illusions about his homeland. Ibrahim Beg, though, pays no attention to such warnings and travels to the Caucuses and there even more adamantly disregards signs of decay and despair in Iranians he sees aboard. Upon his arrival in Iran, with full understanding of the horrors of his homeland, he begins openly to criticize, admonish, and encourage those whom he meets to do something about this misery. But he becomes something of a nuisance and subject to abusive behavior by those who do not wish to hear about the conditions of their country. He finally returns to Egypt and begins writing his travelogue. But in Egypt he does not stop complaining about the conditions of his homeland, and finally one night in the heat of his passion he sets himself and his house on fire and passes out.

A crucial factor in this book is the fact that the protagonist leaves Egypt – and not any European country – in search of his homeland.

This fact completely and categorically de-Orientalizes this genre of literature – dismantling the entire Eurocentric colonial gaze endemic to European travelogues "to the East" (which Qajar scholarship on this body of literature has categorically inherited without a smidgen of critical thinking). This book decenters the Eurocentric world by bringing the itinerary back to the rambunctious world between Egypt and Iran, through Istanbul and the Caucuses, with Europe nowhere in sight. How precious, how extraordinary, is this normal act of forcing the colonized minds to think of the fact of these worlds otherwise concealed under the gaze of the European and colonized thinking hitherto imposed on this body of literature.

The Second Volume of *Seyahat-Nameh-ye Ibrahim Beg* is narrated by Ibrahim Beg's companion, Youssef Amu/Uncle Yousef. Here we learn that Ibrahim Beg comes back to consciousness after passing out, but he has lost his wits and his mental condition fluctuates with the political news that comes from Iran. He finally marries his beloved Mahboubeh and lives in happiness for a while until, upon hearing bad news from his homeland, he passes out and dies, as does his devoted wife. The Third Volume is something of a hallucinatory recollection of various genres that is narrated through a dream of Youssef Amu, who travels first to hell and then to paradise and via the guidance of a Wise man finds his way to Ibrahim Beg and sees him (with a satirical twist to the story) still preaching and complaining about his homeland to people in the other world.

The Original Edition

The original edition of *Siyahat-nameh-ye Ibrahim Beg/Ibrahim Beg's Travelogue*, of which I have obtained a pdf copy from Iran through the gracious help of my good friend Mahmoud Omidsalar, was published in Cairo, and although its initial pages lack any date of publication, we eventually discover this is an offset copy of the very first 1903 edition.[2]

---

[2] Zeyn al-Abedin Maragheh'i, *Seyahat-Nameh-ye Ibrahim Beg Ya Bala-ye Ta'ssob-e Ou/Ibrahim Beg Travelogue or the Calamity of his Prejudice* (Cairo, No Date, Three Volumes under one cover): I: 2–5. I will use this original and complete edition of the book for my reading and references. But there are many other and more recent editions of the book, such as: Zeyn al-Abedin Maragheh'i, *Seyahat-Nameh-ye Ibrahim Beg* (Tehran: Agah Publications, 1384/2005). There is also an English translation: Zayn Al-abidin Maraghahi, *The Travel Diary of Ebrahim Beg* (*Bibliotheca Iranica*. Persian Fiction in Translation Series), translated by James D. Clark (Costa Mesa, CA: Mazda

It begins with the announcement that the proceedings of this publication will be donated to a school in Iran. What follows are the prices of a copy of the book in Egypt (12 Qurush), Iran (5 Qurush), Russia (1 Manat), and India (2 Rupees). This obviously indicates the various domains of the region in which literate Persian-speaking people lived and would be potentially interested in the book. The book then begins with an *Arz-e Makhsus/A Special Introduction,* in which the author praises the significance of the free press and attributes the advances in *Maghreb Zamin/ Western Lands* to this very phenomenon of freedom of the press.

The Author of the book, whom we soon discover is quite a character himself, tells us that before sharing with us the story of his protagonist, he wishes to humor us with a bit of his own background. He (the protagonist, whom we soon realize is the alter ego of the Author himself) was born to a rich and powerful merchant from Azerbaijan who had moved to Cairo and became very successful. But the man was obsessed with Iranian history, had decided not to learn a word of Arabic, and had appointed a certain Mirza Youssef (known also as Uncle Youssef) as the teacher of his son to instruct him about the history and culture of his homeland. The Author then tells us that he became acquainted with the son, the Ibrahim Beg of the title, after the latter's father had passed away, and had visited him in Cairo and spent some time in his library and was impressed by how many copies of *Tarikh-e Naderi/History of Nader Shah* were stocked there. The father and son had a fixation on this book on the life and adventures of the Iranian king Nader Shah (reigned 1736–1747). A key passage we read early in the book is the last will and testament of the father to his son, giving advice of various sorts, particularly his love for his homeland.[3]

Publishers, 2006). This, alas, is only a translation of the First Volume of the three-volume novel, without, evidently, the learned translator being aware that there are two additional volumes to the story he has translated. There is also some excellent secondary literature (mostly in Persian, of course, and by Iranian scholars) on the significance of the book during the Constitutional Revolution – some of which also pays attention to its literary importance. One of the best essays on him in Persian is by Iraj Parsinejad, "Zeyn al-Abedin Maragheh'i: Montaqed-e Adabi/Zeyn al-Abedin Maragheh'i: Literary Critic," *Iran Nameh* 9: 3 (Summer 1991): 427–440. The same author has a book in English, *A History of Literary Criticism in Iran (1866–1951)* (Boston, MA: IBEX Publishers, 2003) in which he devotes a chapter to Zeyn al-Abedin Maragheh'i, which is the English version of the same Persian article in Iran Nameh. The significance of the book is underlined by all major historians of the Constitutional period.
[3] Ibid.: I: 8–11.

The narrative then proceeds on multiple layers, sometimes in the form of a fake letter a friend of Ibrahim Beg pretends he has received from Iran bearing good news of progress, sometimes in the form of a dialogue between him and his friends or relatives about current events in Iran. Ibrahim Beg finally leaves Cairo for Iran, stopping in Istanbul at the Author's home. But he is away, and his protagonist leaves him a note telling him he spent a few days there with his companion Uncle Youssef and borrowed Abd al-Rahim Talebof's (1834–1911) book, *Kebab-e Ahmad*, a famous text popular among the revolutionaries at the time, from him to study on his way to Iran.[4] From the Author we then learn that Ibrahim Beg goes and spends some eight months traveling through Iran, after which he comes back to Istanbul, stops at the Author's place again, and hands him the travelogue he had written while traveling in Iran.[5] The astonishing narrative plot is utterly revolutionary for its time.

"On the 18th of such-and-such month, two hours after the dawn, in the company of my teacher Uncle Youssef, who is indeed like an uncle or even a father to me, we left the Cairo Station on our way to a pilgrimage to the sacred city of Mashhad and a tour of Iran." In the very first lines of this fictive travelogue we find ourselves in the company of a verbose, self-conscious, a bit aggressive and even abrasive persona called Ibrahim Beg, determined to reclaim his homeland and put it on the path of progress. Upon his arrival in Istanbul and everywhere else from there his primary concern is the dire circumstances under which the Iranian expats live. Everything he sees on his way to Iran, from railroads to oil excavations, he uses as occasion to bemoan the circumstances of neglect in which his homeland is left to ruins. The text reads as a clear and purposeful self-critique of the circumstances of a national disaster Iranians face. His "travelogue" reads very much like any other real traveler's account – observant, critical, self-conscious. He arrives in a city, visits its Iranian residence, laments the condition of his homeland, praises the Ottoman and Central Asian advances he witnesses, and moves on. Europe is nowhere in sight – it is not part of his itinerary. The Russian and Ottoman territories, and later Japan, are his main frames of reference for progress.

---

[4] For more on Talebof, see ṬĀLEBUF, ʿABD-AL-RAḤIM, *Encyclopedia Iranica*, available online here: www.iranicaonline.org/articles/talebuf. Accessed January 23, 2018.
[5] Maragheh'i, *Seyahat-Nameh-ye Ibrahim Beg*: I: 20.

Ibrahim Beg and Uncle Youssef finally reach Iran, and the self-exiled patriot stops for a few minutes to kiss the soil of his homeland and chokes with joy. But this does not prevent him from immediately pointing out the corruption of the officials at the border.[6] He spends twenty-two days in Mashhad, making detailed observations about what he sees – and how he feels about them. While in the Shi'a pilgrim city, he is offered a temporary wife, but he refuses, for he is not sure it is done properly according to Shi'a law. He then asks Uncle Yousef to get ready to move toward Tehran, but his companion tries to prevent him from this, telling him he will be deeply disappointed. They travel to Sabzevar, Nishabur, and Damghan, and Ibrahim Beg records the stupidity of the clerics, the corruption of the officials, and the brutality of the security forces. On his way to Tehran he has occasion to praise Shah Abbas, the Safavid monarch, for his legacy.[7] Upon his arrival in Tehran he continues his critical observations of just about everything he sees. There is no "collective will," he says, to work for the national destiny of everyone in the country – every group is preoccupied with their own particular interests.[8]

In Tehran he visits high-ranking merchants and political elites and discusses the calamitous condition of the country with them. He asks them why they don't ask themselves why every year thousands of Iranians move out of their homeland and travel to the Ottoman, Russia, and Indian territories. He severely admonishes them and asks them how they would respond if the Prophet came back and asked what they had done with his faith.[9] The high-ranking officials get offended and order him to shut up. He does not spare the foreign emissaries from his criticism and considers them partially responsible for taking advantage of a weak and corrupt state. Here he appears as a deeply disaffected, cantankerous, belligerent, and even unpleasant interlocutor of everyone and anyone he meets. His criticism is relentless, tireless, bold, and persistent.

Although he does not travel to Europe, Ibrahim Beg repeatedly mentions the fact that he has visited Europe and knows full well of their progress.[10] But eventually we find out Japan is far more a frame of reference for him than Europe. He finally meets a high-ranking official who is willing to listen to him, and he spends a good deal of

---

[6] Ibid.: I: 30–32.   [7] Ibid.: I: 39–43.   [8] Ibid.: I: 58.   [9] Ibid.: I: 69.
[10] Ibid.: I: 76.

his book describing the significance of "rights" to him. Here he discusses constitutional law and the civil rights that it entails for citizens. He divides these rights into four categories: (1) the rights of the nation, (2) the rights of the nationals, (3) the rights of the social collective, and (4) the rights of government.[11] This learned man who is now his chief interlocutor then asks him to stay with him and takes him to his magnificent library in his house, on one side full of books about law in Ottoman, Russian, and European countries, and on the other, Islamic Law. The dignitary gives him a six-volume book that he had written himself in which he had compared Islamic and non-Islamic laws and discarded those that were not compatible with Islam and outlined those that had no problem with Islamic law. It turns out this man is very learned and high-ranking and has studied all various laws that can change his homeland for the better, but there are corrupt officials who will not allow this to happen in this country.[12] The conversation between Ibrahim Beg and this man becomes an occasion to bring two learned Iranians together to discuss the future of their homeland. This part reads like a long treatise on the reformation of a tyranny to a democracy.

The conversation between the two learned and caring men eventually leads to Ibrahim Beg's host giving him a letter written by a fellow Iranian in which he had shared a dream he had long cherished. In this dream, we see an allegory of an old man being harassed and injured by an abusive mob, and we eventually learn the name of this old man; it is of course "Iran Khan/Mr. Iran." As crude an attempt at allegory as this is, it still resonates with a ring of truth in this book.[13] What we read on page 108 of this First Volume is crucial, for when they refer to "Mamalek-e Kharejeh/Foreign countries" they mention Mumbai, Calcutta, Egypt, the Ottoman territories, or Russia. In other words, the idea of "foreign lands" trumps that of "Europe" as where the frame of reference for progress lies. The narrative then continues with a critique of the propaganda press and of the royal travels abroad. Ibrahim Beg's travels to Tehran give him even more occasions to criticize just about everything he sees in the Qajar capital. While in Ardabil, he pays his respect to the founder of the Safavid dynasty Shah Ismail's mausoleum and praises the glories of the Safavid dynasty. In Ardabil he uses the exquisite phrase "Molla-bazi" (being preoccupied with clerical

[11] Ibid.: I: 81–84.   [12] Ibid.: I: 85–89.   [13] Ibid.: I: 105.

leaders).[14] The same story of misery and maleficence is later repeated in
Maragheh.[15] He soon chances upon Protestant missionaries printing
anti-Islam propaganda in a printing shop.[16] He then travels to Urmia
and denounces the stupidity of the people in that city. Upon his arrival
in Tabriz he accuses them of selfishness and pettiness.[17]

   This part of the *Seyahat-Nameh* ends with the Author telling us how,
upon Ibrahim Beg's return to Istanbul and while his protagonist had
gone to bath with Uncle Youssef, he had read the book and was
astonished by it.[18] Upon Ibrahim Beg's return to the Author's home,
they begin a conversation about the journey to Iran. Here the discourse
changes, and we find out that while Ibrahim Beg was in Iran, the Author
had received a letter from Cairo, and he begins to read the letter out
loud. What is important in this letter is how Egypt is considered a far
freer and more liberated country than Iran, on par with any European
state that has been so celebrated.[19] The conversations targeting the
corruption in Iran at this point continue at the Author's home. In his
conclusion to this First Volume of *Seyahat-Nameh*, the Author reiterates
his earlier point that he has agreed to publish this book to alert his
fellow Iranians in and out of their homeland of the dire circumstances of
their country. Here the Author points out that in "Europe" when
authors have something important to say about their homeland, they
freely publish it.[20] This is then followed by an Appendix by another
reader who sees the book in the printing house. He informs us that a
prominent Iranian scholar had just published an essay about the condition of their country, and this reader had asked the printer to include
that essay at the end of this book.[21] This treatise, which this reader adds
to the book in the printing house, is a political analysis of the two
colonial powers of the time, England and Russia. The author of this
treatise has a full critical awareness of British colonialism in India and of
the Russian imperial interests in the region. The author of this appendix
is fully aware of critical thinking of prominent authors in Europe and
keeps citing them anonymously as "a historian says," or a "learned
man observes."[22] Here we have clear evidence that this travelogue is
used to educate its readers of the geopolitics of the region, of alliance
between England and France against Russia, of the strategic interest

---

[14] Ibid.: I: 138.   [15] Ibid.: I: 151.   [16] Ibid.: I: 164.   [17] Ibid.: I: 179.
[18] Ibid.: I: 217.   [19] Ibid..   [20] Ibid.: I: 239.   [21] Ibid.: I: 245.
[22] Ibid.: I: 250.

in Iran for access to India. By the conclusion of the First Volume of the book, we know that the story of this Ibrahim Beg character is just an excuse, a narrative plot to write freely about a whole range of urgent political issues in Iran and its colonial context. But opting for a fictional narrative and consistently changing the voice of the narrators are astonishingly effective, entertaining, plot-twisting devices as we progress from the first to the Second Volume.

Figure 13 "Vintage Engraving of Gate of the Metwaleys, Cairo 19th Century, after David Roberts." Cairo was one of the major cosmopolitan centers of attention for these travelers, as important as Mumbai, Delhi, Tehran, Istanbul, Paris, London, New York, Chicago, Rio de Janeiro, Cape Town, Beirut, or St Petersburg. Mapping these cities together, the topography of an entirely different world emerges than the one imagined by Eurocentric imagination. The travel accounts of these travelers are the textual evidence of that world. Cairo in particular links the Muslim world to Africa and the Mediterranean basin, and by extension farther into the wider Islamic world. Its Islamic and pre-Islamic histories bring the city into the larger frame of Arab, Islamic, Persian, Indian, and Chinese worlds, entirely independent of Europe. Reprinted with permission from Walker Art Libraray/Alamy Stock Photo.

The Second Volume: The Protagonist Burns the House

In the Second Volume, we learn that there has been a vast popular request to find out what happened to our Ibrahim Beg, and in fact someone had sent 200 tumans and promised 800 more if the subsequent account, that was written by Youssef Amu, were to be published.[23] Here we learn that Uncle Youssef had in fact written an account of what had happened to his pupil and companion from Istanbul to Egypt and after. Here we learn that the wife of a prominent Iranian had been listening to a recitation of the First Volume of the travelogue and had asked for a copy to be purchased and kept for her son for when he grew up to realize there were courageous people who wrote about what needed to be done, just like they do in "Europe."[24] The heroism of this lady had prompted the Author to proceed to publish the Second Volume, which is the book that Uncle Youssef had written and sent to him. Perhaps I need to remind you, this is all made up: This is an utterly ingenious fusion of fact and fantasy in a narrative strategy that is so rooted in historical truth that it need not be true to be believable. Maragheh'i is one astonishing narrator of stories he had learned not from reading "Western literature" but from living a real life.

The Second Volume begins with Uncle Youssef as the narrator, and first he tells us something about his own birth in Tabriz, and how after his education he moved to Tbilisi and Istanbul and eventually to Egypt where he was employed by Ibrahim Beg's father as a trusted companion and scribe. Upon Ibrahim's birth, his education is entrusted to Uncle Youssef. He tells us his student had studied Arabic, English, and French (so much for the earlier report that Ibrahim Beg did not speak a word of Arabic). His Persian education, however, is entrusted to Uncle Youssef, who compares Ibrahim Beg to Joseph in the Bible, handsome and virtuous, while many Egyptian women were madly in love with him – thus the Joseph narrative in the Qur'an becomes a model of this description of Ibrahim Beg as the chief protagonist of the story. From Uncle Youssef we also learn more about Ibrahim Beg's family, his mother and sister, and a young slave girl who was purchased by the family when she was a child but raised and educated and freed with the intention that one day she would marry Ibrahim Beg.

---

[23] Ibid.: II: 1.   [24] Ibid.: II: 4.

This young lady, Mahboubeh is her name, was as adamant in her zealous Iranian nationalism as her intended, Ibrahim Beg, was. With Uncle Youssef's account, we enter a much thicker and more elaborate understanding of our protagonist, a more intricate weaving of a story that unfolds itself upon the factual evidence of a regional history that moves from Egypt to the Ottoman capital, through the Caucuses, and into Iran.

At any rate, we now learn that while in Istanbul at the house of the Author, Ibrahim Beg had a heated debate with a local Mulla, and his hat hit a lamp and the house was set on fire. The Mulla was half-burned, and Ibrahim lost consciousness and never fully recovered. Uncle Yousef sends a telegram to Ibrahim Beg's mother in Egypt, gently conveying that her son is not feeling well. She gets on the first available ship and sails from Egypt to Istanbul. But the visit of the distressed mother and her attendant Mas'ud proves ineffective, and Ibrahim Beg remains in this lifeless state of depression and despair. But the severe case of Ibrahim Beg's nervous breakdown is incurable. All he says is "Ya Haq Ya Madad/Oh God Please Help!" They finally sail back to Egypt, where Mahboubeh is waiting impatiently for the return of her beloved.[25] Much of the story here is about the love of Ibrahim Beg and Mahboubeh, which could perhaps be interpreted as a symbol of the love between Iran and its caring intellectuals. One physician finally diagnoses the condition of the patient to be one of desperate love for Iran, though not just as a country but as a metaphor of the beautiful woman Ibrahim Beg loves, and being a witness to her misery and destitution he is now experiencing a nervous breakdown.[26] The only cure for Ibrahim Beg's illness is to bring him good news from Iran, and he would be just fine as long as good news keeps coming from his beloved homeland. The novel at this point thrives on this psychosis of Ibrahim Beg as a caring intellectual and Iran as the object of his desire – with Mahboubeh as a third intermediary forming a ménage à trois.

A recurrent theme in this part of the story, where we learn about Mahboubeh and her love for Ibrahim Beg, is the image of women reading novels as a clear indication of their literary proclivities toward falling in love.[27] In the Second Volume we also learn Japan is the paramount measure of progress for Iranians of this generation, where we are told until very recently they lacked independent press, but now

---

[25] Ibid.: II: 25. [26] Ibid.: II: 46. [27] Ibid.: II: 73.

they enjoy more than one thousand different newspapers![28] References
to Europe are of course widely present, where we learn how in France
the sole title for the presidents of the republic is just "Monsieur," while
in Iran they are boringly tiresome and long.[29] This occasion is used to
denounce the verbose flattery in Persian language as compared to its
simplification in European languages. We also see here the first deroga-
tory references to "Westernization," or what the author calls "Farangi-
ma'ab/Westernized," and the type is ridiculed for having spent enough
time in Europe only to learn to pee standing up![30] Japan, on the
contrary, is offered as an example of both learning from Europe and
yet preserving its own culture. There is of course a lot of hogwash
about how Europeans have learned everything from Muslims, and
their laws are really a verbatim translation of Imam Ali's letters.[31]
The work of fiction, as a result, reads very much like a compendium
of what learned and critically minded Iranian intellectuals thought at
the time.

All these narratives, however, come together as something of a
twisted plot to form long exposés on praising the rule of law in Iran,
with Europe, Russia, China, and particularly Japan as measures of
comparison. Ibrahim Beg's nervous breakdown and Mahboubeh's
unrelenting love for him might, however, be read as a metaphor for
the predicament of Iran and its caring but desperate intellectuals who
wish to cure it but cannot. The news of the fiftieth anniversary coronation of Naser al-Din Shah, the Qajar monarch, is brought to Egypt,
and Uncle Yousef thinks it might cheer Ibrahim Beg up.[32] Like all other
potentially good news, such reports make Ibrahim Beg burst into his
only phrase, "Ya Haq Ya Madad!" Finally, the news of the coronation
of Mozaffar al-Din Shah cures Ibrahim Beg, who comes out of his
nervous breakdown with a famished appetite and orders a huge feast
prepared for him, much to the delight of Uncle Youssef, his mother,
and, of course, Mahboubeh.[33] The story thus oscillates between narratives of Ibrahim Beg's illness, Mahboubeh's love for him, and the
disastrous news of corruption and backwardness from Iran. A key
theme in this part of the story is the useless and expensive trips of
Qajar royalties abroad. The narrative consistency of the First Volume,
to be sure, is much less convincing in this Second Volume, but the

---

[28] Ibid.: II: 92.   [29] Ibid.: II: 101.   [30] Ibid.: II: 112.   [31] Ibid.: II: 116.
[32] Ibid.: II: 136.   [33] Ibid.: II: 149.

oscillation between political pamphleteering and plot progression still works and sustains the novel.

Ibrahim Beg finally agrees to marry Mahboubeh but insists their marriage must be performed through Iranian ceremonies and not based on what "Arabs, Europeans, or the Turks" do.[34] This happy news, though, is buried in between page after page of long panegyrics in praise of homeland and lamentations on its backwardness. We then read a long report on the dialogue between an Iranian traveler and a European in Paris and Berlin, much of which again is about the backwardness of Iranians compared to those of the nations around them, especially Europe, where Iranians are denigrated and their homeland ridiculed.[35] Ibrahim Beg reads this report in Habl al-Matin, the leading oppositional journal, and gets badly depressed again, and this angers Mahboubeh, who bans the famous periodical from their home. The narrative mechanism of getting these reports to Uncle Youssef to read them to Ibrahim Beg is either letters coming from Iran or else news from Habl al-Matin that they read. From these letters we learn about the Qajar monarch's wasteful trips abroad and of the collective fear of both the religious and monarchial elite of public schools or parliament. One cannot help thinking that these extended passages are really intended for mobilization purposes for those who read the book impatiently back in Iran. The novel here in effect acts like a Trojan Horse, carrying within it multiple narratives for immediate political uses.

Finally, after one such crippling crisis, both our protagonist, Ibrahim, and his beloved Mahboubeh die from too much distress.[36] The Second Volume ends with a long treatise on Japan as a model of progress, particularly praising its emperor for having abandoned dictatorship in favor of democracy. Here it is crucial to read how both Europe and Japan are offered as models of progress.[37] A crucial aspect of this book is the ease with which the personal stories of Ibrahim Beg and his wife are interwoven with multiple narratives of critical reflections on the national fate of Iran and Iranians. There are times that these connections are rather bizarre and concocted, and yet there are places that the schizophrenic narratives actually gel together – so, yes, sometimes strange, but never a dull moment.

[34] Ibid.: II: 180.   [35] Ibid.: II: 205–217.   [36] Ibid.: II: 236.
[37] Ibid.: II: 281.

At the end of this volume, the Author returns to the end of the First Volume and the treatise he had attributed to an Iranian scholar about the colonial domination of the region by England and Russia, and updates that treatise.[38] In these pages, there is no sign of any reference to Ibrahim Beg or Mahboubeh. We read a solid account of the geopolitics of imperialism with detailed knowledge of their consequences for the world at large. The treatise then continues with another long panegyric cited from Habl al-Matin and similarly addresses the calamities of colonialism and its consequences. It is important here to keep in mind that to the degree that Europe is present in these pages, it is an icon of global colonialism and its omnipresence in world affairs. In a way, this novel mimics old-fashioned storytelling in a coffeehouse – in which the Naqqal, the Narrator, tells you a principal story and seasons it with various asides, addressing multiple audiences he thinks might be bored with that single story. This volume then concludes with a summary of its points, of the various social strata it has criticized for the calamities that have befallen Iran. These strata include: "ministers, ambassadors, bureaucrats, pseudo-Mullahs, poets, the nobility, physicians, astrologers, police officers, merchants, etc."[39] The Second Volume ends by dating its publication in Ramadan 1323/ October 1905.

The Third Volume: Ibrahim Beg Goes to Paradise

The Third Volume starts by informing its readers that it was published in Calcutta in 1909, at the Habl al-Matin publishing house, at number 4 Medical College Street. It starts the way the Second Volume ends, with yet another long and by now tiresome treatise on how things are terrible in Iran, and the Author does not know any longer what to say and what to complain about – everything is wrong, the country is lost, leaders are corrupt, and the nation has lost all its past glory.[40] This is a further indication that the novel was not meant to be read by one person cover to cover (as I am doing now) but sporadically and in various gatherings with multiple purposes.

The edition I have has two such Introductions with almost (but not entirely) identical wording, in which the Author says he does not know what to say, what to write, and yet he spends page after page

---

[38] Ibid.: II: 290 ff.   [39] Ibid.: II: 304.   [40] Ibid.: III: 1–4.

complaining about everything in his homeland, holding the aristocracy
and the clergy in particular responsible.[41] Then he proceeds to introduce himself as the Author after a lengthy introduction in which he
says that over the last twelve years that the first two volumes of his
book have been published, many people have been suspected to have
been its author, so he now feels obligated to introduce himself. He says
his name is Zeyn al-Abedin, the son of Mashhad Ali, the son of Hajji
Rasul, etc., of Kurdish Sunni descent. He writes briefly about his
education and, as always, belittles and ridicules it. He describes his
youth and tells his readers how he agreed to become a Russian subject
out of desperation.[42] He is deeply troubled by having become a Russian subject and abandoning his nationality. He tells his reader one day
he had put on European clothing and a Russian princess saw it and
reprimanded him. He instantly changed his clothing to his national
habit. He ultimately sells off his business, abandons his Russian citizenship, and moves to Istanbul. On February 8, 1904, he tells us his
request to renounce his Russian citizenship was finally approved. He
was elated and composed a poem for the occasion.[43] He then spends
another few pages still explaining why he had assumed the Russian
citizenship and admonishing others who were doing so, going so far as
to add an "Off" to their last name to pretend they are Russian.[44]
Finally, on page 29 of this last volume, he says the reason he is writing
this book about Ibrahim Beg and his love for his homeland he has
called Mahboubeh is to add it to other love stories of classical Persian
poetry such as Leila and Majnun. What follows is an excellent short
treatise on why "sadeh-nevisi" (writing in a simple prose) is so important at this point in history.[45] Here again, the point of reference for
advancement is Japan and not Europe. These introductory materials
that have nothing to do with the actual story of Ibrahim Beg are crucial
evidence from the text itself as to what the purpose of its Author was
when writing this book. But the fact that its political purposes override
its literary prowess does not preempt looking at this novel as the
pioneering evidence of the manner in which the genre is being cultivated in Persian language and for Persian-speaking audiences. The
novel here reads like a collage of varied and multiple proses serving a
constellation of purposes.

[41] Ibid.: III: 1–5.   [42] Ibid.: III: 11.   [43] Ibid.: III: 18.   [44] Ibid.: III: 20–25.
[45] Ibid.: III: 30 ff.

The story finally begins to be narrated by Uncle Yousef, in which he gives a description of the tragic death of Ibrahim Beg and his bride Mahboubeh and the heart-wrenching mourning that follows. Initially he says he wanted to move to sacred sites in Iraq to spend the rest of his life there, but then he has a dream that changes the course of his life. Here the Author interrupts the narrative and tells us about the significance of dreaming – on the variety of dreams and what they could possibly mean, all by way of an introduction to Uncle Yousef's particular dream.[46] This editorializing aspect of the novel is at once jarring and yet understandable, for the text is a polemical intervention in the dominant issues of the time, with the actual story of Ibrahim Beg occasionally appearing as a mere subterfuge. Be that as it may, the intervention of such expostulating passages opens up a whole new manner of looking at the origin of the novel in Persian, here at its nascent stage.

This finally brings the Author to the actual dream of Uncle Yousef in which he tells us of his vision in first person account. He says he fell fast asleep on his prayer rug, and in his dream he saw a revered old man he knew in life called Sheikh A'ma (The Blind Master), who comes to him and asks him where he is going. He says he is going to the cemetery to pay his respects to Ibrahim Beg and his beloved Mahboubeh. The Sheikh says, don't waste your time, there is no cemetery anymore. Uncle Youssef says, how so, he was there just yesterday. The Blind Master gets incensed and holds him by the hand and takes him to the cemetery where he sees indeed that the site of the two lovers is flooded with water from the Nile, and where the two graves of Ibrahim Beg and Mahboubeh were, now two cypress trees have grown. The Blind Master then tells Uncle Youssef he is taking him to Hell. What Hell, he asks with incredulity; the Hell of Iranians, he is told.[47] They finally enter the pyramids, and through the pyramids they descend into an endless stairway that finally ends in Hell, the Iranian Hell, to be exact. Here Uncle Youssef begins to see people sitting on burning thrones of fire. He describes the scenes to the Blind Master, and he tells him who they are. The first is a king with number 829 on his door, the second a European conqueror with the number 335. This is the conqueror who set Iran on fire (Alexander). Uncle Yousef then sees an Arab conqueror being punished in Hell under the number 316. Then they come to a Mongol conqueror being punished under the number 98. We never

[46] Ibid.: III: 37.   [47] Ibid.: III: 42.

(Reference to *Risalat al-Ghufran*?)

learn the significance of these numbers or what they might represent. But we are consistently given the numerical addresses for these powerful men being burned in Hell.

Uncle Yousef asks the Blind Master who these people are. He tells him to just memorize their numbers and someone will tell him later who they are by their numbers.[48] Then he sees a number of Mullahs being punished. They are many – but still he manages to memorize only three numbers: 982, 6945, and 873. They proceed with various sightings of Iranians burning in hell, as he keeps memorizing their numbers: 599, 1587, 1910, 562. As the Blind Master and Uncle Youssef proceed into the deepest recesses of Hell, we witness various social strata and the way they represent groups that have abused the nation and destroyed their homeland without any hesitation, and now they are being punished for it. Uncle Yousef sees what he sees, describes it to the Blind Master, and he tells him who they are and why are they being punished. All the while he keeps memorizing their numbers. Uncle Yousef's description of Hell in the company of the Blind Master is a complete social pathology of Iranian society as he sees it. Corrupt aristocracy, abusive foreign interventionists, lazy monarchs, retrograde clergy, all the way down to opportunistic careerists of one rank or another. Uncle Yousef finally wakes up and in fear and trembling wonders what to do.[49]

Before he wakes up, Uncle Yousef asks his Blind Master what to do, and he tells him to travel. He flips a coin and decides to go south, where he approaches pleasant environments. Now we realize Uncle Youssef has entered Paradise and is moving along various gates of the heavenly abode, color-coded with various gates, where he sees himself drawn to beautiful gardens, and all he has to say is, Ya Haq Ya Madad, and soon, Ya Iran.[50] He finally meets a beautiful old man who becomes his guide. The old man looks like Iranians, speaks Persian, and shakes hands like Iranians do.[51] The Old Man guides him to an abode on the top of which is written in Arabic, "This is Home of Ibrahim." Presently he hears a trumpet, all the angelic beings gather respectfully, and then two beautiful entities appear and command the respect of all the attendant angelic beings. Then they sit upon a throne and ascend to heavens even higher. It turns out the two angelic characters are none other than Ibrahim Beg and his beloved Mahboubeh, who instantly recognize Uncle Youssef and invite him to come to their heavenly abode

[48] Ibid.: III: 46.   [49] Ibid.: III: 54.   [50] Ibid.: III: 59.   [51] Ibid.: III: 64.

and shower him with love and affection.[52] While in Paradise, Ibrahim Beg asks Uncle Youssef to do certain things for him back on earth. He must marry off his servant and give her a proper dowry. Then he must build a hospital and a school in Iran for poor people. Then he must publish his book of travelogue – the book we are reading. He then informs Uncle Youssef that all the great benevolent kings of Iran are there in Paradise, enjoying their afterlives. While in heaven, Ibrahim Beg still receives travelers from Iran, greets them generously, and asks for the news from his homeland. Uncle Youssef is mesmerized by the love of Ibrahim Beg and Mahboubeh for each other when he is finally awakened and brought back to life.[53] He promises some of his friends to tell them his dream and see what they make of it.

In the next section of the Third Volume, the Author offers us an apologia regarding his criticism of some of his contemporary poets, praises the significance of poetry, and admonishes those who have abused their gifts by praising tyrants.[54] This part of the Third Volume reads alike an old-fashioned biographical dictionary (Tazkireh) of classical poets. For page after page he goes through an alphabetical order of classical poets, offers a quick biography, and then samples their best poems as he has selected them. If we ask ourselves whether this section has anything to do with the subject of the novel, we will be hard-pressed to come up with any explanation, except to think of the emerging genre in Persian effectively mimicking coffeehouse performances of oral traditions of storytelling, in which various asides are introduced to entertain the audience. Here, too, we are dealing with a politically and poetically alert readership that would be delighted by such excursions, though not entirely related to the subject matter. One might surmise here that in this section the Author is in effect recasting a genealogy of the most socially committed poets of the classical period for a renewed readership. He even includes a short section on women poets.[55] He also admonishes Persian poets for openly expressing their love for men and for pederasty. He exempts Europeans from any such "abominable" acts.[56] This section then phases into a "Mirror for Princes" about the things a sovereign should and should not do.[57] This entire section seems to target the ruling monarchs the way the previous

---

[52] Ibid.: III: 73.   [53] Ibid.: III: 87.   [54] Ibid.: III: 88–90.   [55] Ibid.: III: 153.
[56] Ibid.: III: 154.   [57] Ibid.: III: 160 ff.

section was targeting the poets, teaching them the model of good rulership – wise, judicious, and beneficial to the public at large.[58]

What follows then is a Persian translation of Emperor Macao's speech, though done in perfect Persian poetry![59] The content of the poem is quite extraordinary, for it warns of the stratagems of the European colonial power against countries like Japan or Iran or the Arab world and cautions that the verses of the poets such as Sa'di and other classical luminaries are no longer useful in this world. ←— What matters today, the poem warns, is the love of homeland and what is useful to one's country. The rest of this section is devoted to a great admiration for Japan and what it has achieved as a model for the rest of the world – Asia in particular. Japan is here and elsewhere offered as a perfect example and model of progress for other Asian, African, and Latin American countries to emulate.[60] The Author then resumes his categorical denunciation of Iran and all its social institutions for having caused Iranian backwardness. He concludes this section with a discussion of Japanese women and how brave they were in war and struggle for their homeland,[61] and some passages citing the prophet of Islam and his advice to worldly leaders.[62] He then apologizes to the religious leaders if he has offended them, before turning to a friend named Reza Khan who had offered some interpretation of Uncle Youssef's dream that indicates people who are burning in Hell are Zahhak, Alexander, Hajjaj ibn Youssef, and Mahmoud Afghan – all of them warriors who had invaded and occupied Iran.[63] But he does not end here. He still puts forth another long passage about the geopolitics of the region and the Russian and British interests in Iran. He then gives a chronology of "parliaments" that have been established since the time of Adam! This section is a genealogy of how democracy and rule of law and parliament have been at work since the creation of the world. He concludes by dedicating the book to the ruling Qajar monarch.[64]

Mapping and Remapping the World

Reading Zeyn al-Abedin Maragheh'i's *Ibrahim Beg Travelogue* (1903) more than a century after its publication – closely, carefully,

---

[58] Ibid.: III: 170–180.   [59] Ibid.: III: 183.   [60] Ibid.: III: 180–190.
[61] Ibid.: III: 204.   [62] Ibid.. III: 215.   [63] Ibid.: III: 218   [64] Ibid.: III: 245.

completely, and in the original – requires some careful and responsible
consideration.[65] If we were to compare this earliest attempt at writing
a "novel" in the technical sense of the term with its contemporaries in
Russia, France, or England, the result would not be much favorable to
the Iranian author. The comparison with Russian literature of the time
is particularly disappointing because the author must have theoretically been familiar with it. He knew Russian, he lived in Russia, and he
had even for a while become a Russian subject. Just to mention a
couple of Russian landmarks, Gogol's *Dead Souls* (1842), Fyodor
Dostoevsky's *Crime and Punishment* (1866), and Leo Tolstoy's *War
and Peace* (1869) were all available and could have been known to
Maragheh'i. But his book does not come anywhere near those masterpieces. One must be more cautious comparing him to what was
happening in French or English novels, for there is no clear indication
that he could have been seriously familiar with them. But Maragheh'i's
book does compare well with the earliest Arabic novel, Ahmad Faris
al-Shidyaq's *Leg Over Leg* (1855), or with Şemsettin Sami's
(1850–1904) *Tal'at and Fitnat In Love* (1872) – in its more immediate
neighborhood. Be that as it is, there is enough in what we do read in
Maragheh'i to allow a critical attention to what he actually did
achieve.

There is a degree of creative sophistication about his novel that
still makes the taxing exercise of reading him worthwhile. As for
those long asides with no obvious relevance to the main storyline,
one might also compare similar passages to whales and whaling in
Melville's Moby Dick (1851), for example, which are without much
immediate relevance to the actual story. In a similar fashion, one
might suggest these passages are helping the author both reflect and
sustain the world in which the novel is being created. The book is a
self-contained totality and reflects an open-ended world it must
both represent and sustain for the novel to make sense. As I also
mentioned earlier, we might suggest that in a way this novel mimics

[65] An unfortunate example of irresponsible encounters with this seminal text is
the butchered edition prepared by Baqer Momeni, *Zeyn al-Abedin
Maragheh'i's Siyahat-nameh-ye Ibrahim Beg* (Tehran: Nashr-e Andisheh,
1353/1974). No attempt is made in this severely distorted edition to read the
book and consider it in its entirety. Only its social and political contents
are extracted and subjected to a clichéd interpretation in the social context of
the Constitutional Revolution.

old-fashioned storytelling in a coffeehouse – in which the Naqqal, the Narrator, tells you a principal story and seasons it with various asides, addressing multiple audiences he thinks might be bored with that single story. Maragheh'i's audience is mostly distanced from him, and it is amorphous and in formation. If we consider the rise of the novel, as I do, a bourgeois phenomenon and not a "European" phenomenon, each and every formation of transnational bourgeois public sphere has its own particularity, as does the emerging Iranian bourgeoisie, particularly those interested in such typical bourgeois nationalism projects, as is clearly evident in the course of the Constitutional Revolution of 1906–1911.

The social and literary significance of this book and the fact that it was cast as a travelogue, both in this and the world to come, cannot be separated. Some Iranian scholars have compared it (and thus assimilated it backward) to Jean-Jacques Rousseau's *On the Social Contract: Principles of Political Rights/Du Contract Social – ou Principes du droit Politique*, 1762) – a rather cliché, Eurocentric, and useless comparison – but nevertheless pointing to the groundbreaking impact it had at its time. The book had a tremendous impact on its contemporaries – of that there is little doubt. Historical evidence suggests people in Iran were reading it and were deeply moved by its power, more than anything else, because these were facts of their lives written in one coherent volume and made available to them, seasoned by a love story that could have added more power to its punch. The novel may therefore be read as vintage social realism with a tinge of surreal satire. There are Iranian scholars and historians like Ahmad Kasravi, Fereydun Adamiyyat, Karim Keshavarz, and Yahya Aryanpour who all consider his book as seminal in its impact on revolutionary mobilization.[66] The towering intellectual of Maragheh'i's period, Mirza Agha Khan Kerman, may have also been influential in the writing of the text. The book was so important that there were false claims of

---

[66] For a discussion of these Iranian historians' assessments of the book, see the learned Introduction of Mohammad Ali Sepanlou to his edition of Zeyn al-Abedin Maragheh'i, *Seyahat-Nameh-ye Ibrahim Beg Ya Bala-ye Ta'ssob-e Ou/Ibrahim Beg Travelogue or the Calamity of his Prejudice* (Tehran: Asfar Publications, 1364/1985): I–X.

authorship, and the poor author toward the end of his life was nervous people might deny him his authorship.[67]

The structure of the novel might be stipulated in tribular forms: The triangulation among Ibrahim Beg's love for Iran and Mahboubeh's love for Ibrahim Beg holds the love story together and expands into the geopolitics of the region, from Cairo (the Protagonist) to Istanbul (the Author), to Tehran (the Audience and the object of desire) and finds its political manifestation in the fate of colonized countries and their relations with Russia and England – with Japan consistently offering a way out. When we take all these triangulations together, we see how this seminal work of fiction zooms in on the truth of a region that is now casting its own gaze back at Europe. We need to recall here how the European colonialism was as much a project of conquering the physical world and its natural resources as the manners, forms, and epistemic formations of imagining and representing it. Europe used all at its disposal to conquer, think, and imagine the world in a manner that made it its own backyard – to have, hold, explore, and own it at whim. European explorers mapped it; European anthropologists investigated it; European artists, poets, novelists, musicians, composers, scholars, and journalists joined European merchants and colonial officers to explore, and explain, and eroticize it. The world at large – not just "the Orient," or what was to the East of Europe, anything to the North or to the South or to the East or to the West of Europe – became the object of knowledge and desire for "Europe," as "Europe" itself began to fetishize itself. Edward Said's *Orientalism* (1978) took just one such aspect of the European colonial will to know the world by conquering it as conquering it by knowing it. Europe became a knowing subject, the world a knowable thing. What pioneering works of fiction such as Maragheh'i's do is offer solid historical evidence of reversing that gaze, of constituting agency and subjectivity for the (post)colonial person. Iranians became Iranian and could stand up to the colonial conquest of their homeland – in material and moral terms, by virtue of reading Maragheh'i's novel – to put it bluntly.

European colonialism codified, simplified, allegorized, symbolized, and above all mapped out in detail the world it conquered and owned. The Hegelian philosophy of history put the colonized world at the primitive stage of a chronography of conquest, upon which Hegel and

[67] Ibid.: III–IV.

Napoleon sat supreme. The Kantian critique of "pure reason" made the European the knowing subject and the colonized world the knowable world. European anthropology marked the stage of primitive societies awaiting European colonization and conquest. European travelers were instrumental in navigating the routes of conquest for their mercantile class and their military contingencies to follow the same routes. Marco Polo's *Travels*, James Morier's *The Adventures of Hajji Baba of Ispahan*, Jules Verne's *Around the World in Eighty Days*, and Mark Twain's *Innocents Abroad* (among many more) were the literary manifestations of such imaginative geographies of conquest – of knowing and feeling and imagining as owning. There was nothing unusual or strange or unique about this European fascination with mapping and imagining the world in conjunction with their imperial conquest. Muslim and other geographers and travelers had done the same in the heyday of their own empires. These travelogues we are reading together in this book happen at a moment in world history when the European colonial conquest of the world had deeply and widely mapped it – and these travelers, and in Maragheh'i's case, work of fiction, were in the midst of reimagining, remapping, and reclaiming it from a position diametrically opposed to their colonial imaginings.

Mapping the world was to own it; imagining the world while sailing armed through its waters was to conquer it. The rise of European and US exhibitions of the sort some of these travelers saw was to mimic and stage, thereby possess and digest the world in digestible measures. This was the beginning of the tourism industry that eventually sent the European bourgeois class to trips of "discovering" the world for themselves. The tourism industry, visual anthropology, and colonial conquests of Asia, Africa, and Latin America were variations on the same theme of mapping and knowing the world in decidedly European terms. Thus, subjects of the colonial gaze of the European voyeur, the persons of the world anywhere East, West, South, or North of the colonizer were robbed of agency, self-knowledge, and self-assertion. These Persian travelogues we have been studiously examining in this book are evidence of resistance to that gaze, documents of how people stood up against that moral and imaginative subjugation. It was the later colonized mind of the Qajar scholarship that systematically abused and robbed them of that agency – and the only comparison to a book like Zeyn al-Abedin Maragheh'i's *Siyahat-nameh-ye*

Ibrahim Beg that came to their mind was Jean-Jacques Rousseau's *On the Social Contract*. The rise of this literature was somewhere between the fact of that colonial gaze that denied them agency and the fantasy of the colonized minds that failed to read them for the defiance they had mounted.

In their pioneering study, *Reading National Geographic* (1993), Catherine Lutz and Jane L. Collins examined the way a major American institution systematically manufactured an exotic vision of the world that centered around their readers in North America – authenticating them, alienating the subject of their gaze.[68] The authors closely examined thousands of photographs through which forces of Euro–American modernity are set against those of primitivism and exoticism around the world. That world, through this institutional memory of an empire, is set around the epicenter of the United States as its final arbiter of truth and beauty. The world is there to tickle the fancies of this imperial beholder – self-conscious or implied. Almost at the same time, Mary Louise Pratt had published her equally groundbreaking book, *Imperial Eyes: Travel Writing and Transculturation* (1992), in which she went even further to document in detail how US imperial imagination had planted itself at the heart of a global planetary imagination.[69] Pratt acutely dismantled the narrative disposition of manufacturing "the rest of the world" through European travel writing as an "ideological apparatus" of imperial power. Evident in Pratt's critique is the way these European travel writings posited a "European metropole" at the center of a "non-European periphery."

We are nowhere near the archival documentation or theoretical mapping out of the worlds emerging from travel writing of Iranian, Arab, Turk, other Asian, African and Latin American travelers without reducing them to their colonizers' gazes. But as I have tried to argue throughout this book, these Persian travelers subverted the colonial gaze that was cast on them and their worlds. Even in the critical

---

[68] See Catherine A. Lutz and Jane L. Collins, *Reading National Geographic* (Chicago: University of Chicago Press, 1993).
[69] See Mary Louise Pratt, *Imperial Eyes: Travel Writing and Transculturation* (London: Routledge, 1992).

literature that has emerged over the last few decades, the emphasis is rightly on the texture of the colonial gaze and not on how that gaze was resisted as described in exquisite detail by such travelers as those we are reading in this book. This entire book, long and roomy as it has become, is only a critical introduction to that future scholarship.   ✶

Invitation to
graduate
students

12 | *Professor Sayyah Comes Home to Teach*

Set upon my shoulders
Oh the early morning hymns of the Vedas
The whole weight of freshness –
For I'm afflicted
With the warmth of Speech –

Oh, all you olive trees of Palestine:
Address all the abundance of your shades
To me:
To this lonesome traveler
Having just returned
From the vicinity of Mount Sinai
Feverish with
The heat of the Divine Word –

> Sohrab Sepehri (Mosafer/Traveler, Babol, Spring 1966)

From the Vedas to the Hebrew Bible, gathered in one astounding poetic staccato – delivered in a Persian diction that spoke truth to silence. The world came home to Sepehri's poetry, and he brought his poetry home to his people, spoken in Persian as if from the certainty of a divine revelation. By the time in 1966 he composed his "Mosafer/Traveler," that world was so mature and confident in its gestation it had become forgetful of itself. We were worldly without knowing it. Sepehri and his generation of Iranian poets, artists, filmmakers, and literati were there to think and feel and know and enable us that way. That poetry remained by and large a global secret, mostly untranslatable to the afflicted diction of any backward Orientalism that came near it. Above all, it needed some historical excavation to see how we got there – and how he commanded that poetic diction. There is an innate worldliness about Sepehri's poetry, as we read it today, at once material and allegorical, real and parabolic, accessible and distant.

336

Sepehri's poetry is in-the-world in a manner that is innate to his worldliness, domestic to his aesthetic sense of self-transcendence – all placed not in a spatial but in an existential reading of the world, dwelling in the world in and of itself. To be at home in the world is the poetic dwelling of Sepehri, where we found ourselves when we first encountered his poetry. In 1966 when Sepehri wrote this poem I was fifteen years old and had never traveled outside my homeland, but in that poem I was already at home in the world, and I was more than one thousand years old in my happy habitation. How could that be – a halcyon provincial boy in the southern provinces of somewhere, thinking himself the happy epicenter of the world?

The Fruit Too Far from the Tree

In this final chapter, we are coming home, literally, in the life and career of one extraordinary woman, Fatemeh Sayyah (1902–1948), or Fatemeh Reza Zadeh Mahallati, to be exact. She did not write a travelogue, but she was one towering paradoxical conclusion of all the travels and travelogues that had occurred before her and had made her ironic twist possible. She was born, raised, and reached literary and professional maturity in a peripatetic environment that had made her professional character and literary culture possible. If you recall, in Chapter 7 we followed closely the footsteps of Hajj Sayyah during his extensive travels abroad. Fatemeh Sayyah was his niece – the daughter of his brother, and she was also briefly married to his son, Hamid Sayyah. Her father, Sayyah's brother, was a professor of Persian language and literature in Russia, and her mother was Russian, of German origin. She was born and raised in Moscow, received her early and advanced education in Russia, mastered Russian and French languages and literatures, and proceeded to receive her doctorate degree in comparative literature, writing her doctoral dissertation on Anatole France. She then moved to her homeland in 1924, became a prominent professor of comparative literature, and was a pioneering figure in introducing that discipline in her country. As a groundbreaking female professor in a solidly patriarchal society and a deeply cultivated woman, Fatemeh Sayyah became a leading advocate of women's rights in her homeland. She traveled extensively abroad (but left no published travelogue of these journeys), representing Iran in major conferences on peace and the status of women. In doing so, she was the personification and the delivery of all the implied promises and explicit hopes of the travelogues we have examined in this book – and yet with an unanticipated and paradoxical twist. Let us get to know her in more detail – and marvel at her accomplishments during her very short life, fulfilled after a very long period of expectations, and wonder at how she put her puzzling signature on a long letter home. The crowning achievement of a multifaceted cosmopolitan culture evident in the rich body of travel narratives that preceded her, Fatemeh Sayyah thrived at a fanatical Eurocentrism that went against the grain of that literature. In that paradoxical twist, however, dwells the emotive split between the unwavering sovereignty of a rising nation and the vagaries of failed states that have sought and failed to rule it.

The major landmarks of Fatemeh Sayyah's life coincide with world historic events in her two homelands – Iran and Russia. She was born in 1902 in Moscow, during the heat of the preparatory stages of both the Russian and the Iranian revolutions – two cataclysmic events that fed on each other's energy and revealed a larger revolutionary disposition of the period and the region. When at the age of eighteen in 1921 Sayyah married her cousin Hamid Sayyah and for the first time came for a visit back to Iran, her ancestral homeland was in the grip of the dying Qajar aristocracy, the rising colonial domination of the British, and the ambitious ascendency of Reza Shah as the founder of the new Pahlavi dynasty.[1] Neither this marriage nor her first visit to her homeland lasted too long. She soon returned to Russia and resumed her education, as the nascent Soviet Union was emerging as a major superpower in global politics. Her marriage lasted only three years and had resulted in no children. When in 1933 Fatemeh Sayyah received her PhD in European and comparative literature from Moscow University, with a doctoral thesis on Anatole France, the subject of her scholarship was a terra incognita on the Iranian academic scene. Upon receiving her PhD, she returned to Iran permanently in 1934 as Reza Shah was firmly establishing himself as a ruling tyrant at the head of a new dynasty. She is now a single woman, exceptionally erudite and

---

[1] A pioneering study of the life and writings of Fatemeh Sayyah is by Mohammad Golbon (ed.), *Naqd va Siyahat: Majmu'eh Maqalat va Taghrirat-e Dr. Fatemeh Sayyah/Criticism and Traveling: Collected Essays and Writings of Dr. Fatemeh Sayyah* (Tehran: Tus, 1354/1975). I have much benefited from this book.

educated, coming from a learned and respectable family, with a full command of Russian and French languages and literatures, head and shoulders above anything achieved or known before in any Iranian academic institution.

The first very public occasion on which people began to notice Fatemeh Sayyah was in 1934, when she participated in the millennial conference on Ferdowsi, organized on behalf of the new Pahlavi king in part to cultivate national and international legitimacy for his newly minted dynasty. In 1935, she was officially recruited by the Iranian Ministry of Culture and appointed in charge of the education of women. The same year she became a member of the "Kanun-e Bano-van/ Ladies Association" under the same ministry, promoting Reza Shah's "modernization" projects targeting Iranian women. The combination of the changing dynasty and changing demography had brought the previous century of women's rights movement to the forefront of the new monarchy. In 1936, Fatemeh Sayyah began her teaching career in an environment where modern education in Iran had scarcely seen a more erudite professor of literature in the country. The Soviet Union was now a towering imperial presence in Iran, and she was in full command of its language and literature. In the same year, the Ministry of Foreign Affairs sent her to Geneva to participate in a conference at the League of Nations. In her, the new monarchy had a respectable public face to present to the world. In 1938, she became a professor of Russian and Comparative Literature at Tehran University – a first-ever appointment in her homeland. In 1943, she joined the Iran Women's Party and became increasingly more engaged in promoting the cause of women's liberation. In 1943, she became a member of the Soviet Union Cultural Society, fully conscious of the role she could play in facilitating a conversation between her two homelands. In 1944, she was appointed by the Iran Women's Party to attend to the issue of women prisoners. Nothing of the sort had happened before in Iran. In 1944, she was invited by the Turkish government and went to Turkey for 45 days, delivering various lectures on regional and global issues. In 1945, she represented Iran in a conference on women and peace in Paris. Throughout her later years she was the prominent member of multiple and varied organizations devoted to women's social presence. In 1947, she went to Europe for medical treatment – she was suffering from diabetes. She delivered her last lecture in 1947, about the influence of Dostoevsky on French literature. She died on Thursday, March 4, 1948, at the age of forty-five.[2]

Fatemeh Sayyah emerged from a genealogy of towering intellectual figures, all of them men. She brought the legacy of all those figures home – but her ancestral homeland had undergone some serious social changes far beyond what her parentage had left behind. The niece of the famous Hajj Sayyah, and for a short time his daughter-in-law, whom we know by now quite well – one can only imagine the intellectual environment in which she grew up. She was the daughter of Hajj Sayyah's brother Mirza Ja'far Reza Zadeh (died ca. 1940), an accomplished man in his own right. Though not as prominent as his brother, Ja'far was equally committed to the well-being of his homeland, conversant with the top public intellectuals of his time. Mirza Ja'far taught and published books on Persian pedagogy, targeting mostly his Russian students. As you may remember, he was in Russia when the revolutionary rabble-rouser Jamal al-Din Al-Afghan ran away from Iran, and Hajj Sayyah asked his brother to attend to him in Moscow. Mirza Ja'far had moved to Russia in 1873 and established a name and a reputation for himself, learned Russian quite well, and married a Russian/German woman, and among his primary pupils were the Russian diplomatic corps on their way to Iran. Fatemeh Sayyah was the product of this environment, with people like Hajj Sayyah, Zeyn al-Abedin Maragheh'I, and Jamal al-Din al-Afghani in her environment. We also know her father regularly traveled to Istanbul and was in touch with expat intellectuals there. When she married her cousin, Hamid Sayyah, he was the Iranian ambassador to Russia.[3]

As a professor of Russian and comparative literature at Tehran University, Fatemeh Sayyah was deeply loved and widely admired by her students and colleagues, including Ali Akbar Siyasi, the president of University, who upon her passing said that one of her two specialties was literary criticism and that no one after her could teach that subject.[4] But her contributions to her homeland were not limited to this pioneering discipline from a decidedly Russian and French perspective. Between 1923 and 1948, for a quarter of a century, Fatemeh Sayyah spent her life in opening a new chapter in the women's rights movement in her homeland, which was of course deeply rooted in

---

[2] For a quick chronology of her life, see ibid.: Three-Five.
[3] Ibid.: Twenty-two ff.   [4] Ibid.: Forty-three–Forty-four.

social and political mobilization, but had never before her been delivered in succinct scholarly prose. The so-called "unveiling of women" meant of course nothing to her, for she was not veiled to be unveiled. Her Russian upbringing had given her life and character a vastly different conception of liberation. While living in Iran she traveled extensively around the world and was a key member of important international organizations – all of the travel, of course, on official trips was sponsored by Reza Shah's state. In 1944 she was chiefly responsible for drawing attention to women's prisoners in Iran, a virtually non-existent responsibility before her. Soon after the Russian revolution, a center for cultural exchanges between USSR and Iran was established, of which she was an active member. This center published a periodical called Payam-e No/New Message, of which she was a key editorial board member. The achievement in her tragically short life, much of it as she struggled with diabetes, is nothing short of miraculous. In 1944, she was invited to Turkey where she spent six weeks giving lectures on comparative literature, with a focused attention on women, deeply impressing her audiences with her command of languages, cultures, and literatures.[5] In 1948, she joined an Iranian delegation to Paris, and days before her passing from heart failure, she delivered a talk in French at the Iran–France Institute on the impact of Dostoevsky on French literature.

A Pioneering Women's Rights Leader

The biographer of Fatemeh Sayyah informs us that after her graduation, she initially taught in Russia for a few years, and published a few scholarly pieces in Russian, before moving to Iran.[6] Among the first pieces she published in Persian was a critical defense of the genre of novel against the dilettantism of the notorious "reformist" Ahmad Kasravi (1890–1946). Her doctoral dissertation on Anatole France, scores of articles in Persian, a book on Russian language instruction for high school, a manuscript on the history of Russian literature that was left unfinished when she died, and another unpublished manuscript on literary criticism – are among her known outputs. The prominent Iranian novelist Simin Daneshvar (1921–2012) wrote her doctoral

---

[5] Ibid.: Forty-eight.　　[6] Ibid.: Fifty-Fifty-three.

dissertation with her too – and has spoken fondly of her significance in her own academic career.

She was one of the earliest woman scholars in the mostly men's field of Shahnameh scholarship at the time. Her writing on Ferdowsi immediately reveals her command of both Persian and European sources on the Persian epic – though from a decidedly (Russian) Orientalist perspective. She writes a simple and erudite Persian prose. Her essay on the biography of Ferdowsi is solid and thoroughly sourced.[7] She has a deeply informed essay on the European reception of Ferdowsi, in which she shows quite an exceptional command of foreign sources for her time. She has read these sources in Russian, French, German, and English and reports them in a fluent and precise Persian prose.[8] She has an equally compelling essay in what we might call sociology of literature, in which she places the Persian epic in the social and political context of Ferdowsi's own time and region.[9]

The bulk of Fatemeh Sayyah's writing was devoted to women's issues in society, culture, and literature. In an essay on the French writer Germaine de Staël (1766–1817) dated 1926, she traces the relationship between the presence of women in social and political life and their literary ambitions and achievements.[10] Her essay is at once biographical and literary, introducing her to her Persian-speaking readership and discussing her literary importance. In another essay on the hard road European women have traveled to achieve their rights, she praises Reza Shah for having bestowed upon Iranian women their freedom. She says Iranian women ought to be deeply grateful to their king.[11] Here her frame of reference is completely European without any sense of critical awareness of other women's struggles in Asia, Africa, or Latin America. Her gratitude to Reza Shah, perhaps out of political expediency, perhaps out of conviction, exacerbates her Eurocentrism in a crucial moment in Iranian history and marks her as an elitist monarchist. It certainly places her far from the longer history of women's struggles in and out of Iran in the larger Asian, African, and Latin American world, of which she seems to be so utterly ignorant.

In 1939, she wrote a major essay on the place of women in art history. Her concern here is to dismantle the myth that women were

---

[7] Ibid.: 3–20.   [8] Ibid.: 21–39.   [9] Ibid.: 40–48.   [10] Ibid.: 51–64.
[11] Ibid.: 72.

incapable of producing art. She goes through the gamut of various arts – including paintings, drama, opera, dance, and literature – in order to navigate the presence and significance of women in these arts. She is both scholarly and deeply erudite and yet probing and skeptical. She is a realist but also assertive of occasions on which women have been present in such arts in many significant ways.[12] The progressive and feminist dimensions of her arguments are groundbreaking for Iran – solid, convincing, and admirable. But, and there is the rub, the entirety of her examples, without a single exception, come from Europe. She has not a single reference in this entire essay to any Asian, African, Latin American, or, heaven forbid, Arab, Iranian, Indian, Turkish, Muslim, or Hindu women. Nothing. They simply do not occur to her – they are outside her horizons. How did she see herself? What was she doing in Iran? There are, alas, times that she seems to have thought of herself to be on a civilizing mission amongst the barbarians. Iranians had no history of women's struggles before she came to civilize and liberate and educate them about the civilized European ways. This is simply astonishing.

Fatemeh Sayyah's perfectly legitimate concern in this series of essays that she wrote between 1939 and 1940 is the question of what she calls "genius among women." She is investigating whether or not women are capable of "artistic genius." She has very thorough and realistic concerns about women's creativity but (again) it is absolutely astonishing that while she has a few radical parameters about this issue, her entire archive of references, without a single exception, is in the European context. She begins with the Romans and the Greeks, continues with the French, English, and Germans, and she uses detailed examples of these in a European context.[13] The rest of the world does not exist – except as a dark void waiting to be enlightened by Europe. To be sure, her observations are critical and thorough but spoken from a manifestly colonized and Eurocentric mind without the single attention to any woman in Asia or Africa, Latin America, or particularly her own homeland, in fact decidedly dismissing those contexts as backward; they don't even occur to her, they are outside history. Also evident in this series of issues she raises is the apparent elitist, state-sponsored, bourgeois feminism that dovetails with Reza Shah's "modernization" projects that included the violent unveiling of women. This particular

[12] Ibid.: 72–81.   [13] Ibid.: 83–143.

constituency of Fatemeh Sayyah remains definitive to both her erudite scholarship and public pronouncements.

It is only in her own contemporary time that Fatemeh Sayyah becomes adamant about the social status of women in her immediate surroundings. She writes regularly in various periodicals about the role that women ought to play in politics – and she does so eloquently and convincingly. She fights against the rampant patriarchy and misogyny in her country.[14] But she does so not from any understanding of the role that women have historically played in Iranian history – she seems to be entirely oblivious to that. History belongs to Europe, which she knows well and mobilizes convincingly in order to enable Iranian women to fight for their rights. But these women, in and of themselves, in their own homeland, have had no history of their own so far as she is concerned. History is only European. She "and a few other intellectual women," as she used to say, were here to guide and civilize Iranian women, just like women in Turkey, on the European model. Yes, there is a multifaceted cosmopolitan aspect to her character and learning, but she speaks from a deeply colonized mind written into the subconscious of her bourgeois feminism. Her casual defense of Reza Shah pales in comparison to the fact that her brand of feminism could only be of use to the state-sponsored apparatus of the ideological fortification of the ruling monarchy, leaving the rest of the society she had failed to understand to their own historic course.

Comparative Literature as a Potent Ideology

As we read through Fatemeh Sayyah's erudite writings and teachings on "comparative literature," more than ever we see how the discipline at this stage of its vertiginously Eurocentric history was an effective ideology of Euro-universalism that had placed Europe at the center of the universe and the rest of the world at its colonial receiving point – and, as such, a major ideological force in European imperial hegemony around the world, as best argued by Gauri Viswanathan in her pioneering work, *Masks o Conquest: Literary Study and British Rule in India* (1989). Fatemeh Sayyah was not any prophet of this ideology – but she was one exquisitely learned apostle of it. With her command of Russian and French languages and literatures, and her familiarity with

[14] Ibid.: 142–147.

other European languages and literatures, she intimidated her audiences. With her advanced degree in comparative literature from a major Russian university, she had outranked her contemporaries. She used (and subconsciously abused) these privileges to posit the discipline of comparative literature as a civilizing mission to genetically re-engineer a literary consciousness in her homeland that would befit comparison with her European idols. We look at her exquisite learnedness today and we think: Oh, Sister, where art thou?

To be sure, the sort of long essays she wrote on Romanticism and Realism in European literature had no precedent in academic Persian prose.[15] Her critical reflections on Balzac and Zola are at once deeply informed and signs of her sheer brilliance. One must acknowledge the groundbreaking significance of such essays in Persian prose for an audience eager and thirsty to learn about world literature, including European literature. That she was so beholden to European literature was in part because of her academic discipline, Russian upbringing, and perhaps even personal bourgeois taste. If we compare her essays to what was available to Iranian readers at this time, her critical reflections are in fact groundbreaking, opening up a whole horizon of how to read literature. But all of that is from the vantage point of a Russian-educated Europeanist on a civilizing mission in her paternal homeland.

As she says clearly in her essay on Balzac, "The civilized world knows Balzac fairly well."[16] It is only the uncivilized world that is in need of education – one site among it, her own homeland. This is the preface on the basis of which she proceeds to share with her Iranian readers an utterly brilliant essay on the significance of the French novelist and theories of fiction. She does so consciously thinking of young Iranian writers who ought to know Balzac so they could learn how to produce good literature. The point to keep in mind is that scarcely any of the novels she discusses had yet been translated into Persian, and much of theoretical literature in Russian, French, and German at her fingertips was *terra incognita* in Iran. So, no doubt her young and older readers would have much benefited from these essays. But whence and wherefore this civilizational divide, this civilizational mission?

What we are witnessing in her case is how she brings back home a radically Eurocentric worldview from Russia, a lopsided reading of the

[15] Ibid.: 151–188.   [16] Ibid.: 189.

experiences of generations of Iranian travelers, turning her attention almost exclusively to Europe and yet doing so with brilliant literacy. None of her predecessors had the range and depth of her learning, yet they had cultivated a far more global, far more worldly perspective on their time. A crucial reason for this Eurocentrism is no doubt her bourgeois audience and their rising significance as the targeted constituency of Reza Shan's monarchy, to which Fatemeh Sayyah had an entirely uncritical and in fact subservient attitude. She served Reza Shah's monarchy with impeccable scholarship, and Reza Shah's monarchy cultivated a deeply admiring and receptive audience for her – the result was a systematic and overwhelming Eurocentric twist in the emerging worldview of the nascent Iranian bourgeoisie. In 1940, she wrote an excellent essay on "Tradition" in literary history, the content of which is in fact making quite a progressive point about the necessity of innovation in literary forms.[17] But for some strange reason, she feels obligated to begin her essay by saying that when she says "Sonnat" (Persian/Arabic word for "tradition") she means "Tradition" in the French sense! But why? She says so, for it does not even occur to her to question the necessity of beginning with a French point of departure. To be sure, the essay is a perfectly valid reflection on the issue of "tradition and modernity," bringing prominent French authorities to bear witness on the matter. But by the time she comes to a cliché reference to Hafez and Sa'di toward the end of the essay, we are left wondering if Iranians before her had been slumbering in darkness waiting for the French word "Tradition" to awaken them to truth. Something is happening in her mind, in her cast of critical thinking, and, above all, in her bourgeois constituency, that has now introduced a radical epistemic rupture from anything that happened before her for over a century. While she is breaking certain traditions, she is in fact reinstituting a deeply flawed and outdated neo-traditionalism. A crucial cleavage here is that everything progressive in Iran before her arrival was in opposition to the ruling regimes, and everything important about her initiatives is subservient to the ruling monarchy, and even to the colonizing cast of the interwar period when she thrived in her homeland. She was administering a crucial prose into her homeland's history of colonial modernity. But she was far more on the colonizing

---

[17] Ibid.: 217–231.

than on the modernity side of the project. She, in fact, was colonial modernity incarnate.

Perfectly evident in yet another beautiful essay she wrote in 1940 on the presence of daily issues in literature is the theoretical cast of her mind, whereby she persuasively argues the necessity of bringing contemporary social issues into literary domains.[18] All her references are of course, as usual, exclusively to French literature, particularly Anatole France – but the theoretical points she makes are quite powerful and pertinent to her time. On the positive side we see the enormous power of her work shaping the emerging literary concerns of an entire nation. But at the same time, she has not an iota of a critical take on the Eurocentric cast of her own mind. She is theorizing, criticizing, and Europeanizing the very idea of literariness in a country in which no European language has a literary presence.

One of her best essays is the short article she published in 1933 in response to the dilettantism of a leading "reformist," Ahmad Kasravi (1890–1946), and the vulgar attack he had written against fiction.[19] In this short essay (again, entirely based on French and occasionally Russian novels), Sayyah defends the novel as a genre and maps out its significance in the healthy life of a society. We read this essay today, marvel at her pioneering efforts to locate the novel in the moral and imaginative life of a society, and yet wonder at her fanatical Eurocentrism. This could not be just her scholarly limitations in French literature. She does not consider any other non-European literature as a sign of "civilization." In an essay she published in 1943, she does pay a minimal attention to her own contemporary Persian poetry and literature. Here she begins with her favorite phrase that all "civilized countries" of the world know about classical Persian literature. The proof of that? Well, of course: Because they have seen it translated into "major European languages," therefore "the civilized world" knows about it.[20] People who actually produced that literature are not civilized. People who translated into European languages are civilized. At this point we realize this is no longer a mere Eurocentric nervous tic about her colonized mind – this is plain racism, whereby unless something is produced in or translated into a "European language," the "civilized countries" of the world would not know about it – thus categorically equating "civilization" with "Europe." Her knowledge of

---

[18] Ibid.: 232–241.   [19] Ibid.: 245–253.   [20] Ibid.: 253–264.

classical Persian prose and poetry, meanwhile, is astonishingly cliché and deeply Orientalistic. Among her contemporaries, she does mention neoclassicist poets like Mohammad-Taqi Bahar (1886–1951) and Lotf Ali Suratgar (1900–1969) and novelists like Mohammad Ali Jamalzadeh (1892–1997) and Sadegh Hedayat (1903–1951) in brief passing – and even here insisting on the influence of Edgar Alan Poe on Hedayat. But she says nothing about the three masterpieces of her time, Sadegh Hedayat's "The Blind Owl" (1936) and Nima Yushij's two earliest masterpieces, "Qesseh-ye Rang Parideh/The Story of Pale Face" (1921) and "Afsaneh/Myth" (1922), about which she seems to be entirely clueless.

In a speech she delivered to the first Congress of Iranian Writers in 1946, Fatemeh Sayyah mapped out in theoretical detail the necessity of literary criticism as an academic subject, in which she initially begins with French but this time concludes with Russian literature and particularly mentions Vissarion Belinsky (1811–1848) and Nikolay Chernyshevsky (1828–1889) as exemplary models of literary criticism in a socialist realist mode.[21] These seminal Russian literary critics were scarcely known in Iran at this time in any serious way. Two opposite facts emerge from this speech: (1) her extraordinary and, for her time, unique command of the French and Russian literary sources and (2) her categorical ignorance of Persian and Arabic material in the same domain. She thrives at one and is blissfully ignorant of the other. It would not be until a generation later when the eminent literary historian Abdolhossein Zarrinkub (1923–1999) would publish a two-volume book (chief among many more) on the subject of *Naqd-e Adabi/Literary Criticism* (1959). It would take even longer for a seminal literary critic like Mohammad-Reza Shafi'i Kadkani (born 1939) to emerge, retrieving classical sources of literary criticism and advancing them forward. She could have been a forerunner of these literary scholars. She was not. For her time, undeniably impressive is Fatemeh Sayyah's European erudition and consistent engagement with young Iranian scholars and intellectuals, at once criticizing and encouraging them, as best evident in a short response she offers the young Parviz Natal Khanlari, who would later become a major voice in literary modernism.[22] She both praises and criticizes a scholarly talk Parviz Natal Khanlari had given on modern prose. From the short response it

---

[21] Ibid.: 272–275.   [22] Ibid.: 278–281.

is quite evident she did not have the young Khanlari's command of the material he had discussed but is giving him more formal, theoretical, and methodological guidance about his research. Equally impressive is her detailed attention to exhibitions by modern and contemporary young artists whose work she had gone to see, again both praising them and giving them critical tools for how to think about their art.[23]

She of course thrives at introducing giants of Russian literature to her Iranian readers. In an essay she wrote in 1944 on the occasion of the fortieth anniversary of the passing of Anton Chekhov (1860–1904), she uses the occasion to offer the master Russian drama-tist as a model for young Iranian writers.[24] She underlines Chekhov's detailed realism and compares it to Hugo's romanticism, which she says has had an inordinate influence on her contemporary Persian prose. In 1944, Zahra Natel Khanlari, a young literary scholar at the time, translated Dostoevsky's short story "White Night" (1848), and Fatemeh Sayyah wrote a short introduction to this book,[25] in which she introduces Dostoevsky to his Iranian audience, offers a brief biography, and discusses his realism. In another major essay she pub-lished in 1945, she introduces Alexander Pushkin to Iranians. For this essay she chooses the theme of Romanticism and places Pushkin in the tradition of François-René de Chateaubriand and Lord Byron.[26] Here she details the major works of Pushkin and characterizes his fascin-ation with "the East" as the Russian version of European Romanti-cism. Despite her regular admiration for realism, in this essay we see her mapping out in detail Pushkin's romanticism for the rising Iranian bourgeoisie that is now her most potent and immediate audience.

By this point in this excellent collection of Fatemeh Sayyah's writings, I was positively impressed I had not seen many typographical errors or pagination mix-ups in my copy of the book. But I was not to remain under that illusion for too long – for suddenly I ran into the good old habit of clumsy bookbinding, Iranian style, perfectly evident here, too, where pages 311–321 are each printed twice and ordered in a bizarre pagination disorder that takes a few minutes to decipher how in the world the pages work. The poor overworked printer must have fallen asleep and these pages went haywire. But no problem, at least I am not missing any pages. I actually have two copies of each

[23] Ibid.: 281–288.   [24] Ibid.: 291–297.   [25] Ibid.: 297–302.
[26] Ibid.: 302–312.

page, repeated every other page! As I was reading through this excellent collection of Fatemeh Sayyah's writings, edited capably by Mohammad Golbon, I became curious as to when and where I purchased this book, for I am using the copy from my own library. I looked at the back cover of the book and I see a sticker that tells me I purchased the book for £9.99, which means I purchased it in London, which reminded me of this excellent Arab and Iranian bookstore called al-Huda located at the intersection of Charing Cross Road and Shaftesbury, where the theater district of London is located. There used to be a whole row of bookstores there, including the famous Foyles. I used to go to al-Huda in the early 1980s when I was in London during the summer with my family, working on my doctoral dissertation at SOAS. Al-Huda imported excellent collections of books from Iran and stored them in their basement. I bought a whole collection of books in those days and shipped them to the United States – one of them this book on Fatemeh Sayyah. At the time, my mind was entirely on my doctoral dissertation on Prophet Muhammad's charismatic authority. My mind and soul transmigrated to seventh century Arabia; I had no blasted clue who Fatemeh Sayyah was and what she had written. But I was collecting a library for the future scholar I had dreamed in me – then in London, now in New York, far from the capital of my homeland where all these books were published. I don't think at that time in my own journeys away from Iran I was yet ready to reflect on who Fatemeh Sayyah was and what she had written. Some three decades later, her legacy has a whole different resonance for me – as I am collecting my earlier notes and books to write this book from beginning to end.

After figuring out how to sort out those pagination mix-ups, I proceeded to read a major speech Fatemeh Sayyah had delivered in 1946 at the Iran–Soviet Cultural Society, where she offered her audience a detailed account of the life and work of the Soviet writer Mikhail Sholokhov (1905–1984).[27] In her talk on Sholokhov, she delivers a thorough treatment of the Soviet novelist's masterpiece, *Tikhiy Don/And Quiet Flows the Don* (1925–1940). She is intimately knowledgeable of the circumstances of the publication of this major work in Soviet literature. Then she offers a literary context of his work. She considers the book a masterpiece and compares it to Tolstoy's *War*

----

[27] Ibid.: 312–325.

and Peace (1869). Then she gives a volume by volume synopsis of the book, before turning to Sholokhov's other major work (*Podnyataya tselina*, 1932–1960; translated into English as *Virgin Soil Upturned* and *Harvest on the Don*). Her reading of these novels is based on her view that the old and the new world are confronting each other in these seminal Soviet literary works. Her conclusion is that just like Maxim Gorki before him, Sholokhov had emerged from the masses and was practicing the art of "democracy," both in his novels and in society at large. Sholokhov, his literary output, and such close critical analysis were groundbreaking to hear and read in Persian for Fatemeh Sayyah's audience. In her neighboring literary traditions in Russian, the place she could easily also call home, Fatemeh Sayyah had a much more veritable domain to bring to her Iranian contemporaries, where the cosmopolitan worldliness of a much more open possibility could be made available to her audiences.

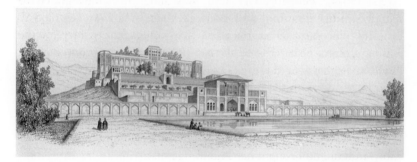

Figure 14 "Perspective view, Castle of Qasr e Qajar, Tehran by Pascal Coste" The Qajar and the subsequent Pahlavi capital of Tehran became the epicenter of attention for these travelers of the late eighteenth to early twentieth century, for whatever they wrote from wherever they went was geared back to the political heartland of their homeland. Without a single exception, all these travelers included Iran in the itinerary of their journeys, and they wrote as detailed accounts of their internal Iranian destinations from North to South and from East to West as they did of any other country they visited. Those accounts were definitive to recasting Iran as a nation upon the global map of the emerging postcolonial world. The image of Tehran that eventually emerges in these traveling narratives is decidedly and consciously against the very grain of the colonial gaze cast upon the Iranian capital. Reprinted with permission from Art Collection 4/Alamy Stock Photo.

The Rise of a Public Intellectual

When we look at the totality of Fatemeh Sayyah's critical output and
the collective result of her work in the last decade of her short but
fruitful life, it becomes unmistakably clear that she was something
much more than a professor of Russian and comparative literature at
Tehran University. She was among the top public intellectuals of her
time – in fact, scarcely anyone even comes close to her, with such
thorough command of European (French in particular) literature;
native familiarity with Russian language, literature, and culture; and
easy facilities with the history, literature, and culture of her own
homeland – albeit from a patently Russian Orientalist perspective.
But all of that was preliminary to the fact that she deeply cared
for her homeland. That unique combination must have dazzled her
contemporaries. Yes, there were more towering public intellectuals,
such as Ali-Akbar Dehkhoda (1879–1956) and Mohammad-Taqi
Bahar (1886–1951), or provocative reformers like Ahmad Kasravi
(1890–1946), whose gender and masculine overconfidence commanded more attention. But none of them was more learned in
decidedly European terms, the terms that were precisely the paradoxical parameters of her rise to the top tier of her generation of public
intellectuals, then in the grips of a Eurocentric monarchy that had
come to power with the British aid and was drawn to the orbit of its
colonial domains. Fatemeh Sayyah was consulted and her thoughts
solicited on the most vital issues of the early Pahlavi period. She was no
revolutionary thinker or political rabble-rouser, but she was impeccably erudite and brought her knowledge of European literature fully
to bear on a variety of issues she and her audience thought important
to their homeland. In 1934, for example, she wrote an excellent essay
in which she discussed the significance of literature in the healthy life of
a society, particularly in the upbringing of children.[28] Although all her
examples in this and all others of her work come from European and
Russian literature, still she is speculating, theorizing, and analyzing
literary issues in Persian and in Iran and to an Iranian audience,
obviously fully conscious of the need of the new society for such urgent
theoretical thinking. The same is the case with another short article she
published in 1938 about Persian prose and what are the pedagogical

[28] Ibid.: 329–342.

principles to be considered in teaching literary prose to young readers.[29] Such timely essays combined with her appointment to crucial governmental committees and delegations abroad made her a key figure in the Pahlavi "modernization" project that nevertheless met with certain crucial social urgencies as well. She was a paradoxical figure – full of positive energies for her time and her audiences, and yet a potent agent in the systematic alienation of a postcolonial culture caught in the grips of superpower rivalries.

When we consider the variety of issues on which Fatemeh Sayyah was publicly sharing her thoughts, it is obvious that she had important things to say about almost every aspect of her homeland, from politics to society, from literature to art, from prose to poetry, from national sovereignty to women's rights. She had an acute theoretical mind that could cut to the chase and dazzle her audiences. In an interview that the *Women's World/Alam Zanan* (a periodical devoted to women's issues) conducted with her in 1944, she is proudly introduced as the first and only female professor at Tehran university, highly educated, in command of multiple European languages, well-traveled, and deeply concerned with women's issues.[30] She was a solid role model for the younger generation of her urban and upwardly mobile compatriots – men and women. In such interviews she projects herself as an Iranian who was born and raised in Russia; attended the University of Moscow; achieved her PhD; writing her dissertation on Anatole France; and having now returned to her homeland to teach and be useful to her country. She says she believes in women's rights but women must also pay attention to their femininity, and to their motherhood. She was a solid bourgeois feminist but not too radical for her time. She says she was the first woman to be sent to Geneva to participate in an international conference. This was indeed an extraordinary feat. She is proud to be part of multiple organizations, particularly one that attends to women prisoners. From this interview we learn that she is interested in music, poetry, and the arts, and that she continues to publish in both Persian in Iran and in Russian in the Soviet Union. One can scarcely think of a more prominent woman in her time. The towering poet of her time, Parvin E'tesami (1907–1941), was of course deeply loved and widely admired too. But Fatemeh Sayyah was of an entirely different cast of character.

[29] Ibid.: 342–348.   [30] Ibid.: 351–362.

In another interview she had granted the same periodical, *Women's World,* later that year in 1944, she gave details of her visit along with a delegation from Women's Party to Turkey. Here she praises the progress Turkish women have made in various professions because of having achieved their equal rights. She also assures her interviewer that "their way of thinking and action one can say is now completely Western and European. For their progress Turkish women consider enlightened European women as their model."[31] She herself is completely beholden to this model, and any progress Iranian or Turkish women may make is of course because they are following and refashioning themselves like European women. How could she be so entirely bereft of any critical backbone – when she thrives at critical thinking in her literary analysis? How could she, with all her intellectual prowess, be so devoid of a more liberated global perspective that would have placed Iranian, Turkish, Asian, African, Latin American, and European women on a more equal critical footing? The answer, I propose, is Reza Shah and the Eurocentric cast of her own mind, and above all her state-sponsored bourgeois feminist constituency, to which she was now actively catering.

Fatemeh Sayyah as a Mixed Metaphor

Let me now pull back a bit and place this detailed reading of Fatemeh Sayyah in the larger context of why I have opted to devote the last chapter of my book to her. My interest in Fatemeh Sayyah in this final chapter is because she was born and raised in Moscow to a family of travelers – the niece and daughter-in-law of the most famous traveler of the nineteenth century – and was a towering critical thinker in her own right, who in her paradoxical character came to define her conflicted age. I was drawn to her because she is a paradoxical ending to a century of travel narratives that had taken Iranians out of their homeland around the globe. It is impossible to overestimate or exaggerate the extraordinary achievements of Fatemeh Sayyah as a scholar, a literary comparatist, a pioneering women's rights activists, and a towering public intellectual – all achieved within the timespan of a relatively short life. She was born to a learned family, raised in a healthy intellectual environment, and was highly educated in

---

[31] Ibid.: 356.

revolutionary Russia. But between her Russian birth and upbringing and Iranian heritage, she exuded a thoroughly colonized mind with "Europe" as the epicenter of her understanding of "civilization." This, I propose, was not a personal failure but the seismic sign of an epistemic change in the early Reza Shah period in which she thrived. She was also beholden to the discipline of "Comparative Literature" as a young graduate student at Moscow University, and ill-equipped so early in the history of that (to this day) pathologically Eurocentric literary thinking to challenge its epistemic foregrounding.

Obviously, women's rights historians and scholars have rightly praised and lionized Fatemeh Sayyah.[32] She was a pioneering women's rights activist in a very powerful position of leadership. She articulated the necessity of gender equality persuasively and in multiple settings. Howsoever her brand of feminism may have been in line with the ruling monarch's policies, still the fact remains she was a woman of enormous capacities and devoted her short but fruitful life to securing women's rights in her homeland. The women's rights movement has had a long and varied history in Iran long before and long after Fatemeh Sayyah, but during her brief life in Iran very few people were as instrumental as she was in advocating and arguing for them. Her Islamist critics, however, are of course hostile, vindictive, and unforgiving toward her.[33] The very same people who saw the picture of Ayatollah Khomeini in the moon and worshipped him like the Hidden Imam find fault with a single vulnerable woman establishing herself as a solid scholar in a new country, and yes, occasionally praising the ruling monarch. They hold her responsible for helping Reza Shah with his unveiling project – as if in and of itself, and entirely independent of Reza Shah's violent, abusive, and arrogant approach, that project was not a worthy cause to allow women freedom of choice. Yes, Reza Shah enforced mandatory unveiling, but the Islamic Republic enforced mandatory veiling – both equally evil and violent superimposition of dress

---

[32] See Mansureh Pirnia, *Salar Zanan-e Iran/Prominent Iranian Women* (Washington, DC: No Publisher, 1995): 88. See also Parvin Paidar, *Women and the Political Process in Twentieth-Century Iran* (Cambridge: Cambridge University Press, 1997): 126–128.

[33] The most damning essay against Fatemeh Sayyah, disguised as a "research paper," is by Reza Ramazan Nargessi, "Zendegi va Andisheh Dr. Fatemeh Sayyah/The Life and Thoughts of Fatemeh Sayyah" (Qom: Center for Research on Women and Family, 1383/2004). Available online here: https://hawzah.net/fa/Magazine/View/6432/6462/73638. Accessed August 10, 2018.

codes on women against their will. Fatemeh Sayyah never advocated mandatory unveiling. She was a leader of women's social presence, and political empowerment, and there was absolutely nothing wrong with that. She was limited and troublingly Eurocentric in her conception of women's rights, with not a single glance at Asia, Africa, or Latin America. But for her time and given the epistemic shift in her country under the British-sponsored military coup that brought Reza Shah to power, she was a leading advocate and a prominent spokesperson for her Iranian sisters.

The Islamists also find fault with her advocacy for land reform and through a bizarre anachronism think it was in support of Reza Shah's son Mohammad Reza Shah's so-called "White Revolution," which included some land reform,[34] which is of course an insanely wrong assumption. Fatemeh Sayyah wrote an essay in support of land reform in 1946 in response to the Azerbaijan separatist movement,[35] while her Islamist nemeses consider it an advocacy for Mohammed Reza Shah's land reform, part of his so-called "White Revolution," in 1963 – almost two decades later when poor Fatemeh Sayyah had been dead for two decades. The sheer inanity of the assertion is mindboggling. During the Soviet-backed separatist movement in Azerbaijan (1945–1946), Fatemeh Sayyah wrote an essay in which she opposed that movement but argued that the land distribution initiated in Azerbaijan during this movement must be implemented throughout the country. It was a simple socialist proposition, perfectly reasonable and praiseworthy. In this essay she praises the Constitutional Revolution of 1906–1911 but rightly points out it was limited to political reforms and left the feudal system of Iranian economy intact. She even finds fault with Reza Shah for his concerns being entirely political and not having attended to these more fundamental economic issues. She concludes this essay with a brilliant defense of women's political participation. The book in which this essay is reprinted, namely Golbon's volume, was published under the Pahlavis in 1975, and because of Pahlavi censorship of anything critical of their regime, one full page of the essay was censored, and the conscientious editor is good enough at least, in a footnote on page 364, to tell us that a whole page was deleted.[36] Under these circumstances, these illiterate militant Islamists,

[34] See Nargessi, "The Life and Thoughts of Fatemeh Sayyah."
[35] Golbon (ed.), *Criticism and Traveling*: 361–370.   [36] Ibid.: 364.

who oppose any such just distribution of land, find fault with Fatemeh Sayyah's proposal, which is fine and perfectly in line with their current militant liberal capitalism, but to then denounce her anachronistically as if she wrote it two decades later in support of Mohammad Reza Shah's Kennedy-inspired reforms, when in fact she was dead, is sheer charlatanism or else malignant illiteracy. Their pettiness and hostility know no limits. They even accuse her of not knowing Persian well, and writing her essays in Russian and someone translating them for her. Even if true (I have seen no conclusive evidence to that effect), that does not compromise the significance of her work, especially coming from monolingual seminarians who, after a whole lifetime in Shi'a seminaries, cannot put two Arabic sentences together. Particularly incensed are these seminarians with Sayyah's position on women's liberation, from the vantage point of a male patriarchy that decides what is good for women, from a position of power heavily subsidized by the Islamic Republic.

A far more balanced and fair criticism (though still limited within the confinements of a Eurocentric mind) comes from Iraj Parsinejad, a prominent historian of literary criticism in Persian, who has written insightfully about Fatemeh Sayyah's work in literary criticism, marking her commitment to Socialist Realism as a major flaw in her critical thinking at the expense of more balanced awareness of other literary traditions evident in the work of James Joyce or Marcel Proust.[37] Parsinejad does not accuse Fatemeh Sayyah of not writing her own Persian essays, but he believes her Persian prose was flawed and could have been better! He too points to the fact that she was born, raised, and educated in Russia as the reasons for her "flawed" Persian prose. Parsinejad's own literary frame of reference is of course entirely European literature and literary movements. So, if Fatemeh Sayyah were a bit even more Eurocentric and more evenhanded in her awareness and commitments to even more European literary movements, she would have been flawless in this literary historian's perspective.

Such tendentious assessments and conflicting perspectives on Fatemeh Sayyah are in part because of her own literary and intellectual

[37] See Iraj Parsinejad, "Fatemeh Sayyah va Naqd-e Adabi" (*Bokhara*, 1390/2011). Available here: http://bukharamag.com/1390.02.14103.html. Accessed June 15, 2019. For a fuller treatment, see Iraj Parsinejad's book on the subject, *Fatemeh Sayyah va Naqd-e Adabi/Fatemeh Sayyah and Literary Criticism* (Sokhan, 1389/2010).

legacies and partly the spirit of the age in which she lived and the world in which she is now being received. She came to Iran highly respected and admired by her peers and her students and was put to effective use by the rising Pahlavi regime for its own propaganda purposes. But she had no conception of the genealogy of worldly travelers that had come before and during the time that her Iranian father and German/Russian mother met and married in Moscow. In her life and extraordinary achievements, we have spectacular evidence of a major epistemic shift in her ancestral homeland – to which she was integral. If she were only more self-aware of her own intellectual parentage and less beholden to Europe! But the issue is not *ad hominem*. Upon her arrival in Iran, a decadent dynasty was falling and an ambitious new monarchy was ascendant. She was a single woman in a deeply and irredeemably patriarchal society. Being in line with the ruling monarch's politics and seeking the company of other progressive (albeit Eurocentric) bourgeois feminists were not just ideological choices, but also a matter of survival.

It is epistemologically wrong to put undue emphasis on Fatemeh Sayyah and disregard the emerging spirit of her age – which is the condition in which she thrived. In her blindfolded Eurocentrism, Fatemeh Sayyah marks and represents a major epistemic shift early in the twentieth century intellectual history of Iran that leaves the magnificent worldly disposition of the nineteenth century evident in these travelogues we have read together behind and catapults the political culture of the country into two opposing camps: the Eurocentric monarchists and the Europhobic Islamists (both pathologically fixated on the allegory of "the West.") It was not until 1962 and the publication of Jalal Al-e Ahmad's powerful essay *Gharbzadegi/Westoxification* that the Eurocentric fanaticism of Fatemeh Sayyah and her time was contested by a serious intellectual. But the coincidence of the date of that seminal essay and the first revolutionary uprising by Ayatollah Khomeini in June 1963 unfairly and incorrectly cast *Gharbzadegi* in an Islamist shade. The successful takeover of the Iranian revolution of 1977–1979 by the Islamists further exacerbated this anachronistic reading of Al-e Ahmad's essay. In both her brilliance and her blindfolded Eurocentrism, Fatemeh Sayyah brought the preceding century of world discovery to a closure and marked an epistemic shift toward a major cultural schizophrenia. She placed her exquisite erudition at the service of the ideological foregrounding of the Pahlavi monarchy – at a time when the towering literary and poetic prophets of her time (Nima Yushij and Sadegh Hedayat) were rooting it further in the cosmopolitan imagination Sayyah had actively forgotten. But at the same time, she exponentially advanced the literary consciousness of her nation – even beyond her own expectations. She introduced comparative literature to her homeland as if on a civilizing mission amongst the barbarians – entirely oblivious of what world-historic literary and poetic events were happening in Iran. She knew little to nothing of what Nima Yushij and Sadegh Hedayat had inaugurated in their homeland. But in both her brilliance and in her ignorance, she opened up the horizons of a literary consciousness beyond her age and timespan. She remained mostly an obscure figure except among those who were documenting the history of bourgeois feminism in Iran – or else opposing it. But her significance, hidden and miasmatic, is far more widespread than hitherto assayed or imagined.

In a paradoxical twist that best captures the spirit of her age, Fatemeh Sayyah personifies the emotive split between the unwavering sovereignty of a rising nation and the vagaries of miscarried states that have sought and failed to rule it. She happened somewhere in between those two opposing facts – and thus her legacies go both ways. I have mentioned already how there are those who have accused Fatemeh Sayyah of not writing her Persian prose herself but writing her essays in Russian and others translating it into Persian, and there are those who find fault with her Persian prose because of her birth and upbringing outside Iran. There is no evident validity to either of these two charges. But scarcely anyone has pointed out the plausible evidence of looking at the matter the other way around, that her Persian had inflected her Russian and French. This, in fact, is even more perfectly plausible. She was born and raised in a multilingual family in which her mother was German/Russian and her father Iranian/Russian, so presumably remnants of at least two actives (Persian and Russian) and a third passive language (German) must have been evident in her Persian. If so, then in Fatemeh Sayyah we have the first Persian presence in two European languages and a Russian language, which brings a Persian inflection into the Euro-universalism of a cosmopolitan culture at the roots of her birth and upbringing. I am, as I write my English with a decidedly Persian twist to it, a direct descendent of Fatemeh Sayyah. In the Russian trace in her Persian prose, you might say, she is the intellectual grandmother to the Persian trace in my English.

Be that as it may, still the question remains, what happened to that cosmopolitan worldliness of her previous generations – when she helped the ruling monarchy and its comprador base and its bourgeois feminism plunge so deeply into a fanatical Eurocentrism? It was, in short, sublated into the poetic consciousness of her nation, which is precisely the reason why I have begun every one of these chapters with a solid and sustainable piece of poetry by Sohrab Sepehri, for whom traveling and worldliness, and returning the colonial gaze by a magnificent, sublime look at the world, were coterminous with his poetic consciousness. But more of that in my conclusion.

Conclusion

We must cross and wander –
We can hear
The wind blowing –
We must cross and wander –
I'm a traveler –
All you perennial winds!
Carry me to the vastness of where
The leaves are formed!
Take me to the childhood of salty waters!
And fill my shoes
With the mobile beauty of
Humility: Until I reach
The full maturity of the body of grapes!
Soar all my minutes high
To the white skies of instincts
Where flocks of pigeons are flying!
And transform the accident of my being
To a pure lost connection
By a tree!
And in the breathing of my solitude
Flap the windowpanes of my intelligence!
On that day
Send me running after a kite!
Take me to the solitude
Of the hidden proportions of life
And show me the gentle presence of
Nothingness!

Sohrab Sepehri (Mosafer/Traveler, Babol, Spring 1966)

Nothingness! Nothingness? Imagine the audacity of coming to *nothing* – the subjective authority, the poetic presence of it – not out of any mystical convictions but through the sheer experience of living. Aware of the gentle presence of *nothing*, discovering a solitude evident in life itself, Sepehri's poetry, here and elsewhere, formed the filled commotion of existence to the brim. The word *obur/cross* in Persian is mobility in verbal register; it is when we are neither here nor there – always somewhere in between. It is a state of existence. *Obur bayad kard*, "we need to move forward," "we need to cross," is as much imperative as it is subjunctive. This is how it is. This is how it should be. We must heed the call. Sepehri taught a whole poetic diction how to run after a wild joyous kite – not as an incidental day off from work. But as life itself, life as it is. Being-in-the-world in Sepehri's poetry becomes proverbial to existence. There is no *being* except *being-in-the-world*, traveling through it. Sepehri did not discover that world. He invented it. We woke up to that world in his poetry and discovered our worldliness upon reading it. This poetic intuition had not fallen from the heavens. It had come home to Sepehri after he completed the journeys others had started long before him.

Traveling the Globe

I have asked you to come along for a long journey and read these travel accounts with me, page after page and cover to cover, to show you where they went and what they thought – most particularly and against the grain of the abusive reading that they did not travel exclusively to Europe. Europe was part but not parcel of their destiny or destination – they were remapping the world they had inherited. The world was their oyster – with and without Europe. The very idea of "Europe," I have had reasons and occasions to argue, was a gradual and manufactured entity – a metaphor that became a metonymy for something entirely amorphous. It was not "there" waiting to be discovered or visited or desired or loved or hated or emulated or resented. Europe was and remains metonymic and differential. These very travel accounts have been abused in the manufacturing of that phantasm – for if these travelers went to Europe, then Europe was there waiting to be visited, discovered, emulated, desired. I have, instead, read these texts as the evidence of reversing the colonial gaze, reclaiming the world in its entirety, enabling, in effect, their readers to imagine themselves integral to, not the subjects of, that world by way of recapturing "the whole presence of the world," to paraphrase Frantz Fanon. Without this owning, and owning up to, this world these travelers visited, there would not be a person, a persona, beyond the terror of European colonization, to stand up and say one day: "I exist."

My reading of these travelogues stands in sharp contrast to the continued abuse of these texts. In a recent study in Persian we read there are more than one hundred unpublished manuscripts of travelogues from the Qajar period, written between 1779 and 1925.[1] A four-volume collection of some of these travelogues have recently been published, of a total of a projected nineteen-volume collection – each consisting of the edited manuscripts of these travelogues plus explanatory notes and commentaries. Although the general contour of this extraordinary project still remains that very same flawed category of travels "to Europe," the very existence of this endeavor shows the exceptional significance of this genre in Persian language and in the Qajar period, the most vital period of Iranian encounters with colonial modernity. Add to such projects the ever-increasing number of special issues of Persian scholarly journals, learned conferences, doctoral dissertations, and edited volumes on Iranians from various walks of life traveling around the globe and making a written record of their experiences. Iranian and non-Iranian scholars continue to study these travelogues apace and cast them all in the flawed frame of "encounter with the West," or "discovery of Europe," or some such falsifying category.

Such flawed framing is in sharp contrast with the actual content of the books thus edited and published. One such edited volume, for example, is about a travel around the world in the late nineteenth century.[2] The traveler, one Ibrahim Sahhafbashi Tehrani, began his journey on Wednesday, May 12, 1897 to Anzali, continuing to Astara and eventually reaching Moscow and from there traveling to Berlin, and from there to London and then Paris and back to London. He starts writing his travelogue from the moment he leaves his homeland until his return, much of which has nothing to do with Europe. On Saturday, July 10, 1897, Sahhafbashi tells us in plain beautiful Persian he boards a luxurious ship called "New York" from London and sails to New York. A week later, on Saturday, July 17, he reaches New York. From there he takes trains and eventually reaches San Francisco and from there to Vancouver where he boards a ship and travels to

---

[1] See Harun Vahuman (ed.), *Safarnameh-ha-ye Khati Farsi/Persian Travelogue Manuscripts*, First Volume (Tehran: Akhtaran Publishers, 1388/2009).

[2] See Mohammad Moshiri (ed.), *Safarnameh Ibrahim Sahhafbashi Tehrani* (Tehran: Sherkat Moallefan va Motarjeman-e Iran, 1357/1978).

Japan. Is Japan Europe? He sails through the Pacific Ocean for twelve days with nothing to do except read Sa'di's poetry. On Sunday, August 15, 1897, he arrives at Yokohama port. He spends six weeks in Japan and then takes a ship to Hong Kong. Hong Kong is not in Japan, and he continues to write. On October 21 of 1897 he sails to Mumbai, via Singapore and Sri Lanka. The travelogue of Sahhafbashi ends when he moves toward Karachi, without any mention of his trip back to Iran. He is the first Iranian to have an account of a cinematographer in London.[3] He evidently opened a shop in Tehran, selling merchandise he had brought from abroad and showing films in a small room behind his shop.

My arguments in this book have been informed by a scrupulously close reading of an extended sample of travelogues written in Persian throughout the nineteenth and early twentieth centuries, trying to retrieve the spirt of the age in which they were written. I have not disregarded the parts before and the parts after their short or long visits to Europe. I have not ignored their visits to Europe either. I have placed their presence in Europe, short or long, in the larger contexts of their journeys before and after, and thus these journeys I have not identified as "going to Europe" but going abroad. Meanwhile I have anchored my reading of these travelogues in a detailed reading of just one among countless pieces of poetry, Sepehri's "Traveler," as evidence of how that age went into the poetic subconsciousness of the nation while its political discourse was trapped inside that Eurocentrism – in both Europhilia and Europhobia – of the state ideologies. I have concluded my book in its last chapter by a close examination of a counter-text, a seminal thinker who was exactly the opposite of what I have detected and argued – for she was put squarely at the service of the ruling state ideology. The crowning achievement of a multifaceted cosmopolitan culture that preceded her, Fatemeh Sayyah thrived at a fanatical Eurocentrism that went against the grain of the literature of which she seems to have known next to nothing, though her own uncle and father-in-law was a prominent figure in its genre. In that paradoxical twist, however, became evident the emotive split between the unwavering sovereignty of a rising nation and the vagaries of abortive states that have sought but failed to rule it. The more regional, global, and comparative was the public sphere on which the nation was formed,

---

[3] Ibid: 14–15.

the more fanatical and Eurocentric (in Europhilia or Europhobia) became the ruling state ideologies.

In making my arguments, I have also been conscious of the larger historical frame of refence in which these travelogues will have to be located. Yes, the encounter with colonial modernity was crucial and

Figure 15 Abbas Kiarostami, Untitled, from the Roads series, 1989, C Print, 91 × 122 cm, © Abbas Kiarostami – [Reprinted with permission] – Everything in these travelogues we have read together in this book points to such recasting of an allegorical picture of the world and worldliness, evident in this photograph by Abbas Kiarostami (1940–2016) from his Road Series. Here, in the winding road of a passage from here to an eternity, truth of worldliness has finally become allegorical, the factual fantastic, geography brought home to the absolute interiority of intuitive truth. The eye of the world is in Kiarostami's camera here. Just like Sohrab Sepehri's poetry, Abbas Kiarostami's cinema and photography, as well as the other Iranian artist Parviz Kalantari's artwork, imagine a time and space, the factual fusion of a spatial temporality at once global, local, worldly and yet rooted in the historical consciousness of the home and habitat that are thus pictured, imagined, intuited. The poetry of Sepehri, the photography and cinema of Kiarostami, and the artwork of Kalantari are chief among many other forms in the aesthetic intuition these travelers had enabled for their posterity. It is in this artworld that the colonial gaze is forever overcome and transcended and the postcolonial person made possible, agential, imaginative, authorial.

informative. But Iranians as a people were not born the day before that
encounter. In the course that encounter, we have been quite conscious
of the long tradition of travel writing in Persian prose, beginning at
least with the seminal philosopher Naser Khosrow (1004–1088)
down to Sa'di (ca. 1208–1294). From Shahab al-Din Yahya Suhrawardi (115–1191) to Mulla Sadra Shirazi (ca. 571–1640), these travel
writings have also assumed allegorical and philosophical dimensions.
The nineteenth century travelers, however, discovered a whole new
world and reclaimed it for and into their Persian prose. In the twentieth
century, towering public intellectuals like Jalal Al-e Ahmad, Gholamhossein Saedi, and Sohrab Sepehri brought all those traditions home.
Through reading these travelers and their prose and purpose, we are in
fact reliving and relocating ourselves over our own fast dwindling
worlds, the spaces we have traversed, agencies we have sought, the
subjects of our own histories we have discovered and lived.

The Center Cannot Hold

The principal thesis of my book has been quite simple: Based on the
detailed reading of these texts cover to cover, from the moment they
leave home until they return, these travels were not exclusively to
Europe. Europe was not their destination, though Europe was part of
their itinerary. These travelers did not fly to Europe or, Orientals as
they were, board their magic carpets. They traveled on foot, mules,
horses, camels, or trains when they were on land and then on boats and
ships when on sea. They were curious, observant, and copious in their
notes wherever they went. They usually started taking notes when they
were still in their own homeland, and thereafter they continued taking
notes city after city, region after region, from Iran to Russia to Ottoman territories to Eastern and Western European cities and then some
of them off to the Americas and Japan and back to the Indian subcontinent and the Arab and Muslim world. By definition, therefore, these
journeys were not "travels to Europe." Sometimes these travelers went
all the way to the United States, to Japan, to South America, or to
Africa. Many of them went to the Arab and Muslim world on their
way back to Iran. An unpardonable epistemic violence is therefore
perpetrated on these texts when we consider them "travel to Europe."
India, the Arab and Muslim world, South Africa, and South America
are not Europe. Privileging Europe over all other destinations they

visited has done irreparable damage to the manner in which they have been read.

The obvious question is, why has the factual evidence of these travelers' accounts been so systematically ignored and their journeys categorically cast as "travels to Europe?" Why have they been so consistently distorted and compromised? Two answers immediately suggest themselves: (1) a colonized mind that takes Europe as the center of the universe and only looks for segments of the text that deal with a visit to Europe and (2) a shabby and lazy reading habit of primary sources, where the dominant assumptions and prejudices within a mode of thinking decide what parts are highlighted and privileged. Let us put aside the factor of ill-equipped Orientalist readers who have a vested interest in reading these texts solely to prove Europe was the center of the universe. If you begin with a colonized mind and have a lazy reading habit, then inevitably you enter these texts and fish for a few passages in which they indeed do write about their visits to Europe and disregard the rest. Reading these texts cover to cover, as I have spent years doing before writing this book, reveals a whole different body of evidence that immediately dispenses with the myth, the colonial delusion, that these are travelogues "to Europe." The result is an intentional or hysterical blindness conditioned by the supreme fiction of "the West and the Rest." You see the words, and you read them, one by one – but they don't register any meaning, you subconsciously disregard them, you could not care less what they actually say, or mean – for your mind, your thinking is trapped and foregrounded on the colonial epistemology of "the West and the Rest."

But still the question is why this would happen, and how come the original authors wrote decidedly about their traveling experiences abroad (and not just about Europe) true to where they went and what they saw? Why did they start writing long before they reached Europe and long after they left Europe? Why were they so open-minded and receptive to the entirety of the world they visited and not just "to Europe?" Here is where the final chapter, on Fatemeh Sayyah, is important, for this preoccupation with Europe has nothing to do with the content of these travelogues or with the intelligence of those who are reading them now, but with the frame of their minds and, by extension, the audience they are addressing and the epistemic shift in the general consciousness of the society. Fatemeh Sayyah, the first woman professor at Tehran University, is in effect the mother of all subsequent Eurocentric scholarship on Qajar history, and these travelogues in particular.

What would happen if we did what we have done in this book – actually read a solid constellation of these texts and not just one or two of them haphazardly (and only a fraction of those texts – and not cover to cover) to write about "Muslims going to see Jane Austen's country," or "to discover Europe?" Suppose we read these texts with a decolonized mind, determined to retrieve the world their authors had inherited, and the world they were mapping out with every stroke of their pen, with the turn of every page they wrote? What then? If we did so, I have proposed the following hermeneutic horizons will open up.

First and foremost, we find ourselves in the midst of an age of discovery, discovery not of Europe as the notorious Orientalist Bernard Lewis would say, but the discovery of a vastly changing world – from one end to another. These travelers are traveling through the world they did not know existed in such changing details. There is almost a pornographic fixation in these travel accounts on seeing and describing everything they see – in Asia, Africa, Europe, and the Americas. It is not even clear to whom they are addressing these texts. They are effectively addressed to a generation, to a generalized audience, they scarcely knew even existed. They are in effect crafting that ideal reader for themselves as they write. There is a dialectic between the world they are discovering and describing and the readership they are crafting and creating as they write. This is where both authorial agency and readership are being subjectively formed at one and the same time. Between these traveling writers and their emerging readers, they are discovering and mapping the world they knew existed only generically and never in such exquisite and enabling detail. It is precisely in these details that these travelers are mapping, peopling, and historicizing the world, beyond any fictive fixation with Europe or the "West." This mapping is planetary, historical, real, detailed, and peopled with actual events instead of imagined attributes; and it discovers the world, not as "Modern versus Traditional," but as a whole, the world they are making their own, fully conscious of the coloniality of their conditions but also transcending them by writing, by claiming it. They know Russia, England, and the Ottomans are imperial powers – but they also know of the Indian and the Japanese resistance and rebellion against those empires. These travelogues are the earliest evidence of the emerging geopolitics of the world rising to map the world.

There is no doubt these travelers are fully conscious of Europe, particularly of its imperial and colonial conquests and consequences, and the calamities it has caused around the globe. Yes, they are aware and they write about European advances in various fields, but also of the costs of those advances for the rest of the world. Crucial is the fact that they are equally conscious and aware of India, Russia, Japan, the Ottoman Empire, the Arab and Muslim World, the rest of Asia, and then of Africa, and the Americas. They are not fixated on Europe. They put one world against the other and make them all theirs by reading them together, integral to their consciousness and worldliness. Every conceivable binary dissolves in the pages of these travelogues, "Tradition versus Modernity, "the West and the Rest," "Secular versus Religious." Most importantly, the act of traveling becomes integral to the critical consciousness of the nation these travelers inform at the very moment of its inception. It is as if they cannot think unless they move. Their conception of the nation as a result also becomes mobile, aterritorial, formed on the transnational public sphere these travelers are mapping as they write. Yes, they love and miss their homeland wherever they travel, but travel they do, and a map of the newly discovered world is now always on their mind when they speak of their homeland. The more the state becomes myopic, nativist, and tyrannical, the more open, transnational, mobile, and agile becomes their conception of the nation. The radical and irreconcilable bifurcation between *the nation* and *the state* occurs right here on the tumultuous pages of these travel narratives, as the nation is narrated regionally, globally, and comparatively, while the state becomes archaic, static, statist, clumsily ethnocentric, and nativist.

In their simplified Persian prose, these travel narratives link the idea of Iran as a postcolonial nation back to much earlier travel narratives of poets and philosophers, such as Naser Khosrow, Sa'di, Suhrawardi and Mulla Sadra – whether they wrote in factual or allegorical diction. Through this narrative connection, the roots of pre- and post-colonial ideas of "Iran/Persia" link together, and their symbolic registers become historical, mythical, and heroic. This is in stark contrast to the clumsy racialized nationalism of the state, and thus the fate of the nation and nationhood are systemically severed from the abuses of political nationalism as a state-building ideology that comes to full fruition during the first and second Pahlavi monarchies and then with the Islamic Republic. The body of travelogues we have read together in this book is the most enduring evidence of that crucial bifurcation between the healthy and robust nation and the stale and reactionary state, against the fabricated colonial connection of "the nation-state."

[is such a bifurcation possible?]

Purgatorial Passages

The logic and rhetoric, the prose and poetry, of these travelogues ultimately find their most allegorical expression in a twin volume by a prominent Shi'a cleric bringing this and other worldly travels together, somewhat reminiscent of what Maragheh'i had done in his work of fiction, but this time deeply rooted in Shi'a eschatology. Seyyed Mohammad Hassan Aqa Najafi Quchani (1878–1943) was a politically active Shi'i cleric during the Constitutional period who received his early education in his village of Karva, and then in Quchan, Mashhad, Isfahan, and finally in Najaf.[4] By 1908, at the age of thirty, he had completed his scholastic learnings. Following his teacher Akhund Khorasani's politics, Quchani was an active supporter of the Constitutional movement, too. He spent the rest of his life in his hometown of Quchan as a well-respected cleric. Among his mostly cliché publications, Quchani has two volumes that are of relevance to us he here: one is his autobiography (up to 1928), *Siyahat-e Sharq: Zendegi-nameh Aqa Najafi Quchani/Traveling East: The Biography of Aqa Najafi Quchani*, and the second volume, *Siyahat-e Gharb: Sarnevesht-e Arvah ba'd az Marg/Traveling West: The Fate of Souls after Death*, is his memoir about "afterlife" – that is right, his travelogue of "afterlife"!

In *Traveling East*, we read the memoir of a young man going through the thick and thin of his life, with a simple, occasionally delightful, always entertaining account.[5] Aqa Najafi thrives at a folkloric prose, full of stories from his childhood and youth, expanded from Iran to Iraq in pursuit of scholastic knowledge. The book offers an excellent first-person account of the rural and urban childhood life of late nineteenth century Iran. With wit and a gift for storytelling, Aqa Najafi gives an account of his birth and upbringing in rural areas near

---

[4] For a short biographical account, see the entry in *Encyclopedia Iranica* under the title of "ĀQĀ NAJAFĪ QŪČĀNI." Available online here: www.iranicaonline.org/articles/aqa-najafi-qucani-sayyed-mohammad-hasan-b. Accessed August 15, 2018.

[5] See Aqa Najafi Quchani, *Siyahat-e Sharq/Traveling East*. Edited by R. A. Shakeri (Tehran: Amir Kabir Publishers, 1362/1983).

Quchan, his eventual move to Quchan, and from there to Sabzevar and Mashhad, and eventually Isfahan, and from there to Najaf. All the while we read his observations about the changing times and emergence of Iran from its social slumbers. He gives details of his teacher Akhund Khorasani (1839–1911) and his support for the Constitutional revolution, to which he too was drawn. He describes in some detail the Ottoman rule over Iraq eventually giving way to British colonial domination. The book continues until his return to Quchan, where he becomes a prominent cleric. The prose is cast in the form of a fusion of memoir and travelogue, full of advice and admonition of how to lead a pious and morally upright life. What becomes evident in this book is how mobility, traveling, being away from one's birthplace, and above all the genre of travel writing even for those who did not travel much, are all the necessary conditions for living, for being, and for writing. It is as if without traveling, thinking is made impossible.

The second volume, *Traveling West*, is an allegorical fiction, reminiscent of the third volume of Maragheh'i's *Siyahat-nameh-ye Ibrahim Beg/Ibrahim Beg's Travelogue*, or Dante's *Divine Comedy*. Chances are, Aqa Najafi knew the former and not the latter. *Traveling West* is cast in first-person narrative, and the prose is rich with Islamic (Shi'i in particular) wisdom literature, Quranic passages, and Prophetic traditions used on various occasions.[6] The book is mostly based on Islamic (Shi'a) eschatological accounts of afterlife. The world he portrays is the purgatorial space (Barzakh) between heaven and hell. Through the purgatory, the narrator is guided by a young man whom he calls Hadi ("the Guide") and identifies with the Love of Ali – the first Shi'a Imam. In this account we even have a premonition of Skype, namely a phone conversation in which we see the person on the other side. There is even a movie made on the basis of this book.

The combination of these two "travelogues" by a Shi'a cleric who really did not travel much beyond his homeland or to Iraq to study jurisprudence is a remarkable testimony to the power of "journey" as a metaphor to navigate an imaginative geography on which an entire nation was now imagining their worldly existence. Aqa Najafi Quchani reaches deeply onto Shi'a eschatology to link his modest

---

[6] See Aqa Najafi Quchani, *Siyahat-e Gharb: Sarnevesht-e Arvah ba'd az Marg/ Traveling West: Or the Fate of Soul after Death* (Tehran: Pol Publications, 1379/ 1990).

worldly existence to the world to come. The two volumes are cast in
the geographical terms of East and West, entirely different from the
later ideological meaning these terms assumed. "East" here is the
domain of earthly existence, basically Iran and Iraq; while "West" is
the purgatorial space of the afterlife. Put together, these two "journeys" East and West posit the postcolonial person on an epistemic
domain beyond the reach of any state-sponsored ideology.

Traveling in Poetry

From the Preface and the Introduction forward, I have had multiple
occasions to emphasize and explain the larger context in which I have
written this book on Persian travelogues of the nineteenth and early
twentieth centuries. The historic formation of the postcolonial public
sphere and its contingent subject have been at the heart of my scholarship of the last decade or so. What is the global context in which
specific postcolonial public spheres and their corresponding subjects
have emerged? I propose that the uniting of "nation-states" with fixed
colonial boundaries has confused and distorted these far more important units of analysis. In the transnational landscape these travelers
have mapped out, we see the postcolonial public sphere upon which
"nation-states" have been colonially concocted and imposed. That
public sphere has been transnational, and the subject it has enabled
supple, miasmatic, multidimensional, and open-ended. The liminality
and conflation of worlds that have come together to form a new world
correspond to a cosmopolitan worldliness mapped out on an imaginative geography that is transnational in its character and far beyond the
very assumption of any nation-state. In this manner I wish to expose
the ideological grain of "the West and the Rest" as a potent delusion
that has bewitched and mesmerized the world – willed by a colonial
power determined to shape the world in its own best interests. Upon
these interpolated worlds I propose the active formation of a cosmopolitan public sphere and an organically multifaceted subject that has
asserted historical agency beyond the pale of any coloniality.

Postcolonial states of even opposing ideologies have been contingent
on abusing this transnational public sphere to procure legitimacy for
themselves. The Pahlavi monarchy was founded on the delusion of
"the West and the Rest," and its successor and archenemy, the Islamic
republic, was launched on the identical premise but against
"the West," further exacerbating that delusion. In one seminal text,

Gharbzadegi/Westoxication, Jalal Al-e Ahmad sought to dismantle that delusion but ended up further validating it. Instead of reading the history backward and going to the nineteenth century as the origin of this false binary and fake hostility, as is often done, I have done precisely the opposite. I went back to the nineteenth century and came forward, mapping out in unprecedented details how the world these travelers traversed, discovered, mapped, and narrated was in fact polypolar, plural, widely open, neither ignored nor privileged Europe, and brought back to Persian prose an open horizon of an expansive geography. I concluded with a chapter that pinpointed when exactly it was at the dawn of the Pahlavi dynasty when, in the figure of one exquisitely learned Europeanist named Fatemeh Sayyah, that world came to a crushing end when the Pahlavi dynasty wedded its monarchy to a Eurocentric perception of the world, ruling Iran with that ideology for half a century until the rise of the Islamic republic reversed that ideology by an ideology whose "Islamism" was even more "Westoxicated" than the Westoxicated ideology it wanted to dismantle.

While the Pahlavis falsely Europeanized Iran, the Islamic Republic violently over-Islamized Iran. They were both pulling and pushing the same tug of war, the same rope that ideologically cut through the lived experiences of more than a century of worlding the Iranian lives upon the transnational public sphere where the postcolonial person had a much more global, far worldlier claim on this world. But as the ruling states waged this false war as state ideology, the nation itself sublated its lived historical memory into its poetic intuition of the sublime and the beautiful. Poetry under the Pahlavis and cinema under the Islamic republic sustained the course of that poetic intuition, tucking away the public sphere in a parapublic sphere and that subject into the collective subconscious of a nation – a people always already traveling the known and unknown world guided by their poets:

> Where are my shoes?
> Did someone say Sohrab? ...
> I can smell the air of migration.
> And my pillow is filled
> With the songs of swallows' feathers.[7]

---

[7] Sohrab Sepehri, "Neda-ye Aghaz/Sound of the Beginning," in Sohrab Sepehri, *Hasht Ketab/Eight Books* (Tehran: Tahuri Publishers, 2536/1356/1977): 390–391.

Index

34

Suratgar, Lotf Ali, 348
Suwar al-Aqalim (al-Balkhi), 165–166
Sweden, 296–298
Swift, Jonathan, 310
Switzerland
   in *Hayat-e Yahiya/The Life of Yahiya*
      (Dowlatabadi), 286–287, 289–292
   in *Safarnameh/Travelogue* (Hajj
      Sayyah), 210
   in *Safar-Nameh/Travelogue* (Naser
      al-Din Shah), 167–168, 173
   view of, 175
   See also specific cities
Syria, 246–247, 254
   See also specific cities

Tabataba'i, Zia al-Din, 302
Tabriz, 87, 318
Tabrizi, Haji Ali, 268
*Tadhkereh-ye Shushtar/History of
   Shushtar*, 30–32
Taghizadeh, Seyyed Hassan, 298, 303
Taken for Wonder (N. Sohrabi), 6–7
Tal'at and Fitnat In Love (Sami), 330
Talbot, G. F., 156
Talebof Tabrizi, Mirza Abd al-Rahim, 284
Tanzimat reforms (1839–1876), 168
Tarikh-e Afranj/History of the Franks
   (Rashid al-Din Fazlollah), 148
Tbilisi
   in *Hayat-e Yahiya/The Life of Yahiya*
      (Dowlatabadi), 281–282
   in *Heyrat-Nameh/Book of Wonders*
      (Ilchi), 92
   in *Safar-Nameh/Travelogue* (Naser
      al-Din Shah), 167–168, 174
Tehran
   in Abd al-Samad Mirza's travelogues,
      231
   in Haji Pirzadeh's travelogues,
      244–245
   in *Hayat-e Yahiya/The Life of Yahiya*
      (Dowlatabadi), 267, 284, 299
   in *Khaterat/Memoirs* (Hajj Sayyah),
      187–188, 194–196
   in *Safar-Nameh/Travelogue* (Naser
      al-Din Shah), 168
   in *Siyahat-nameh-ye Ibrahim Beg/
      Ibrahim Beg's Travelogue*
      (Maragheh'i), 316–317

view of, 351
Tikhiy Don/And Quiet Flows the Don
   (Sholokhov), 350–351
Tipu Sultan, Fateh Ali Khan Sahib, 38
Tobacco Revolt (1890–1891), 156,
   158, 177–178, 198, 268–269
Tocqueville, Alexis de, 57–58
*Tohfat al-Alam/The Gift from the
   World* (Shushtari)
   Abu Taleb in, 53, 58–59
   Aql-e Salim/Sound Reason in, 42
   as autobiography, 28–29
   on British colonialism in India in,
      37–40
   cosmopolitan wordliness of, 44–48
   on creation and Shushtar as center of
      the universe, 1–2, 25–26, 28–30
   literary context of, 40–41
   narrative style of, 32–35
   scholarship on, 104
   sources and "plagiarism" in, 30
   structure of, 27
Tolstoy, Leo, 330, 350–351
Totality and Infinity (Levinas), 150–153
tourism industry, 333
Tours, 213
Travel Theory, 121–123
Travelogues
   autobiographical voice in, 28–29
   cosmopolitan wordliness of, 7–10,
      14, 22–24, 42–46, 71–72
   desire for the invisible and, 150–153
   deterritorialization/
      reterritorialization and,
      127–130
   Europe and "the West" in, 2–7,
      13–14, 47–48, 362–370
   Ghanoonparvar on, 240–243
   Iran as nation-state and, 181–184,
      223–226, 266–267, 277,
      369–370
   itineraries of, 104–105
   journey as metaphor in, 10–13
   origin of genre, 40–42
   as "reverse travelogues" and "reverse
      ethnography," 48–53
   scholarship on, 4–7, 13–14, 104–105
   unpublished manuscripts and
      editions of, 363
Travels (Polo), 333